Evolutionary Economic Geography

T0300364

Economic geographers increasingly consider the significance of history in shaping the contemporary socio-economic landscape and believe that experiences and competencies, acquired over time by individuals and entities in particular localities, to a large degree determine present configurations as well as future regional trajectories. Attempts to trace, understand, and investigate the pathways from past to present have given rise to the thriving and exciting sub-field of Evolutionary Economic Geography (EEG).

EEG highlights the important factors that initiate, inhibit, or consolidate the contextual settings and relationships in which regions and their respective agents, which comprise and shape economic activity and social reproduction, change over time. It has at its core the production and destruction of novelty in space, and the links between innovation and regional economic fortunes. The creation of knowledge, its movement and recombination within different regional ensembles of economic agents and institutions plays a critical role in the evolution of the space-economy. EEG provides a framework to disentangle the complexity of technological change and regional economic development based on a variety of theoretical and methodological approaches.

In only a short time, EEG has established itself as a promising and rapidly evolving research framework with its focus on the driving forces of regional development across various scales and its attempt to translate findings into public policy. This book advances the theoretical foundations of EEG, and demonstrates how EEG utilises and operationalises conceptual frameworks, both established and new. Contributions also point to future research avenues and extensions of EEG, attempting to build stronger ties between theory, empirical evidence, and relevance to policy. This book was originally published as a special issue of *Regional Studies*.

Dieter F. Kogler is a Lecturer in Economic Geography at University College Dublin, Ireland. His research focus is on the geography of innovation and evolutionary economic geography, with a particular emphasis on knowledge production and diffusion, and processes related to technological change and innovation. He is the co-editor of *Global and Regional Dynamics in Knowledge Flows and Innovation* (with Van Egeraat and Cooke, Routledge, 2014), and *Beyond Territory: Dynamic Geographies of Knowledge Creation, Diffusion, and Innovation* (with Bathelt and Feldman, Routledge, 2011).

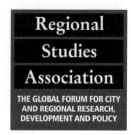

Regions and Cities

Series Editor in Chief
Susan M. Christopherson
Cornell University, USA

Editors
Maryann Feldman
University of Georgia, USA
Gernot Grabher
HafenCity University Hamburg, Germany
Ron Martin
University of Cambridge, UK
Martin Perry
Massey University, New Zealand

In today's globalised, knowledge-driven and networked world, regions and cities have assumed heightened significance as the interconnected nodes of economic, social and cultural production, and as sites of new modes of economic and territorial governance and policy experimentation. This book series brings together incisive and critically engaged international and interdisciplinary research on this resurgence of regions and cities, and should be of interest to geographers, economists, sociologists, political scientists and cultural scholars, as well as to policy-makers involved in regional and urban development.

For more information on the Regional Studies Association visit www.regionalstudies.org

There is a **30% discount** available to RSA members on books in the *Regions and Cities* series, and other subject related Taylor and Francis books and e-books including Routledge titles. To order just e-mail alex.robinson@tandf.co.uk, or phone on +44 (0) 20 7017 6924 and declare your RSA membership. You can also visit www.routledge.com and use the discount code: **RSA0901**

Evolutionary Economic Geography

Theoretical and empirical progress

Edited by
Dieter F. Kogler

Routledge
Taylor & Francis Group
LONDON AND NEW YORK

First published 2016
by Routledge
2 Park Square, Milton Park, Abingdon, Oxon, OX14 4RN, UK

and by Routledge
711 Third Avenue, New York, NY 10017, USA

First issued in paperback 2017

Routledge is an imprint of the Taylor & Francis Group, an informa business

British Library Cataloguing in Publication Data
A catalogue record for this book is available from the British Library

ISBN 13: 978-1-138-29517-9 (pbk)
ISBN 13: 978-1-138-95318-5 (hbk)

Typeset in Bembo
by RefineCatch Limited, Bungay, Suffolk

Publisher's Note
The publisher accepts responsibility for any inconsistencies that may have arisen during the conversion of this book from journal articles to book chapters, namely the possible inclusion of journal terminology.

Disclaimer
Every effort has been made to contact copyright holders for their permission to reprint material in this book. The publishers would be grateful to hear from any copyright holder who is not here acknowledged and will undertake to rectify any errors or omissions in future editions of this book.

Contents

Citation Information

The chapters in this book were originally published in *Regional Studies*, volume 49, issue 5 (May 2015). When citing this material, please use the original page numbering for each article, as follows:

Chapter 8
What Makes Clusters Decline? A Study on Disruption and Evolution of a High-Tech Cluster in Denmark
Christian Richter Østergaard and Eunkyung Park
Regional Studies, volume 49, issue 5 (May 2015) pp. 834–849

Chapter 9
Path Renewal in Old Industrial Regions: Possibilities and Limitation for Regional Innovation Policy
Lars Coenen, Jerker Moodysson and Hanna Martin
Regional Studies, volume 49, issue 5 (May 2015) pp. 850–865

Chapter 10
Education-Job (Mis)Match and Interregional Migration: Italian University Graduates' Transition to Work
Simona Iammarino and Elisabetta Marinelli
Regional Studies, volume 49, issue 5 (May 2015) pp. 866–882

Chapter 11
Knowledge Neighbourhoods: Urban Form and Evolutionary Economic Geography
Gregory M. Spencer
Regional Studies, volume 49, issue 5 (May 2015) pp. 883–898

For any permission-related enquiries please visit:
http://www.tandfonline.com/page/help/permissions

Notes on Contributors

Ron Boschma is a Professor in Regional Economics at Utrecht University, The Netherlands, and Professor in Innovation Studies at Lund University, Sweden, where he is also the Director of the Centre for Innovation, Research and Competence in the Learning Economy (CIRCLE). His research interests include evolutionary economic geography, the spatial evolution of industries, regional systems of innovation, and Italian industrial districts. He is the co-editor of *The Handbook on Regional Innovation and Growth* (with Cooke, Asheim, Martin, Schwarz and Todtling, 2011).

Stefano Breschi is a Professor in the Department of Management and Technology at Bocconi University, Milan, Italy. His areas of research include industrial dynamics, social networks, clusters and knowledge spillovers, the economics of science, and the economics and econometrics of patents. He is the editor of *Clusters, networks and innovation* (with Franco Malerba, 2005).

Carolina Castaldi is an Assistant Professor in Economics of Innovation at the School of Innovation Sciences of Eindhoven University of Technology. Her research focus is on conceptualizing and measuring innovation from an evolutionary economic perspective. She has published articles in a variety of journals, including *Regional Studies, Research Policy and Industry and Innovation*.

Lars Coenen is Professor in Innovation Studies at the Centre for Innovation, Research and Competence in the Learning Economy (CIRCLE), Lund University, Sweden, and (part-time) Research Professor at the Nordic Institute for Studies in Innovation, Research and Education. His research interests converge around the geography of innovation and sustainability transitions. His work has been published in leading international journals such as *Research Policy, Environment and Planning A*, and *Economic Geography*.

Jürgen Essletzbichler is based in the Department of Geography at University College London, UK. His research interests include the theoretical development of evolutionary economic geography, metropolitan economic growth and resilience in the USA, the quantitative analysis of the role of industrial diversity and industrial branching for urban economic transformation, and the analysis of the causes of increasing income inequality at the metropolitan scale.

Maryann P. Feldman is the Heninger Distinguished Professor in the Department of Public Policy at the University of North Carolina, Chapel Hill, NC, USA. Her research and teaching interests focus on the areas of innovation, the commercialization of academic research and the factors that promote technological change and economic growth. She has written extensively on the process and mechanics of the commercialization of academic research, publishing in *Management Science, Organization Science, Research Policy*, and *The Journal of Technology Transfer*.

Rune Dahl Fitjar is Professor of Innovation Studies in the Copernicus Institute of Sustainable Development at Utrecht University, The Netherlands.

Koen Frenken is Professor of Innovation Studies in the Copernicus Institute of Sustainable Development at Utrecht University, The Netherlands.

Simona Iammarino is Professor of Economic Geography and Head of the Department of Geography & Environment at the London School of Economics, UK. She was one of the editors of *Regional Studies* (2008–2013), and is currently on the editorial board of *Environment and Planning C*. Her book, *Multinational Corporations and European Regional Systems of Innovation* (Routledge, 2003), co-authored with John Cantwell, is highly cited in the academic literature, and has attracted the interest of government agencies in the UK and elsewhere.

Dieter F. Kogler is a Lecturer in Economic Geography at University College Dublin, Ireland. His research focus is on the geography of innovation and evolutionary economic geography, with a particular emphasis on knowledge production and diffusion, and processes related to technological change and innovation. He is the co-editor of *Global and Regional Dynamics in Knowledge Flows and Innovation* (with Van Egeraat and Cooke, Routledge, 2014), and *Beyond Territory: Dynamic Geographies of Knowledge Creation, Diffusion, and Innovation* (with Bathelt and Feldman, Routledge, 2011).

Camilla Lenzi is an Associate Professor of Regional and Urban Economics at the Politecnico di Milano, Milan, Italy. She has published several papers in international peer-reviewed journals in the fields of innovation and urban and regional growth, entrepreneurship, human capital mobility and technology transfer.

Bart Los is an Associate Professor in the Faculty of Economics and Business at the University of Groningen, The Netherlands. His research expertise lies in the productivity effects of R&D, dynamic input-output models, data envelopment analysis, and evolutionary growth theory. He is the author of *Harmful monitoring* (with Haan and Riyanto, 2007) and *The Weakest Link: a field experiment in rational decision making* (with Haan, Riyanto, and van Geest, 2002).

Elisabetta Marinelli, Ph.D., is a Scientific Officer at the Institute of Prospective Technological Studies of the Joint Research Centre of the European Commission.

Hanna Martin is a Ph.D. candidate in Economic Geography in the Centre for Innovation, Research and Competence in the Learning Economy (CIRCLE) at Lund University, Sweden. Her dissertation deals with the development of cleantech industries in Sweden. In particular, she is interested in studying the regional contexts in which clean technologies emerge and the factors that trigger and hinder their development and diffusion.

Ron Martin is Professor of Economic Geography, and a Professorial Fellow of St. Catharine's College, at the University of Cambridge, UK. His research interests focus on the geographies of work and financial systems, regional economic development, evolutionary economic geography, and the policy relevance of economic-geographic research. He has published nearly 30 books and more than 200 papers on these and related themes. He co-edited the *Handbook of Evolutionary Economic Geography* (2010) with Ron Boschma. He is also co-editor of the *The Handbook on Regional Innovation and Growth* (with P. Cooke, B. Asheim, R. Boschma, P. Schwarz and F. Todtling, 2011). Forthcoming books include *The Handbook of the Geographies of Money and Finance* (edited with J. Pollard, 2016), and *Britain's Unbalanced Economy: Spatial Divisions of Growth, Work and Welfare* (with P. Sunley, 2016).

Jerker Moodysson is Professor of Innovation Studies, and Deputy Director of the Centre for Innovation, Research and Competence in the Learning Economy (CIRCLE), at Lund University, Sweden. His research focuses on regional economies, transformation of industries and regions, and regional innovation policy.

Christian Richter Østergaard is an Associate Professor in the Department of Business and Management at Aalborg University, Denmark, where he is a member of the Innovation, Knowledge, and Economics Dynamics (IKE) Group. He is also a member of the DRUID network. He has published articles in journals such as *Research Policy, Industry and Innovation, Structural Change and Economic Dynamics,* and the *Journal of Engineering and Technology Management.*

Eunkyung Park is a Research Assistant in the Department of Business and Management at Aalborg University, Denmark. She has published in the *Regional Studies* journal.

David L. Rigby is a Professor in the Department of Geography at UCLA, Los Angeles, California, USA. His research interests are in evolutionary economic geography, geographies of innovation and knowledge flow, technological change, and regional economic growth. He is the co-editor of *Elementary Statistics for Geographers* (with Burt and Barber, 2009).

Andrés Rodríguez-Pose is a Professor of Economic Geography at the London School of Economics, UK. He has a long track record of research in regional growth and disparities, fiscal and political decentralization, regional innovation, and development policies and strategies. His research is widely cited in academic circles and has also been frequently used by policy- and decision-makers. He is the editor of *Technology and Industrial Parks in Emerging Countries* (with Daniel Hardy, 2014), and the co-editor of the *Handbook of Local and Regional Development* (with Andy Pike and John Tomany, 2010).

Gregory M. Spencer is the Manager of Local IDEAs (Indicator Database for Economic Analysis) in the Munk

School for Global Affairs at the University of Toronto, Canada. His research broadly deals with the economies of cities in a global context.

Peter Sunley is Professor of Economic Geography, and Director of Research and Enterprise for Geography and Environment, at the University of Southampton, UK. His research interests include regional growth and development, venture capital, geographies of labour and social enterprise, and evolutionary economic geography. He is the co-editor of the *The SAGE Handbook of Economic Geography* (with Andrew Leyshon, Roger Lee and Linda McDowell, 2011). He is co-authoring *Britain's Unbalanced Economy: Spatial Divisions of Growth, Work and Welfare* (with Ron Martin, forthcoming).

Evolutionary Economic Geography – Theoretical and Empirical Progress

DIETER F. KOGLER

School of Geography, University College Dublin, Dublin, Ireland.

INTRODUCTION

Economic geographers increasingly consider the significance of history in shaping the contemporary socio-economic landscape. Inspired by evolutionary economics (NELSON and WINTER, 1982), it is acknowledged that we have now arrived at a new stage in economic geography, i.e. the 'evolutionary turn' (GRABHER, 2009). Simply put, it is believed that experiences and competencies acquired over time by individuals and entities in particular localities to a large degree determine present configurations as well as future regional trajectories. In order to trace, understand and investigate the pathways from past to present, economic geographers have sought insights from a number of closely related fields, including regional science, the geography of innovation approach (FELDMAN and KOGLER, 2010), other disciplines such as heterodox economics, and to some extent also the natural sciences (BOSCHMA and MARTIN, 2010a). The results of these efforts have given rise to a thriving and exciting sub-field within the larger discipline, entitled evolutionary economic geography (EEG).

The common point of departure in EEG is the concept of 'creative destruction', and along with it the principal idea that the capitalist economy is in constant flux, evolving through 'constant changes that transform the economic structure from within' (SCHUMPETER, 1942, p. 82). The notion of creative destruction describes the ongoing process whereby firms strive to achieve market power through innovation, which essentially means producing better goods than their competitors. While this appears a rational argument, what is less understood are the non-equilibrium processes that transform the economy from within (WITT, 2003). SCHUMPETER (1934, p. 64) conceptualized the phenomenon of innovation and the processes inherent to it as 'spontaneous and discontinuous change in the channels of the flow, disturbance of equilibrium, which forever alters and displaces the equilibrium state previously existing'. Essentially, embedded in the socio-economic realities and imaginations that drive the continuous search for novelty and competitive advantage, technological change arises endogenously

from within the system, and through transformative and adaptive mechanisms shapes the evolution of the space economy. The consequence is that the economic landscape is in constant unrest, pushed and pulled by processes of competition that both trap capital, labour and routines within some sectors and regions while at the same time encouraging experimentation and discovery in others, resulting in an uneven geography of knowledge production and innovation. Thus, technological change also has a decidedly geographic dimension that affects regional economic growth and prosperity (ASHEIM and GERTLER, 2005).

Evolutionary research approaches frequently focus on history as an explanation for the persistent patterns of uneven regional development. It is understood that the spatial distribution of economic activity is an outcome of largely connected and path-dependent historical processes (DOSI and NELSON, 2010). Indeed, long-term investigations into the patterns of technological change confirm that local technology trajectories are for the most part rigid and path dependent, and without constant reinvention tend to enter a state of technological lock-in, followed by economic decline that is difficult for a locality to escape. Nevertheless, historic accounts also point to islands of innovation at certain times, which indicates that there are windows of opportunities for places and regions to elevate their knowledge production and innovativeness under particular circumstances (SCOTT and STORPER, 2003). Empirical accounts that take a dynamic approach are insightful in this regard, but it is studies that draw on key theories in evolutionary economics and EEG (BOSCHMA and FRENKEN, 2006; FRENKEN and BOSCHMA, 2007; BOSCHMA and MARTIN, 2010a) that really provide the potential to disentangle further the complexity of technological change in the economic landscape (MARTIN and SUNLEY, 2007).

EEG offers a broad, though still evolving, framework that has at its core the production and destruction of novelty in space and the links between novelty and regional economic fortunes (BOSCHMA and MARTIN, 2010b). The creation of technological knowledge, its movement and recombination within different regional ensembles of economic agents and institutions plays a critical role in the evolution of the space-economy (RIGBY and ESSLETZBICHLER, 1997). Theorizing and empirical analysis in EEG often focuses on networks of agents and institutions, rather than just taking the region, or any other spatial entity, as the sole unit of analysis. Also, the firm or public entities are frequently considered the locus of development and change. In this framework, economic evolution is understood to be the result of innovations leading to new organizational routines, and of their subsequent selective transmission amongst agents, and across entities and localities.

In only a short time period, EEG has established itself as a promising and rapidly evolving research framework. Its focus on the driving forces of regional development processes across various scales (micro-, meso-, macro-level) of economic activities, and its attempt to translate findings regarding uneven development, and related consequences, into public policy, puts this stream of enquiry at the centre of the socio-economic research project. There are three primary key approaches and theoretical foundations that have guided EEG-focused research efforts in the recent past. These include, 'Generalised Darwinism', especially the key concepts of variety, selection and retention (ESSLETZBICHLER and RIGBY, 2007, 2010). 'Complexity Theory' thinking, in particular in the context of processes related to the emergence and adaptation of knowledge and innovations, and system properties more generally, is another micro-foundation that frequently guides EEG studies (FRENKEN, 2006; MARTIN and SUNLEY, 2007). The most prevalent applied approach in this line of enquiry, however, is the theory of 'Path Dependency', which circumscribes a whole array of concepts, including branching, path creation and lock-in, among others (BOSCHMA and LAMBOOY, 1999; MARTIN and SUNLEY, 2006, 2010). Other frequently consulted and applied theories include the nature and extent of localized and sectoral knowledge spillovers (JAFFE et al., 1993; BRESCHI and LISSONI, 2001), and the recombinant knowledge/innovation concept (FLEMING and SORENSON, 2001; FRENKEN et al., 2012). The study of localized learning processes (MASKELL and MALMBERG, 1999), properties of different regional knowledge bases (ASHEIM et al., 2012), and knowledge/technology spaces (QUATRARO, 2010; KOGLER et al., 2013; RIGBY, 2013), provide further theoretical insights in this regard.

Based on these foundations, the rationale is that knowledge exchange is predicated on common frameworks of reference and understanding of basic principles and thus most effective between similar, i.e. related, parts in the system. Thus, if knowledge exchange is indeed constrained by technological, cognitive, social and geographical distance, the expectation is that the existing set and composition of knowledge and technologies, along with the stock of knowledge, including institutional expertise and absorptive capacity (COHEN and LEVINTHAL, 1990), at a given place and time, will shape the future path of regional technological change (BOSCHMA et al., 2015). While this logic of path dependency suggests that there are significant limitations with regards to the extent a system can transform due to technological lock-in, at least in the short run this also indicates that there are potential opportunities for branching out into closely related knowledge or technology domains, which may not be part of the regional portfolio at present. While this is a very elementary outline of how EEG reasoning and conceptualization is operationalized, it displays the wide array of theoretical foundations that provide insights for EEG-driven empirical investigations.

Despite the increasing number of studies that apply an EEG framework, the debate surrounding the potential challenges associated with this new paradigm in economic geography is ongoing.[1] On the one hand, there have been calls for a more systematic approach and research agenda, frequently guided by the principal question of what constitutes and identifies an EEG-based study (JOURNAL OF ECONOMIC GEOGRAPHY, 2007; BOSCHMA and MARTIN, 2007). On the contrary, there is a strong and legitimate push for engaged pluralism that will actually expand the theoretical foundations of EEG with insights from related fields, such as geographical political economy, and in particular the role of regional institutions (MACKINNON et al., 2009; PIKE et al., 2009), and more recently relational economic geography (HASSINK et al., 2014).

EVOLUTIONARY ECONOMIC GEOGRAPHY – AN EVOLVING PROJECT

This special issue echoes these calls on several accounts by offering 11 contributions that advance the theoretical foundations of the EEG project in economic geography, and that demonstrate how empirical EEG investigations utilize and operationalize established and new conceptual frameworks. Furthermore, a number of contributions in this special issue point to possible extensions and future research avenues in EEG, and also attempt to establish a stronger link between theory, empirics and policy relevance.[2]

In their contribution, MARTIN and SUNLEY (2014, in this issue) engage in the type of epistemological pluralism that has been called for (MACKINNON et al., 2009), and suggest a path towards a developmental turn in EEG. At the centre of this approach is the reality of uneven geographical development, which is a well-established stylized fact in the field of economic geography. Uneven geographical development is then set in the intersection of three intellectual frameworks, i.e. EEG, institutional economic geography and geographical political economy. While adding yet another, and possibly very important, dimension to the theoretical EEG framework, the paper also implicitly counters past claims that the EEG project is in a state of solidification where the door that allows for engaged pluralisms seems to shut (BARNES and SHEPPARD, 2010).

In the following contribution by BOSCHMA (2014, in this issue), the key argument is for a move towards an evolutionary perspective on regional resilience, which reinvigorates a number of claims and suggestions brought forward in the previous paper by Martin and Sunley. This is a timely and welcome addition to the discussions concerning the concept of regional resilience (CHRISTOPHERSON *et al.*, 2010). Resilience usually refers to the responsiveness of individuals, organizations or systems to shocks, as well as the ability to return to a pre-existing stable equilibrium state after the shock. However, a return to a previous equilibrium state contradicts the basic notions of EEG thinking where the economy is understood as an evolving system in constant change. Thus, it is suggested that an evolutionary approach to regional resilience needs to adopt two meanings within one framework; one that relates to the short-term capacity of a region to absorb shocks, but also another that focuses on the long-term capacity of a region to develop new growth paths.

ESSLETZBICHLER's (2013, in this issue) study of relatedness, industrial branching and technological cohesion in US metropolitan areas offers a methodological and empirical extension of the previous efforts in EEG-related research that investigates the role of industry relatedness for regional economic development. The concept of relatedness, either measured by input linkages between industries, as in this case, or by means of co-occurrence analysis in general, has become an important analysis tool in EEG. Based on the methodology applied in the studies by FRENKEN *et al.* (2007), HAUSMANN and KLINGER (2007) and HIDALGO *et al.* (2007), investigations in this realm test for levels of regional specialization or cohesion in order to examine questions about economic growth and uneven development. The results of the study confirm that technological relatedness is positively correlated to metropolitan industry entry, whereas it is negatively associated with industry exit. Furthermore, Essletzbichler finds that the selection of related incumbent industries complements industry entry and exit as the main drivers of change in metropolitan technological cohesion.

CASTALDI *et al.* (2014, in this issue) investigate how variety affects the innovation output of a region. The results confirm the positive relationships between related variety and economic performance. Additionally, 'unrelated variety' is considered as a potential avenue to generate novel combinations of previously unconnected knowledge domains. It is hypothesized that unrelated variety is positively associated with the regional ability to produce breakthrough inventions. The findings show that there is a positive relationship between the degree of unrelated variety and the share of breakthrough innovation, measured by the share of

superstar patents that receive substantially more forward citations than regular patented products and processes, in a state's total innovation output. These insights advance the related variety hypothesis that has been widely applied in EEG, but also in economic geography more generally.

BRESCHI and LENZI (2014, in this issue) investigate the role of external linkages and gatekeepers for the renewal and expansion of US cities' knowledge bases. The main foundation in considering the importance of external knowledge linkages rests on the fact that knowledge is highly localized and embedded in individuals at a given place. Over time local learning opportunities, and thus possibilities to recombine different knowledge sets, potentially start to diminish, resulting in a decline in creativity and innovative output. The findings confirm the importance of direct external relations for the renewal of local knowledge bases, and also show that these outperform external links mediated by gatekeepers. Gatekeepers are especially important for cities characterized by a localized and specialized knowledge base due to their ability to transcode and absorb externally sourced knowledge into the local innovation system. Investigations into the role of non-local linkages, in the form of co-inventorship, labour (skill) mobility, among others, in shaping inventive potential and innovation performance provide a fruitful avenue for future EEG research endeavours.

A defining moment in the establishment of the modern biotechnology industry was the development of the recombinant DNA (rDNA) method in the 1970s. The technology was patented in 1980, which marks the point of departure for FELDMAN *et al.* (2014, in this issue) in their investigation of the spatial diffusion and adoption of rDNA methods across metropolitan areas over the following 25 years. In this work, space takes different forms, and while it is always geographical, it is also constituted through sets of social relationships and the shifting character of regional knowledge bases. Utilizing a combination of several proximity measures, i.e. spatial, cognitive and social proximity, the analysis employs event history models to examine the timing of a city's first rDNA patent. Feldman *et al.* show that patterns of diffusion and adoption were mainly directed by social contacts developed among co-inventors and by the absorptive capacity of host cities, measured through the structure of a city's knowledge space and its cognitive proximity to the technology class of interest. They conclude that while these results further one's understanding of technology diffusion and adoption mechanisms, important questions in this stream of enquiry remain unanswered, e.g. how does the diffusion of technology alter knowledge variety within regions, and thus the evolution within the space-economy?

In their contribution, FITJAR and RODRÍGUEZ-POSE (2015, in this issue) explore how different types of interaction are related to the ability of firms to innovate in different sectors of the economy. The motivation for this investigation is one's limited understanding of how interaction affects firm adaptation and evolution, and how different forms of interaction shape the genesis of new knowledge and innovation in firms. The findings confirm some of the theoretical expectations, but not others. For example, interaction with universities and research institutes is closely connected with both product and process innovation, and this holds not only for manufacturing, but also for construction and retail firms. Contrary, supplier and customer relations are found to exhibit a negative relationship to innovation in the trade, retail and professional services sector. It is noted that the mismatch between empirical findings and the theoretical expectations point to the need for further research in this regard, a call that should be taken up by the EEG agenda considering the implications for both research and policy on innovation.

ØSTERGAARD and PARK (2015, in this issue) are interested in why clusters decline, a reversal of the usual focus on the genesis and growth of clusters. Firm creation and spinoff activities, along with role of foreign multinational corporations, are taken into account as important drivers of cluster evolution. The results of the analysis reveal that technological and cognitive lock-in, and the exit of focal firms, significantly hampered the adaptive capabilities of the investigated cluster. The lack of new firm formation is found to be another factor that led to the decline of the cluster. It is noted that, in order to generalize these findings, comparable studies are needed. While scholars have produced an abundant amount of cluster and location specific studies that provide fascinating and important insights into how the space-economy evolves, rarely are exact replicas of such studies available, which in turn prohibits a comparative exercise that would allow for a separation of place bound properties from industry-specific trajectories, and from more universal factors altogether.

Policy relevance is usually an implicit part of every EEG-driven analysis, but rarely is regional innovation policy the focal point of interest. This is the case in the contribution by COENEN et al. (2014, in this issue), where the aim is to evaluate the possibilities and limitations for regional innovation policy in facilitating industrial renewal in old industrial regions. Taking a specific policy programme as the point of departure, a case study approach is pursued, with the objective to disentangle empirically the mechanisms which directly affect the processes of path dependency and lock-in, and opportunities for path renewal by means of policy intervention. One of the main insights to be gained from this policy evaluation is that there certainly are mechanisms at work that transcend the regional level, including wider industrial transition and regulatory frameworks, and thus particular attention should be given to support that encourages changes in firm routines and institutional adaptation. Technology-push initiatives

alone appear not to be sufficient for path creation, but need to be supplemented by non-technical, social learning processes. How to initiate and support regional transition from a locked-in mature and declining industry, towards related new industries with growth potential, remains one of the key questions on the EEG agenda.

In their contribution, IAMMARINO and MARINELLI (2014, in this issue) investigate the transition of Italian university graduates to the workforce, and in particular the education–job (mis)match in the context of interregional migration. The objective is to enhance one's understanding of how a territorial perspective can provide insight into the learning processes that influence economic evolution. The findings highlight the regional socio-economic structural differences that persist in the Italian economy. The North, considered vibrant and advanced, seems be a winner in two ways: it benefits from the public investment in higher education made elsewhere, and it also extracts a higher productivity from these investments compared with other regions in the country. This has significant implications if one considers regional innovation policy, which frequently provides extra support for local education systems in the hope of sustained economic development. However, if demand conditions do not match these efforts, and the need for local economic upgrading and diversification is ignored, these efforts most likely will be fruitless.

In the final contribution of this special issue, SPENCER (2015, in this issue) takes up a topic in EEG research that has not been explicitly investigated previously, i.e. urban form. In essence, this study examines the connection between urban forms of neighbourhoods in relation to the EEG of knowledge-intensive industries. The overall finding is that creative industries tend to be located in dense, mixed-use neighbourhoods near the city core, opposed to science-based industries that are mainly located in the suburbs, characterized by low-density and single-use neighbourhoods. This is in line with the understanding that inter-firm relationships that lead to interaction and learning are of particular importance in the creative industries. There is much to be gained from these insights for future investigations. The process of innovation between industries in the creative field and those driven by science and technology may operate quite differently. The latter appears the predominant focus in most contemporary EEG studies, and thus empirical research pertaining to the evolutionary patterns of knowledge production and innovation in the creative sector is still scarce. Perhaps this is due to the lack of easily accessible data, but this certainly should not prevent one from pursuing this EEG research avenue in the future.

REMARKS

EEG highlights the important factors that initiate, prevent or consolidate the contextual settings and relationships in which regions and their respective agents, which comprise and shape economic activity and social reproduction, change over time. While it has become more common in the recent past to investigate economic activity in a dynamic setting, EEG goes beyond this by examining the factors that influence these dynamics rather than just describing them. Overall, EEG provides a framework to disentangle the complexity of technological change and regional economic development based on a variety of theoretical and methodological approaches.

Technological change, the focal process in this context, is a multifaceted phenomenon that is inseparable from the complex structure of socio-economic life (CARLSSON and STANKIEWICZ, 1991). It is a process that is largely cumulative and path dependent, but can sometimes also be radical and spur the birth of entire new industry sectors by means of paradigm changes (COHEN, 2010). The uncertainties regarding the process of technological change explain the obvious difficulties attached to theory building and the collection of empirical evidence in the field of economic geography, and EEG more specifically. Overall, the spatial clustering or agglomeration of economic activity is viewed as a sign of increasing returns and competitive advantage. While economic geographers have explored why agglomeration and knowledge production occur in some places rather than others, they have said little about the emergence of agglomerations, how the benefits of agglomeration may shift over time, and about what types of firms and other economic agents are most likely to capture different returns to co-location.

The arguments embedded in EEG seem well suited for the analysis of these issues, by linking the heterogeneity of economic agents, knowledge systems, political, institutional and organizational forms to the competitive environments that give rise to that heterogeneity, while simultaneously being shaped by them. In essence, EEG explains the spatial evolution of firms, industries, networks, cities and regions from elementary processes such as the entry, growth, decline and exit of firms, and their locational behaviour. While EEG has recently drawn a great deal of attention, much work remains to be done. One of the main concerns that was debated at the special sessions where the idea for this special issue was conceived is that a potential disconnect between theory-making and empirical studies exists, and that this significantly hampers the advancement of the ambitious EEG research agenda. Another concern is that research in this line of enquiry frequently does not attend to policy-relevant questions regarding uneven development. For example, will EEG eventually provide insights to enable the identification of regional lock-in before it occurs in order to apply measures to avoid it? Thus, one of the main objectives that has guided the compilation of this special issue was to address these concerns by means of studies that aim to bridge theory with empiricism, in order to set a future research agenda for this field.

To what extent this endeavour was successful, only time will tell, but certainly the collection of contributions featured in this special issue demonstrate the wide-ranging theoretical and methodological foundations of contemporary research in EEG. A lack of engaged pluralism or cross-sub-disciplinary exchange appears less of a problem than BARNES and SHEPPARD (2010) suggest; a simple bibliometric analysis of the diversity of references and the variety of techniques utilized in the present papers would confirm this. What seems to remain problematic is how empirics in this line of enquiry will keep up with the rapidly evolving and expanding theoretical foundations in order to produce comparative studies that will allow for the separation of place-bound properties from more universal ones. Only then will it be possible to establish a set of stylized facts similar to what has been produced in other related sub-disciplines of economic geography (FELDMAN and KOGLER, 2010). The evolutionary project in economic geography has come a long way since the influential reference point provided by BOSCHMA and FRENKEN (2006), but the journey is far from over: this special issue aims to provide some direction and foundation in this regard.

Acknowledgements – The Guest Editor thanks Ron Boschma and the editorial team of *Regional Studies* for their support with this special issue. He benefited from the comments made by Boschma and David Rigby on earlier drafts of this editorial.

Disclosure statement – No potential conflict of interest was reported by the guest editor.

NOTES

1. A number of special issues have been dedicated to EEG research over the past decade, including: JOURNAL OF ECONOMIC GEOGRAPHY (2007, issue 5; BOSCHMA and MARTIN, 2007) and ECONOMIC GEOGRAPHY (2009, issue 2). In addition, there have been engaged discussions about theoretical foundations that should guide EEG research (e.g. GRABHER, 2009). Also, a number of scholars have contributed to books that aim to outline the EEG research agenda (FRENKEN, 2007), most prominent among these the *Handbook of Evolutionary Economic Geography*, edited by BOSCHMA and MARTIN (2010).
2. The idea for this special issue was born at the Annual Meetings of the Association of American Geographers (AAG) in New York (February, 2012) following a series of 'Evolutionary Economic Geography' sessions.

REFERENCES

ASHEIM B. T. and GERTLER M. S. (2005) The geography of innovation: regional innovation systems, in FAGERBERG J., MOWERY D. and NELSON R. (Eds) *The Oxford Handbook of Innovation*, pp. 291–317. Oxford University Press, Oxford.

ASHEIM B., ISAKSEN A., MOODYSSON J. and SOTARAUTA M. (2012) Knowledge bases, modes of innovation and regional innovation policy, in BATHELT H., FELDMAN M. P. and KOGLER D. F. (Eds) *Beyond Territory: Dynamic Geographies of Knowledge Creation, Diffusion, and Innovation*, pp. 227–249. Routledge, London.

BARNES T. and SHEPPARD E. S. (2010) 'Nothing includes everything': towards engaged pluralism in Anglophone economic geography, *Progress in Human Geography* **34**, 193–214. doi:10.1177/0309132509343728

BOSCHMA R. (2014) Towards an evolutionary perspective on regional resilience, *Regional Studies* **49**, 733–751. doi:10.1080/00343404.2014.959481

BOSCHMA R. A., BALLAND P. A. and KOGLER D. F. (2015) Relatedness and technological change in cities: the rise and fall of technological knowledge in US metropolitan areas from 1981 to 2010, *Industrial and Corporate Change* **24**, 223–250. doi:10.1093/icc/dtu012

BOSCHMA R. A. and FRENKEN K. (2006) Why is economic geography not an evolutionary science? Towards an evolutionary economic geography, *Journal of Economic Geography* **6**, 273–302. doi:10.1093/jeg/lbi022

BOSCHMA R. A. and LAMBOOY J. G. (1999) Evolutionary economics and economic geography, *Journal of Evolutionary Economics* **9**, 411–429. doi:10.1007/s001910050089

BOSCHMA R. and MARTIN R. (2007) Editorial: Constructing an evolutionary economic geography, *Journal of Economic Geography* **7**, 537–548. doi:10.1093/jeg/lbm021

BOSCHMA R. A. and MARTIN R. L. (Eds) (2010a) *Handbook of Evolutionary Economic Geography*. Edward Elgar, Cheltenham.

BOSCHMA R. A. and MARTIN R. L. (2010b) The aims and scope of evolutionary economic geography, in BOSCHMA R. and MARTIN R. L. (Eds) *The Handbook of Evolutionary Economic Geography*, pp. 3–39. Edward Elgar, Cheltenham.

BRESCHI S. and LENZI C. (2014) The role of external linkages and gatekeepers for the renewal and expansion of US cities' knowledge base, 1990–2004, *Regional Studies* **49**, 782–797. doi:10.1080/00343404.2014.954534

BRESCHI S. and LISSONI F. (2001) Knowledge spillovers and local innovation systems: a critical survey, *Industrial and Corporate Change* **10**, 975–1005. doi:10.1093/icc/10.4.975

CARLSSON B. and STANKIEWICZ R. (1991) On the nature, function and composition of technological systems, *Journal of Evolutionary Economics* **1**, 93–118. doi:10.1007/BF01224915

CASTALDI C., FRENKEN K. and LOS B. (2014) Related variety, unrelated variety and technological breakthroughs: an analysis of US state-level patenting, *Regional Studies* **49**, 767–781. doi:10.1080/00343404.2014.940305

CHRISTOPHERSON S., MICHIE J. and TYLER P. (2010) Regional resilience: theoretical and empirical perspectives, *Cambridge Journal of Regions, Economy and Society* **3**, 3–10. doi:10.1093/cjres/rsq004

COENEN L., MOODYSSON J. and MARTIN H. (2014) Path renewal in old industrial regions: possibilities and limitations for regional innovation policy, *Regional Studies* **49**, 850–865. doi:10.1080/00343404.2014.979321

COHEN W. M. (2010) Fifty years of empirical studies of innovative activity and performance, in HALL B. and ROSENBERG N. (Eds) *Handbook of the Economics of Innovation*, pp. 129–213. Elsevier, Oxford.

COHEN W. M. and LEVINTHAL D. (1990) Absorptive capacity: a new perspective on learning and innovation, *Administrative Science Quarterly* **35**, 128–152. doi:10.2307/2393553

DOSI G. and NELSON R. R. (2010) Technical change and industrial dynamics as evolutionary processes, in HALL B. and ROSENBERG N. (Eds) *Handbook of the Economics of Innovation*, pp. 51–127. Elsevier, Oxford.

ESSLETZBICHLER J. (2013) Relatedness, industrial branching and technological cohesion in US metropolitan areas, *Regional Studies* **49**, 752–766. doi:10.1080/00343404.2013.806793

ESSLETZBICHLER J. and RIGBY D. L. (2007) Exploring evolutionary economic geographies, *Journal of Economic Geography* **7**, 549–571. doi:10.1093/jeg/lbm022

ESSLETZBICHLER J. and RIGBY D. L. (2010) Generalized Darwinism and evolutionary economic geography, in BOSCHMA R. A. and MARTIN R. L. (Eds) *The Handbook of Evolutionary Economic Geography*, pp. 43–61. Edward Elgar, Cheltenham.

FELDMAN M. P. and KOGLER D. F. (2010) Stylized facts in the geography of innovation, in HALL B. and ROSENBERG N. (Eds) *Handbook of the Economics of Innovation*, pp. 381–410. Elsevier, Oxford.

FELDMAN M. P., KOGLER D. F. and RIGBY D. L. (2014) rKnowledge: the spatial diffusion and adoption of rDNA methods, *Regional Studies* **49**, 798–817. doi:10.1080/00343404.2014.980799

FITJAR R. D. and RODRÍGUEZ-POSE A. (2015) Interaction and innovation across different sectors: findings from Norwegian city-regions, *Regional Studies* **49**, 818–833. doi:10.1080/00343404.2015.1016415

FLEMING L. and SORENSON O. (2001) Technology as a complex adaptive system: evidence from patent data, *Research Policy* **30**, 1019–1039. doi:10.1016/S0048-7333(00)00135-9

FRENKEN K. (2006) Technological innovation and complexity theory, *Economics of Innovation and New Technology* **15**, 137–155. doi:10.1080/10438590500141453

FRENKEN K. (Ed.) (2007) *Applied Evolutionary Economics and Economic Geography*. Edward Elgar, Cheltenham.

FRENKEN K. and BOSCHMA R. A. (2007) A theoretical framework for evolutionary economic geography: industrial dynamics and urban growth as a branching process, *Journal of Economic Geography* **7**, 635–649. doi:10.1093/jeg/lbm018

FRENKEN K., IZQUIERDO L. R. and ZEPPINI P. (2012) Branching innovation, recombinant innovation, and endogenous technological transitions, *Environmental Innovation and Societal Transitions* **4**, 25–35. doi:10.1016/j.eist.2012.06.001

FRENKEN K., VAN OORT F. G. and VERBURG T. (2007) Related variety, unrelated variety and regional economic growth, *Regional Studies* **41**, 685–697. doi:10.1080/00343400601120296

GRABHER G. (2009) Yet another turn? The evolutionary project in economic geography, *Economic Geography* **85**, 119–127. doi:10.1111/j.1944-8287.2009.01016.x

HASSINK R., KLAERDING C. and MARQUES P. (2014) Advancing evolutionary economic geography by engaged pluralism, *Regional Studies* **48**, 1295–1307. doi:10.1080/00343404.2014.889815

HAUSMANN R. and KLINGER B. (2007) *The Structure of the Product Space and the Evolution of Comparative Advantage.* CID Working Paper No. 146. Center for International Development (CID), Harvard University, Cambridge, MA.

HIDALGO C. A., KLINGER B., BARABASSI A.-L. and HAUSMANN R. (2007) The product space conditions the development of nations, *Science* **317(5837)**, 482–487. doi:10.1126/science.1144581

IAMMARINO S. and MARINELLI E. (2014) Education–job (mis)match and interregional migration: Italian university graduates' transition to work, *Regional Studies* **49**, 866–882. doi:10.1080/00343404.2014.965135

JAFFE A. B., TRAJTENBERG M. and HENDERSON R. (1993) Geographic localization of knowledge spillovers as evidenced by patent citations, *Quarterly Journal of Economics* **63**, 577–598. doi:10.2307/2118401

KOGLER D. F., RIGBY D. L. and TUCKER I. (2013) Mapping knowledge space and technological relatedness in US cities, *European Planning Studies* **21**, 1374–1391. doi:10.1080/09654313.2012.755832

MACKINNON D., CUMBERS A., PIKE A., BIRCH K. and MCMASTER R. (2009) Evolution in economic geography: Institutions, political economy, and adaptation, *Economic Geography* **85**, 129–150. doi:10.1111/j.1944-8287.2009.01017.x

MARTIN R. L. and SUNLEY P. (2006) Path dependence and regional economic evolution, *Journal of Economic Geography* **6**, 395–437. doi:10.1093/jeg/lbl012

MARTIN R. L. and SUNLEY P. (2007) Complexity thinking and evolutionary economic geography, *Journal of Economic Geography* **7**, 573–601. doi:10.1093/jeg/lbm019

MARTIN R. L. and SUNLEY P. (2010) The place of path dependence in an evolutionary perspective on the economic landscape, in BOSCHMA R. A. and MARTIN R. L. (Eds) *The Handbook of Evolutionary Economic Geography*, pp. 62–92. Edward Elgar, Cheltenham.

MARTIN R. and SUNLEY P. (2014) Towards a developmental turn in evolutionary economic geography?, *Regional Studies* **49**, 712–732. doi:10.1080/00343404.2014.899431

MASKELL P. and MALMBERG A. (1999) The competitiveness of firms and regions: 'ubiquitification' and the importance of localized learning, *European Urban and Regional Studies* **6**, 9–25. doi:10.1177/096977649900600102

NELSON R. R. and WINTER S. G. (1982) *An Evolutionary Theory of Economic Change.* Belknap, Cambridge, MA.

ØSTERGAARD C. R. and PARK E. (2015) What makes clusters decline? A study on disruption and evolution of a high-tech cluster in Denmark, *Regional Studies* **49**, 834–849. doi:10.1080/00343404.2015.1015975

PIKE A., BIRCH K., CUMBERS A., MACKINNON D. and MCMASTER R. (2009) A geographical political economy of evolution in economic geography, *Economic Geography* **85**, 175–182. doi:10.1111/j.1944-8287.2009.01021.x

QUATRARO F. (2010) Knowledge coherence, variety and economic growth: manufacturing evidence from Italian regions, *Research Policy* **39**, 1289–1302. doi:10.1016/j.respol.2010.09.005

RIGBY D. L. (2013) Technological relatedness and knowledge space: entry and exit of US cities from patent classes, *Regional Studies*. doi:10.1080/00343404.2013.854878

RIGBY D. L. and ESSLETZBICHLER J. (1997) Evolution, process variety, and regional trajectories of technological change in U.S. manufacturing, *Economic Geography* **73**, 269–284. doi:10.2307/144484

SCHUMPETER J. A. (1934) *The Theory of Economic Development.* Harvard University Press, Cambridge, MA.

SCHUMPETER J. A. (1942) *Capitalism, Socialism and Democracy.* Harper, New York, NY.

SCOTT A. J. and STORPER M. (2003) Regions, globalization, development, *Regional Studies* **37**, 579–593. doi:10.1080/0034340032000108697a

SPENCER G. M. (2015) Knowledge neighbourhoods: urban form and evolutionary economic geography, *Regional Studies* **49**, 883–898. doi:10.1080/00343404.2015.1019846

WITT U. (2003) *The Evolving Economy: Essays on the Evolutionary Approach to Economics.* Edward Elgar, Cheltenham.

Towards a Developmental Turn in Evolutionary Economic Geography?

RON MARTIN and PETER SUNLEY

Department of Geography, University of Cambridge, Downing Place, UK.
Geography and Environment, University of Southampton, University Road, UK.

MARTIN R. and SUNLEY P. Towards a developmental turn in evolutionary economic geography?, *Regional Studies*. Over the past couple of decades or so there have been increasing moves within evolutionary theory to move beyond the neo-Darwinian principles of variety, selection and retention, and to incorporate development. This has led to a richer palette of concepts, mechanisms and models of evolution and change, such as plasticity, robustness, evolvability, emergence, niche construction and self-organization, This opens up a different framework for understanding evolution. This paper sets out the main characteristics of the recent and ongoing 'developmental turn' in evolutionary theory and suggests how these might inform a corresponding 'developmental turn' in evolutionary economic geography.

MARTIN R. and SUNLEY P. 演化经济地理中的发展转向？ 区域研究。过去数十年来，演化理论中，有越来越多超越新达尔文主义有关变异、选择与维持准则之转变，并纳入了发展。此一转变导致了更为丰富的概念、机制，以及演化和变迁的模式，诸如可塑性、坚实、可进化性、浮现、利基建立与自我组织。此一趋势，开启了不同的框架来理解演化。本文阐述晚近在演化理论中持续进行的"发展转向"的主要特征，并指出这些特征如何告知演化经济地理中相应的"发展转向"。

MARTIN R. et SUNLEY P. Vers une tournure dans la géographie économique évolutionniste?, *Regional Studies*. Au cours des deux dernières décennies ou presque, il y a eu une augmentation des démarches au sein de la théorie évolutionniste en faveur d'aller au-delà des principes néo-darwiniens de variété, de sélection, et de conservation, et d'y intégrer le développement. Cela a amené à une riche palette de notions, de mécanismes et de modèles de l'évolution et de la mutation, telles la plasticité, la robustesse, le caractère évolutive, l'émergence, la construction de créneaux et l'auto-organisation. Cela crée un cadre différent pour comprendre l'évolution. Cet article élabore les principales caractéristiques de la récente 'tournure' courante dans la théorie évolutionniste et suggère comment elles pourraient informer une 'tournure' correspondante dans la géographie économique évolutionniste.

MARTIN R. und SUNLEY P. Auf dem Weg zu einer Entwicklungswende in der evolutionären Wirtschaftsgeografie?, *Regional Studies*. In den letzten Jahrzehnten gab es innerhalb der Evolutionstheorie verstärkte Bewegungen zur Weiterentwicklung der neodarwinistischen Prinzipien der Vielfalt, Auswahl und Beibehaltung sowie zur Berücksichtigung der Entwicklung. Dies hat zu einer reichhaltigeren Palette von Konzepten, Mechanismen und Modellen der Evolution und Veränderung geführt, wie z. B. der Plastizität, Robustheit, Evolvierbarkeit, Emergenz, Nischenbildung und Selbstorganisation, was einen unterschiedlichen Rahmen zum Verständnis der Evolution eröffnet. In diesem Beitrag werden die wichtigsten Merkmale der aktuellen und andauernden 'Entwicklungswende' in der Evolutionstheorie beschrieben, und es wird dargelegt, wie diese Merkmale eine entsprechende 'Entwicklungswende' in der evolutionären Wirtschaftsgeografie gestalten könnten.

MARTIN R. y SUNLEY P. ¿Hacia un cambio en el desarrollo de la geografía económica evolutiva?, *Regional Studies*. En las dos últimas décadas se han observado cada vez más intentos en la teoría de la evolución de ir más allá de los principios neodarwinianos de variedad, selección y retención para considerar también el desarrollo. Esto ha conducido a una paleta más rica de conceptos, mecanismos y modelos de la evolución y el cambio, tales como plasticidad, solidez, evolutividad, emergencia, construcción de nichos y auto-organización, lo que abre vías diferentes para entender la evolución. En este artículo se presentan las características principales del 'giro del desarrollo' reciente y continuo en la teoría de la evolución y se indica cómo estas podrían contribuir a un 'giro del desarrollo' correspondiente en la geografía económica evolutiva.

INTRODUCTION: RETHINKING EVOLUTIONARY ECONOMIC GEOGRAPHY

Perhaps it is not too much to say that what we need is an evolutionary theory worthy of the best social theory, not a social theory trimmed to fit a rapidly receding, overly simplistic evolutionary theory.

(DEPEW and WEBER, 1995, p. 495)

I remonstrate that only one side of the Darwinian narrative is currently being told – the eliminative aspects that derive from competition. It is the neglected half of evolution – i.e. the growth side – that more resembles developmental theory and deserves greater emphasis.

(ULANOWICZ, 2012, p. 281)

Explaining how 'space makes possible the particular, which then unfolds in time', to use the pithy phrase with which August Lösch begins the Epilogue to his masterpiece on *The Economics of Location*, has long been a recurring focus of enquiry in economic geography. Most often this focus has been subsumed under the general rubric of 'regional development', and over the years various theories have been advanced purporting to capture the characteristic patterns and processes involved. The recent rise of 'evolutionary economic geography' (EEG) can in one sense be seen as the latest attempt in this ongoing endeavour (BOSCHMA and FRENKEN, 2006; BOSCHMA and MARTIN, 2007, 2010). Advocates of the new EEG – ourselves included – have championed the exploration of this perspective on the grounds that it pushes the analysis of regional economic *change and evolution* to centre stage, and have argued that much of the distinctiveness of the approach derives not just from giving primary emphasis to the 'historical unfolding' of the economic landscape, but also from the deliberate exploration and use of explicitly *evolutionary* concepts, analogies and metaphors inspired by evolutionary ideas and thinking developed in biology, physics, ecology and other such fields of enquiry. Of course, care must be exercised in using ideas from other disciplinary fields as metaphors and analogies for how one thinks about change in the economic landscape. For one thing, there may well be ontological limits to such abductions: as Alfred Marshall once quipped, 'analogies may help one into the saddle, but are encumbrances on a long journey' (MARSHALL, 1898, p. 39). For another thing, and equally importantly, different evolutionary concepts embody or imply different models of change, with the consequence that their application in economic geography likewise implies different models of how regional economies

change over time: such models of change, sometimes recognized explicitly, sometimes merely left implicit, include gradualism, path dependence, punctuated equilibrium, branching, emergence and life cycles. Thus far, evolutionary economic geographers – again, ourselves included – have given relatively little attention to how far and in what ways these different underlying models of change, and the theoretical perspectives from which they are drawn, relate to each other. Different models of evolutionary sequence may be applicable to some types of economic process and spatial scales and not others. This raises the question of whether and to what extent some sort of synthesis is possible, and thus whether, as a consequence, EEG can be given a more comprehensive and more integrated conceptual basis.

There is another compelling reason for posing this question. If there is one single conceptual approach that above others has tended to inform and motivate EEG, it is some invocation of the key Darwinian notions of variation, selection and retention (VSR) (ESSLETZBICHLER and RIGBY, 2007).[1] These same notions have played a formative role in the development of evolutionary economics, so it is not surprising that economic geographers should have been drawn to them in developing their own 'evolutionary turn'. Indeed, in this respect, both disciplines have been heavily influenced by a wider movement that has sought to construct a new overarching research strategy of 'Generalized Darwinism' based on the assumption of a close homology between evolution in nature and the evolution of the socio-economy (HODGSON, 1993). Advocates of Generalized Darwinism invoke VSR as the central defining principles governing social and economic evolution. Evolutionary economic geographers have tended to adopt the same strategy: in their work, too, the notions of variety (and more recently 'related variety'), selection and retention have been used to construct an evolutionary perspective on the spatial economy, including studies of how industries emerge and develop across space, how regional economies function as 'selection' environments, how far and in what ways various 'retention' mechanisms lead to the 'lock-in' of particular regional patterns of economic activity, and how spatial networks of economic relations and forms of spatial economic agglomeration (from clusters to cities) evolve through time, to name but some of the topics of interest.

However, within economics and other disciplines, the project of Generalized Darwinism has recently come under increasing critical examination. Even some of those evolutionary economists who previously drew extensively on the basic Darwinian framework in their work now seem to argue that invoking the concepts of VSR may not only be ontologically problematic, but also that these three principles of themselves do not suffice to explain economic evolution. There is growing doubt about how far Darwinism can be 'generalized' to the economic realm, and certainly whether its abstract principles provide an adequate basis for an evolutionary approach to economics. At the very least, the view seems to be emerging that additional principles and concepts for explaining the processes of economic change and evolution also need to be considered.

To compound matters, recent debates in evolutionary biology itself involve a major reassessment of the Darwinian-infused model. The Modern Synthesis, essentially a synthesis of neo-Darwinism and Mendelism, has defined evolutionary theory since the 1940s (FUTUYMA, 1988). Over recent decades, however, there have been increasing moves to overcome what an expanding number of evolutionary theorists see as key limitations of the Modern Synthesis, including the tenets of VSR. These limitations are seen by a growing number of theorists as deriving in large part from the relative isolation of developmental biology from evolutionary biology. How to reconcile and integrate these two sciences has been discussed intermittently for some time, but recently two new synthesizing endeavours have emerged that represent major steps in this direction, namely: Evolutionary Developmental Biology (EDB), or 'evo-devo' to use its commonly employed sobriquet, and Developmental Systems Theory (DST). Both, in their different ways, seek to expound how developmental processes effect evolutionary change and how development itself has evolved. Both seek to move beyond the 'gene-centred' approach of the Darwinian Modern Synthesis to recognize the multilevel and non-genetic aspects of evolution. And, importantly, both allow environmental and contextual resources and influences to have a formative role in how development and evolution co-interact. Of the two approaches, EDB retains the closest links with the Modern Synthesis, whereas DST is more radical in its approach. Furthermore, although EDB and DST derive from different basic conceptualizations of how evolution and development are (or should be) related, some of their tenets are not that dissimilar, and there is increasing interest in creating bridges between the two perspectives. Both seem to offer the prospect of a more pluralistic and systemic or holistic theory of evolution, one that incorporates additional levels of explanation than that provided by the Darwinian Modern Synthesis. Interestingly, some evolutionary anthropologists and cultural theorists have begun to examine EDB to ascertain what its implications might be for their disciplines (e.g., MESOUDI et al., 2006; WIMSATT, 2006; SMITH and RUPPLE, 2011), and behavioural psychologists are applying DST in their field

(e.g., LERNER, 2006; MASTEN and OBRADOVIC, 2006). Economists appear about to embark on similar exploratory expeditions (for example, see PELIKAN, 2011, and COCHRANE and MACCLAURIN, 2012, on the relevance of EDB for evolutionary economics). It is worth exploring, therefore, what the implications might be for EEG.

The more so because current EEG has already come in for some criticism. It has been charged as being too narrowly focused and for claiming to be an approach quite different from others in economic geography. Its critics argue that what one should be seeking to develop is not 'evolutionary economic geography', but the treatment of 'evolution in economic geography' and the integration of EEG with existing theoretical frameworks, such as geopolitical economy or institutional economic geography, which, it is claimed, not only incorporate various historical arguments of their own, but also, unlike EEG, take power and agency into explicit account (MACKINNON et al., 2009; BARNES and SHEPPARD, 2010; COE, 2011; OOSTERLYNCK, 2012).[2] Evolutionary economic geographers – ourselves included – would not only argue that such criticisms are somewhat premature (after all, the field of EEG is still in its infancy), but that power relations, embedded agents and institutions can all in principle be incorporated into an evolutionary perspective. The fact that progress has yet to be made on this front should not be taken to mean that evolutionary economic geographers view these features as unimportant or incompatible with their approach (BOSCHMA and FRENKEN, 2009; MARTIN, 2011). At the same time, however, evolutionary economic geographers – again, ourselves most certainly included – would also refute any suggestion that they are seeking to construct some all-embracing alternative 'meta-theory'. Rather, the ambition is more modest. Capitalism is a dynamic system of ongoing change and transformation, of incessant and uneven 'creative destruction', to use Schumpeter's famous phrase: or, as KNIGHT (1923, p. 184) once put it, 'there is evolution in the nature of capitalism'. The aim of EEG, as we see it, is to explore what evolutionary principles can be identified that help to explain change and transformation in the economic landscape. To this end, and this is the key point, whether the aim is to develop the treatment of 'evolution in economic geography' or to prosecute 'evolutionary economic geography' as a distinctive paradigm, it is surely important that the ideas utilized and adapted reflect the latest thinking in evolutionary theory. Writing over a decade ago, METCALFE (1998) argued that 'as economists applying evolutionary ideas to economic phenomena, we can learn from the debates on evolution in biology [...] without in any sense needing to absorb the associated biological context' (pp. 21–22). That is precisely the sentiment here.

But our purpose needs to make clear. We are not arguing that 'Generalized Darwinism' (largely via its use in evolutionary economics) has been the *only* source of inspiration in EEG; obviously that is not the case. Some authors have expressed interest in ideas borrowed from the theory of complex adaptive systems; indeed we have explored such ideas ourselves (MARTIN and SUNLEY, 2007, 2011, 2012). And of course the notion of path dependence is frequently invoked in EEG accounts: again, we have contributed to the development of this notion for studying change and continuity in the economic landscape (MARTIN and SUNLEY, 2006; MARTIN, 2010, 2013). However, it is the case that, explicitly or implicitly, ideas from Generalized Darwinism have played, and continue to play, a significant role in EEG, and it is this body of evolutionary notions and metaphors that has recently attracted reappraisal from within evolutionary biology and evolutionary economics. This reappraisal, moreover, involves the incorporation of ideas from complex adaptive systems. These developments provide the motivation for this paper. In our view there are two main tasks: to update the range of evolutionary concepts and constructs that might be deployed, to take account of new developments within evolutionary theory itself; and to develop an expanded theoretical architecture that allows engagement with relevant ideas and arguments to be found in other approaches to economic geography, particularly those that focus on uneven regional development. Each task is itself a major exercise: to accomplish both successfully is far beyond a single paper. What follows, therefore, is merely an initial attempt to chart one possible route by which to travel towards that destination, namely the idea of constructing what might be called an 'evolutionary developmental economic geography'.[3] The focus is on establishing an expanded evolutionary–geographical conceptual apparatus, since that is the vital first step; the discussion of how to put that apparatus into empirical action, the second step, is beyond the scope (and length) of this paper, though brief thoughts are offered on this issue. The next section begins with an examination of the limits of Generalized Darwinism as a basis for EEG.

EVOLUTIONARY ECONOMIC GEOGRAPHY: MOVING BEYOND GENERALIZED DARWINISM

As noted above, neo-Darwinian evolutionary ideas have been important to the emergence of EEG in two main ways. Firstly, the subfield has drawn much inspiration from the way that evolutionary economists have used Darwinian-infused notions in a metaphorical and analogical manner (such as NELSON and WINTER, 1982; METCALFE, 1998; and WITT, 2003). In particular, most of the foundational contributions to EEG have drawn upon NELSON and WINTER's (1982) argument that in the economic sphere it is business routines that demonstrate the key neo-Darwinian processes of

variation, selection and replication or retention (BOSCHMA 2004; BOSCHMA and FRENKEN, 2006). Just as genes are the main replicators of biological information, so business routines are frequently viewed by evolutionary economists and evolutionary economic geographers as playing an analogous role in the economy:

> The appropriate unit of selection is, I suggest, an organizational cum technological complex: a set of instructions for translating input into output for a purpose. This complex is constituted by the set of routines to guide behaviour, routines which collectively constitute the knowledge base of the particular activity. We shall call this complex a business unit […].
>
> (METCALFE, 1998, p. 27)

Heterogeneity and variety in routines are argued to fuel a selection process driven by competitive markets (what Metcalfe calls a process of 'competitive selection').

Secondly, the influence of neo-Darwinian thought has been strengthened in recent years by the consolidation of what has been called 'Generalized Darwinism' (HODGSON, 2002; HODGSON and KNUDSEN, 2006, 2010; ALDRICH et al., 2008). This approach argues that all evolutionary processes, including those in the economic domain, are characterized by the operation of the three key principles of VSR. Although it is recognized that the specific nature and operation of these principles are quite distinct in different fields, and that economic instances differ from their biological counterparts, nevertheless according to HODGSON and KNUDSEN (2006, 2010) one cannot have satisfactory explanations of how economic systems evolve that do not refer to these three principles (also see METCALFE, 1998). This assumption has been carried over into EEG, where the challenge is seen as one of identifying the specific instances of VSR responsible for spatial economic change (ESSLETZBICHLER and RIGBY, 2007).

In recent years, however, the appeal to neo-Darwinian ideas has been subject to growing reassessment within evolutionary economics. This critique is partly rooted in a concern about the difficulties in translating these ideas into social theories. WITT (2004), for example, highlights how the metaphors of VSR are in some ways ill-suited to understanding processes of human creativity and learning. In his view, 'The selection metaphor may therefore divert attention from what seems to be crucially important for economic evolution – the role played by cognition, learning and growing knowledge' (p. 128). Others point out that such metaphors yield an approach that is overly micro-focused and which fail to consider the more holistic features of an economic system (FOSTER, 2010). Such questioning has been intensified by the recent critical reaction to Generalized Darwinism (NELSON, 1995, 2007; BUENSTORF, 2006; VROMEN, 2007, 2008; LEVIT et al., 2011). Interestingly, while maintaining that neo-Darwinian evolutionary theory illuminates some aspects of economic change, even Richard Nelson now warns that socio-cultural evolution should not be shoehorned into a standard Darwinian framework, and that fundamental differences exist between the biological and socio-cultural realms: 'Indeed it seems to me that the differences are as interesting as the similarities, and I would like to urge a broad and flexible view of evolutionary theories of change' (NELSON, 2007, p. 92).

But in part the critique of an overreliance on the principles of VSR has also claimed that Generalized Darwinism is too abstract and too 'top down'. While HODGSON and KNUDSEN (2006, 2010) acknowledge that there are significant differences between biological and economic systems, they argue that the differences relate to domain-specific details rather than to the general principles propounded by Generalized Darwinism. In other words, details that are specific for the economic domain are to be added to the three principles in order to get fully fledged causal explanations of economic evolutionary processes. The problem with this position, as VROMEN (2007, 2008) points out, is that if the three basic tenets of Generalized Darwinism are still necessary for explaining economic evolution but free of any biological connotation or analogy, then the form of Generalized Darwinism invoked will have to be of a very high level of generality and abstraction indeed. Yet this then means that even more 'domain-specific' hypotheses have to be added than Hodgson and Knudsen envisage in order to arrive at detailed causal theories of how economic systems evolve.

In this view, as the neo-Darwinian principles of VSR are forced to become ever more abstract in order to apply across all aspects of the economy, so they lose their explanatory power in the process (CORDES, 2006). Similarly, LEVIT et al. (2011) argue that Generalized Darwinism is too 'top-down', trying in vain to proceed from an abstract hull to auxiliary hypotheses about economic processes. Instead, they argue, a better research strategy might be a 'bottom-up' approach that starts with concrete details:

> If so, the recommendation for evolutionary economics would be to focus on analyzing the huge variety of specific evolutionary processes in the economy at a concrete level, and only when explanatory progress has been made at that concrete level, to engage in a (bottom-up) discourse of how the complex set of specific hypotheses can be organized into a more coherent causal and functional structure.
> (p. 559)

In their opinion, this approach – which obviously bears a close similarity with the methodologies of 'appreciative theorising' and 'grounded theory' – is the more appropriate for deriving general principles with which to understand economic evolution.

To many economic geographers this call to engage with 'concrete variety' will feel rather like a rendezvous with an old acquaintance. The debate about whether to start with concrete details or with abstract theory, and

the potential dangers entailed in either approach, has a long history in economic geography. It is tempting to agree with Levit et al. by arguing that a 'bottom up' approach should be adopted in EEG by first analysing the 'huge variety of specific evolutionary processes in the [spatial] economy at the concrete level', and then seeking to develop general principles and theory from this basis. In our view, however, the 'bottom-up' strategy recommended by these (reconstructed) evolutionary economists is not unproblematic, as it carries the danger of veering too closely towards an inductive approach that does little more than generate a welter of empirical studies that might claim to be 'evolutionary', and which may use 'evolutionary' terms and phrases, but which actually fail to advance the theoretical or conceptual foundations of an evolutionary perspective. This is not to dismiss Levit et al.'s persuasive critique of Generalized Darwinism and its rather constricting set of principles. But we are wary that a 'bottom-up' research strategy alone would find enough conceptual direction and momentum to drive the coherent development of EEG. Although important, the accumulation of an increasing array of empirical case studies of the historical spatial development of specific industries and technologies is not of itself a guarantee that a coherent body of evolutionary economic–geographic theory or principles will emerge as a result. In any case, a 'bottom-up' approach surely presupposes that we have at least some idea of what the 'evolutionary processes' we are seeking to analyse actually are. A 'bottom-up' approach – whether a form of 'appreciative theorising' (NELSON, 1995) or what is now becoming known in evolutionary economics as 'history-friendly models' (CASTELLACCI, 2006; MALERBA et al., 1999; MALERBA, 2010) – based on the close empirical examination of concrete specific cases and trends, must almost inevitably involve the use of some sort of guiding theoretical principles or concepts, and these presumably will be evolutionary in nature. After all, if one is interested in economic evolution, it makes sense to think in 'evolutionary' terms, however loosely such ontological preconceptions are framed. It is doubtful that good inductive research, including even what might appear to be straightforward historical narratives of regional industrial–technological change, can ever be wholly 'theory free' or devoid of metaphorical constructions.

In other words, there is a continuing role for evolutionary metaphors and analogies, even in 'bottom-up' approaches, because such metaphors can guide the process of theorizing *and* empirical work. Evolutionary metaphors and analogies, in other words, can help historical change to be conceptualized, and guide the search for evolutionary processes. The purpose of an evolutionary perspective in economic geography is *not* in searching for direct and exact economic–geographic equivalents of biological processes. Rather, the value of an evolutionary perspective is as *a way of thinking*, in our case about the unfolding and transformation of economic landscapes over time. Evolutionary ideas and concepts taken from biology, ecology or some other related discipline may suggest principles that are more generic in nature, that have an interpretation and relevance in fields like economics and economic geography quite different from those in which they were first expounded.

To this end, it is important that one engages with the latest ideas and concepts emerging in evolutionary theory. And one such area where new ideas and principles are being forged is the new 'developmental turn' in evolutionary thinking as found in EDB and DST. EDB and DST do not reject or abandon the principles of VSR, but seek to embed them in a larger, more expansive repertoire of concepts and 'organizing principles' used to explain evolution, and thereby to create space for the role of other factors and mechanisms in shaping the process and pathways of evolution. Potentially, then, these new fields may offer a wider body of ideas for use in EEG, and perhaps may even assist with integrating the study of economic evolution with that of (uneven) geographical development. To begin to move towards this framework, the next section examines the 'developmental turn' that is currently underway in evolutionary theory.

THE 'DEVELOPMENTAL TURN' IN EVOLUTIONARY THEORY

Much has been written about how the neo-Darwinian Modern Synthesis entrenched a separation between evolutionary and developmental biology. Evolutionary biology has classically been concerned with phylogeny, the evolutionary history of organismal populations, drawing heavily on the population genetic formalism of the neo-Darwinian Modern Synthesis. Developmental biology, on the other hand, is concerned with ontogeny, with the origin and development of an individual organism through its life span. Reconciling the evolutionary science of VSR with the science of development has troubled biologists for decades. Over the past 20 years or so, however, increasing attention has been directed to integrating evolution and

development as part of a search for what some have called a 'New Synthesis' (ENDLER and MCLELLAN, 1988), others a new 'Extended Synthesis' (PIGLIUCCI and MÜLLER, 2010), and still others a new 'epistemic space' (MÜLLER, 2007; PIGLIUCCI, 2007, 2008; 2009; WEBER, 2011).

As mentioned above, this synthesizing endeavour has found expression in two main research programmes, namely EDB and DST.[4] Of these, EDB is the more theoretically articulated, and is explicitly aimed at building on and extending the Modern Synthesis (RAFF, 1996; HALL, 1999, 2003; CARROLL, 2000; LAUBICHLER and MAIENSCHEIN, 2007; MÜLLER, 2007, 2008; FUSCO and MINELLI, 2008). DST is less well formulated but more expansive in orientation, and has its roots in psycho-biology and behavioural psychology (OYAMA, 2000; OYAMA et al., 2001; GRAY, 2001; ROBERT et al., 2001; GRIFFITHS and GRAY, 1994, 2005). Although these two perspectives have different origins, several recent papers have addressed the relationship between them and in general conclude that EDB and DST are essentially complementary (ROBERT et al., 2001; JABLONKA and LAMB, 2002; GILBERT, 2003; GRIFFITHS and GRAY, 2004, 2005). Considered together, these two approaches embrace a number of key departures from the Modern Synthesis.

First, each advocates a much more *holistic* perspective on evolution, an approach that allows evolutionary and developmental processes to interact both with each other and with the environment. This implies a systems-orientated view that goes beyond the 'gene-centrism' of the Modern Evolutionary Synthesis to allow several other factors, mechanisms and interactions to play an equally vital role in shaping the evolutionary process. In EDB this new (sometimes called 'epigenetic') approach to evolution focuses on aspects of an organism's development that lead to adjustment when its environment or internal organization changes (BRAKEFIELD, 2006) (Table 1). An explicit allowance is made for environmental induction, that is for environmental influences to impact on development and evolution (MÜLLER, 2007). Central to this new focus is the interplay between the developmental features of *robustness* and *plasticity*, and how these processes themselves evolve (BATESON and GLUCKMAN, 2011). In this

Table 1. Some key concepts in Evolutionary Developmental Biology (EDB)

Concept	Main focus or definition
Robustness	Ability of an organism or system to maintain certain functionalities when subjected to substantial environmental or internal perturbation or disruption, and may involve or necessitate changes in the structure or components of the system
Plasticity	Ability of an organism or system to adjust its behaviour, function or form in response to mutations and environmental disturbances and disruptions
Niche construction	Ability of an organism to modify, shape or control its own immediate environment so as to ensure its own evolutionary success
Evolvability	Capacity of a developmental system to evolve, which is primarily a function of its ability to generate variation in form in a way that potentially enhances survival and reproduction

Sources: MÜLLER (2007), PIGLIUCCI and MÜLLER (2010), and BATESON and GLUCKMAN (2011).

respect, biologists view organisms as complex adaptive systems, the *robustness* of which is defined as the maintenance through time of an organism's core purpose and performance or functionality despite environmental perturbation. Robustness does *not* mean that an organism or system remains completely unchanged in the face of disruptions or perturbations in its environment; rather some structural or other features may *need* to change in order preserve *core* functions:

> Robustness is often misunderstood to mean staying unchanged regardless of stimuli or mutations, so that the structure and components of the system, and therefore the mode of operation, are unaffected. In fact, robustness is the maintenance of specific functionalities of the system against perturbations, and it often requires the system to change its mode of operation in a flexible way. In other words, robustness allows changes in the structure and components of the system owing to perturbations, but specific functions are maintained.
>
> (KITANO, 2004, p. 827)

Robustness, therefore, may require and involve *plasticity*, which describes an organism's or entity's malleability, its capacity to change or adapt its form or behaviour in response to changing external or internal conditions. Plasticity involves developmental 'reaction norms' that relate the response of an organism's internally coded, inheritable information (its genotype) to a particular environmental perturbation or system input. As WEST-EBERHARD (2005) puts it: 'I consider genes followers rather than leaders in adaptive evolution. […] We forget that […] environmental factors constitute powerful inducers and essential raw materials whose geographically variable states can induce developmental novelties as populations colonise new areas' (p. 6547). In this account, new traits may appear for a variety of reasons (including environmental induction, and learning) and give rise to novel organismal forms and behaviours. If the novelty is advantageous, and affects the organism's fitness, natural selection 'fixes' it by stabilizing the alteration of the genetic architecture (the genetic frequencies that make populations). Thus plasticity is not necessarily the opposite of robustness, or the closely related idea of developmental *canalization*, whereby organisms remain on their developmental pathways regardless of the variability in their environment, or at least up to certain degrees of environmental disruption. Further, robustness – the maintenance of certain core functions or performances – is often generated by plastic mechanisms, and plasticity is often regulated by robust mechanisms. It is the interplay between developmental robustness and developmental plasticity that shapes the pace and direction of evolutionary change (WAGNER, 2008).

According to plasticity theory, then, environmental factors can elicit innovation through their direct influence on developmental systems (also REID, 2007). But at the same time the environment does not simply set

a problem to which the organism has to find a solution: an organism can often do a great deal to create an environment to which it is best suited. Many organisms change the physical or social conditions with which they (and their descendants) have to cope. These ideas are now referred to as *niche construction* theory (ODLING-SMEE, 2010). Virtually all organisms modify their immediate environments to some degree, and in many cases such impacts sum up across individuals to affect the evolution of their descendants. The evolution of organisms is now viewed as depending on natural selection *and* niche construction. Adding niche construction to evolutionary theory connects evolution to ecosystem-level ecology (ODLING-SMEE, 2010), and contributes to an 'eco-evo-devo' relationship by introducing a recursive dynamic interaction between environment and organisms and thence populations.

This 'developmental challenge' to the neo-Darwinian Modern Synthesis is taken further within DST (Table 2). For most DST theorists, what changes over evolutionary time is a *developmental system*, consisting of the organism *embedded in a broader 'developmental context'*, much of which would traditionally have been regarded as an external (and autonomous) 'environment' (GRIFFITHS and GRAY, 2005). In DST, genes must be deeply contextualized. As OYAMA (2000), a leading exponent of DST, puts it, 'if development is to re-enter evolutionary theory, it should be development that integrates genes into organisms, and organisms into the many levels of the environment that enter into their ontogenetic construction' (p. 113). In this task of *deep contextualization* the 'developmental system' is the key construct, defined as the dynamic set of all the interacting entities and influences on development at all levels, including the molecular, cellular, organismal, ecological, social and bio-geographical (OYAMA, 2000).[5] This interactive matrix of entities and resources is seen as contingent and possibly spatio-temporally discontinuous, multilayered and relational. This view implies that clear distinctions between organism and environment cannot be sustained, and emphasizes several additional key principles (Table 2).

First, the developmental importance of non-genetic factors implies a model of *multiple and dispersed systemic causality*. Causality does not reside in any one particular entity or class of entities but rather in the relations between developmental 'interactants'. DST advocates a *constructionist interactionism* in which the outcomes of different types of causes are interdependent and spatially and temporally contingent. This refocuses developmental enquiry on a multitude of factors, forces and mechanisms, without insisting that genes are ontogenetically or ontologically primary: no single source of influence has central control over an organism's development. Evolutionary change results from the constructive interaction between all developmental resources: the various elements of developmental systems co-evolve. As noted above, organisms are not independent of or just

Table 2. Some major tenets of Developmental Systems Theory (DST)

Developmental system as unit of evolution	Developmental system consists of the organism embedded in a broader developmental context, all of which is subject to evolutionary processes. Evolution is not a matter of organisms or populations adapting to their environments but of organism–environment systems co-evolving over time
Deep contextualization	Defined as the dynamic set of all the interacting entities and influences on development at all levels
Constructionist interactionism	Development is the product of multiple interacting causes. No single source of influence has central control over an organism's development. The significance of any one causal process is contingent upon context and the state of the rest of the system: time and space matter
Contingent developmental history	Development is spatially and historically contingent, shaped by interactions among causal antecedents and inherited resources
Extended inheritance	Process of reconstruction, at each generation, of the developmental process through the nonlinear interactions among inherited developmental factors. This constructive process is autocatalytic and self-organizing
Emergence	Development is a process of emergence whereby the organismal or systems forms at one level emerge from interactions of components at lower levels, and with their environment, but are not simply reducible to those components. Environment is a major generator of emergent evolutionary novelty, whereas natural selection engenders stasis
Self-organization	Pattern and order emerge from the interactions of the components of a complex system without explicit directive instructions either in the organism itself or from the environment. Self-organization involves processes that by their own activities change themselves

Sources: OYAMA *et al.* (2001), ROBERT *et al.* (2001) and others.

passively dependent on their environments; they actively construct their developmental niches which are an integral part of the whole developmental system. This introduces new resources for variation and innovation, beyond mutation and recombination, and points to the ways in which developmental processes situated in their ecological niche can produce novel organismal forms and behaviours. A further principle is that of *contingent developmental history*. DST emphasizes the contingent and historical nature of developmental processes so that time and space matter. The key idea here is that the constellation and characteristics of any developmental system should be explained by the prior interactions between a range of causal antecedents. Interactions and learning at one stage of development are often critical to what happens in subsequent stages. In this way contingent experiences and resource changes can have long-lasting effects. At the same time, however, DST emphasizes that both predictability and stability occur within developmental history. That is, despite the importance of contingent events, developmental systems also are marked by the repeated assembly of patterns of interaction. Evolution selects those developmental systems that reliably assemble all the necessary resources for the fulfilment of their life cycle.

A third feature of DST is its *extended version of inheritance*. EDB itself operates with a wider model of inheritance – epigenetic inheritance – than that found in the Modern Synthesis. In the latter, the gene is the sole unit of hereditary transmission. The genetic–developmental network and the phenotype it generates are not inheritable, and hence cannot be a unit of evolution. In epigenetic inheritance theory information transfer can take place between organisms through social learning, symbolic communication, and the interactions

between the individual and its environment that are involved in niche construction. The inheritance of developmentally induced and regulated variations is recognized as important. DST theorists go further and move to a concept of 'expanded inheritance' by replacing the notion of transmission with the notion of the reproduction of developmental resources and interactions in successive generations (GRIFFITHS and GRAY, 2004). As a consequence, for DST theorists the notion of 'replicator' is not used to refer to special factors able to produce reliable copies of themselves, but to designate the process of *reconstruction*, at each generation, of the developmental process through the interactions among inherited developmental factors.[6]

Fourth, both EDB and DST destabilize the selection-centred framework of modern evolutionary theory and place greater emphasis on the idea of *emergence*. In the Modern Synthesis, the problem of innovation was treated as part of the variation issue by calling all change in form 'variants'. Accordingly, morphological novelties were seen as 'major variants'. In EDB and DST, innovation and novelty are not treated in the same way as variation. EDB adopts a systems-orientated view of innovation ('epigenetic innovation theory') in which novelty origination is not based on the continuous variation of pre-existing characteristics, but appears *de novo* from developmental system reactions. Thus, novelty is a product of interactive emergence during the process of development.

Emergence also figures in the evolutionary development of organisms and other complex systems in another way, namely in its association with *self-organization*, that is the process in which order, pattern and structure at a higher level of an organism or system *emerges* solely from numerous interactions among lower-level or subunit components making up that organism or system (JOHNSON and LAM, 2010;

CAMAZINE et al., 2003). Moreover, the rules and processes specifying interactions among the system's components are executed using only local information, without reference to the macro-level pattern or to the organism's or system's environment. The subunits in biological systems acquire information about the local properties of the system and *behave* according to particular genetic programmes that have been subjected to natural selection. This adds an extra dimension to self-organization in biological systems, because in these systems selection can fine-tune the rules of interaction. By tuning the rules, selection shapes the patterns that are formed and thus the products of group activity can be adaptive. Self-organization involves processes that by their own activities change themselves. The greater the role of self-organization in the generation of life's adaptive order, the less the creative role of cumulative selection and the less the overall evolutionary process can be strictly termed 'Darwinian' (EDELMANN and DENTON, 2007).

What is obvious from this (necessarily brief and non-technical) survey of EDB and DST is that evolutionary theory is moving beyond the neo-Darwinian Modern Synthesis. This makes debates about the applicability of Generalized Darwinism to both evolutionary economics and EEG too restrictive. As DEPEW and WEBER (1995) have argued in a more general context, the 'developmental turn' underway in evolutionary biology should be a warning to all social scientists interested in constructing their own evolutionary approaches based upon only natural selection analogies:

> These reflections suggest that it should be at least a mild constraint on any evolutionary theory that claims to explain human phenomena that it should throw light on, rather than eliminate or reduce away, the interactional, relational, intentional, and symbolic features that interpretative social scientists have already discovered about social reality. Perhaps it is not too much to say that what we need is an evolutionary theory worthy of the best social theory, not a social theory trimmed to fit a rapidly receding, overly simplistic evolutionary theory.
>
> (p. 495)

So what then might be gained by thinking through the implications of this 'developmental turn' in evolutionary theory for EEG? Are the ideas advanced by the new developmental approach to evolutionary theory useful in some way to our discipline?

A DEVELOPMENTAL TURN IN EVOLUTIONARY ECONOMIC GEOGRAPHY?

The first implications are ontological and epistemological. To date, EEG has tended to focus on the micro-level of the firm, on the spatial evolution of the population of firms that make up a particular industry: in short it has been mainly concerned with the construction of a sort of 'evolutionary industrial geography' rather than an explicit evolutionary theory of uneven regional development. There have been studies of how particular industries have evolved across space; studies of the evolution of one or more industries in a given place (such as a cluster or industrial district); and studies of the evolving geography of technological innovation by firms (including knowledge networks). Such studies have proved highly informative, and have yielded valuable insights. What has been much less in evidence is a concern with the synergy of different economic processes and structures in particular places and with the systemic tendency towards uneven regional development. Hence EEG has struggled to connect micro-scale processes with large-scale processes, patterns and regularities (STORPER, 1997). The primary implication of the 'developmental turn' in evolutionary theory is that one needs to move to a *more systemic and holistic* understanding of spatial economic evolution, one that considers not just industrial evolutionary dynamics but also the wider economic, institutional, and socio-political structures produced by and constitutive of uneven geographical development (Table 3).

This in turn suggests that the typical focus (implicit if not explicit) in evolutionary economics and EEG on sets or bundles of rules and routines (typically interpreted as technologies or competences) as the basic 'units of variety' and the 'units of selection' might be incorporated into a more expansive focus on *economic developmental systems*. DOPFER (2005) suggests an ontology for evolutionary economics based on a model involving three 'scales' or levels of abstraction, those of micro-, meso- and macro-rules, moving epistemologically from the former to the latter. We also envisage an ontology based on a multilevel abstraction, but of nested, interacting and co-evolving spatial–economic developmental *systems*, rather than simply units defined by rules or routines.[7] Economic developmental systems are complex systems, and come in different forms and scales: workers and households, firms, industries, production networks, supply chains, clusters, cities, regions and nations are all types of (interconnected) economic developmental systems, all evolving over time through the interaction of their constituent developmental systems, and their co-interaction and co-evolution with their respective 'environments', that is other developmental systems of which they are themselves a component. No one ontological level takes precedence: there is no priority of the micro over the macro, or vice versa. And defining the nature and 'boundaries' of the developmental systems that make up the economy, and how they interrelate, may not be straightforward. Economic developmental systems are spatially distributed but also spatially discontinuous, have fuzzy boundaries, and are not easy to separate from their 'environment': these are precisely

Table 3. Some implications of the 'developmental turn' in evolutionary theory for evolutionary economic geography

Implication	New/additional focus
Need for a more holistic and systemic ontology for evolutionary economic geography	Moving from routines and rules as the basic units of variety and selection to the notion of multi-scalar spatial–economic developmental systems as the 'units of evolution' Focus is on differential emergence, reproduction and adaptation of spatial economic developmental systems, and on the (co)evolution of their developmental pathways
Need for 'deep contextualization' in evolutionary analyses	Consideration of the whole set of influences and entities, internal and external, local and non-local, structural and contingent, that enter into the evolution of a spatial economic developmental system. This implies, where appropriate, analysis both 'downwards' (the role of agency and purposive behaviour) as well as 'upwards' and 'outwards' (the influence of socio-institutional structures and regulatory conditions impinging on the system under study).
Need to view spatial economic developmental systems as self-organizing entities with emergent properties	Recognition that many spatial economic developmental systems are self-organizing, arising out of the interactions between their components and their connectedness. This process is not directed or controlled by any agent or subsystem inside or outside the system, although the path followed by the process, and its initial conditions, may have been chosen or instigated by certain (perhaps more influential) agents. Those same interactions can give rise to emergent properties and innovations that are not simply reducible to the individual components, and which then feedback to shape the evolution of those components
Need to examine the degree to which spatial economic developmental systems can construct their own environments	Consideration of the processes by which agents, firms and institutions do not simply react to their developmental, competitive and institutional environments but modify and even construct those environments ('niches') in their own favour. This demands an understanding of the power structures involved, and the regulatory and other conditions that both allow and obstruct these processes
Need to operate with an extended view of the influence of inherited legacies (economic and institutional structures and practices) on the evolution of spatial economic developmental systems	Appreciation of the formative role of path dependence across the set of components making up a spatial economic developmental system, where path dependence is construed as involving the adaptive reconstruction of the developmental process through the nonlinear and autocatalytic interactions among inherited developmental factors
Need to account for and trace the implications of the robustness and plasticity of developmental paths	Analysis of the processes making for robustness and/or plasticity of a spatial economic developmental system's evolutionary trajectory in the context of constant or periodical changes in the system's 'environment', and how robustness and plasticity influence the adaptive resilience of the system over time. This includes examining how critical stresses have long-lasting impacts on resources and potential for future change

the features found in many complex systems which are neither completely closed nor entirely open (MARTIN and SUNLEY, 2007).

Integral to a more holistic and systemic approach, and the layered multi-scalar ontology it involves, is the need for evolutionary analysis to engage in *deep contextualization*. That is, evolutionary accounts in economic geography should consider the full set of entities, factors and influences, including internal (endogenous) and external (exogenous), local and non-local, and structural and contingent, that have conditioned and shaped the evolutionary dynamics and trajectory of the spatial economic developmental system under study. This requires analysis 'downward', to micro-level processes including where appropriate the role, decisions and purposive behaviour of individual key agents; 'upward' to take account of the meso- and macro-level circumstances and influences that might have constrained or facilitated a particular evolutionary path of the system in question; and 'outward' to consider the system's and its components' (firms', workers' and institutions') connections with and dependencies on other systems elsewhere. This is not an appeal to some sort of ontological relativism,

where everything that might impinge upon the evolutionary development of, say, a particular local or regional economy has to be considered, or where no one factor is given more explanatory weight than any other. Rather, it is to argue that local and regional economies are complex, multilayered systems, both connected to and in part also constitutive of their (competitive) environments, and that to understand fully their evolutionary development over time requires analysis of their multi-scalar and interdependent character.

Take the example of the firm. Firms are open and 'deeply contextual' developmental systems, comprising resources, activities and organizational forms, not just economic but also institutional, social and cultural. They are made up of interactions between several categories of phenomena including: physical and ecosystem resources; technologies; firm capabilities and organization, industry structures; and institutions (including both markets and non-market regulatory, legal, financial and public institutions) (NELSON, 2011; CHILD *et al.*, 2012). The mutual interdependence of these factors means that they show reciprocal causality. The concept of a developmental system also emphasizes that the competences and capabilities of firms are so strongly interpenetrated by exogenous 'environmental' factors, such as competitive pressures from rivals, collaborations with cognate firms, micro- and micro-regulatory arrangements, and the like, that it is impossible to draw a clearly defined boundary around the firm. And while the evolution of a firm – in terms of changes in its technologies, its products, its labour inputs and its locational dynamics – obviously reflects imperatives arising from within, many such changes will be induced by pressures and opportunities arising in the firm's 'environment'. In addition, while some inter-actions and relationships that make up a firm will be local, others may be quite geographically remote so that the firm's evolution will inevitably involve the assembly of spatially distributed networks and relation-ships at different scales (TER WAL and BOSCHMA, 2011). In this way, these ideas allow insights from rela-tional economic geography and its focus on relationships and networks to be merged with an evolutionary under-standing of firms.

Or consider the case of a business cluster, an archety-pical example of a spatial economic developmental system. There has been growing interest in how clusters evolve (MENZEL and FORNAHL, 2010; REGIONAL STUDIES, 2011; MARTIN and SUNLEY, 2011, 2012). What has often been accorded insufficient examination is any proper contextualization of cluster evolution both in terms of the role of agency in shaping what in reality can be quite heterogeneous, even divergent, develop-mental strategies by individual firms in a cluster, and in terms of the relationships of individual cluster firms with their respective external competitive and colla-borative environments[8]: too often clusters are studied in isolation from the wider system of similar and related clusters of which they are both a part and with which they co-evolve.

A developmental, complex systems perspective on spatial economic evolution would also assign importance to explicating the roles of *self-organization* and *emergence*. As argued elsewhere (MARTIN and SUNLEY 2007, 2012), self-organization and emergence are key mechanisms in the evolution of economic landscapes. The idea of self-organization is related to the notion of autopoiesis, which refers to the dynamics of a non-equilibrium system that produces the components which in turn con-tinue to maintain the organized structure that gives rise to those components. The geographical forms that consti-tute the economic landscape – cities, centre–periphery patterns, clusters, industrial districts and so forth – can, in a certain sense, be viewed as emergent, self-organizing phenomena. Cities, clusters and regional economies arise out of the myriad individual actions and interactions of economic agents (firms, workers, households, institutions, etc.) that generate outcomes (daily behaviours, invest-ment and employment decisions, knowledges, profits, incomes, and expenditures) that serve to reproduce

those same spatial systems. But, in contrast to biological systems, where self-organization is often regarded as a 'spontaneous' process, in the socio-economic realm the development of cities, clusters and spatial structures in general is the complex outcome of the *intentional* beha-viours and learning of economic agents pursuing their own objectives. In so doing, some agents may possess and exert more influence and power than others over the precise form and function of spatial economic 'self-organization'.[9] Thus, the idea of 'self-organization' in a evolutionary–developmental perspective on the econ-omic landscape is necessarily a political economy one in which the imperatives and logics of capitalist accumu-lation inexorably tend to 'self-organize' the economic landscape unevenly, but where the precise form of that unevenness will vary from place to place and over time, depending on the opportunities afforded in particular places and how economic actors respond to those oppor-tunities. *Self-organization in the economic landscape is quintes-sentially a power-inflected evolutionary process.*

Self-organization in the economic landscape is closely bound up with various processes and forms of emergence. The idea of emergence is attracting increasing interest within economics (e.g., JOURNAL OF ECONOMIC BE-HAVIOUR AND ORGANISATION, 2012). Different economists interpret the notion in slightly different ways (HARPER and LEWIS, 2012), but the basic idea is that emergence occurs when wholes (e.g., the economy) form from, and take on properties and produce outcomes that differ from, and are not simply reducible to, the actions of and properties possessed by their constituent individual parts (human agents and organizations) (DE HAAN, 2006, p. 294). In economic geography, a good example of emergence is how the spatial agglomeration of economic activity – in cities or in business clusters – gives rise to various localized extern-alities that do not reside in firms themselves but become 'macro-level' features of the agglomeration as a whole, available to (that is, which have 'downward causal influ-ence' on) those firms as sources of productivity gain and competitive advantage. Properties of the firms, and the interactions between the firms, become represented in and give rise to agglomeration-level system-type proper-ties, especially externalities, which then exert influence on the performance of the firms concerned (Table 4). A similar point was made by MASSEY (1992) when discuss-ing the 'politics of space/time':

> Spatial form as 'outcome' […] has emergent powers which can have effects on subsequent events. Spatial form can alter the future course of the very histories that have produced it. […] One way of thinking about all of this is to say that the spatial is integral to the production of history […] just as the temporal is to geography.
> (p. 84)

Emergence is a source of innovative and evolutionary change, and is itself a dynamic, recursive process. It thus both shapes and reshapes the structural and

Table 4. Types of 'downward causation' and some spatial economic examples

Type of downward causation	Examples of spatial economic effects (e.g., in an agglomeration)
Effects of system organization Boundaries and patterns of organization of a system shape which causal powers of their constituent components are activated (or deactivated)	Spatial agglomeration of firms opens up local market niches and supplier opportunities for the firms concerned. Though generally positive, such local orientation may also restrict the export reach of local firms
Effects of external system consequences Emergent impact of a system on its external environment influences properties and interactions of system components	A local cluster can shape the wider industry of which it is a part, and acquire an external reputation that in turn influences the resources available to its firms, their performance and market position
Effects of system-level dynamics Properties and constraints emergent at system level become internalized by system components	Conventions and practices may emerge at the agglomeration or cluster level which then become internalized in the routines and decisions of the constituent firms
Effects on generative processes Properties, processes and constraints emergent at system level alter selection pressures on, and hence sources of constructive variation in, lower level components	The form and degree of specialization of a local agglomeration or cluster, and the nature of local competition and collaboration, may shape the scope for and direction of innovation among constituent firms

Source: After MARTIN and SUNLEY (2012).

organizational legacies that influence the historical evolution of economic landscapes. The emergence of various types of externalities through the spatial agglomeration of economic activity may shape the generation, viability and selection of new products and new firms within such spatial economic developmental systems. And these processes in turn reshape or reinforce the nature of the externalities arising from agglomeration. The recursive nature of this process involves the interaction between two key features of emergent systems, namely 'memory', or path dependence, and selection (MARTIN and SUNLEY, 2006, 2012) (Fig. 1). Path dependence effects occur through several mechanisms and across scales (firm, industry, spatial agglomeration or cluster, and external 'environment'). Firm properties shape the properties of the regional economy or spatial agglomeration in question, which in turn influence firm properties. At the same time, firms themselves carry over products and practices from one period to the next, whilst also embodying learning effects and knowledge spillovers arising from interactions with other local firms. And to the extent that a region's firms compete or collaborate with similar firms in other regions and locations, they influence their wider competitive and technological environment, which feeds back to influence the local firms' developmental trajectories. Further these processes will impact differently on different local firms, such that selection will occur, and the population of local firms will change as some cease to compete, decline and disappear, while new ones are created. *Path dependence, then, can itself be viewed as an emergent property of the economic landscape, while at the same time acting as a key mechanism by which the spatial forms of that landscape themselves emerge.* The issue, however, is how 'strong' that path dependence is, and what the relative roles are of low-level components (firms, institutions), and higher-level (regional)

emergent forms and processes (MARTIN and SUNLEY, 2006, 2012; MARTIN, 2010).

Of course, while the notion of evolutionary emergence appears to capture the recursive way in which economic evolution may operate, it needs to be remembered that there are also limits to the analogy between biological evolutionary emergence and emergence in economic systems. In social and economic systems, both self-organization and emergence typically arise from (power) relationships between individuals (LAWSON, 2011; SAYER, 2010), and relationships are undoubtedly fundamental to many economic capabilities. In addition, socio-economic self-organization and emergence are much more reflexive: agents are aware of the context in which they operate and seek to modify their behaviour as a consequence. This suggests that economic self-organization and emergence will be essentially knowledge-based and knowledge-driven, and that one should be especially concerned with processes by which agents sample, select, and build upon past and existing knowledges in particular locations (FOSTER, 2010).

TOWARDS AN ANALYTICAL AGENDA: THE FUSION OF ECONOMIC EVOLUTION AND DEVELOPMENT

Precisely how far this idea of a 'developmental evolutionary economic geography' can be taken, both conceptually and especially empirically, of course remains to be seen. It is not possible here to map out a detailed research programme. But some issues can be offered for future discussion. The analytical implication for EEG of the developmental turn in evolutionary theory outlined above is that by arguing that EEG should be made more contextual, developmental and

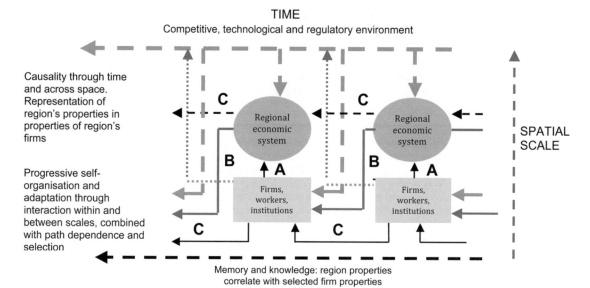

A - Morphological emergence of spatial agglomeration of firms, workers, institutions
B - Emergence of agglomeration-level properties that influence existing firms and workers and attract new
      firms and workers
C - Involves memory effects within firms and memory and selection effects arising at agglomeration and
      extra-region levels. Developmental-evolutionary path dependence

Fig. 1. *Evolutionary emergence and path dependence in the economic landscape*
Source: Adapted from MARTIN and SUNLEY (2012)

holistic in orientation, the possibility is opened not only for embracing a more expansive set of evolutionary notions – extending the 'analytical toolkit' – but also for linking the approach more constructively to other perspectives or 'analytical frameworks' in economic geography, that is for engaging in epistemological pluralism. A fusion of economic evolution and development might release substantial analytical and empirical energy.

In making their influential case for EEG, BOSCHMA and FRENKEN (2006) saw it as separate from but having interfaces with institutional economic geography, on the one hand, and what they called Neoclassical Economic Geography, on the other. We agree with the interface and connection with institutional economic geography. A developmental EEG would view institutions (at all scales), not only as developmental systems in their own right, but as systems that permeate all other economic developmental systems, from households to firms to industries, to local economies and so on. Not only do institutions of all kinds and at all scales condition, constrain and enable the operation of evolutionary mechanisms in the economy, but also these same institutions are themselves subject to similar such evolutionary mechanisms and processes: an economy and its institutional forms and arrangements co-evolve. *Institutions are both context and consequence of economic evolution.* How institutions co-evolve with the economy is thus a key issue requiring analysis (SETTERFIELD, 1998). How robust, plastic and adaptive are institutions? In what ways and how quickly do institutional forms adapt to changing economic conditions

and circumstances? On the one hand, stability of institutional structures and arrangements is needed in order for economic systems to function and reproduce themselves: institutions serve to reduce uncertainty regarding future organizational, regulatory and related conditions. In DAVID's (1994) words institutions are 'carriers of history' and act as a key means of extended economic inheritance and path dependence. Institutions help determine the balance between competition and cooperation and thus strongly shape the emergence of economic developmental systems across space (MARTIN, 2000; NELSON, 2006). On the other hand, institutional rigidities and dysfunctional institutional forms can hinder economic development. Institutions can hold back economic innovation and change. As a growing catalogue of evidence on recent institutional crises – from the global scale to the national to the local – indicates only too vividly, institutions can fail, and such failures can seriously destabilize economies.[10] A developmental EEG would necessarily examine the co-evolutionary dynamics of institutions and the economic systems of which they are a part.

BOSCHMA and FRENKEN (2006) suggest that the interface of EEG with Neoclassical location theory derives from a shared interest in the usefulness of formal modelling strategies: in other words, the interface is primarily a methodological one, since EEG, they argue, also employs modelling and quantitative techniques. While evolutionary economics, and some versions of EEG, do indeed employ such techniques, for us the key connections between different perspectives in economic geography should first and foremost be conceptual and ontological, not methodological. On this basis, with its adherence to the assumption of equilibrium, its neglect of history, its decontextualized mode of abstraction and its unrealistic model of rational maximizing human behaviour, Neoclassical location theory has little ontological relevance to EEG, or indeed to the real world of economic growth and development (this same criticism can be levied at the latest incarnation of neoclassical location theory, namely the 'new economic geography'; MARTIN, 1999, 2011; GARRETSEN and MARTIN, 2010). If EEG is about improving our understanding of uneven geographical development, as it should be, then the more appropriate interface and connection is with geographical political economy, given the latter's core focus on capitalism as a dynamic yet crisis-prone process of economic growth and development that is inherently spatially uneven. Now whether geographical political economy is superior to EEG, and whether it provides a more compelling explanation of economic evolution, as implied for example by OOSTERLYNCK (2012) and MACKINNON et al. (2009), are claims that are themselves open to debate (MARTIN, 2012a). Further, we suspect different economic geographers would in any case subscribe to somewhat different versions of what they regard as 'geographical political economy', and would not necessarily view the approach as synonymous with Marxist political economy (SHEPPARD, 2011). There is no single unified, integrated or generally agreed form of geographical political economy, just as there is no single unified version of evolutionary economics (DOPFER and POTTS, 2004, p. 195); nevertheless common themes of most versions of geographical political economy include an explicit focus on uneven development and an emphasis on 'large' systemic processes (such as regimes of accumulation, crises, etc.) and 'big' structures (such as modes of regulation, the state, etc.). It is fair to say that, to date, EEG has given insufficient attention to such systemic processes and structures. Yet such 'big' processes and 'large' structures play key roles in shaping the processes, rhythms and directions of economic change (TILLY, 1984). The labour processes, wage relations, regulatory architectures and technological systems that make up an historical regime of capital accumulation function to enable, constrain, and influence the dynamics and interaction of the various developmental systems (firms, industries, labour markets, institutions, regional patterns of development) that make up (the space economy of) that phase of capitalism. For instance, the dynamics of capital investment in particular industries and the ways in which these shape demand for other industries are fundamental to the process of adaptive structural growth (METCALFE et al., 2006). Likewise, the forms of state–economy relations, economic governance structures and political institutions that define the mode of regulation associated with a particular regime of accumulation also condition the scope and pace of evolutionary change in the economy. As such, some of the core ideas that underpin geographical political economy could certainly inform and enrich EEG, and provide a more systemic and holistic orientation to our analyses.

But equally, the processes and mechanisms of economic evolution shape the dynamics and trajectory of capitalist development. The 'big' processes and 'large' structures of capitalism are more than just the aggregates or 'averaged sums' of the micro-changes and parts (firms, institutions, workers, spatial structures, etc.) on which they are based. They are also emergent in nature (FOSTER, 2010). In the context of capital, emergence pertains to the dependence of system properties at various levels (scales) in the capital structure on the mode of composition and organization of lower-level elements in that structure. Emergence occurs at each level of the capital structure where elements are connected to form new systemic 'wholes' (e.g., capital goods, firm-level capital combinations, industry-level structures, and spatial patterns and structures of various kinds), and those 'wholes' take on properties that are not simply reducible to the elements of which they are composed. Thus, industry-wide capital structures, though synchronic with, cannot simply be reduced to, the capital combinations of individual firms. Further, and importantly, the interactions between processes occurring at all scales of the capital structure – within firms, between firms, within and between industries, and within and between places – give rise to diachronic emergence or the appearance of novel systemic properties that shape the evolution of an economy over time. Emergence is ubiquitous in the economic landscape, and occurs every time there is an appearance of a qualitatively new good or service, technology, design, firm, network, market or industry. Emergence is key to understanding uneven geographical development and its evolution over time.

In short, EEG, institutionalist economic geography and geographical political economy should not be seen as competing alternative paradigms, but as complementary perspectives each capable of informing the other (Fig. 2). Each perspective sees capitalism through a different lens, each emphasizing different particular features, structures and processes. Yet they also overlap, and can help inform one another. Both institutional economic geography and geographical political economy can assist in the 'deep contextualization' it has been argued is necessary in EEG. Institutional forms and practices (from individual social–cultural norms, to social networks, to the state), on the one hand, and 'big' systemic processes and structures, such as regimes of capital accumulation, modes of regulation and crisis tendencies, on the other, influence and condition the mechanisms of economic evolution and their spatial outcomes. In turn, those evolutionary mechanisms shape the formation and reformation of institutional arrangements and the nature and dynamics of capital accumulation. Economic evolution and economic

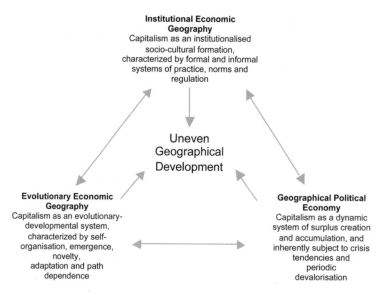

Fig. 2. Multiple perspectives in economic geography: towards a synthesis?

development should be seen as inextricably intertwined: nothing makes sense in economic geography except in the light of evolution *and* development.

The ideas central to a new 'developmental' EEG – robustness, plasticity, self-organization, emergence and evolvability – should not, therefore, be seen as antithetical to geographical political economy, but as helping to shed new light on how the process of uneven regional development plays out across economic landscapes. According to HARVEY (2006) the 'coercive laws' of capital accumulation and competition produce perpetual instability within the geographical landscape of capitalism:

> capitalism is about growth not stationary state equilibrium. The problem is to see how spatially confined market structures evolve in relation to both growth and technological dynamism. […] Capitalist producers in competition with each other seek to gain advantage and higher profits by adopting superior technologies and organizational forms. […] But the search for excess profits generates a locational dynamism within production that parallels technological and organizational dynamism. Trade-offs exist between these two ways of gaining competitive advantage. […] The coercive laws of competition nevertheless produce perpetual instability within the geographical landscape of capitalism.
>
> (pp. 97–98)

Evolutionary concepts can help explain this instability and the spatial forms it produces; why some firms and places are more or less 'robust' to the ever-shifting pressures of competition; why some firms and places are more able to adapt (are more 'plastic'); and why some firms and places are more able to initiate technological and organizational change than others (i.e. why evolvability varies across firms, industries and places).

Take, for example, the concept of robustness. The notion of robustness, recall, is not about stasis or the preservation of existing functions and structure in the face of perturbation or change (whether arising from within or without), but about the capacity of a system such (as a local economy) to *maintain core functionality and performance* (say economic growth, and full employment and rising real incomes for its residents) – under conditions of a constantly changing (competitive and technological) environment. The recent EDB literature identifies four different pathways to robustness in the face of perturbations in natural systems: homeostasis, adaptive plasticity, environment tracking and environment shaping (e.g., WHITACRE, 2012). First, *homeostasis* refers to the stabilizing regulation of internal system states that buffers stresses through altered uses of components in order to preserve viability. Second, *adaptive plasticity* modifies traits in order to regulate responses to a changing environment, and often involves context-dependent changes in the function and structure of networks. Both types of response can occur through reorganization or forms of self-organization that experiment with solutions. Third, *environment tracking* maintains stability through either temporal or spatial movement, which may be to avoid threatening conditions or to maintain the acquisition of key resources. Fourth, *environment shaping* involves controlling and shaping the environment through co-evolution, inheritance and niche construction with the aim of creating more amenable conditions and reducing system vulnerabilities. It may be helpful to begin to approach economic robustness and resilience by envisaging economic equivalents of these types of pathway (Fig. 3).

For instance, homeostasis through altered use of components and feedback controls on economic processes is a basic type of response used by firms to economic changes. Yet this appears to be a limited and incremental type of response, which may not be sufficient to cope with more fundamental changes. It may well lead over time to 'lock-in' and increased

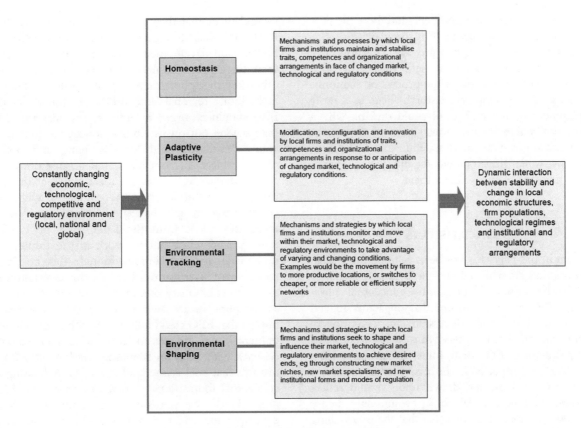

Fig. 3. Pathways to local economic robustness

vulnerability to more profound negative shocks. *Adaptive plasticity*, on the other hand, involves the modification of routines, practices and activities either through feedback and regulation or through processes of internal reorganization and self-organization (GRABHER and STARK, 1997). The functions of economic networks may be just as context dependent as those in biology, so one needs to examine how inter-firm networks, industrial–technological paths and institutional structures adjust and adapt with changing economic conditions (STRAMBACH, 2008; VISSERS and DANKBAAR, 2013). This type of economic plasticity allows a wider range of responses and could include or generate radical process innovations. *Environment tracking* would involve relocation of firms to other locations – an example of Harvey's 'locational dynamism' – which, of course, has been widely seen in labour-intensive assembly firms that move overseas to take advantage of cheaper wages or a more pliant workforce. Alternatively, it could involve a switch in market focus to maintain the viability of certain products.

However, the *environment shaping* route to robustness is probably the most important in economic terms as it involves a very broad range of strategies including marketing and advertising, creating new markets or market niches through technological innovation (Harvey's 'technological dynamism'), and the production of human and business ecosystem resources. Collaboration with universities and technical institutions in order to construct a skilled or expert labour supply is a good example. One fundamental form of environment shaping involves co-evolution, e.g. where economic systems and their 'natural' environments shape each other (NORGAARD and KALLIS, 2011). Over the long-term one might expect economic resilience to depend heavily on the degree to which environment-shaping activities by firms are successful, rather than inadvertently dysfunctional and leading to a long-term loss of adaptability (MARTIN, 2012b). In any spatial economic developmental system these different forms of response by firms will be combined in various ways, and their relative prevalence may determine whether and to what extent an economic system proves adaptive and resilient. A firm preoccupied with homeostasis will restrict its potential for environment shaping so that spinoffs are created precisely to experiment with market-shaping activities. Structural and macro-economic changes will also be influenced by these types of strategic choices. A developmental EEG would seek to understand the institutional and cultural contexts that shape these types of decision-making and pathway.

Ultimately, economic development is about the capacity of an economic system – be it a firm, an industry or a local economy – to adapt over time in response to or in anticipation of a changing market, technological and regulatory conditions and opportunities. How such adaptability arises, the forms it takes and the direction(s) it assumes all help shape the 'big processes' and 'large structures' of capitalist development, and those big processes and large structures in turn stimulate and condition the process of adaptive growth. The notion of economic robustness may be a useful organizing principle by which to investigate the process of economic adaptation. A key empirical research focus in a more developmentally inflected EEG could thus be why it is that different robustness strategies tend to emerge and dominate in different firms, industries and places, and why some firms, industries and places exhibit greater adaptive plasticity than others.

CONCLUSIONS

The aim in this paper has not been to undermine what EEG has thus far achieved. To the contrary, the argument has been for a widening of the conceptual apparatus of EEG so as to ensure that apparatus reflects current thinking and discussion in evolutionary theory. For whether the objective is to construct a distinct paradigm of EEG or to infuse evolutionary ideas into existing perspectives, the evolutionary concepts and metaphors used and drawn upon should reflect the latest thinking and debates in evolutionary theory itself. Furthermore, it is our belief that the overarching aim of EEG should be to contribute to the understanding of geographically uneven development. Within evolutionary biology – a major source of the Darwinian-inspired ideas frequently used in evolutionary economics and EEG – a significant reappraisal, extension and reorientation is underway, what has been termed here a major 'developmental turn', as found in EDB and DST. These two new streams of evolutionary thinking are not only leading to a reconsideration of the three key tenets of neo-Darwinian evolutionary theory – variety, selection and retention (VSR) – but also are beginning to reveal how the processes of evolution and development in biological systems are inextricably interrelated. In so doing, a whole range of new concepts, principles, and mechanisms are being explored and elaborated. These may have suggestive implications for how one might think about economic evolution in general and about the evolution of the economic landscape more specifically. While some of these concepts and principles, such as self-organization and emergence, have begun to find their way into the writings of certain economic geographers, our own included, those discussions (and very definitely our own!) have thus far been rudimentary; and other ideas found in EDB and DST, such as robustness, plasticity, niche construction and evolvability, have yet to be examined at all for their potential usefulness. And, most importantly, the focus in EDB and DST on holistic and deeply contextualized accounts is also suggestive for EEG.

It is not being suggested here that the three basic neo-Darwinian evolutionary concepts of VSR are

redundant or that they should be jettisoned: far from it. But the dual message of evolutionary development biology and developmental system theory is both that these three principles need reappraisal and that several other key metaphors may help shed valuable light on how local, regional and urban economies evolve. EEG should be urged to embrace this message rather than staying put on its familiar conceptual terrain. Of course 'evolution' and 'development', and notions such as selection, robustness, self-organization, plasticity, emergence, and so on, mean different things in the socio-economic realm as compared with their counterparts in the biological–natural: our use of metaphors taken from the latter must be carefully reinterpreted when put to work in the former. But non-trivial and tendentious though this task is, it could repay investigation. Further, the 'developmental turn' in evolutionary theory, it is contended, serves as a metaphor in its own right, in the sense that it implies that EEG could follow suit with its own 'developmental turn' and seek to integrate ideas on economic *evolution* with ideas on economic *development*. Moving towards that goal is a second reason for extending the conceptual foundations of EEG, in order to focus it more directly on the issue of geographically uneven development, which is taken to be a fundamental concern for our discipline.

NOTES

1. The terms 'inheritance', 'replication' and 'retention' are often used interchangeably in the evolutionary literature, and likewise also in evolutionary economics. But according to CAMPBELL (1965), in socio-economic contexts 'retention' is preferable to 'inheritance' or 'replication' since the latter two are too loaded with biological connotations.
2. A not dissimilar argument has been made by certain mainstream economists against the need for a separate discipline of evolutionary economics. They are of the view that conventional economic theory can in fact explain evolutionary phenomena and processes (KRUGMAN, 1996).
3. The paper is the latest in an ongoing series in which the aim has been to explore and evaluate the scope and limits of various conceptual approaches to evolutionary economic geography, not in any belief that there is a single superior all-embracing framework to be discovered, but to identify novel evolutionary metaphors, notions and principles that seem to be potentially useful in expanding the conceptual reach and empirical concerns of the subject.
4. The discussion that follows can only provide a brief, simplified and non-technical overview of some of the main ideas and insights that characterize EDB and DST. We have endeavoured to identify the main ideas that may have relevance for evolutionary economic geography.
5. The adoption by DST of this much more inclusive vision of the components and limits of the development system,

than that found in EDB, is a key difference between the two approaches. In DST, aspects of the environment are a product of evolution as well as a cause of evolution.

6. This extended view of inheritance has not gone uncontested by other evolutionary theorists. However, DST theorists have argued that such critiques misunderstand this approach to development and evolution (GRIFFITH and GRAY, 2005).

7. Of course, it might be argued that everything in the socio-economy consists of, or can be reduced to, 'rules' and 'routines' (some institutional theorists subscribe to this view). But to our mind, to reduce a complex system like an economy to rules and routines is akin to the problem of gene-centrism that the proponents of evolutional developmental biology and developmental theory are seeking to avoid.

8. Different economic agents and firms in an industrial cluster may react quite differently to changes in the

market and technological environment in which they compete, and hence may pursue different developmental and evolutionary trajectories. Understanding this heterogeneity requires deep contextualization, 'downwards', 'upwards' and 'outwards'.

9. The conceptions of self-organization and emergence thus differ from the use of these notions in Austrian economics, where they are ascribed to the 'spontaneous' workings of abstract competitive market forces.

10. It is intriguing that the recent surge of interest by economic geographers in institutions comes at a time of mounting institutional failure and growing public disenchantment with, and distrust of, many of the institutions that govern everyday economic and social life. The financial crisis that has afflicted many counties in 2008 was in part the result of the failure of the regulatory institutions to curb the excessive risk-taking and leverage activities of the banks.

REFERENCES

ALDRICH H., HODGSON G., HULL D., KNUDSEN T., MOKYR J. and VANBERG V. (2008) In defence of generalized Darwinism, *Journal of Evolutionary Economics* **18**, 577–596.
BARNES T. and SHEPPARD E. S. (2010) 'Nothing includes everything': towards engaged pluralism in Anglophone economic geography, *Progress in Human Geography* **34**, 193–214.
BATESON P. and GLUCKMAN P. (2011) *Plasticity, Robustness, Development and Evolution*. Cambridge University Press, Cambridge.
BOSCHMA R. (2004) Competitiveness of regions from an evolutionary perspective, *Regional Studies* **38**, 1001–1014.
BOSCHMA R. and FRENKEN K. (2006) Why is economic geography not an evolutionary science?, *Journal of Economic Geography* **6**, 273–302.
BOSCHMA R. and FRENKEN K. (2009) Some notes on institutions in evolutionary economic geography, *Economic Geography* **85**, 151–158.
BOSCHMA R. and MARTIN R. L. (2007) Constructing an evolutionary economic geography, *Journal of Economic Geography* **7**, 537–548.
BOSCHMA R. and MARTIN R. L. (Eds) (2010) *Handbook of Evolutionary Economic Geography*. Edward Elgar, Chichester.
BRAKEFIELD P. M. (2006) Evo-devo and constraints on selection, *Trends in Ecology and Evolution* **21**, 362–368.
BUENSTORF G. (2006) How useful is generalized Darwinism as a framework to study competition and industrial evolution?, *Journal of Evolutionary Economics* **16**, 511–527.
CAMAZINE S., DENEUBOURG J. L., FRANKS N. R., SNEYD J., THERAULAZ G. and BONABEAU E. (2003) *Self Organisation in Biological Systems*. Princeton University Press, Princeton, NJ.
CAMPBELL D. T. (1965) Variation and selective retention in sociocultural evolution, in BARRINGER H. R., BLANKSTEN G. I. and MACK, R. W. (Eds) *Social Change in Developing Areas: A Reinterpretation of Evolutionary Theory*, pp. 19–49. Schenkmann, Cambridge, MA.
CARROLL R. L. (2000) Towards a new evolutionary synthesis, *Trends in Ecology and Evolution* **15**, 27–32.
CASTELLACCI F. (2006) A critical realist interpretation of evolutionary growth theorizing, *Cambridge Journal of Economics* **30**, 861–880.
CHILD J., RODRIGUES S. and TSE K. (2012) The dynamics of influence in corporate co-evolution, *Journal of Management Studies* **49**, 1246–1273.
COCHRANE T. and MACCLAURIN J. (2012) Evolvability and progress in evolutionary economics, *Journal of Bioeconomics* **14**, 101–114.
COE N. (2011) Geographies of production, 1: an evolutionary revolution?, *Progress in Human Geography* **35**, 81–91.
CORDES C. (2006) Darwinism in economics: from analogy to continuity, *Journal of Evolutionary Economics* **16**, 529–541.
DAVID P. (1994) Why are institutions 'the carriers of history': path dependence and the evolution of conventions, *Organizations and Institutions, Structural Change and Economic Dynamics* **5**, 205–220.
DE HAAN J. (2006) How emergence arises, *Ecological Complexity* **3**, 293–301.
DEPEW D. J. and WEBER B. R. (1995) The fate of Darwinism: evolution after the Modern Synthesis, *Biological Theory* **6**, 89–102.
DOPFER K. (2005) Evolutionary economics: a theoretical framework, in DOPFER K. (Ed.) *The Evolutionary Foundations of Economics*, pp. 3–55. Cambridge University Press, Cambridge.
DOPFER K. and POTTS J. (2004) Evolutionary realism: a new ontology for economics, *Journal of Economic Methodology* **11**, 115–212.
EDELMANN J. B. and DENTON M. J. (2007) The uniqueness of biological self organisation: challenging the Darwinian paradigm, *Biological Philosophy* **11**, 579–601.
ENDLER J. A. and MCLELLAN T. (1988) The process of evolution: towards a new synthesis, *Annual Review of Ecological Systematics* **19**, 395–421.
ESSLETZBICHLER J. and RIGBY D. (2007) Exploring evolutionary economic geographies, *Journal of Economic Geography* **7**, 549–572.
FOSTER J. (2010) Evolutionary macroeconomics: a research agenda, *Journal of Evolutionary Economics* **21**, 5–28.

FUSCO G. and MINELLI A. (2008) *Evolving Pathways: Key Themes in Evolutionary Developmental Biology*. Cambridge University Press, Cambridge.

FUTUYMA D. (1988) *Sturm und drang* and the evolutionary synthesis, *Evolution* **42**, 217–226.

GARRETSEN H. and MARTIN R. L. (2010) Rethinking (new) economic geography: taking geography and history more seriously, *Spatial Economic Analysis* **5**, 127–160.

GILBERT S. F. (2003) The morphogenesis of evolutionary developmental biology, *International Journal Developmental Biology* **47**, 467–477.

GRABHER G. and STARK D. (1997) Organising diversity: evolutionary theory, network analysis and postsocialism, *Regional Studies* **31**, 533–544.

GRAY R. D. (2001) Selfish genes or developmental systems?, in SINGH R., KRIMBAS K., PAUL D. and BEATTY J. (Eds) *Thinking about Evolution: Historical, Philosophical and Political Perspectives: Festschrift for Richard Lewontin*, pp. 184–207. Cambridge University Press, Cambridge.

GRIFFITHS P. E. and GRAY R. D. (1994) Developmental systems and evolutionary explanation, *Journal of Philosophy* **91**, 277–304.

GRIFFITHS P. E. and GRAY R. D. (2004) The developmental systems perspective: organism–environment systems as units of development and evolution, in PIGLIUCCI M. and PRESTON K. (Eds) *Phenotypic Integration – Studying the Ecology and the Evolution of Complex Phenotypes*, pp. 409–431. Oxford University Press, Oxford.

GRIFFITHS P. E. and GRAY R. D. (2005) Discussion: Three ways to misunderstand Developmental Systems Theory, *Biology and Philosophy* **20**, 417–425.

HALL B. K. (1999) *Evolutionary Developmental Biology*. Kluwer, Dordrecht.

HALL B. K. (2003) Evo-devo: evolutionary developmental mechanisms, *International Journal of Developmental Biology* **47**, 491–495.

HARPER D. A. and LEWIS P. (2012) New perspectives on emergence in economics, *Journal of Economic Behaviour and Organization* **82** [Special Issue: Emergence in Economics], 329–335.

HARVEY D. (2006) *Spaces of Global Capitalism: Towards a Theory of Uneven Geographical Development*. Verso, London.

HODGSON G. (1993) *Economics and Evolution: Bring Life Back into Economics*. Policy Press, Cambridge.

HODGSON G. (2002) Darwinism in economics: from analogy to ontology, *Journal of Evolutionary Economics* **12**, 259–281.

HODGSON G. and KNUDSEN T. (2006) Why we need a generalised Darwinism and why generalised Darwinism is not enough, *Journal of Economic Behavior and Organization* **61**, 1–19.

HODGSON G. and KNUDSEN T. (2010) *Darwin's Conjecture: The Search for General Principles of Social and Economic Evolution*. University of Chicago Press, Chicago, IL.

JABLONKA E. and LAMB M. J. (2002) The changing concept of epigenetics, *Annals of the New York Academy of Sciences* **981**, 82–96.

JOHNSON B. R. and LAM S. K. (2010) Self-organisation, natural selection and evolution, *Bioscience* **60**, 872–885.

JOURNAL OF ECONOMIC BEHAVIOUR AND ORGANISATION (2012) Emergence in economics, *Journal of Economic Behaviour and Organisation* **82** [Special Issue].

KITANO H. (2004) Biological robustness, *Nature Reviews* **5**, 826–837.

KNIGHT F. (1923) The ethics of competition, *Quarterly Journal of Economics* **37**, 579–624.

KRUGMAN P. (1996) What economists can learn from evolutionary theorists. Paper presented at the European Association for Evolutionary Political Economy (available at: http://web.mit.edu/krugman/www/evolute.html).

LAUBICHLER M. and MAIENSCHEIN J. (Eds) (2007) *From Embryology to Evo-Devo: A History of Developmental Evolution*. MIT Press, Cambridge, MA.

LAWSON T. (2011) *Ontology and the Study of Social Reality: Emergence, Organization, Community, Social Relations and Artefacts*. Mimeo. Faculty of Economics, University of Cambridge, Cambridge.

LERNER R. M. (2006) Resilience as an attribute of the developmental system, *Annals of the New York Academy of Sciences* **1094**, 40–51.

LEVIT G. S., HOSSFELD U. and WITT U. (2011) Can Darwinism be 'generalised' and what use would this be?, *Journal of Evolutionary Economics* **21**, 545–562.

LÖSCH A. (1954) *The Economics of Location*. Yale University Press, New Haven, CT.

MACKINNON D., CUMBERS A., PIKE A., BIRCH K. and MCMASTER R. (2009) Evolution in economic geography: institutions, political economy, and adaptation, *Economic Geography* **85**, 129–150.

MALERBA F. (2010) Industry evolution and history-friendly models. Plenary Paper presented at the International Schumpeter Society Conference on Innovation, Organisation, Sustainability and Crisis, Aalborg, Denmark, 21–24 June 2010 (available at: http://www.schumpeter2010.dk/index.php/schumpeter/schumpeter2010/paper/viewFile/491/208).

MALERBA F., NELSON R., ORSENIGO L. and WINTER S. (1999) History-friendly models of industrial evolution: the computer industry, *Industrial and Corporate Change* **8**, 3–40.

MARSHALL A. (1898) Distribution and exchange, *Economic Journal* **8**, 37–59.

MARTIN R. L. (1999) The new 'geographical turn' in economics: some critical reflections, *Cambridge Journal of Economics* **23**, 65–91.

MARTIN R. L. (2000) Institutional approaches to economic geography, in SHEPPARD E. and BARNES T. (Eds) *A Companion to Economic Geography*, pp. 77–94. Blackwell, Oxford.

MARTIN R. L. (2010) The Roepke Lecture in Economic Geography: Rethinking regional path dependence: beyond lock-in to evolution, *Economic Geography* **86**, 1–27.

MARTIN R. L. (2011) The 'new economic geography': credible models of the economic landscape?, in LEYSHON A., LEE R., MCDOWELL L. and SUNLEY P. (Eds) *The Sage Handbook of Economic Geography*, pp. 53–71. Sage, London.

MARTIN R. L. (2012a) (Re)placing path dependence: a response to the debate, *International Journal of Urban and Regional Research* **36**, 179–192.

MARTIN R. L. (2012b) Regional economic resilience, hysteresis and recessionary shocks, *Journal of Economic Geography* **12**, 1–32.

MARTIN R. L. (2013) Path dependence and the spatial economy: a key concept in retrospect and prospect, in EZCURRA R. and RODRIGUEZ-POSE A. (Eds) *Handbook of Regional Science*, pp. 609–629. Springer, Berlin.

MARTIN R. L. and SUNLEY P. J. (2006) Path dependence and regional economic evolution, *Journal of Economic Geography* **6**, 395–435.

MARTIN R. L. and SUNLEY P. J. (2007) Complexity thinking and evolutionary economic geography, *Journal of Economic Geography* **7**, 573–602.

MARTIN R. L. and SUNLEY P. J. (2011) Conceptualising cluster evolution: beyond the life cycle model?, *Regional Studies* **45**, 1299–1318.

MARTIN R. L. and SUNLEY P. J. (2012) Forms of emergence and the evolution of economic landscapes, *Journal of Economic Behaviour and Organisation* **82**[Special Issue: Emergence in Economics], 338–352.

MASSEY D. (1992) Politics and space/time, *New Left Review* **196**, 65–84.

MASTEN A. and OBRADOVIC J. (2006) Competence and resilience in development, *Annals of the New York Academy of Sciences* **1094**, 13–27.

MENZEL M. and FORNAHL D. (2010) Cluster lifecycles – dimensions and rationales of cluster evolution, *Industrial and Corporate Change* **19**, 205–238.

MESOUDI A., WHITEN A. and LALAND K. (2006) Towards a unified science of cultural evolution, *Behavioural and Brain Sciences* **29**, 329–383.

METCALFE J. S. (1998) *Evolutionary Economics and Creative Destruction*. Routledge, London.

METCALFE J. S., FOSTER J. and RAMLOGAN R. (2006) Adaptive economic growth, *Cambridge Journal of Economics* **30**, 7–32.

MÜLLER G. (2007) Six memos for evo-devo, in LAUBICHLER M. D. and MAIENSCHEIN J. (Eds) *From Embryology to Evo-Devo*, pp. 499–524. MIT Press, Cambridge, MA.

MÜLLER G. B. (2008) Evo-devo as a discipline, in MINELLI A. and FUSCO G. (Eds) *Evolving Pathways: Key Themes in Evolutionary Developmental Biology*, pp. 3–29. Cambridge University Press, Cambridge.

NELSON R. R. (1995) Recent evolutionary thinking about economic change, *Journal of Economic Literature* **33**, 48–90.

NELSON R. R. (2006) *Economic Development from the Perspective of Evolutionary Economic Theory*. Working Papers in Technology Governance and Economic Dynamics No. 2. Other Canon Foundation, Norway.

NELSON R. R. (2007) Universal Darwinism and evolutionary social science, *Biology and Philosophy* **22**, 73–94.

NELSON R. R. (2011) Economic development as an evolutionary process, *Innovation and Development* **1**, 39–49.

NELSON R. R. and WINTER S. (1982) *An Evolutionary Theory of Economic Change*. Harvard University Press, Cambridge, MA.

NORGAARD R. B. and KALLIS G. (2011) Coevolutionary contradictions: prospects for a research programme on social and environmental change, *Geografiska Annaler Series B* **93**, 289–300.

ODLING-SMEE J. (2010) Niche inheritance, in PIGLIUCCI M. and MÜLLER G. B. (Eds) *Evolution: The Extended Synthesis*, pp. 175–208. MIT Press, Cambridge, MA.

OOSTERLYNCK S. (2012) Path dependence: a political economy perspective, *International Journal of Urban and Regional Research* **36**, 158–165.

OYAMA S. (2000) Causal democracy and causal contributions in Developmental Systems Theory, *Proceedings of the PSA* **67**, S332–S347.

OYAMA S., GRIFFITHS P. E. and GRAY R. D. (2001) *Cycles of Contingency: Developmental Systems and Evolution*. MIT Press, Cambridge, MA.

PELIKAN P. (2011) Evolutionary developmental economics: how to generalize Darwinism fruitfully to help comprehend change, *Journal of Evolutionary Economics* **21**, 341–366.

PIGLIUCCI M. (2007) Do we need an extended evolutionary synthesis?, *Evolution* **61**, 2743–2749.

PIGLIUCCI M. (2008) Is evolvability evolvable?, *Nature Reviews Genetics* **9**, 75–82.

PIGLIUCCI M. (2009) An extended synthesis for evolutionary biology, *Annals of the New York Academy of Sciences* **1168**, 218–228.

PIGLIUCCI M. and MÜLLER G. B. (Eds) (2010) *Evolution: The Extended Synthesis*. MIT Press, Cambridge, MA.

RAFF R. A. (1996) *The Shape of Life: Genes, Development and the Evolution of Animal Forms*. University of Chicago Press, Chicago, IL.

REGIONAL STUDIES (2011) Cluster life cycles, *Regional Studies* **45**[Special Issue], 1295–1402.

REID R. G. (2007) *Biological Emergences: Evolution by Natural Experiment*. MIT Press, Cambridge, MA.

ROBERT J., HALL B. and OLSON W. (2001) Bridging the gap between Developmental Systems Theory and Evolutionary Developmental Biology, *BioEssays* **23**, 954–962.

SAYER A. (2010) Reductionism in social science, in LEE R. E. (Ed.) *Questioning Nineteenth Century Assumptions about Knowledge*, pp. 5–39. SUNY Press, New York, NY.

SETTERFIELD M. (1998) *Rapid Growth and Relative Decline: Modelling Macroeconomic Dynamics with Hysteresis*. Macmillan, Basingstoke.

SHEPPARD E. (2011) Geographical political economy, *Journal of Economic Geography* **11**, 319–332.

SMITH C. M. and RUPPELL J. C. (2011) What anthropologists should know about the new extended synthesis, *Structure and Dynamics* **5**, 1–13.

STORPER M. (1997) *The Regional World, Territorial Development in a Global Economy*. Guilford Press, London.

STRAMBACH S. (2008) *Path Dependence and Path Plasticity: The Co-Evolution of Institutions and Innovation – The German Customised Business Software Industry*. Working Papers on Innovation and Space No. 2.08. Department of Geography, University of Marburg, Marburg.

TER WAL A. and BOSCHMA R. (2011) Co-evolution of firms, industries and networks in space, *Regional Studies* **45**, 919–933.

TILLY C. (1984) *Big Structures, Large Processes, Huge Comparisons*. Russell Sage Foundation, New York, NY.

ULANOWICZ R. E. (2012) Widening the third window, *Axiomathes* **22**, 269–289.

VISSERS G. and DANKBARR B. (2013) Path dependence and path plasticity: textile cities in the Netherlands, *Zeitschrift für Wirtschaftsgeographie* **57**, 83–95.

VROMEN J. (2007) *Generalised Darwinism in Economics – The Devil is in the Details*. Papers on Economics and Evolution No. 0711. Max Planck Institute of Economics, Jena.

VROMEN J. (2008) *Ontological Issues in Evolutionary Economics: The Debate between Generalised Darwinism and the Continuity Hypothesis*. Papers on Economics and Evolution No. 0805. Max Planck Institute of Economics, Jena.

WAGNER A. (2008) Robustness and evolvability: a paradox resolved, *Proceedings of the Royal Society, B: Biological Sciences* **275**, 91–100.

WEBER B. H. (2011) Extending and expanding the Darwinian synthesis: the role of complex systems dynamics, *Studies in the History and Philosophy of Science Part C: Studies in the History and Philosophy of Biological and Biomedical Sciences* **42**, 75–81.

WEST-EBERHARD M. J. (2005) Developmental plasticity and the origin of species differences, *Proceedings of the National Academy of Sciences, USA* **102(Suppl. 1)**, 6543–6549.

WHITACRE J. M. (2012) Biological robustness: paradigms, mechanism and systems principles, *Frontiers in Genetics* **3**, 1–15. doi:10.3389/fgene.2012.00067

WIMSATT W. (2006) Generative entrenchment and an Evolutionary Developmental Biology for culture, *Behavioural and Brain Sciences* **29**, 364–366.

WITT U. (2003) *The Evolving Economy: Essays on the Evolutionary Approach to Economics*. Edward Elgar, Cheltenham.

WITT U. (2004) On the proper interpretation of 'evolution' in economics and its implications for production theory, *Journal of Economic Methodology* **11**, 125–146.

Towards an Evolutionary Perspective on Regional Resilience

RON BOSCHMA

*Center for Innovation, Research and Competence in the Learning Economy (CIRCLE), Lund University,
Sweden.*
*Urban and Regional Research Centre Utrecht (URU), Utrecht University,
the Netherlands.*

BOSCHMA R. Towards an evolutionary perspective on regional resilience, *Regional Studies.* This paper proposes an evolutionary perspective on regional resilience. It conceptualizes resilience not just as the ability of a region to accommodate shocks, but extends it to the long-term ability of regions to develop new growth paths. A comprehensive view on regional resilience is proposed in which history is key to understand how regions develop new growth paths, and in which industrial, network and institutional dimensions of resilience come together. Resilient regions are capable of overcoming a trade-off between adaptation and adaptability, as embodied in related and unrelated variety, loosely coupled networks and loosely coherent institutional structures.

BOSCHMA R. 迈向区域恢復力的演化观点，区域研究。本文提出一个区域恢復力的演化观点。该观点不仅将恢復力概念化为区域调适冲击的能力，更将此延伸至区域建立新的成长路径的长期能力 。本研究将提出一个区域恢復力的综合视角，在该视角中，历史是理解区域如何发展新的成长路径的关键，且恢復力的产业、网络 与制度面向融合在一起 。具恢復力的区域，有能力克服适应与调适力之间的权衡，并体现在相关与不相关多样性，以及鬆弛连结的网络和鬆散协调的制度结构中。

BOSCHMA R. Vers une perspective évolutive de la capacité d'adaptation régionale, *Regional Studies.* Cet article propose une perspective évolutive de la capacité d'adaptation régionale. On conceptualise la capacité d'adaptation non seulement comme la capacité d'une région de s'ajuster aux chocs, mais aussi la capacité à long terme des régions de développer de nouveaux sentiers de croissance. On cherche à donner un aperçu global de la capacité d'adaptation régionale où l'histoire s'avère un facteur clé pour comprendre comment les régions développent de nouveaux sentiers de croissance, et où les aspects industriels, réseautés et institutionnels de la capacité d'adaptation se réunissent. Les régions qui s'adaptent peuvent surmonter le conflit entre, d'un côté, la capacité d'adaptation et, de l'autre côté, l'adaptabilité, tel qu'il figure dans les notions de variétés connexe et sans rapport, dans les réseaux à couplage faible et dans les structures institutionnelles peu cohérentes.

BOSCHMA R. Auf dem Weg zu einer evolutionären Perspektive der regionalen Resilienz, *Regional Studies.* In diesem Beitrag wird eine evolutionäre Perspektive der regionalen Resilienz vorgeschlagen. Die Resilienz wird nicht nur als die Fähigkeit einer Region zur Verarbeitung von Schocks konzeptualisiert, sondern auf die langfristige Fähigkeit von Regionen zur Entwicklung neuer Wachstumspfade erweitert. Es wird eine umfassende Perspektive der regionalen Resilienz vorgeschlagen, in der die Geschichte eine Schlüsselrolle beim Verständnis der Frage spielt, wie Regionen neue Wachstumspfade entwickeln, und in der Branchen-, Netzwerk- und institutionelle Dimensionen der Resilienz miteinander kombiniert werden. Resiliente Regionen können einen Kompromiss zwischen Anpassung und Anpassungsfähigkeit überwinden, der sich in verwandter und nichtverwandter Varietät, lose gekoppelten Netzwerken und lose kohärenten institutionellen Strukturen verkörpert.

BOSCHMA R. Hacia una perspectiva evolutiva sobre la resiliencia regional, *Regional Studies.* En este artículo se propone una perspectiva evolutiva de la resiliencia regional. Se conceptualiza la resiliencia no solo como la capacidad de una región para acomodar choques, sino también teniendo en cuenta la capacidad a largo plazo de las regiones para desarrollar nuevas vías de crecimiento. Se propone una visión completa de resiliencia regional donde la historia es fundamental para entender cómo las regiones nuevas desarrollan vías de crecimiento, y dónde se combinan las dimensiones industriales, institucionales y de redes de la resiliencia. Las regiones con resiliencia son capaces de superar una compensación entre la adaptación y adaptabilidad, tal como está representado en la variedad relacionada o no, en las redes sin conexión directa y las estructuras institucionales poco coherentes.

INTRODUCTION

The concept of regional resilience has drawn a lot of attention in the context of the current economic crisis. This has brought about more clarity about the definition and meaning of resilience, but no consensus. In economic geography, there is a tendency to refute the engineering, equilibrium concept of resilience, in which resilience is regarded as a response to external disturbances and a move back to a steady state. Scholars have advocated an evolutionary approach to regional resilience instead, in which the focus is on the long-term capacity of regions to reconfigure their socio-economic structure (e.g. CHRISTOPHERSON et al., 2010; SIMMIE and MARTIN, 2010; COOKE et al., 2011). However, MARTIN (2012) argues that the long-term adaptive capacity of regions is still 'largely unresearched' (p. 11). As such, an evolutionary perspective on regional resilience is still work very much in progress.

The objective of the paper is to show that an evolutionary perspective can bring additional insights to the expanding literature on regional resilience. First, regional resilience is conceptualized not just as the ability of a region to accommodate shocks, as is common in the literature, but it is extended to the ability of regions to reconfigure their socio-economic and institutional structures to develop new growth paths. Second, a comprehensive view on regional resilience is proposed in which industrial, network and institutional dimensions of resilience come together and are combined. Doing so, the question is taken up of how related variety may be linked to regional resilience, how networks can be made part of it (VICENTE et al., 2011), an issue that has received little attention in the regional resilience literature despite some focus on complex adaptive systems, and an effort is made to tackle the critique that the resilience literature has drawn too little attention to institutions (e.g. SWAN-STROM, 2008; PIKE et al., 2010; DAVIES, 2011). Third, history is made a key input to the understanding of regional resilience. There is a tendency in the literature that resilience means to avoid path dependence, or a move away from it, as if new growth paths are detached from their past, and as if regions need to escape from their historical legacy to achieve that. A conceptualization of regional resilience is proposed in which history is key to understand how regions

develop new growth paths, as pre-existing industrial, network and institutional structures in regions provide opportunities but also set limits to the process of diversification. Fourth, the evolutionary literature on regional resilience has drawn attention to a trade-off between adaptation and adaptability (e.g. HASSINK, 2010; PIKE et al., 2010). How this trade-off may be overcome is explored, as this is seen as a key challenge for regions to become resilient, that is, how to secure adaptability and adaptation simultaneously.

The paper is organized as follows. The second section briefly discusses the treatment of resilience in the economic geography literature. An evolutionary approach to regional resilience is proposed in which structural change is the guiding principle, and which explores how the trade-off between regional adaptation and adaptability may be overcome. The third section discusses how regional resilience can be associated with configurations of the industrial structure in a region. The fourth section discusses how networks can be made part of regional resilience; and the fifth section will incorporate the institutional dimension. The sixth section draws conclusions and sets out some unresolved issues that an evolutionary approach to regional resilience needs to take up.

TOWARDS AN EVOLUTIONARY CONCEPTUALIZATION OF REGIONAL RESILIENCE

When social scientists speak about resilience, they refer to the responsiveness of individuals, organizations or systems to shocks. There is an almost endless list of shocks the resilience literature has dealt with, and the nature of these disturbances varies widely.[1] Shocks can occur as sudden and discrete events, or evolve more gradually, as 'slow-burn challenges' (PENDALL et al., 2010). Examples are individual traumas, terrorist attacks, natural disasters, natural developments like global warming, global economic crises, major plant closures, technologies becoming obsolete, the fall of complete industries, political transformations, and so forth.

Triggered by the current economic crisis, economic geographers have shown a strong interest in the topic of regional resilience. This has led to many empirical papers, ranging from case studies on particular regions (e.g. TREADO, 2010), to comparative analyses of two or more regions (e.g. SWANSTROM et al., 2009; SIMMIE and MARTIN, 2010; WOLFE, 2010; HILL et al., 2012) to more systematic approaches analysing the resilience of many regions (e.g. DIODATO and WETERINGS, 2014; FINGLETON et al., 2012; MARTIN, 2012). However, this interest has also led to fierce debate.

CHRISTOPHERSON et al. (2010) state that the 'question of regional resilience is, at base, a very old and enduring question' (p. 3). Indeed, many economic geographers have investigated in the past how regions responded differently to, for instance, de-industrialization, the shift from Fordist to neo-Fordist types of production (PIORE and SABEL, 1984; SCOTT, 1988; CHAPPLE and LESTER, 2010), and economic recessions in general (DOMAZLICKY, 1980). Some scholars have come to the conclusion that the resilience concept has little to add to existing concepts like path dependence and lock-in (HASSINK, 2010; PIKE et al., 2010; DAVIES, 2011). Other scholars have stated that the resilience concept is at risk of being a fuzzy concept (PENDALL et al., 2010) that is in of more precision and clarity (MARTIN, 2012). One of the crucial issues is how to relate resilience to regions, as regions (at whatever spatial scale) are collections of individuals, organizations, industries, networks and institutions, each of which may have their own distinctive features of resilience.[2] Another issue is that it is not always clear in the regional resilience literature what is cause and what is effect. For instance, is institutional resilience a sign of regional resilience, or is it a determinant?

The regional resilience literature differentiates between three types of approaches. The engineering-based concept of resilience (ROSE, 2004; FINGLETON et al., 2012) refers to the ability of a system to return to a pre-existing stable equilibrium state after a shock. In this framework, regional economies (at whatever spatial scale) show different levels of resilience in terms of 'whether or not, and to what degree, and in what time frame an economy can return to its pre-existing shock position and level of output' (PIKE et al., 2010, p. 61). Economic geographers tend to refute this equilibrium approach, as it makes no reference to changes in the structure and function of regions, among other reasons (MARTIN, 2012).

There is more ambiguity about the second approach, which is the ecological concept of resilience that is based on multiple equilibria (e.g. REGGIANI et al., 2002; SWANSTROM et al., 2009; ZOLLI and HEALY, 2012). Here a region can change its structure and function in the face of an external shock, and move into a new equilibrium state. Still, this approach adopts an equilibrium perspective in which a resilient region shifts from one possible steady growth path or equilibrium to another. Crucial issues like the role of human agency, institutions and structural change are not well captured by such an equilibrium perspective, but are key to understand the long-term economic evolution of regions

(MACKINNNON and DRISCOLL DERICKSON, 2012). Moreover, this approach fails to see resilience as much broader than just assessing the sensitivity of a regional economy to shocks, and it often misleadingly portrays the region as an autonomous spatial unit (CHRISTOPHERSON et al., 2010).

There is increasing interest in an evolutionary approach to regional resilience (e.g. CHRISTOPHERSON et al., 2010; CLARK et al., 2010; PIKE et al., 2010; SIMMIE and MARTIN, 2010; COOKE et al., 2011). In an evolutionary framework, resilience in the meaning of the capacity of a region to sustain long-term development is regarded as important as the capacity of a region to respond positively to short-term shocks. This approach focuses more on the long-term evolution of regions and their ability to adapt and reconfigure their industrial, technological and institutional structures in an economic system that is restless and evolving. Here, 'resilience is considered as an ongoing process rather than a recovery to a (pre-existing or new) stable equilibrium state [...]' (SIMMIE and MARTIN, 2010, p. 31). This basic need for fundamental economic renewal is ever present, though in times of crises, this is felt more pressing. Resilience then depends on the ability of regions to cope with structural change, that is, to create new growth paths, in order to offset inevitable processes of stagnation and decline in their regional economy (SAVIOTTI, 1996), as 'no region can rely on its legacy of past successes to succeed in the future' (SWANSTROM, 2008, p. 1).[3]

When conceptualizing resilience in terms of a region's capacity to develop new growth paths, the evolutionary approach tends to fall back on the distinction made by GRABHER (1993) between adaptation and adaptability (CHRISTOPHERSON et al., 2010; PIKE et al., 2010; BRISTOW et al., 2012). Adaptation concerns changes within preconceived paths, while adaptability is about developing new pathways, i.e. departures from existing paths. In this framework, scholars argue there is a trade-off between the two. As GRABHER (1993) put it:

adaptation leads to an increasing specialization of resources and a pronounced preference for innovations that reproduce existing structures. And while the system optimizes the 'fit' into its environment, it loses its adaptability. [...] Adaptability crucially depends on the availability of unspecific and uncommitted capacities that can be put to a variety of unforeseeable uses: redundancy.

(p. 265)

Here, regional resilience has been associated primarily with long-term adaptability, how history can stand in the way of true economic renewal, and how to overcome negative lock-in (BOSCHMA and LAMBOOY, 1999). This has led to a tendency in the literature to depict history as something negative that one has to get rid of, or to escape from, to secure regional resilience.

It is argued in this paper that the evolutionary approach of regional resilience is still underdeveloped for at least five reasons. First, there is a need to integrate the two meanings of resilience, that is, the short-term capacity of a region to absorb shocks and the long-term capacity of a region to develop new growth paths (MARTIN and SUNLEY, 2013). The ability of regions to respond to shocks will be redefined in terms of how shocks affect the capacity of regions to develop new growth paths like new industries or technological breakthroughs. New growth paths can be understood as new path creation but also path renewal, as long as these are distinct from existing regional paths (MARTIN and SUNLEY, 2006; GARUD et al., 2010). Second, this requires better understanding of how regions develop new growth paths. However, there is still little understanding of what determines the long-term adaptive capacity of regions (MARTIN, 2012). Accordingly, a key task is to identify the main determinants of a region's ability to develop new growth paths. Third, there is a misleading tendency in the literature to associate regional adaptability with new growth paths that are detached from their past, as if path dependency will cause only problems of adjustment (MAGNUSSON and OTTOSSON, 2009; HENNING et al., 2013).[4] There is a need to redefine the role of history here. It is argued that the legacy of the past has a strong imprint on regional resilience not only in terms of constraints but also in terms of opportunities, as it sets the scope for re-orientating technologies, skills and institutions in regions.[5] Drawing on recent empirical work (e.g. NEFFKE et al., 2011a; KOGLER et al., 2013), it is claimed that pre-existing resources and capabilities in regions often shape new growth paths in regions, as these are rejuvenated and redeployed in new combinations. Fourth, this requires a rethinking of regional resilience as the capacity of regions to overcome the trade-off between adaptability and adaptation. While a lot has been said on how adaptation may preclude adaptability, the evolutionary approach has drawn little attention to the other side of the trade-off, though there are good reasons to believe that adaptability may also hurt adaptation, as, for instance, explorative search for new things may go at the expense of focus and local cohesiveness, and therefore positive externalities in a region may fail to materialize. This requires a better understanding of how regions can achieve adaptation without a loss of adaptability, and adaptability without compromising on adaptation. And fifth, an evolutionary approach to regional resilience needs to account for the complex and multidimensional nature of resilience (PENDALL et al., 2010). Regions (at whatever spatial scale) are collections of individuals,[6] organizations,[7] industries, networks and institutions, each of which, and in combination, can display their own processes of path dependence, and each of which can be associated with this tension between adaptation and adaptability. This paper limits its attention to the industrial, network and institutional dimensions of regional resilience, and it is explained for each of these dimensions how this trade-off may be overcome.

The aim of this paper is to incorporate regional resilience in a long-term evolutionary perspective that is theoretically, but above all, empirically informed. This requires understanding of how regions develop new growth paths, and whether, and how history plays a role here. Instead of arguing that resilience means to avoid path dependence, or a move away from it, it is argued that the long-term adaptability of regions is conditioned by its industrial, network and institutional legacy which provides opportunities but also sets limits for local actors to be resilient. Doing so, the aim is to develop a regional resilience concept that goes beyond this trade-off thinking. This requires a clarification of how this tension can be overcome at the level of industries, networks and institutions and, thus, how particular industrial, network and institutional structures in regions, alone or in combination, impact on the resilience of regions. This will be taken up one by one in the subsequent sections.

TECHNO-INDUSTRIAL VARIETY AND REGIONAL RESILIENCE

The resilience literature has drawn a lot of attention to the industrial composition in a region. Focus is often exclusively on the sensitivity of regions to negative[8] sector-specific shocks, like a fall in demand.[9] In this context, specialized regions are perceived to be less vulnerable to sector-specific shocks, as their regional economies are dominated by one principal industry. Nevertheless, when hit, such a shock is more likely to damage large parts of the regional economy. In contrast, diversified regions have a higher chance to be hit by a sector-specific shock, as they house a range of industries that may become victim. Nevertheless, despite this higher risk, a diversified region has a lower probability that a sector-specific shock has a negative impact on the local economy as a whole. In other words, industrial variety in a region spreads risks and can better accommodate idiosyncratic sector-specific shocks (DISSART, 2003; ESSLETZBICHLER, 2007; DAVIES and TONTS, 2010; DESROCHERS and LEPPALA, 2011).

However, this effect of industrial variety as shock-absorber will only become manifest when other conditions are met. First, local industries have to be disconnected in terms of input–output relationships, otherwise, the decline in one industry will still trigger decline in other local industries (DIODATO and WETERINGS, 2014). It could also be argued that local industries have to be disconnected in cognitive terms, which has been referred to as unrelated variety (FRENKEN et al., 2007), so the fall of one industry will not affect the learning opportunities available to other industries in a diversified region. However, there is increasing awareness that industrial variety will work better as a shock-absorber when the local industries are skill related, that is, when industries require similar skills, as this enhances regional labour matching (NEFFKE and HENNING, 2013).[10] Regional variety in skill-related industries is expected to speed up the recovery from sector-specific shocks, as the redundant employees can find more easily new jobs in a region with a local supply of skill-related industries in which their skills are still found relevant (DIODATO and WETERINGS, 2014). This also prevents the destruction of human capital in a region as well as the outflow of high-skilled people to other regions.

This variety effect covers only one aspect of regional resilience, that is, the capacity of a region to resist a shock, and the speed with which it can recover from that (e.g. DAVIES, 2011; MARTIN, 2012). It ignores another crucial aspect of regional resilience, as it says little on how shocks affect regional competitiveness more in general, and the ability of regions to create new growth paths and to make crossovers across technologies and industries in regions, out of which new economic activities may develop. This leads to the other important meaning of resilience, which is the capacity of a region to develop new growth paths. It will be argued here that this depends on the existing industrial structure in a region, which provides opportunities, or not, to make new combinations that evolve into new growth paths.

To start with, a specialized region has less options at its disposal to develop new growth paths, as it has basically one principal sector (possibly with a few sectors that developed around it), out of which a new industry can branch. It has few recombinatory options available at the regional scale, as there is little (related) variety between knowledge domains in the region that might be recombined. In other words, specialized regions have few potential sources for renewal and diversification. What is more, their ability to diversify into new growth paths might be negatively affected by their specialized industrial structure (BOSCHMA and LAMBOOY, 1999; HASSINK, 2005; MARTIN and SUNLEY, 2006). Once a region specializes in a knowledge base, this offers opportunities to local firms for further improvements, but regions may also become myopic for opportunities that lay beyond their own development paths, and sunk costs may prevent them from switching to new growth tracks (MALMBERG and MASKELL, 1997; MASKELL and MALMBERG, 1999). Here, perfect adaptation to the local environment leads to reproduction and locks a region into a specific trajectory that goes at the expense of a region's adaptability. Here, the classic trade-off is found between adaptation and adaptability in specialized regions in which the former undermines the latter, and which has been described by GRABHER (1993) as the 'trap of rigid specialization'.

In diversified regions, this type of conflict, in which adaptation harms adaptability, has less chance to become manifest, at least at the regional scale (at the industry and technology scale, the same lock-in processes might still occur). Diversified regions are considered to have more potential to make new recombinations across local industries, and to develop new growth paths, also known as 'Jacobs' externalities', after the seminal work of JACOBS (1969). So, diversified regions may score high on adaptability, but adaptability may go at the expense of adaptation, as diversified regions may suffer from a lack of industrial focus, a lack of critical mass for each of its industries (no localization externalities), and a lack of cognitive proximity between local industries. Doing many things may not lead to excellence in any of those parts in the region, especially when these parts do not provide complementary resources either, that is, they suffer from unrelated variety. Under these conditions, local industries are more likely to decline and disappear, as these are loosely embedded in the regional context. This is in line with empirical evidence that shows that sectors that are unrelated to other local industries are more likely to fail and exit a region (NEFFKE et al., 2011a; ESSLEZTBICHLER, 2013; NEFFKE et al., 2014). In other words, in these circumstances, diversified regions suffer from a trade-off between adaptability and adaptation that has received little attention in the literature so far.

In the evolutionary literature, there is a tendency to equate regional resilience with adaptability (e.g. PIKE et al., 2010). It is claimed instead that adaptability is a necessary but not a sufficient condition for regional resilience, as being resilient depends on the capacity of a region to overcome the tension between adaptability and adaptation. It is claimed that related variety in a region has the potential to secure both adaptation and adaptability, and thus, may make a region more resilient. Related variety means that a region has a wide range of related industries that provide potentials for inter-industry learning and new recombinations (FRENKEN et al., 2007): the higher related variety is, the more opportunities for local industries to learn from each other, and the more potential combinations across local industries can be made. In this context, related variety guarantees adaptation because of the local presence of a high number of related industries which provides a supportive local environment. This makes related industries can benefit from each other's co-presence, as each of them can draw from a local pool of relevant capabilities and skills, and so benefit from what might be referred to as 'local related externalities'. Recent studies have indeed demonstrated that industries are less likely to exit a region when these are technologically related to other local industries (NEFFKE et al., 2011a), and that especially young firms have higher survival rates in a region that is well endowed with related industries (NEFFKE et al., 2012).

But more importantly, related variety also enhances the adaptability of regions. FRENKEN *et al.* (2007) claimed that the recombinatory potential of diversified regions is enhanced by related variety, and not necessarily by variety per se. There is indeed evidence that related variety appears to be a key ingredient for regions to diversify and develop new growth paths, as new industries tend to branch out of and recombine resources from existing local industries to which they are technologically related. There is a lot of case-study evidence that the long-term capacity of regions to develop new growth paths is depending on the reconfiguration and reorientation of existing regional assets (e.g. BATHELT and BOGGS, 2003; BELUSSI and SEDITA, 2009; MORISET, 2009). GLAESER (2005) described how Boston was able to reinvent itself by reconfiguring its skill-related assets over a long period of time. Pittsburgh lost most of its steelmaking capacity but not its steelmaking expertise which laid the foundations of a strong economic recovery (TREADO, 2010). Entrepreneurial studies have demonstrated that the pre-entry experience of entrepreneurs in related industries and a location with related industries increase the life chances of firms in new industries (KLEPPER, 2007; BUENSTORF and KLEPPER, 2009).[11] Studies on the evolution of a technology show that technological competences in regions shape patterns of technological diversification in fuel cells (TANNER, 2011, 2014), nanotechnology (COLOMBELLI *et al.*, 2014) and biotechnology (BOSCHMA *et al.*, 2014a). Empirical studies on diversification show systematically that new industries emerge from related industries, and thus, that the industrial structure of a regional economy has an impact on diversification opportunities of regions (KLEPPER and SIMONS, 2000; NEFFKE *et al.*, 2011a; RIGBY, 2012; VAN DER WOUDEN, 2012; BOSCHMA *et al.*, 2013, 2014b; ESSLETZBICHLER, 2013; MUNEE-PEERAKUL *et al.*, 2013). NEFFKE *et al.* (2011a) found that sectors that are technologically related to other local sectors are more likely to emerge in a region. So, breakthroughs are often novelties that depend on pre-existing technologies that are recombined at the regional scale (e.g. ARTS and VEUGELERS, 2012). In sum, these studies confirm that the resilience of regions depends on their industrial history to a considerable degree.

The question is whether a shock may undo the positive effects of related variety on the capacity of a region to develop new paths. This depends on whether the collapse of one industry in a region will also damage other local industries to which it is technologically related. When a shock concerns a complete shift to another technological paradigm or general purpose technology that concerns the whole underlying knowledge base of all related industries in a region, it will seriously undermine regional resilience. Moreover, if the underlying knowledge base of a region is more specialized (that is, there is related variety within only one group

of industries), related variety in a region may be weakened by a sector-specific shock, and it might undermine the recombinatory and labour matching potential of a region. However, if the underlying knowledge base in a region is truly diverse, a sector-specific shock is less likely to lead to the decline of other local related industries, and related variety will remain to function as a key source for regional economic renewal. This is the case when the region consists of groups of related activities in which there is a high degree of relatedness within each group (i.e. related variety within each group) but a low degree of relatedness between the groups (i.e. unrelated variety between groups). In this case, the loss of one industry might lower the degree of related variety within the group to which that industry belongs, but it will not affect related variety in the other local groups, as these groups of local industries are unrelated, and thus, it will not undermine related variety of the region as a whole. This also shows that, next to related variety, it might be beneficial to have unrelated variety in a region as well to protect the recombinatory potential of a region against shocks.

So far, it has been argued that unrelated variety, as well as related variety in a region may enhance the region's adaptability, as both increase the potential to make new recombinations. It is expected that related variety acts more often as a key source for regional renewal, as new industries can build on and draw resources from local industries to which they are technologically related. In other words, adaptability and adaptation go hand in hand in regions with related variety. This is not the case in regions with unrelated variety only, as recombinations between unrelated knowledge domains also imply more risks and higher switching costs, as there is no local supportive environment. Therefore, unrelated diversification is more likely to fail, and successful unrelated diversification will be a more rare event. Having said that, it makes relevant the question whether regions can keep relying on recombinations between related industries (i.e. related diversification) to develop new growth paths in the long run, or whether regions have to diversify in more unrelated activities now and then, that is, making new combinations between unrelated domains that become related as soon as these domains connect (SAVIOTTI, 1996; SAVIOTTI and FRENKEN, 2008; QUATRARO, 2010). As regions have a tendency to diversify into related activities and shake off unrelated activities (NEFFKE *et al.*, 2011a; ESSLETZBICHLER, 2013; BOSCHMA *et al.*, 2013; NEFFKE *et al.*, 2014), it could be argued that regions need to develop new unrelated activities to increase their variety. CASTALDI *et al.* (2013) have claimed that regions with unrelated variety are more likely to produce technological breakthroughs, as it provides opportunities to recombine previously unrelated knowledge domains, while incremental innovations benefit from related variety in a region, as these arise out of recombinations of more closely related knowledge domains along well-defined paths. This would imply that unrelated variety (unrelated knowledge domains) guarantees adaptability while related variety (within each knowledge domain) secures adaptation. Having both types of variety then would make a region truly resilient, as it would overcome the trade-off between adaptability and adaptation.

To sum up, the resilience of a region is enhanced when a region has: (1) a variety of skill-related industries that have little local input–output relationships with one another, which increases the capacity to respond to sector-specific shocks; and (2) related variety which enhances the recombination potential of a region but, above all, provides local (related) resources on which new growth paths can build and develop. Consequently, related variety relaxes the trade-off between adaptability and adaptation that might occur in diversified regions. It is still an open question though whether related variety is sufficient, or whether a mixture of related variety within groups of local industries/technologies and unrelated variety between groups is beneficial, as it might protect the recombination potential of a region from shocks. In contrast to diversified regions, specialized regions combine high adaptation with a low adaptability to develop new growth paths, due to a lower recombination potential and a possible state of negative lock-in. Specialized regions may overcome this trade-off by: (1) activating uncommitted local resources or redundancies like skills; (2) using their specialized knowledge base to diversify into new related activities, like Pittsburgh (TREADO, 2010); and (3) connecting to industries and technologies in other regions, from which they can draw (related) resources and recombine those with their own local knowledge base (BOSCHMA and CAPONE, 2014).

The discussion on regional resilience so far has been partial, as it left out other dimensions that need to be integrated in a comprehensive view on regional resilience. The paper now turns to network and institutional dimensions of regional resilience in the fourth and fifth sections respectively.

REGIONAL RESILIENCE AND KNOWLEDGE NETWORKS

So far, the paper has looked at regions as collections of competences and industries that are technologically related or not, but it was left open whether these local resources actually connect. Regions may also be viewed as what LAWSON (1999) refers to as 'ensembles of competences that emerge from social interaction' (p. 157) in which regional actors have knowledge networks of relationships with other local actors but also with actors outside the region (ANTONELLI, 2000; HUGGINS and THOMPSON, 2014). In the regional resilience literature, little attention has been drawn to the

role of knowledge networks so far, despite some focus on complex adaptive systems.[12] Few studies in economic geography (yet) exist that have applied systematically the adaptive system approach, although scholars have used it as a background or as a source of inspiration (e.g. SIMMIE and MARTIN, 2010; COOKE et al., 2011; WINK, 2012; BRISTOW and HEALEY, 2013).[13] It is explained below how regional resilience may depend on network structures in regions. This section focuses on knowledge networks, not on other types of networks like urban transport networks (e.g. REGGIANI, 2012) or regional trade networks (THISSEN et al., 2013), to which the resilience concept has also been applied.

The internal structure of knowledge networks in a region, as well as their openness to the outside world, matter for regional resilience, because they impact on the sensitivity of regions to shocks (i.e. some network structures are more sensitive to the removal of a tie or a node), but also on the capacity of regions to develop new growth paths (i.e. some network structures have a higher capacity to induce radical change). Moreover, the trade-off between adaptation and adaptability outlined in the previous section has its network analogy in what SIMMIE and MARTIN (2010) described as a conflict between connectedness and resilience. Local network structures may become excessive and inward-looking, and network partners may become too proximate on various dimensions. These types of networks make regions score high on adaptation. The predominance of a closely tied core in the local network and a high degree of proximity between network partners (like cognitive and social proximity) favour control and efficiency, as they enhance information transmission and coordination, and lower the risk of opportunistic behaviour. However, the downside of this type of local network is a low score on adaptability: it suffers from a lack of recombination possibilities, it prevents lock-out, and it is vulnerable to shocks (CRESPO et al., 2013). This typical network state in which adaptation undermines adaptability has been especially found in specialized regions where the local connectedness (as embodied in interlocking corporate boards and strong social networks) may become so excessive that fundamental renewal is not on the mindset and is even heavily contested by local network players (GRABHER, 1993; BOSCHMA and FRENKEN, 2010). These networks will also result into an excess of cognitive proximity between the local network partners, which contribute further to this regional network lock-in. HERRIGEL (1990) proposed the concept of 'autarkic firm-based industrial order', as opposed to a 'decentralised region-based industrial order', to describe the adverse consequences of a regional network comprising of hierarchically organized corporations with standardized supplier linkages.

Local network structures may also be too fragmented, with many nodes that have few connections, and with a lack of proximity between the various (potential) nodes in the region. These local networks score high on adaptability, as these provide opportunities to accommodate shocks, and these give access to new and non-redundant knowledge. Here, the other side of trade-off (i.e. adaptability harming adaptation) is likely to prevail, as there is a lack of regional cohesiveness that weakens the efficiency and control of collective behaviour in the network, and there is hardly any mutual learning taking place, as agents are just too distant to each other (geographical proximity being the exception). This might come close to what SAXENIAN (1994) referred to as 'independent firm-based industrial systems', as opposed to 'regional network-based industrial systems' that actually promote learning and adjustment.

In the network literature, there are suggestions of how these trade-offs between adaptation and adaptability might be overcome at the level of structural properties of networks. FLEMING et al. (2007) argue that the trade-off between adaptation (for the sake of control and efficiency) and adaptability (for the sake of openness) can be overcome by a network structure in which embedded relationships within cliques co-exist with strategic 'structural hole' relationships among cliques. Likewise, BALLAND et al. (2013) have described a core/periphery network structure in which a cohesive structure of knowledge interactions (for the sake of coordination and circulation of knowledge) is mixed with a periphery of loosely connected organizations that are poorly tied with the core of the network (to promote new and fresh ideas). CRESPO et al. (2013) have explored how to solve potential conflicts between efficiency and resilience in knowledge networks in terms of the relative importance of closure and bridging network strategies. When closure strategies prevail, the structure of the network will exhibit tightly couplings in a core-component and a loosely connected periphery of nodes. This favours technological lock-in and efficiency but prevents regional lock-out which is bad for resilience. Instead, bridging strategies are more open for more disruptive relations between the core and periphery of nodes, but they undermine cohesiveness that weakens the control of collective behaviour in the network. In the core/periphery and resilient network described by CRESPO et al. (2013), there are high levels of connection between the core and periphery which prevent shocks on core members to weaken the whole network structure. At the same time, explorative behaviour can diffuse more easily from periphery to core members, due to the ability of key nodes to mix closure and bridging ties for overlapping explorative and exploitive phases in their relational patterns.

To overcome the trade-off between adaptation and adaptability in regional networks, one can also look at the nature of the network relationships, next to the structural properties of networks. The proximity framework is useful to describe the nature of network ties in terms of various dimensions of proximity, and how that

enhances, or not, regional resilience (BOSCHMA and FRENKEN, 2010; BALLAND, 2012a, 2012b). Proximity between agents favours the formation of knowledge network ties, as proximity decreases costs and risks, but too much proximity may lead to lock-in and be bad for breakthroughs. To overcome this proximity trade-off between efficiency and resilience, one could think of optimal levels of proximity between agents on the various proximity dimensions (BOSCHMA and FRENKEN, 2010). The optimal level of cognitive proximity follows from the need to keep some cognitive distance (for the sake of new ideas) and to secure some cognitive proximity (to enable effective communication) (COHENDET and LLERENA, 1997; NOOTE-BOOM, 2000; GILSING et al., 2008; BROEKEL and BOSCHMA, 2012). Such optimal levels of proximity are likely to exist for the other forms of proximity as well. For geographical proximity, one could argue that a combination of local buzz and global pipelines is beneficial for the long-term evolution of regions (ASHEIM and ISAKSEN, 2002; BATHELT et al., 2004; MOODYSSON, 2008; DAHL FITJAR and RODRÍ-GUEZ-POSE, 2011), while an optimal level of organizational proximity could be accomplished by loosely coupled networks that combine flexibility and coordination (GRABHER and STARK, 1997).

Besides looking at network structures as a whole, studies have investigated the strategic role of key agents in networks to ensure coordination and induce real change at the same time (CATTANI and FERRIANI, 2008). These studies focus on gatekeepers in regions, and on the extent to which local agents benefit or not from the presence of gatekeepers and their global linkages (GIULIANI and BELL, 2005; CANTNER and GRAF, 2006; MORRISON, 2008; MORRISON and RABELLOTTI, 2009; GRAF, 2011; MUNARI et al., 2012). Gatekeepers can prevent a region to enter into a situation of lock-in, as they have strong external linkages through which external knowledge diffuses widely to local actors. In doing so, they can overcome the trade-off between what has been called embeddedness and structural holes, as they facilitate: 'the formation of a network structure that combines the benefits of local clustering (i.e., high trust and cooperation) with the existence of short pathways to external sources (i.e., rapid and facilitated access to novel information)' (VERSPAGEN and DUYSTERS, 2004, quoted in MORRISON et al., 2013, p. 81). MORRISON et al. (2013) have claimed that global pipelines enhance knowledge accumulation in clusters when there is high-quality local buzz that makes this external knowledge circulate, or when the cluster is small and has a weak knowledge base. BRESCHI and LENZI (2014) found evidence that the transcoding function of gatekeepers is especially important in cities with a specialized knowledge base, while in cities with a diversified knowledge base, direct linkages to external knowledge are more important for innovation, and the role of gatekeepers as translators and circulators of external knowledge is less pronounced. GILLY et al. (2014) have pointed out the importance of local authorities and hub firms to activate new network relationships to make new recombinations of know-how.

In the regional resilience literature, it is remarkable how little attention has been paid to the sensitivity of regional networks to the removal of specific nodes or the dissolution of particular linkages. One can depict a regional economy as a knowledge network in which the nodes stand for industries/technologies and the ties reflect the degree of technological relatedness between these nodes (e.g. NEFFKE et al., 2011a, 2011b; BOSCHMA et al., 2014b), as described in the third section. Then, one can identify how resilient a region is to changes in this network structure. For instance, in a tight local network that connect many technologically related industries, one may expect that the loss of one industry will not have huge consequences, as the technological cohesiveness of the region will be lowered only marginally, and thus the recombination capacity of a region remains more or less intact. However, when a boundary-spanning industry, that is, an industry that bridges two distinct technology fields, disappears from the region, the recombination potential of the region may be more seriously affected. Following such a network approach, one can directly link the issue of sensitivity of regions to shocks to the ability of regions to develop new growth paths.

In summary, regional resilience is enhanced in network terms when a region has: (1) a core/periphery network structure with a balance between embedded relationships within cliques and strategic 'structural hole' relationships among cliques, as proposed by FLEMING et al. (2007) among others, as this might provide a solution for trade-off between adaptation (control and efficiency) and adaptability (openness); (2) a network structure with combinations of optimal levels of proximities (e.g. combinations of local and non-local ties, cognitively proximate and distant ties, loosely coupled networks), as proposed by BOSCHMA and FRENKEN (2010) among others, as this may overcome the trade-off between adaptation (efficiency) and adaptability (novelty) in the network; and (3) key agents in the network who ensure access to novel information and enable its wide diffusion to other local actors, as this secures adaptation (local clustering) and adaptability (short links to external knowledge).

REGIONAL RESILIENCE AND INSTITUTIONS

The conceptualization of regional resilience is not complete without accounting for institutions. There is widespread agreement that the resilience literature has drawn too little attention to the role of institutions and the state (e.g. SWANSTROM et al., 2009; BRISTOW, 2010;

HASSINK, 2010; WOLFE, 2010; PIKE et al., 2010; DAVIES, 2011; MacKINNON and DRISCOLL DERICKSON, 2012; WINK, 2012).[14] In the author's evolutionary perspective, institutions are closely intertwined with the two other dimensions of regional resilience, that is, techno-industrial variety and networks, as institutions like laws, norms and cultural attitudes enable, or not, interactions across knowledge bases and local industries (HUGGINS et al., 2012; CRESCENZI and PERCOCO, 2013). Second, institutional structures may be subject to shocks (like the erosion of social capital, the loss of property rights, a sudden change in economic policy, the downsizing of public gatekeepers) that have a direct impact on the capacity of regions to develop new growth paths, and thus, on regional resilience (e.g. DAWLEY, 2014). Third, institutions can be linked to the trade-off between adaptation and adaptability, as there is a strong historical and path-dependent dimension to institutions. When new industries develop, new institutions come into being that fulfil a specific need, but once these institutions become firmly established, they may hinder the development of new growth paths, due to institutional hysteresis and inertia (SETTERFIELD, 1997; MURMANN, 2003). This requires a search for institutional structures that can cope with this tension between adaptability and adaptation.

So, new institutions tend to co-evolve with new industries in a region (FREEMAN and PEREZ, 1988; NELSON, 1994; COENEN et al., 2013). The more regions specialize, the more the institutional structure will be geared towards and customized to the specific needs of the local industries. Gradual adjustments in local institutions in order to meet the changing needs of these industries can be more easily accommodated in specialized regions. EBBINGHAUS (2009) refers to this type of gradual institutional change as path stabilization. However, this adaptation tends to undermine the adaptability of the region, as it might impede the development of new institutions to support the growth of new industries. So, regions may become victim of institutional lock-in, when the institutional structure is entirely focused on the specific needs of the principal industries. This is reinforced when the local political elite is completely interwoven in the tight and rigid network described in the fourth section. OLSON (1982) referred to this as 'institutional sclerosis', when powerful special-interest organizations take over a local economy and slow down the capacity of a region to reallocate resources to new activities. Specialized regions may be subject to what GRABHER (1993) called 'political lock-in', which refers to a conservative culture of long-standing relations between vested players like large firms and public authorities that show rent-seeking behaviour and actively opposes radical change. A prime example is Detroit (HILL et al., 2012).

Thus, the possibilities of institutional adaptability may be higher in regions with a more heterogeneous industrial mix. In those circumstances, it may harder for industries or powerful players to monopolize and dominate the design of regional institutions (NEFFKE *et al.*, 2011b). So, diversified regions may be in a better position to make institutional change in order to support new growth paths, as one expects less opposition in these regions from vested players, and there might be more redundant institutional capacity around that can be put to unexpected uses (GRABHER, 1993). This might come close to what HOLLINGSWORTH (2009) called a 'weak' institutional environment which allows for greater variation in organizations and the development of more radical innovations, as opposed to strong and rigid institutional environments. However, in diversified regions, the other side of trade-off may prevail (that is, adaptability may go at the expense of adaptation), as there is lack of institutional cohesiveness with too many interests that harms local institutional focus, coordination and control. In other words, regions with such a fragmented institutional structure may well be more responsive to experimentation and newcomers, but the problem is that these creative actions will remain unnoticed and too isolated, as the new institutions have to be built from scratch, and local public support is hard to get due to many competing local claims.

The question is how to tackle these trade-offs between adaptation and adaptability in regions in institutional terms, as to enhance the resilience of regions.[15] It is proposed that some industries and knowledge bases may have complementarities or overlap in institutional terms, that is, they have similar, though not identical institutional requirements, like a new patent regulation may be relevant for a whole set of technologies and industries. It is expected that regions with such institutional overlap across industries are better equipped to exploit new recombinations between those industries and to develop new growth paths, without compromising on adaptation, as the overarching institutional framework is not fundamentally challenged, and can even be put to use effectively to accommodate the demands of new industries. In this case, adaptability does not preclude adaptation, because the region can keep it overall institutional focus, as new institutions do not have to be built from scratch but can draw on existing institutions, and little local resistance to institutional change is expected.

This comes close to the notion of institutional complementarity (AMABLE, 2000; HOLLINGSWORTH, 2000; HALL and SOSKICE, 2001), which is about institutions that reinforce each other and make one another more efficient (see also GRILLITSCH, 2014). The Varieties of Capitalism literature is very relevant here, as it claims that institutional systems at the national level make feasible only a kind of economic specialization, like Germany's focus on high-quality engineering, and the focus of the United States on science-driven industries (HALL and SOSKICE, 2001). Moreover, this is in

line with literature that argues that institutional change is often created alongside existing structures. Scholars have proposed taxonomies of institutional change like institutional layering and conversion that fall under this type of institutional change (THELEN, 2003; STREECK and THELEN, 2005; MARTIN, 2010). So, developing new growth paths in regions does not necessarily mean breaking with the past. On the contrary, EBBINGHAUS (2009) defines path departure as a partial renewal of current institutions that does not challenge or redirect its underlying core principles. STRAMBACH (2010) proposed the notion of institutional *plasticity* to emphasize that an institutional system has a range of options for new paths within the dominant institutional framework. Agents can deviate from the established path by creating new institutions but not breaking with the overarching institutional system (STRAMBACH and KLEMENT, 2012; ZEITSCHRIFT FUR WIRTSCHAFTSGEOGRAPHIE, 2013).

It was discussed above that new industries tend to branch out of existing activities to which new industries are technologically related. The underlying idea was that the local industrial structure makes the emergence of some (but not all) industries more feasible, depending on whether they are technologically related to other local industries. A similar idea can be applied to institutions, as the existing institutional legacy (e.g. at the national and regional level) sets sharp limits to the type and direction of institutional change. This makes the creation of some institutions more feasible, depending on whether they are coherent with the existing set of institutions (again, at various spatial scales), while other combinations of institutions will not work (AMABLE, 2000). Taking these ideas together, it is expected that regional branching is facilitated when new industries require institutions similar (though not identical) to those of other related industries in the region, so new institutions do not have to build from scratch, and this new institution–building will not be contested heavily by (local) agents.

There is a recurrent claim in the literature (e.g. ACEMOGLU *et al.*, 2014) that some overarching institutional frameworks are believed to be more responsive to radical change. HALL and SOSKICE (2001) claimed that the institutional system in liberal market economies is more inclined to generate radical innovations than coordinated market economies, as the latter are characterized by specific assets that cannot be readily put to another use (as opposed to generic assets in the liberal variant).[16] MENZEL and KAMMER (2012) claimed that the formation of new industries is therefore more tightly connected to established resources and industries in coordinated market economies. BOSCHMA and CAPONE (2014) have argued that the overarching institutional framework will affect the intensity but, above all, the nature of industrial diversification. Their preliminary findings show that some macro-institutions enable countries to make a jump in their industrial evolution over time: their overarching institutional framework gives countries more freedom to diversify in more unrelated activities.

As stated above, the role of the state has been neglected in the resilience literature (BRISTOW, 2010; HASSINK, 2010; PIKE et al., 2010). DAVIES (2011) has made a laudable attempt to assess the effects of the last economic downturn on the resilience of European regions by looking at their dependence on the public sector. Studies have investigated whether some governance structures in regions (like civic capital or quality of government) can better accommodate and facilitate change (e.g. CHRISTOPHERSON et al., 2010; PENDALL et al., 2010; RODRÍGUEZ-POSE and DI-CATALDO, 2014). Scholars have explored proactive public strategies to enhance resilience of regions (BAILEY and MACNEILL, 2008; HILL et al., 2012). According to WOLFE (2010), resilient regions engage in collaborative processes to implement change within the constraints dictated by their existing regional assets. In other words, the past conditions the range of possibilities that are available to regions. Other studies have focused more on the role of human agency and institutional leadership (SOTARAUTA et al., 2012; BRISTOW and HEALEY, 2013), as key actors (either individually or collectively) can make changes in institutions, rather than being subject to an institutional environment that is favourable or not (MACKINNON et al., 2009; GERTLER, 2010). Shocks can also trigger new leadership that brings about the necessary changes. WINK (2012) has conceptualized institutions as embedded into complex feedback interactions with other institutions. This makes it necessary to look at institutional change and adaptive capabilities on different levels and with different speed potentials. In this respect, SWANSTROM (2008) claimed that 'a resilient system is one where […] smaller scale processes are able to deal with the stressor without having to reorganize the larger scale structures' (p. 9).

To sum up, regional resilience is enhanced in institutional terms when a region has: (1) a loosely coherent institutional structure. In this context, there is institutional diversity but still overlap across local industries that favours institutional change to enable the development of new growth paths (adaptability), while the new institutions can build on and expand within an overarching institutional framework (adaptation); (2) an overarching institutional framework that is more open to radical change (adaptability), but that still provides a supportive basis to facilitate institutional change (adaptation); and (3) key institutional agents that can take the lead and implement the necessary institutional reforms when confronted by shocks.

SYNTHESIS AND DISCUSSION

It is impossible to give a full and comprehensive account of what makes a region resilient. Attention here is limited to the meaning of resilience as the extent to which a shock may affect the ability of regions to develop new growth paths. Focusing on structural change and long-term economic renewal, an equilibrium concept of resilience was left behind in which resilience is simply regarded as a response to shocks and a move back to a steady state. Instead, an evolutionary concept of resilience is proposed that connects shocks to the determinants of the ability of regions to develop new growth paths.

Taking an evolutionary perspective, regional resilience was redefined in terms of adaptation and adaptability. It is claimed that the resilience of regions is strongly rooted in their past legacy, as embodied in their industrial, network and institutional structures. While adaptation has been closely associated with the notion of path dependency (either in terms of positive or negative lock-in), there is a tendency in the resilience literature to define adaptability as a move away from path dependency, as if new growth paths are detached from their past, as if regions need to deviate from their past to achieve that, and as if path dependency will cause insurmountable problems of adjustment. Instead, it was argued that history is key to understand how regions develop new growth paths, as its past not only sets limits but also provides opportunities for making new combinations and diversifying into new pathways.

An attempt was made to develop a more comprehensive concept of regional resilience that captures industrial, network and institutional dimensions of regions that have been either ignored in the resilience literature, or treated separately. This also enabled a more sharp distinction to be made between causes and effects of regional resilience. Structures of industries (e.g. related variety), networks (e.g. a loosely coupled network) and institutions (e.g. a loosely coherent institutional structure) have been treated as the main determinants of regional resilience. The argument has moved away from the meaning of resilience as the ability of regions to recover from a shock, and regional resilience has been redefined in terms of the impact of a shock on the capacity of a region to develop new growth paths. What is crucial for an understanding of regional resilience is to investigate how a shock in the industrial structure (e.g. collapse of an industry), network structure (e.g. loss of a node or dissolution of a tie) and institutional structure (e.g. the erosion of a functional or dysfunctional institution) impacts on the capacity of a region to develop new growth paths. In the proposed framework, shocks can have an impact on all three determinants, like lower related variety, the loss of a public node that bridged the core and periphery in a network, or the erosion of trust or property rights. This also requires that the three determinants of regional resilience become more fully integrated, as a change in an institution may lead to a change in the knowledge network which subsequently leads to a change in the industrial structure that all affect regional resilience.

The attempt to propose an evolutionary concept of regional resilience opens up a whole set of new research challenges (e.g. BALLAND *et al.*, 2014). The remainder briefly discusses a few.

It is argued that the industrial composition matters for regional resilience. First, the claim that regions with a high variety of skill-related industries with few local input–output relationships have indeed a stronger capacity to respond to sector-specific shocks has to be tested empirically. And will redundant labour be employed more readily in local skill-related industries, and will labour flows across skill-related industries lead to new and unexpected combinations (BOSCHMA *et al.*, 2013)? Second, studies have reported that regions with related variety have higher economic growth rates (FRENKEN *et al.*, 2007; BOSCHMA *et al.*, 2012), but no study, to the author's knowledge, has yet tested whether diversified regions, as compared to specialized regions, diversify more successfully into new (related) activities.[17] Third, there is a need to examine systematically the extent to which specialized regions are resilient in the long-run, and how they prevent or overcome a state of negative lock-in. How successful are specialized regions to develop new growth paths, to what extent do they exploit their specialized knowledge base when diversifying into new activities, and to what extent do they draw on resources from other regions and recombine those with their local knowledge base? Fourth, studies on regional resilience have to test empirically whether regions with related variety or unrelated variety have a stronger capacity to develop new growth paths, or whether a mixture of related and unrelated variety is required. This is closely connected to the question whether regions can keep relying on related diversification to sustain development in the long-run, or whether regions have to diversify in more unrelated activities to remain resilient. There is no *a priori* reason to believe that it is inevitable that related diversification in a region will come to a halt, as (combinations of) existing industries might give birth to new industries in an almost endless sequence. However, unrelated diversification (i. e. a jump into a completely new field) rather than related diversification might be needed to secure long-term regional development, as regions have a tendency to diversify into related activities and shake off unrelated activities (NEFFKE *et al.*, 2011a). This would also shed light on the nature of these two types of new growth paths (i.e. new combinations between predominantly related activities, and new combinations between previously unrelated activities). Finally, it is crucial to investigate which types of agents (e.g. new firms, diversifying firms, relocating firms) are key drivers behind such new growth paths in regions. Findings suggest that new establishments, especially from outside the region, induce structural change in regions (NEFFKE *et al.*, 2014).

It is also argued that the structure of knowledge networks matters for regional resilience, but there are few regional studies that have tested this claim. First, there is a need to determine whether local knowledge networks with optimal levels of proximity on its various dimensions (geographical, organizational, cognitive, social, institutional) are indeed more resilient to shocks, and whether these networks have a higher capacity to develop new growth paths. In theory, one can think of many possible combinations of network structures in such a proximity framework, but one needs to explore which combinations are more resilient. Second, it has to be tested whether core/periphery network structures in regions that consist of embedded relationships within cliques and strategic 'structural hole' relationships among cliques are indeed more resilient (FLEMING *et al.*, 2007). And are boundary-spanning industries affecting the capacity of a region to develop new growth paths? And third, few studies have investigated whether related industries in regions actually connect and exchange knowledge and skills. Another promising research line is to investigate whether labour mobility between skill-related industries boosts regional resilience (HEUERMANN, 2009; BOSCHMA *et al.*, 2014c).

It has also been claimed that institutions matter for regional resilience, but this needs to be worked out more thoroughly, especially with regard to the impact of shocks. First, there is a need to investigate more systematically which institutional structures in regions are more responsive to develop new growth paths. One way to do that is to investigate a direct relationship with the quality of government in regions (RODRÍGUEZ-POSE and DI-CATALDO, 2014). And is a region with what has been called here a loosely coherent institutional structure more likely to develop new growth paths? Second, to what extent is institutional change required for the development of new growth paths in regions, and to what extent are pre-existing institutions in regions shaping that process of institutional change (STREECK and THELEN, 2005)? Are diversified regions more successful in restructuring their institutions, and which types of agents (political leaders, private entrepreneurs, coalitions of private and public players) are driving institutional change (SOTARAUTA *et al.*, 2012)? Third, to exploit the potential of related variety in a region, institutions are needed to connect related industries and make new combinations. This recombinatory process is facilitated when sector-specific institutions have institutional overlap. It was discussed above that new industries tend to branch out of local activities to which new industries are technologically related. Yet, there is little understanding about which institutional factors facilitate this branching process. It could be that regions branch in new related industries because these require institutions similar to those that sustain related industries. To what extent is there institutional overlap between industries in a region, can one actually define and measure institutional overlap, and if so, is such institutional overlap in a region more likely to generate new recombinations between industries? And to what extent do related industries draw on similar sets of institutions? This would provide an institutional explanation (besides cognitive proximity) for why related industries might benefit from each other's co-presence at the regional level. And fourth, there is a need to investigate how macro institutional structures affect the intensity and nature of diversification in countries and regions. BOSCHMA and CAPONE (2014) have found preliminary evidence that some macro-institutions enable countries to make a jump in their industrial evolution, and thus give countries freedom to diversify in more unrelated activities. This has major implications for the long-term resilience of regions, as shocks might lead to instability in macro-institutions that could undermine the capacity of regions to develop new growth paths.

Funding – This work was conducted as part of a project granted under the Open Research Area in Europe for the Social Sciences (ORA): 'Territories and Technologies in an Unstable Knowledge Economy: An Evolutionary Framework of Regional Resilience'. The authors are grateful to NWO (Netherlands), ANR (France), ESRC (UK) and DFG (Germany) for funding this project.

NOTES

1. Because there are so many different shocks, it is impossible to generalize about how a shock may affect the resilience of a region. It may well be that a region is capable of responding to one type of shock, but not to another.
2. The question of how to relate a region to resilience is a crucial one, but not peculiar to the topic of regional resilience (for a similar discussion on the usefulness of the regional competitiveness concept, see, for example, LAWSON, 1999; and CAMAGNI, 2002). Studies on regional resilience often tend to take a rather pragmatic approach: a region is viewed as a collection of heterogeneous units (individuals, organizations and institutions) that interact or not within predefined boundaries, but that is also part of a wider system outside the region that affects its resilience.
3. Every year, more than 10% of all companies in the United States disappear (ORMEROD 2005), and only very few firms grow old (BROUWER, 2005). There is also no industry in a region that will thrive forever. Even when it survives for a longer period, the nature of that industry (as embodied in its products, technologies, firms and surrounding institutions) will change dramatically over time.
4. There is a tendency to perceive resilience as freeing itself from path dependence, as if it stands in the way of true economic renewal. MAGNUSSON and OTTOSSON (2009) argue instead that one should leave behind the view that 'path dependence and (radical) change cannot go together', as if radical change can be explained only by an exogenous event. EBBINGHAUS (2009) advocates 'a not-too-narrowly defined, nondeterministic concept of path dependence, in which different forms of change can come about, and the emergence of new structures is not restricted to chance events'; and proposes that the nature of change should therefore be object of study, and that one should go 'beyond the heuristics of the path dependence metaphor' (p. 203).
5. BRISTOW et al. (2012) argue that the path dependency concept is not well equipped to help one understand the process of adaptability. Instead, they propose the notion of path interdependence, which refers to unforeseen innovations due to crossovers and recombinations of knowledge between firms and industries.
6. In psychology, individuals are characterized as resilient or not. In economic geography, there is increasing attention on key individuals who can make a difference in regions, such as influential entrepreneurs, top managers, star scientists, political leaders, etc. (e.g. FELDMAN et al., 2005; SOTARAUTA et al., 2012; TRIPPL, 2013; BLOMKVIST et al., 2014).
7. At the organizational level, this is known as the 'competency trap' (LEVITT and MARCH, 1996), or what MARCH (1991) calls a tension between 'exploration of new possibilities' and 'exploitation of old certainties' in organizational learning, as 'becoming quite good at doing any one thing reduces the organization's capacity to absorb new ideas and to do other things' (LAWSON and LORENZ, 1999, p. 311). BEUNZA and STARK (2003) propose 'generative redundancy' to overcome this tension in organizations, like more ways of doing things. However, when incorporating organizations into the concept of regional resilience, there is a need to leave behind such an atomistic view and embed organizations in their wider socio-economic context. For instance, there is evidence that diversification strategies of firms are influenced by their local environment, as firms tend to diversify into new products that are technologically related to existing products in their own region (NEFFKE et al., 2014).
8. When the resilience literature refers to shocks, in almost all cases it concerns a negative shock to the region. The analysis concentrates then on the duration and extent to which a full recovery process unfolds. However, one could also think of positive shocks, such as lower corporate taxes, or the rise of the Chinese economy, and the extent to which regions are capable of fully benefiting from that.
9. Studies have identified particular industries that are expected to be most sensitive to general shocks. Scholars have, for instance, determined the shares of recession-sensitive industries like manufacturing in the total output of regions to estimate the effect of global recessions (e.g. GROOT et al., 2011). DAVIES (2011) finds that resilience to the 2009 downturn was lower in regions with overvalued housing markets, a high dependence on construction, strong export dependency, asset bubbles on public debts and openness to risky assets on financial markets.
10. The unemployed might also move to other regions. This brings to light the question what is actually meant by resilience, and what indicators are most appropriate to grasp that. If resilience is defined as a return to previous regional output levels (as it often is), then the rapid absorption of the unemployed in the local labour market favours that.

However, if all the unemployed move to other regions, this will negatively affect regional output (a bad sign of resilience) but will also lower regional unemployment (which might be a good sign of resilience).

11. Scholars (e.g. ANDERSSON and KOSTER, 2011) have argued that regions also have distinct entrepreneurship cultures that persist over time. FRITSCH and WYRWICH (2012) demonstrate that regional entrepreneurship cultures persisted in Germany in the period 1925–2005, despite drastic shocks, such as the Second World War, the economic crises of the 1930s, German unification and socialist regime change. So, history seems to matter for regional resilience, but a crucial question remains whether the local knowledge base impacts on this geographical persistence of new firm formation. COLOMBELLI and QUATRARO (2013) find that entrepreneurship in Italian regions is related to the exploitation of technological knowledge in regions. Moreover, there is a need to investigate whether these persistent regional patterns of entrepreneurship also induce structural change in regions.

12. When taking a network perspective on regional resilience, it is appealing to look at complex adaptive systems that make use of evolutionary properties like emergence, self-organization, non-linear dynamics and co-evolution (MARTIN and SUNLEY, 2007; BRISTOW et al., 2012). SWANSTROM et al. (2009) claim that the study of resilience requires that regions are viewed as composed of complex interlinked processes with powerful feedback effects. Interesting for this discussion is that adaptive systems accommodate the conflict between connectedness and resilience through panarchy which is a system state with high connectedness that is still open to experiments (GUNDERSON and HOLLING, 2002; SWANSTROM, 2008). PENDALL et al. (2010) adopt the adaptive cycle model to propose a dynamic perspective to resilience in which 'resilience levels vary continually as the systems adapts and changes' (p. 77).

13. This comprehensive concept of systemic resilience has its analogy in the literature on sustainability transitions. There, the emphasis is on the formation and transformation of socio-technical systems to support the emergence of radically new modes of sustainable production and consumption. It is about defining the preconditions of radical path-breaking change or the development of new niches that still suffer from a poor alignment with existing technologies, institutions and user practices (GEELS, 2002). Emphasis is on the link with established, dominant practices and socio-technological regimes that

might enable but also inhibit such large-scale system shifts. TRUFFER and COENEN (2012) explain that this transition literature has to incorporate a spatial dimension, as regions differ in their potentials to sustainable transformations, and transition processes are multi-scalar phenomena in which changes co-occur at different spatial scales (see also BINZ et al., 2014).

14. SWANSTROM (2008) argues that the concept of ecological resilience is 'fundamentally anti-statist' (p. 15), as social affairs are not driven by natural but by human forces, like man-made institutions and policies.

15. WINK (2012) distinguishes between two types of institutions that embody the conflict between adaptation and adaptability. Path-dependent institutions keep their stability for a time, but due to their inability to change they collapse and lose their functions. In contrast, resilient institutions are capable of adjusting to new challenges caused by external disruptions or internal conflicts, and to maintain their functionality which is to stabilize expectations.

16. HALL and SOSKICE (2001) did not mention explicitly which of the two institutional systems is more capable of developing new growth paths. All they claim is that both institutional systems generate different economic specializations that reflect a different nature of innovation. Liberal market economies, for instance, specialize in science-driven sectors like biotechnology, where radical types of innovations are especially important. What is missing but crucial for an understanding of regional resilience are the following questions: (1) Is there more technological and industrial variety in liberal market economies, as these are considered to have a higher propensity to induce radical change?; (2) Are liberal market economies better capable of developing new growth paths, as these are considered to concentrate more on radical change, whereas coordinated market economies tend to focus more on incremental change? (e.g. TAYLOR, 2004; AKKERMANS et al., 2009); (3) If so, would there be more of a tendency in liberal market economies to diversify in unrelated activities, while coordinated market economies would focus on more related diversification?; and (4) Are liberal market economies better equipped to support institutional change to enable the development of new industries?

17. There are studies, though, that have demonstrated that young industries are more likely to be found in diversified regions, while more mature industries tend to be located in specialized regions (NEFFKE et al., 2011b).

REFERENCES

ACEMOGLU D., AKCIGIT U. and CELIK M. A. (2014) *Young, Restless and Creative: Openness to Disruption and Creative Innovations.* PIER Working Paper No. 14-004. PIER, Philadelphia, PA.

AKKERMANS D., CASTALDI C. and LOS B. (2009) Do 'liberal market economies' really innovate more radically than 'coordinated market economies'? Hall and Soskice reconsidered, *Research Policy* **38**, 181–191. doi:10.1016/j.respol.2008.10.002

AMABLE B. (2000) Institutional complementarity and diversity of social systems of innovation and production, *Review of International Political Economy* **7**, 645–687. doi:10.1080/096922900750034572

ANDERSSON M. and KOSTER S. (2011) Sources of persistence in regional start-ups. Evidence from Sweden, *Journal of Economic Geography* **11**, 179–201. doi:10.1093/jeg/lbp069

ANTONELLI C. (2000) Collective knowledge, communication and innovation. The evidence of technological districts, *Regional Studies* **34**: 535–547. doi:10.1080/00343400050085657

ARTS S. and VEUGELERS R. (2012) *The Technological Origins and Novelty of Breakthrough Inventions*. Working Paper. Faculty of Economics and Business, KU Leuven, Leuven.

ASHEIM B. T., ISAKSEN A. (2002) Regional innovation systems. The integration of local 'sticky' and global 'unbiquitous' knowledge, *Journal of Technology Transfer* 27, 77–86. doi:10.1023/A:1013100704794

BAILEY D. and MACNEILL S. (2008) The Rover Task Force: a case study in proactive and reactive policy intervention, *Regional Science Policy and Practices* 1, 109–124. doi:10.1111/j.1757-7802.2008.00007.x

BALLAND P. A. (2012a) Proximity and the evolution of collaboration networks: evidence from research and development projects within the Global Navigation Satellite System (GNSS) industry, *Regional Studies* 46, 741–756. doi:10.1080/00343404.2010. 529121

BALLAND P. A. (2012b) *Promoting Knowledge Transfer and the Economic Resilience of Regions*. Working Paper. Utrecht University, Utrecht.

BALLAND P. A., RIGBY D. and BOSCHMA R. (2014) *The Technological Resilience of U.S. Cities*. Working Paper. Utrecht University, Utrecht.

BALLAND P. A., SUIRE R. and VICENTE J. (2013) Structural and geographical patterns of knowledge networks in emerging technological standards: evidence from the European GNSS industry, *Economics of Innovation and New Technology* 22, 47–72. doi:10.1080/10438599.2012.699773

BATHELT H. and BOGGS J. S. (2003) Towards a reconceptualization of regional development paths: is Leipzig's media cluster a continuation of or a rupture with the past?, *Economic Geography* 79, 265–293. doi:10.1111/j.1944-8287.2003.tb00212.x

BATHELT H., MALMBERG A. and MASKELL P. (2004) Clusters and knowledge. Local buzz, global pipelines and the process of knowledge creation, *Progress in Human Geography* 28, 31–56. doi:10.1191/0309132504ph469oa

BELUSSI F. and SEDITA S. R. (2009) Life cycle versus multiple path dependency in industrial districts, *European Planning Studies* 17, 505–528. doi:10.1080/09654310802682065

BEUNZA D. and STARK D. (2003) The organization of responsiveness: innovation and recovery in the trading rooms of Lower Manhattan, *Socio-Economic Review* 1, 135–164. doi:10.1093/soceco/1.2.135

BINZ C., TRUFFER B. and COENEN L. (2014) Why space matters in technological innovation systems – mapping the global knowledge dynamics of membrane bioreactor technology, *Research Policy* 43, 138–155. doi:10.1016/j.respol.2013.07.002

BLOMKVIST K., KAPPEN P. and ZANDER I. (2014) Superstar inventors – towards a people-centric perspective on the geography of technological renewal in the multinational corporation, *Research Policy* 43, 669–682. doi:10.1016/j.respol.2013.12.003

BOSCHMA R., BALLAND P. A. and KOGLER D. F. (Forthcoming 2014b) Relatedness and technological change in cities: the rise and fall of technological knowledge in US metropolitan areas from 1981 to 2010, *Industrial and Corporate Change*. doi:10.1093/icc/dtu012

BOSCHMA R. and CAPONE G. (2014) *Relatedness, Diversification and Institutions*. Working Paper. Utrecht University, Utrecht.

BOSCHMA R., ERIKSSON R. H. and LINDGREN U. (2014c) Labour market externalities and regional growth in Sweden. The importance of labour mobility between skill-related industries, *Regional Studies* 48, 1669–1690. doi:10.1080/00343404.2013.867429

BOSCHMA R. A. and FRENKEN K. (2010) The spatial evolution of innovation networks. A proximity perspective, in BOSCHMA R. A. and MARTIN R. (Eds) *The Handbook of Evolutionary Economic Geography*, pp. 120–135. Edward Elgar, Cheltenham.

BOSCHMA R. HEIMERIKS G. and BALLAND P. A. (2014a) Scientific knowledge dynamics and relatedness in biotech cities, *Research Policy* 43, 107–114. doi:10.1016/j.respol.2013.07.009

BOSCHMA R. and LAMBOOY J. (1999) The prospects of an adjustment policy based on collective learning in old industrial regions, *Geojournal* 49, 391–399. doi:10.1023/A:1007144414006

BOSCHMA R., MINONDO A. and NAVARRO M. (2012) Related variety and regional growth in Spain. Papers *in Regional Science* 91, 241–256.

BOSCHMA R., MINONDO A. and NAVARRO M. (2013) The emergence of new industries at the regional level in Spain. A proximity approach based on product-relatedness, *Economic Geography* 89, 29–51. doi:10.1111/j.1944-8287.2012.01170.x

BRESCHI S. and LENZI C. (2014) *The Returns of External Linkages: The Role of Gatekeepers for the Renewal and Expansion of U.S. Cities' Knowledge Base, 1990–2004*. Papers in Evolutionary Economic Geography No. 14.14. Utrecht University, Utrecht.

BRISTOW G. (2010) Resilient regions: re-'place'ing regional competitiveness, *Cambridge Journal of Regions, Economy and Society* 3, 153–167. doi:10.1093/cjres/rsp030

BRISTOW G. and HEALEY A. (2013) *Regional resilience: An Agency Perspective*. Working Paper. Cardiff University, Cardiff.

BRISTOW G., PORTER J. and COOKE P. (2012) *Path Interdependence, Firm Innovation and Resilience. A Complex Adaptive Systems Perspective*. Working Paper. CASS, Cardiff University, Cardiff.

BROEKEL T. and BOSCHMA R. (2012) Knowledge networks in the Dutch aviation industry: the proximity paradox, *Journal of Economic Geography* 12, 409–433. doi:10.1093/jeg/lbr010

BROUWER A. E. (2005) *Old Firms in the Netherlands. The Long-Term Spatial Implications of Firms' Identities and Embeddedness*. KNAG/FRW, RUG. Netherlands Geographical Studies No. 329. Utrecht/Groningen.

BUENSTORF G. and KLEPPER S. (2009) Heritage and agglomeration. The Akron tyre cluster revisited, *Economic Journal* 119, 705–733. doi:10.1111/j.1468-0297.2009.02216.x

CAMAGNI R. (2002) On the concept of territorial competitiveness: sound or misleading?, *Urban Studies* 39, 2395–2411. doi:10.1080/0042098022000027022

CANTNER U. and GRAF H. (2006) The network of innovators in Jena: an application of social network analysis, *Research Policy* 35, 463–480. doi:10.1016/j.respol.2006.01.002

CASTALDI C., FRENKEN K. and LOS B. (2013) *Related Variety, Unrelated Variety and Technological Breakthroughs, An Analysis of U.S. State-Level Patenting*. Papers in Evolutionary Economic Geography No. 13.02. Utrecht University, Utrecht.

CATTANI G. and FERRIANI S. (2008) A core/periphery perspective on individual creative performance: social networks and cinematic achievements in the Hollywood film industry, *Organization Science* **19**, 824–844. doi:10.1287/orsc.1070.0350

CHAPPLE K. and LESTER T. W. (2010) The resilient regional labour market? The US case, *Cambridge Journal of Regions, Economy and Society* **3**, 85–104. doi:10.1093/cjres/rsp031

CHRISTOPHERSON S., MICHIE J. and TYLER P. (2010) Regional resilience: theoretical and empirical perspectives, *Cambridge Journal of Regions, Economy and Society* **3**, 3–10. doi:10.1093/cjres/rsq004

CLARK J. HUANG H. I. and WALSH J. P. (2010) A typology of 'innovation districts': what it means for regional resilience, *Cambridge Journal of Regions, Economy and Society* **3**, 121–137. doi:10.1093/cjres/rsp034

COENEN L., MOODYSSON J. and MARTIN H. (2013) *Renewal of Mature Industry in an Old Industrial Region: Regional Innovation Policy and the Co-evolution of Institutions and Technology*. CIRCLE Working Papers No. WP 2013/07. Centre for Innovation, Research and Competence in the Learning Economy (CIRCLE), Lund University, Lund.

COHENDET P. and LLERENA P. (1997) Learning, technical change and public policy: how to create and exploit diversity, in EDQUIST C. (Ed.) *Systems of Innovation*, pp. 223–241. Pinter, London.

COLOMBELLI A., KRAFFT J. and QUATRARO F. (Forthcoming 2014) The emergence of new technology-based sectors at the regional level: a proximity-based analysis of nanotechnologies, *Research Policy*.

COLOMBELLI A. and QUATRARO F. (2013) *The Properties of Local Knowledge Bases and Entrepreneurship: Evidence from Italian NUTS 3 Regions*. Papers in Evolutionary Economic Geography No. 13.03. Utrecht University, Utrecht.

COOKE P., BRISTOW G. and PORTER J. (2011) Regional resilience literature review. Paper presented at Bordeaux, France, September 2011.

CRESCENZI R. and PERCOCO M. (Eds) (2013) *Geography, Institutions and Regional Economic Performance*. Springer, Berlin.

CRESPO J., SUIRE R. and VICENTE J. (2013) Lock-in or lock-out? How structural properties of knowledge networks affect regional resilience, *Journal of Economic Geography*. doi:10.193/jeg/lbt006

DAHL FITJAR R. and RODRÍGUEZ-POSE A. (2011) When local interaction does not suffice; sources of firm innovation in urban Norway, *Environment and Planning A* **43**, 1248–1267. doi:10.1068/a43516

DAVIES S. (2011) Regional resilience in the 2008–2010 downturn: comparative evidence from European countries, *Cambridge Journal of Regions, Economy and Society* **4**, 369–382. doi:10.1093/cjres/rsr019

DAVIES A. and TONTS M. (2010) Economic diversity and regional socio-economic performance, *Geographical Research* **48**, 223–234. doi:10.1111/j.1745-5871.2009.00627.x

DAWLEY S. (2014) Creating new paths? Offshore wind, policy activism, and peripheral region development, *Economic Geography* **90**, 91–112. doi:10.1111/ecge.12028

DESROCHERS P. and LEPPALA S. (2011) Opening up the 'Jacobs spillovers' black box: local diversity, creativity and the processes underlying new combinations, *Journal of Economic Geography* **11**, 843–863. doi:10.1093/jeg/lbq028

DIODATO D. and WETERINGS A. B. R. (Forthcoming 2014) The resilience of regional labour markets to economic shocks: exploring the role of interactions among firms and workers, *Journal of Economic Geography*. doi:10.1093/jeg/lbu030

DISSART J. C. (2003) Regional economic diversity and regional economic stability: research results and agenda, *International Regional Science Review* **26**, 423–446. doi:10.1177/0160017603259083

DOMAZLICKY B. (1980) Regional business cycles: a survey, *Regional Science Perspectives* **10**, 15–34.

EBBINGHAUS B. (2009) Can path dependence explain institutional change? Two approaches applied to welfare state reform, in MAGNUSSON L. and OTTOSSON J. (Eds) *The Evolution of Path Dependence*, pp. 191–218. Edward Elgar, Cheltenham.

ESSLETZBICHLER J. (2007) Diversity, stability and regional growth in the United States, 1975–2002, in FRENKEN K. (Ed.) *Applied Evolutionary Economics and Economic Geography*, pp. 203–299. Edward Edgar, Cheltenham.

ESSLEZTBICHLER, J. (Forthcoming 2013) Relatedness, industrial branching and technological cohesion in US metropolitan areas, *Regional Studies*. doi:10.1080/00343404.2013.806793

FELDMAN M. P., FRANCIS J. and BERCOVITZ J. (2005) Creating a cluster while building a firm. Entrepreneurs and the formation of industrial clusters, *Regional Studies* **39**, 129–141. doi:10.1080/0034340052000320888

FINGLETON B., GARRETSEN H. and MARTIN R. (2012) Recessionary shocks and regional employment: evidence on the resilience of U.K. regions, *Journal of Regional Science* **52**, 109–133. doi:10.1111/j.1467-9787.2011.00755.x

FLEMING L., MINGO S. and CHEN D. (2007) Collaborative brokerage, generative creativity and creative success, *Administrative Science Quarterly* **52**, 443–475.

FREEMAN C. and PEREZ C. (1988) Structural crisis of adjustment, business cycles and investment behaviour, in DOSI G., FREEMAN C., NELSON R., SILVERBERG G. and SOETE L. (Eds) *Technical Change and Economic Theory*, pp. 38–66. Pinter, London.

FRENKEN K., VAN OORT F. G. and VERBURG T. (2007) Related variety, unrelated variety and regional economic growth, *Regional Studies* **41**, 685–697. doi:10.1080/00343400601120296

FRITSCH M. and WYRWICH M. (2012) *The Long Persistence of Regional Entrepreneurship Culture: Germany 1925–2005*. Papers in Evolutionary Economic Geography No. 12.14. Utrecht University, Utrecht.

GARUD R., KUMARASWAMY A. and KARNOE P. (2010) Path dependence or path creation, *Journal of Management Studies* **47**, 760–774. doi:10.1111/j.1467-6486.2009.00914.x

GEELS F. W. (2002) Technological transitions as evolutionary reconfiguration processes: a multi-level perspective and a case-study, *Research Policy* **31**, 1257–1274. doi:10.1016/S0048-7333(02)00062-8

GERTLER M. (2010) Rules of the game: the place of institutions in regional economic change, *Regional Studies* **44**, 1–15. doi:10.1080/00343400903389979

GILLY J. P., KECHIDI M. and TALBOT D. (2014) Resilience of organisations and territories: the role of pivot firms, *European Management Journal* **32**, 596–602.

GILSING V., NOOTEBOOM B., VANHAVERBEKE W., DUYSTERS G. and VAN DEN OORD A. (2008) Network embeddedness and the exploration of novel technologies. Technological distance, betweenness centrality and density, *Research Policy* **37**, 1717–1731. doi:10.1016/j.respol.2008.08.010

GIULIANI E. and BELL M. (2005) The micro-determinants of meso-level learning and innovation. Evidence from a Chilean wine cluster, *Research Policy* **34**, 47–68. doi:10.1016/j.respol.2004.10.008

GLAESER E. L. (2005) Reinventing Boston: 1630–2003, *Journal of Economic Geography* **5**, 119–153. doi:10.1093/jnlecg/lbh058

GRABHER G. (1993) The weakness of strong ties: the lock-in of regional development in the Ruhr area, in GRABHER G. (Ed.) *The Embedded Firm*, pp. 255–277. Routledge, London.

GRABHER G. and STARK D. (1997) Organizing diversity: evolutionary theory, network analysis and postsocialism, *Regional Studies* **31**, 533–544. doi:10.1080/00343409750132315

GRAF H. (2011) Gatekeepers in regional networks of innovators, *Cambridge Journal of Economics* **35**, 173–198. doi:10.1093/cje/beq001

GRILLITSCH M. (2014) *Institutional Change and Economic Evolution in Regions*. Working Paper. Lund University, Lund.

GROOT S. P. T., MÖHLMANN J. L., GARRETSEN J. H. and DE GROOT H. L. F. (2011) The crisis sensitivity of European countries and regions: stylized facts and spatial heterogeneity, *Cambridge Journal of Regions, Economy and Society* **4**, 437–456. doi:10.1093/cjres/rsr024

GUNDERSON L. and HOLLING C. S. (Eds) (2002) *Panarchy: Understanding Transformations in Human and Natural Systems*. Island Press, Washington, DC.

HALL P. A. and SOSKICE D. (Eds) (2001) *Varieties of Capitalism. The Institutional Foundations of Comparative Advantage*. Oxford University Press, New York, NY.

HASSINK R. (2005) How to unlock regional economies from path dependency? From learning region to learning cluster, *European Planning Studies* **13**, 521–535. doi:10.1080/09654310500107134

HASSINK R. (2010) Regional resilience: a promising concept to explain differences in regional economic adaptability?, *Cambridge Journal of Regions, Economy and Society* **3**, 45–58. doi:10.1093/cjres/rsp033

HENNING M., STAM E. and WENTING R. (2013) Path dependence research in regional economic development: cacophony or knowledge accumulation?, *Regional Studies*. doi:10.1080/00343404.2012.750422

HERRIGEL G. B. (1990) Industrial organization and the politics of industry. Centralized and decentralized production in Germany. PhD thesis, MIT, Cambridge, MA.

HEUERMANN D. F. (2009) *Reinventing the Skilled Region. Human Capital Externalities and Industrial Change*. Working Paper. University of Trier, Trier.

HILL E., CLAIR T. S., WIAL H., WOLMAN H., ATKINS P., BLUMENTHAL P., FICENEC S. and FRIEDHOFF A. (2012) Economic shocks and regional economic resilience, in PINDUS N., WEIR M., WIAL H. and WOLMAN H. (Eds) *Building Resilient Regions: Urban and Regional Policy and Its Effects*, vol. 4, pp. 193–274. Brookings Institution Press, Washington, DC.

HOLLINGSWORTH J. R. (2000) Doing institutional analysis: implications for the study of innovations, *Review of International Political Economy* **7**, 595–644. doi:10.1080/096922900750034563

HOLLINGSWORTH R. (2009) The role of institutions and organizations in shaping radical scientific innovations, in MAGNUSSON L. and OTTOSSON J. (Eds) *The Evolution of Path Dependence*, pp. 139–165. Edward Elgar, Cheltenham.

HUGGINS R. and THOMPSON P. (2014) A network-based view of regional growth, *Journal of Economic Geography* **14**, 511–545. doi:10.1093/jeg/lbt012

HUGGINS R., THOMPSON P. and JOHNSTON A. (2012) Network capital, social capital, and knowledge flow: how the nature of inter-organisational networks impacts on innovation, *Industry and Innovation* **19**, 203–232. doi:10.1080/13662716.2012.669615

JACOBS J. (1969) *The Economy of Cities*. Vintage, New York, NY.

KLEPPER S. (2007) Disagreements, spinoffs, and the evolution of Detroit as the capital. of the U.S. automobile industry, *Management Science* **53**, 616–631. doi:10.1287/mnsc.1060.0683

KLEPPER S. and SIMONS K. L. (2000) Dominance by birthright. Entry of prior radio producers and competitive ramifications in the US television receiver industry, *Strategic Management Journal* **21**, 997–1016. doi:10.1002/1097-0266(200010/11)21:10/11<997::AID-SMJ134>3.0.CO;2-O

KOGLER D. F., RIGBY D. L. and TUCKER I. (2013) Mapping knowledge space and technological relatedness in US cities, *European Planning Studies* **21**, 1374–1391. doi:10.1080/09654313.2012.755832

LAWSON C. (1999) Towards a competence theory of the region, *Cambridge Journal of Economics* **23**, 151–166. doi:10.1093/cje/23.2.151

LAWSON C. and LORENZ E. (1999) Collective learning, tacit knowledge and regional innovative capacity, *Regional Studies* **33**, 305–317. doi:10.1080/713693555

LEVITT B. and MARCH J. (1996) Organizational learning, in COHEN M. D. and SPROULL, L. S. (Eds) *Organizational Learning*, pp. 516–541. Sage, Thousand Oaks, CA.

MACKINNON D., CUMBERS A., PYKE A., BIRCH K. and MCMASTER R. (2009) Evolution in economic geography. Institutions, political economy and adaptation, *Economic Geography* **85**, 129–150. doi:10.1111/j.1944-8287.2009.01017.x

MACKINNON D. and DRISCOLL DERICKSON K. (2012) *From Resilience to Resourcefulness: A Critique of Resilience Policy and Activism*. Papers in Evolutionary Economic Geography No. 12.12. Utrecht University, Utrecht.

MAGNUSSON L. and OTTOSSON J. (Eds) (2009) *The Evolution of Path Dependence*. Edward Elgar, Cheltenham.

MALMBERG A. and MASKELL P. (1997) Towards an explanation of regional specialization and industry agglomeration, *European Planning Studies* **5**, 25–41. doi:10.1080/09654319708720382

MARCH J. G. (1991) Exploration and exploitation in organizational learning, *Organization Science* **2**, 71–87. doi:10.1287/orsc.2.1.71

MARTIN R. (2010) Roepke Lecture in Economic Geography: Rethinking regional path dependence. Beyond lock-in to evolution, *Economic Geography* **86**, 1–27. doi:10.1111/j.1944-8287.2009.01056.x

MARTIN R. (2012) Regional economic resilience, hysteresis and recessionary shocks, *Journal of Economic Geography* **12**, 1–32. doi:10.1093/jeg/lbr019

MARTIN R. and SUNLEY P. (2006) Path dependence and regional economic evolution, *Journal of Economic Geography* **6**, 395–437. doi:10.1093/jeg/lbl012

MARTIN R. and SUNLEY P. (2007) Complexity thinking and evolutionary economic geography, *Journal of Economic Geography* **7**, 573–601. doi:10.1093/jeg/lbm019

MARTIN R. and SUNLEY P. (2013) *On the Notion of Regional Economic Resilience: Conceptualisation and Explanation*. Papers in Evolutionary Economic Geography No. 13.20. Utrecht University, Utrecht.

MASKELL P. and MALMBERG A. (1999) Localised learning and industrial competitiveness, *Cambridge Journal of Economics* **23**, 167–186. doi:10.1093/cje/23.2.167

MENZEL M.-P. and KAMMER J. (2012) *Industry Evolution in Varieties of Capitalism: A Survival Analysis on Wind Turbine Producers in Denmark and the USA*. Papers in Evolutionary Economic Geography No. 12.20. Utrecht University, Utrecht.

MOODYSSON J. (2008) Principles and practices of knowledge creation: on the organization of 'buzz' and 'pipelines' in life science communities, *Economic Geography* **84**, 449–469. doi:10.1111/j.1944-8287.2008.00004.x

MORISET B. (2009) A high-tech cluster revisited: An evolutionary perspective on Grenoble, France. Paper presented at the Economie et geographie de l'innovation et de la creativite conference, University of Lille, Lille, France, 11 December 2009.

MORRISON A. (2008) Gatekeepers of knowledge within industrial districts: who they are, how they interact?, *Regional Studies* **42**, 817–835. doi:10.1080/00343400701654178

MORRISON A. and RABELLOTTI R. (2009) Knowledge and information networks in an Italian wine cluster, *European Planning Studies* **17**, 983–1006. doi:10.1080/09654310902949265

MORRISON A., RABELLOTTI R. and ZIRULIA L. (2013) When do global pipelines enhance the diffusion of knowledge in clusters?, *Economic Geography* **89**, 77–96. doi:10.1111/j.1944-8287.2012.01167.x

MUNARI F., SOBRERO M. and MALIPIERO A. (2012) Absorptive capacity and localized spillovers: focal firms as technological gatekeepers in industrial districts, *Industrial and Corporate Change* **21**, 429–462. doi:10.1093/icc/dtr053

MUNEEPEERAKUL R., LOBO J., SHUTTERS S. T., GOMEZ-LIEVANO A. and QUBBAJ M. R. (2013) Urban economies and occupation space: can they get 'there' from 'here'?, *PLoS ONE* **8**, e73676. doi:10.1371/journal.pone.0073676

MURMANN J. P. (2003) *Knowledge and Competitive Advantage. The Co-Evolution of Firms, Technology and National Institutions*. Cambridge University Press, Cambridge.

NEFFKE F., HARTOG M., BOSCHMA R. and HENNING M. (2014) *Agents of Structural Change: The Role of Firms and Entrepreneurs in Regional Diversification*. Papers in Evolutionary Economic Geography No. 14.10. Utrecht University, Utrecht.

NEFFKE F. and HENNING M. (2013) Skill-relatedness and firm diversification, *Strategic Management Journal* **34**, 297–316. doi:10.1002/smj.2014

NEFFKE F., HENNING M. and BOSCHMA R. (2011a) How do regions diversify over time? Industry relatedness and the development of new growth paths in regions, *Economic Geography* **87**, 237–265. doi:10.1111/j.1944-8287.2011.01121.x

NEFFKE F. M. H., HENNING M. and BOSCHMA R. (2012) The impact of aging and technological relatedness on agglomeration externalities: a survival analysis, *Journal of Economic Geography* **12**, 485–517. doi:10.1093/jeg/lbr001

NEFFKE F., HENNING M., BOSCHMA R. A., LUNDQUIST K. J. and OLANDER L. O. (2011b) The dynamics of agglomeration externalities along the life cycle of industries, *Regional Studies* **45**, 49–65. doi:10.1080/00343401003596307

NELSON R. R. (1994) The co-evolution of technology, industrial structure, and supporting institutions, *Industrial and Corporate Change* **3**, 47–63. doi:10.1093/icc/3.1.47

NOOTEBOOM B. (2000) *Learning and Innovation in Organizations and Economies*. Oxford University Press, Oxford.

OLSON M. (1982) *The Rise and Decline of Nations. Economic Growth, Stagflation and Social Rigidities*. Yale University Press, New Haven, CT.

ORMEROD P. (2005) *Why Most Things Fail. Evolution, Extinction and Economics*. Pantheon, New York, NY.

PENDALL R., FOSTER K. A. and COWELL M. (2010) Resilience and regions: building understanding of the metaphor, *Cambridge Journal of Regions, Economy and Society* **3**, 71–84. doi:10.1093/cjres/rsp028

PIKE A., DAWLEY S. and TOMANEY J. (2010) Resilience, adaptation and adaptability. *Cambridge Journal of Regions, Economy and Society* **3**, 59–70. doi:10.1093/cjres/rsq001

PIORE M. J. and SABEL C. E. (1984) *The Second Industrial Divide. Possibilities for Prosperity*. Basic, New York, NY.

QUATRARO F. (2010) Knowledge coherence, variety and productivity growth: manufacturing evidence from Italian regions, *Research Policy* **39**, 1289–1302. doi:10.1016/j.respol.2010.09.005

REGGIANI A. (2012) Network resilience for transport security. Some methodological considerations, *Transport Policy*. http://dx.doi.org/10.1016/j.transport.2012.09.007

REGGIANI A., DE GRAAF T. and NIJKAMP P. (2002) Resilience: an evolutionary approach to spatial economic systems, *Networks and Spatial Economics* **2**, 211–229. doi:10.1023/A:1015377515690

RIGBY D. (2012) *The Geography of Knowledge Relatedness and Technological Diversification in U.S. Cities*. Papers in Evolutionary Economic Geography No. 12.18. Utrecht University, Utrecht.

RODRÍGUEZ-POSE A. and DI-CATALDO M. (2014) *Quality of Government and Innovative Performance in the Regions of Europe*. Papers in Evolutionary Economic Geography No. 14.16. Utrecht University, Utrecht.

ROSE A. (2004) Defining and measuring economic resilience to disasters, *Disaster Prevention and Management* **13**, 307–314. doi:10.1108/09653560410556528

Saviotti P. P. (1996) *Technological Evolution, Variety and the Economy*. Edward Elgar, Cheltenham.

Saviotti P. P. and Frenken K. (2008) Trade variety and economic development of countries, *Journal of Evolutionary Economics* **18**, 201–218. doi:10.1007/s00191-007-0081-5

Saxenian A. (1994) *Regional Networks: Industrial Adaptation in Silicon Valley and Route 128*. Harvard University Press, Cambridge, MA.

Scott A. J. (1988) *New Industrial Spaces. Flexible Production Organization and Regional Development in North America and Western Europe*. Pion, London.

Setterfield M. (1997) *Rapid Growth and Relative Decline. Modelling Macroeconomic Dynamics with Hysteresis*. Macmillan, London.

Simmie J. and Martin R. (2010) The economic resilience of regions: towards an evolutionary approach, *Cambridge Journal of Regions, Economy and Society* **3**, 27–43. doi:10.1093/cjres/rsp029

Sotarauta M., Horlings L. and Liddle J. (Eds) (2012) *Leadership and Change in Sustainable Regional Development*. Routledge, Abingdon.

Strambach S. (2010) Path dependency and path plasticity. The co-evolution of institutions and innovation – the German customized business software industry, in Boschma R. A. and Martin R. (Eds) *Handbook of Evolutionary Economic Geography*, pp. 406–431. Edward Elgar, Cheltenham.

Strambach S. and Klement B. (2012) Cumulative and combinatorial micro-dynamics of knowledge. The role of space and place in knowledge integration, *European Planning Studies* **20**, 1843–1866. doi:10.1080/09654313.2012.723424

Streeck W. and Thelen K. (2005) Introduction: Institutional change in advanced political economies, in Streeck W. and Thelen K. (Eds) *Beyond Continuity. Institutional Change in Advanced Political Economies*, pp. 1–39. Oxford University Press, Oxford.

Swanstrom T. (2008) *Regional Resilience: A Critical Examination of the Ecological Framework*. Working Paper No. 2008–07. Institute of Urban and Regional Development, University of California – Berkeley, CA.

Swanstrom T., Chapple K. and Immergluck D. (2009) *Regional Resilience in the Face of Foreclosures: Evidence from Six Metropolitan Areas*. Report Prepared for the MacArthur Foundation's Building Resilient Regions Project, Working Paper No. 2009–05. Institute of Urban and Regional Development, University of California – Berkeley, CA.

Tanner A. N. (2011) *The Place of New Industries: The Case of Fuel Cell Technology and its Technological Relatedness to Regional Knowledge Bases*. Papers in Evolutionary Economic Geography No. 11.13. Utrecht University, Utrecht.

Tanner A. N. (2014) Regional branching reconsidered: emergence of the fuel cell industry in European regions, *Economic Geography*. doi:10.1111/ecge.12055

Taylor M. Z. (2004) Empirical evidence against varieties of capitalism's theory of technological innovation, *International Organization* **58**, 601–631. doi:10.1017/S0020818304583066

Thelen K. (2003) How institutions evolve, in Mahoney J. and Rueschemeyer D. (Eds) *Comparative Historical Analysis in the Social Sciences*, pp. 208–240. Cambridge University Press, Cambridge.

Thissen M., van Oort F., Diodato D. and Ruijs A. (2013) *Regional Competitiveness and Smart Specialization in Europe. Place-Based Development in International Economic Networks*. Edward Elgar, Cheltenham.

Treado C. D. (2010) Pittsburgh's evolving steel legacy and the steel technology cluster, *Cambridge Journal of Regions, Economy and Society* **3**, 105–120. doi:10.1093/cjres/rsp027

Trippl M. (2013) Scientific mobility and knowledge transfer at the interregional and intraregional level, *Regional Studies* **47**, 1653–1667. doi:10.1080/00343404.2010.549119

Truffer B. and Coenen L. (2012) Environmental innovation and sustainability transitions in regional studies, *Regional Studies* **46**, 1–21. doi:10.1080/00343404.2012.646164

Verspagen B. and Duysters G. (2004) The small worlds of strategic technology alliances, *Technovation* **24**, 563–571. doi:10.1016/S0166-4972(02)00123-2

Vicente J., Balland P. A. and Brossard O. (2011) Getting into networks and clusters: evidence from the Midi-Pyrenean Global Navigation Satellite Systems (GNSS) collaboration network, *Regional Studies* **45**, 1059–1078. doi:10.1080/00343401003713340

Wink R. (2012) *Institutions and Regional Economic Resilience*. HTWK, Leipzig.

Wolfe D. A. (2010) The strategic management of core cities: path dependence and economic adjustment in resilient regions, *Cambridge Journal of Regions, Economy and Society* **3**, 139–152. doi:10.1093/cjres/rsp032

Van der Wouden F. (2012) The role of relatedness in economic variety on knowledge production of U.S. cities between 1975 and 2005. MA thesis, Department of Economic Geography, Utrecht University, Utrecht.

Zeitschrift fur Wirtschaftsgeographie (2013) Special issue on Reconceptualizing Change: Path Dependency, Path Plasticity and Knowledge Combination, *Zeitschrift fur Wirtschaftsgeographie* **57**, 1–96.

Zolli A. and Healy A. M. (2012) *Resilience. Why Things Bounce Back*. Headline, London.

Relatedness, Industrial Branching and Technological Cohesion in US Metropolitan Areas

JÜRGEN ESSLETZBICHLER

Department of Geography, University College London, Gower Street, UK.

ESSLETZBICHLER J. Relatedness, industrial branching and technological cohesion in US metropolitan areas, *Regional Studies*. Work by evolutionary economic geographers on the role of industry relatedness for regional economic development is extended into a number of methodological and empirical directions. First, relatedness is measured as the intensity of input–output linkages between industries. Second, this measure is employed to examine industry evolution in 360 US metropolitan areas. Third, an employment-weighted measure of metropolitan technological cohesion is developed. The results confirm that technological relatedness is positively related to metropolitan industry portfolio membership and industry entry and negatively related to industry exit. The decomposition of technological cohesion indicates that the selection of related incumbent industries complements industry entry and exit as the main drivers of change in metropolitan technological cohesion.

ESSLETZBICHLER J. 美国大都会地区中的关联性、产业扩展分支与技术整合，区域研究。演化经济地理学者对产业关联性之于区域经济发展的角色之研究，延伸至下列数个方法与经验面向。首先，关联性以产业间的投入—产出连结密集度量测之。再者，此一方法被用来检视美国三百六十个大都会地区的产业发展。第三则建立一个大都会地区技术整合的就业加权测量法。研究结果证实，技术关联性与大都会产业组合关系及产业进入呈现正相关，与产业退出则为负相关。解构技术整合，指出与当前在位产业有关的选择，与产业进入及退出相互补充，做为大都会技术整合变革的主要驱力。

ESSLETZBICHLER J. La parenté, la ramification industrielle et la cohésion technologique dans les zones métropolitaines aux États-Unis, *Regional Studies*. Le travail des géographes économiques évolutionnaires sur le rôle de la parenté industrielle ayant égard pour le développement économique régional s'étend à un nombre d'orientations méthodologiques et empiriques. Primo, on mesure la parenté comme l'intensité des échanges inter-industriels. Secundo, on emploie cette mesure afin d'examiner l'évolution de l'industrie dans 360 zones métropolitaines aux États-Unis. Tertio, on développe une mesure de la cohésion technologique métropolitaine pesée en termes d'emploi. Les résultats confirment que la parenté technologique est en corrélation positive avec l'adhésion au portefeuille industrielle métropolitaine et l'entrée de l'industrie, et en corrélation négative avec la sortie de l'industrie. La décomposition de la cohésion technologique indique que le choix d'industries connexes en place complète l'entrée et la sortie de l'industrie comme forces motrices du changement à la cohésion technologique métropolitaine.

ESSLETZBICHLER J. Verwandtschaft, Branchenbildung und technische Kohäsion in Metropolitangebieten der USA, *Regional Studies*. In diesem Beitrag wird die Arbeit von evolutionären Wirtschaftsgeografen über die Rolle der Branchenverwandtschaft für die regionale Wirtschaftsentwicklung in verschiedene methodologische und empirische Richtungen erweitert. Erstens wird Verwandtschaft als Intensität von Input-Output-Verknüpfungen zwischen Branchen gemessen. Zweitens wird dieser Maßstab zur Untersuchung der Branchenevolution in 360 Metropolitangebieten der USA verwendet. Drittens wird ein nach Beschäftigungsniveau gewichteter Maßstab der metropolitanen technischen Kohäsion entwickelt. Die Ergebnisse bestätigen, dass die technische Verwandtschaft in einem positiven Zusammenhang mit der Mitgliedschaft im metropolitanen Branchenportfolio und mit dem Branchenzugang sowie in einem negativen Zusammenhang mit Branchenaustritten steht. Aus der Zusammensetzung der technischen Kohäsion geht hervor, dass die Auswahl der verwandten etablierten Branchen den Branchenzugang und die Branchenaustritte als wichtigste Faktoren der Veränderung bei der metropolitanen technischen Kohäsion ergänzt.

ESSLETZBICHLER J. Relación, ramas industriales y cohesión tecnológica en las áreas metropolitanas de EE.UU., *Regional Studies*. En este estudio el trabajo de geógrafos económicos evolutivos sobre el papel de las relaciones de la industria para el desarrollo económico se extiende a una serie de direcciones metodológicas y empíricas. Primero se mide la relación en cuanto a la intensidad de los vínculos de entrada/salida entre las industrias. Segundo, se emplea esta medida para analizar la evolución de la industria en 360 áreas metropolitanas de Estados Unidos. Tercero, se desarrolla una medida ponderada según el empleo de la cohesión tecnológica metropolitana. Los resultados confirman que la relación tecnológica está positivamente vinculada a la representación en la cartera industrial metropolitana y la entrada industrial, y negativamente vinculada a la salida industrial. La descomposición de la cohesión tecnológica indica que la selección de las industrias establecidas relacionadas complementa la entrada y salida en las industrias como los principales impulsores de cambio en la cohesión tecnológica metropolitana.

INTRODUCTION

Regions evolve through a process of creative destruction of technological and industrial variety (SCHUMPETER, 1939; STORPER and WALKER, 1989; ESSLETZBICHLER and RIGBY, 2005; RIGBY and ESSLETZBICHLER, 2006; NEFFKE et al., 2011b) mirroring rapid churning at the plant level (DAVIS et al., 1996; BALDWIN, 1998, FOSTER et al., 1998). Creative destruction reflects an imperfect trial-and-error process where firms enter markets with the hope of selling products at a profit. Evidence for the US manufacturing sector indicates that between 1963 and 1982, 39.8% of manufacturing firms registered in a particular census year were not yet active five years earlier. Those high entry rates were matched by slightly lower exit rates varying between 30.8% and 39.0% (DUNNE et al., 1988). Underpinning long-term structural change, the high rates of churning at the national level are also observed at the state and metropolitan area levels (RIGBY and ESSLETZBICHLER, 2000; ESSLETZBICHLER and RIGBY, 2002; ESSLETZBICHLER 2004). While some regions are able to harness the process to rejuvenate their industrial base, others fail to diversify and become locked into a process of industrial decline (GRABHER, 1993; HASSINK and SHIN, 2005; MARTIN, 2010).

MARTIN and SUNLEY (2006) discuss a number of ways for regions to create new paths of development, including processes of recombinant innovation (FRENKEN et al., 2012) based on existing industrial or technological diversity, investment and technology transfer from outside the region (BATHELT et al., 2004) and technological change and endogenous transformation of firms in the region (TÖDTLING and TRIPPL, 2004). How regions grow and decline is also a key research question in new geographical economics. Debates in economics have centred on the relative importance of urbanization and localization economies to generate regional and urban economic growth. The importance of urban diversity to generate novel ideas and knowledge through spillovers among different

rather than similar industries leading to urban economic growth was advocated by Jane Jacobs (JACOBS, 1969), but has since been examined empirically by economists (GLAESER et al., 1992; HENDERSON et al., 1995; DURANTON and PUGA, 2001; ROSENTHAL and STRANGE, 2004) complementing their work on the impact of localization economies and urban size. Numerous empirical studies on the importance of diversity versus specialization as drivers of regional and urban economic growth produced inconclusive evidence at best (BEAUDRY and SCHIFFAUEROVA, 2009; DE GROOT et al., 2009). Perhaps one reason for this inconclusive evidence is the treatment of industries as quantitatively distinct but qualitatively similar. Localization economies enter empirical models as absolute or relative concentration of employment in any industry ignoring the (dis)similarity of those industries. Similarly, urbanization economies are approximated through urban size, population density or the number of plants with little regard for the relationship among sectors making up those regions.

One of the recent contributions of the work by evolutionary economic geographers is the importance attributed to the concept of relatedness between industries highlighting the need to consider not only the number and employment shares of regional industries, but also the similarity among them to understand regional economic evolution. While sectoral diversity may increase the potential for radical innovations because of the exchange of different ideas, too much dissimilarity between sectors may impede knowledge exchange because some overlap in knowledge bases and competences is required to communicate effectively. NOOTEBOOM (2000) thus postulates a trade-off between diversity and similarity: too much similarity may result in cognitive lock-in while too little similarity may impede knowledge exchange altogether. The notion of cognitive distance points towards the idea of relatedness between sectors and forces researchers to capture the technological similarity between sectors empirically rather than simply tallying the number of sectors or employment shares in sectors.

Industries are related through different channels of information and knowledge exchange: labour flows, supplier–customer relationships and knowledge 'spillovers' (MARSHALL, 1920; POTTER and WATTS, 2012). Geographic proximity is assumed to facilitate this exchange. Cities with local pools of skilled labour are more likely to boost firm performance (BOSCHMA et al., 2009) and regional economic growth. As firms are more likely to diversify into industries requiring similar skill sets to take full advantage of their workforce (NEFFKE and HENNING, 2013) and workers are more likely to exchange information if they possess related skills, cities are likely to add industries employing workers with related skill sets. The second channel of knowledge exchange is through supplier–customer linkages as the presence of competent suppliers increases the productivity of their customers, while the presence of competent customers pushes up competition and innovation among suppliers. Thus, regions are likely to branch into related industries as those industries can take advantage of the local supplier and customer base (FRENKEN and BOSCHMA, 2007). And finally, technology spillovers may be more likely to occur between technologically related industries, rather than within a single industry or between technologically unrelated industries (BOSCHMA and FRENKEN, 2011).

In order to examine the impact of relatedness on regional performance, FRENKEN et al. (2007) distinguish between 'related' and 'unrelated' variety and link variety to regional employment, output and productivity growth. Employing an entropy measure of industry concentration, 'related variety' refers to the concentration of employment in SIC-5-digit sectors within SIC-2-digit sectors and 'unrelated variety' refers to the concentration of employment in SIC-2-digit sectors.[1] Their findings indicate that for Dutch regions 'related variety' is positively related to employment growth, while 'unrelated variety' is negatively related to unemployment growth suggesting the operation of a portfolio effect. BOSCHMA and IAMMARINO (2009) found similar results for Italian regions. Building on entropy-based measures of variety, BOSCHMA et al. (2009) show the importance of related skill portfolios of a plant's workforce for its productivity growth in Sweden; QUATRARO (2010) demonstrates that related but not unrelated variety exerts a positive impact of total factor productivity (TFP) growth in Italian regions; and BOSCHMA et al. (2012) find positive effects on value added and employment growth in Spanish regions. HARTOG et al. (2012) find that the positive effect of related variety on employment growth in Finnish regions is restricted to high-technology sectors only.

Subsequent work developed relatedness measures based on co-occurrences of country exports (HIDALGO et al., 2007), co-production of products in plants (NEFFKE and HENNING, 2008), and co-citation of patents in patent applications (RIGBY, 2012).

HAUSMANN and KLINGER (2007) and HIDALGO et al. (2007) establish a link between a country's export portfolio and its subsequent potential for economic development as countries expand their export portfolio into industries related to their existing export mix. Countries of the Global North occupying densely connected parts of the product/industry space have thus better opportunities to diversify into new industries than countries of the Global South. The lack of opportunities to diversify into a large number of sectors then impedes rapid growth and catch-up processes. The impact of complementary knowledge flows through labour mobility has been examined by BOSCHMA et al. (2009) who demonstrate that firm productivity increases only if workers with complementary rather than different or identical skills are hired. They show that hiring workers with identical skills decreases firm productivity suggesting that only the import of related knowledge results in competitive advantages.

Because complementary knowledge flows bridge existing, but different, knowledge and technology fields, FRENKEN and BOSCHMA (2007) and BOSCHMA and FRENKEN (2011) suggest that regions diversify into industries related to the existing portfolio of industries. New, but related, forms of knowledge and organizational routines can be generated through spin-off dynamics (KLEPPER, 2007; BOSCHMA and WENTING, 2007), new firm entry in related industries, inflow of labour with complementary skills, or the co-location of suppliers and/or customers to take advantage from learning by doing, learning by using and learning by interacting (VON HIPPEL, 1988). Regional branching into related industries suggests a gradual build up of technological and industrial variety not dissimilar to Charles Darwin's notion of speciation and evolution driven primarily by gradual change.[2] The branching of regions into related manufacturing industries has been studied systematically for 170 Swedish regions (NEFFKE et al., 2011a). Using a measure of relatedness based on co-occurrence of different products in firms, NEFFKE et al. (2011a) highlight substantial change in regional industrial structure over a thirty-year period driven by entry of industries related to existing industries in the region and exit of less related industries from the region.

This paper builds on and complements this work as follows. First, it attempts to corroborate empirically the findings of NEFFKE et al. (2011a) in a different geographic context and with a different measure of relatedness. The different mechanisms of knowledge exchange identified above require different measures of relatedness that will in turn capture one particular channel linking sectors. Although the impact of different measures of relatedness on the process of regional branching may differ in magnitude, by sector and metropolitan area, theory suggests that the general result of regional evolution as industrial branching into related industries should hold independently of the channel of knowledge transfer studied and relatedness measure employed. It is important to notice that the focus on a single measure of relatedness impedes a proper evaluation of the sources of differences in results, whether differences are due to different empirical implementation of relatedness or different economic–geographic contexts. The measure of technological relatedness employed in this paper is developed from input–output flows between 362 US manufacturing sectors. This measure is applied to examine the impact of technological relatedness on the entry and exit of new industries in 360 US metropolitan areas over the period 1977–1997. The second contribution of this paper is an analysis of the main components of change in metropolitan technological cohesion. Change in technological cohesion is shown to be the result of changes in technological relatedness among incumbent industries, selection or differential growth of incumbent industries, and the entry and exit of industries. While NEFFKE et al. (2011a) focus on the entry and exit of industries as drivers of structural change in regions resulting in relatively stable patterns of regional technological cohesion over time, the reallocation of employment towards better connected incumbent industries may also contribute to the evolution of technological cohesion that may result in negative technological lock-in if not counterbalanced by industry entry.

The paper is structured as follows. The second section briefly outlines different approaches to measuring relatedness and explains how relatedness is measured in the context of this paper. The third section discusses the empirical findings linking relatedness to structural change and technological cohesion in 360 US metropolitan areas. The fourth section discusses an employment share-weighted measure of metropolitan technological cohesion and decomposes change in technological cohesion into selection, entry and exit effects. The fifth section concludes the paper.

MEASURING INTER-INDUSTRY RELATEDNESS

Three broad approaches to measure relatedness are distinguished in the literature (NEFFKE and HENNING, 2013). The first relies on the hierarchy of industry classifications and defines industries that fall into the same broad industry classes as related. For instance, SIC-4-digit industries belonging to the same SIC-2-digit industry are considered as related. This is the approach chosen by FRENKEN et al. (2007), BOSCHMA and IAMMARINO (2009), BOSCHMA et al. (2009, 2012), QUATRARO (2010), and HARTOG et al. (2012). This method is relatively easy to implement and available for a large number of secondary data for different countries and regions. However, the method is criticized on theoretical grounds, as classification of

industries into broader industry groups does not necessarily mean that the industries are related technologically or knowledge is exchanged more easily between those sectors.

The second strategy that gained popularity in the recent literature defines relatedness through co-occurrence examining how often two industries are found together in the same economic entity. This work includes the co-occurrence of industries in a country's or a region's export portfolio (HIDALGO et al., 2007; BOSCHMA et al., 2013), the likelihood of co-production of different products in the same plant said to reveal economies of scope through technological spillovers (NEFFKE and HENNING, 2008; NEFFKE et al., 2011a), or the co-occurrence of patent citations (RIGBY, 2012). However, co-occurrence assumes technological or cognitive proximity leading to co-production or diversification into related products/sectors and obscures the sources of economies of scope that may emerge from co-occurrence. As a result, it is difficult to determine the type of relatedness that has been measured (NEFFKE and HENNING, 2013).

The third approach defines relatedness through similarity in resource use or flow of resources between firms and/or sectors focusing on the role of human capital and the similarity in occupation profiles (FARJOUN, 1994; DUMAIS et al., 1997), technological resources using patent analysis (BRESCHI et al., 2003), and material resources using commodity flows measured through input–output linkages (FAN and LANG, 2000; FESER, 2003). Resource-based similarity measures suffer from bias because of the strategic relevance given to some resources. Patent-based indicators shed light on relatedness among patent-intensive industries, while input–output-based measures may be more useful for an investigation of manufacturing rather than service industries. Each of the approaches has advantages and disadvantages and the utility of them in various historical, geographical and sectoral contexts needs to be explored further through systematic accumulation of empirical material.

In order to examine whether resource-based measures result in similar conclusions on the link between relatedness and regional industrial branching, this paper follows the literature on input–output relations and adopts a measure of relatedness based on the relative strengths of value flows between pairs of industries.[3] The inter-industry relatedness measure is derived from the 'Make Table' and 'Use Table' of the detailed 1987 benchmark input–output tables supplied by the Bureau of Economic Analysis (BEA) that include input–output flows between 563 industries. The 'Make Table' includes the value of commodities c, produced by industry i. The 'Use Table' contains the value of commodities c consumed by industry j. In order to obtain value flows between industries (rather than commodities that are produced by several industries), the following transformation was carried out.

First, the 'Make Table' was used to find out how much of a commodity c was produced by various industries i. More specifically, s_{ic} refers to the share of one unit of commodity c produced by industry i. Second, the 'Use Table' was required to reveal the value, F_{cj}, of commodity c consumed by industry j. In order to obtain the value flows between industries i and j, F_{cj} was multiplied by the industry-commodity shares, s_{ic}. Third, summing the resulting values over industries i and j then yields an estimate of input–output flows, F_{ij} between industries i and j (in US$). Following FAN and LANG (2000), the input–output relatedness between industries i and j, IOR_{ij}, is measured as:

$$IOR_{ij} = \frac{1}{2}\left(\frac{F_{ij}}{\sum_{j=1}^{n} F_{ij}} + \frac{F_{ji}}{\sum_{i=1}^{m} F_{ji}} \right) \times 100 \qquad (1)$$

One of the drawbacks of input–output tables is the lack of detailed industry classifications for non-manufacturing industries. Hence, the analysis was restricted to the 362 manufacturing sectors (IO Industry numbers 130100–641200) included in the BEA input–output tables. Unfortunately, those 362 IO industry numbers are only a subset of the 453 SIC codes used in census statistics. Because some IO numbers correspond to various SIC codes (for example, 141900 (Sugar) corresponds to SIC codes 2061, 2062 and 2063), the SIC sectors were aggregated to the IO industries resulting in a 362×362 industry matrix.[4]

This measure of IO–industry relatedness can now be used to examine the role of industry relatedness on structural change in the US space economy. As it is generally assumed that metropolitan areas most closely mirror functional economic spatial entities, the empirical analysis examines industrial branching in 360 US metropolitan statistical areas.[5] In order to examine structural change in those metropolitan areas and the components of change of regional technological cohesion, it was necessary to identify the presence or absence of industries in a metropolitan area. County business patterns provide this information. For each year they include information on employment, number of plants and annual payroll for SIC-4-digit sectors per county. For confidentiality reasons, employment figures for small industries in small counties are often omitted and replaced with employment size bands. However, using the information on the number of plants in different plant size categories (which is not suppressed), ISSERMAN and WESTERVELT (2006) suggest a data-imputation method that reduces substantially the uncertainty in county–industry employment numbers. Following ISSERMAN and WESTERVELT (2006), data imputation was carried out for all years of the analysis to reduce the uncertainty in county–industry–employment figures. The second potential data

problem arises from a change in industry classification system between 1987 and 1988. In order to analyse structural change, consistent industry classifications are required. A consistent set of industries between 1977 and 1997 was obtained by converting 1972 SICs into 1987 SICs using the Bartelsman–Becker–Gray conversion tables.[6] Unfortunately, a more severe reclassification took place in 1997. Despite existing conversion tables, the new North American Industry Classification System (NAICS) is entirely different from the old SIC system such that consistency over time is compromised and the analysis presented in this paper is restricted to the twenty-year period from 1977 to 1997. For this period, a consistent set of 362 manufacturing industries for 360 metropolitan areas was constructed.

Combining the data on IO relatedness from the BEA input–output tables and industry employment data from the County Business Patterns allows for an analysis of the impact of industry relatedness on structural change in metropolitan areas.

STRUCTURAL CHANGE AND TECHNOLOGICAL COHESION IN US METROPOLITAN AREAS

Before examining structural change in metropolitan areas, Fig. 1 reveals the IO relatedness between 362 manufacturing sectors in 1987. In order to facilitate readability, the relatedness measure IOR_{ij} was reduced to three categories using the values for the 90th (0.237) and 75th (0.024) percentiles as cut-off criteria. The white/light purple cells are those with an IOR_{ij} measure of less than 0.024, medium grey/medium purple values represent those industry pairs with IOR_{ij} values between 0.024 and less than 0.237, while the dark grey/dark purple values represent those industry pairs with values ≥ 0.237. There are a number of clusters along the main diagonal (food, textile/apparel) and some industries which are tied to most other industries (such as metallurgy and machine tools, petroleum refining, industrial inorganic and organic chemicals).

As the main objective of this paper is to uncover the extent of structural change at the metropolitan level, Fig. 2 depicts the change in metropolitan industry composition between 1975 and 1997. The solid line represents the share of industries in metropolitan areas that were present in those areas in 1975. The original set of industry–regions in 1975 constitutes 77.2% of metropolitan industries in 1997. Or put another way, one-quarter of industries that were present in 1975 disappeared from metropolitan industry portfolios by 1997. The dashed line represents the share of industries in metropolitan areas that were present in 1997 and reveals that only 61.0% of industry–regions present in 1997 existed in 1975. These values are similar to those observed for the Swedish case reported by NEFFKE et al. (2011a).

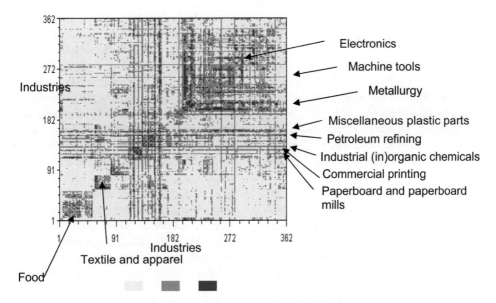

Fig. 1. *Relatedness matrix based on the 1987 input–output table*
Note: IOR: 90 percentile = 0.237; and 75th percentile = 0.024; dark grey/dark purple: IOR values > = 0.237; medium grey/medium purple: 0.0237 < = IOR values < 0.24; and white/light purple: IOR values < 0.024

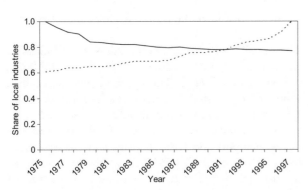

Fig. 2. *Structural change in US metropolitan areas, 1975–1997*
Note: The solid line represents the shares of industries present in a metropolitan area in 1975; the dashed line represents the shares of industries present in a metropolitan area in 1997

The IOR measure reports the relatedness between industry pairs. As metropolitan areas host more than one industry, it is necessary to examine how strongly a single industry in a metropolitan area is related to all other industries that make up a regional portfolio. A regional portfolio of region r, RPF_r, in any given year is defined as the set of industries with non-zero employment in the region. In order to count links only to closely related industries, the number of links to industries with IOR values above a certain threshold are counted. The closeness of a particular industry i to all other industries j comprising a regional portfolio r is then defined as:

$$closeness_{ir} = \sum_{j \in RPF_r} I\left(IOR_{ij} > 0.237\right) \qquad (2)$$

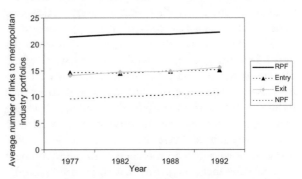

Fig. 3. *Evolution of metropolitan technological cohesion*
Note: The vertical axis depicts the average number of related industries *(IOR > 0.237)* (see equation 3) averaged over all metropolitan areas; the solid line depicts the values for regional portfolio members; the dashed line depicts the closeness of absent industries to the regional portfolio members; the line with the upward-pointing triangles depicts the closeness of entrants; and the line with diamonds depicts the closeness of exits to the regional portfolio. Values for entry are significantly higher than those for exit in 1977 and significantly lower than those for exit in 1992. The differences in 1982 and 1988 are not statistically significant

where $I(.)$ is an indicator function that takes the value of 1 if the argument is true and 0 if the argument is wrong. Any threshold value could be used to obtain the closeness index. A total of 0.237 is somewhat arbitrary but has been chosen because it constitutes the 90% percentile, that is, 10% of industry pairs have $IOR_{ij} > 0.237$.[7]

For each region, technological cohesion is then defined as the average closeness value of industries present in a regional portfolio:

$$Technological\ cohesion_r = \frac{1}{N_r} \sum_{i \in RPF_r} closeness_{ir} \qquad (3)$$

where N_r is the number of industries belonging to regional portfolio RPF_r. Fig. 3 depicts the technological cohesion of regional portfolios for the years 1977, 1982, 1988 and 1992 (solid line).[8] In addition, the dotted line depicts the average closeness of industries belonging to a regional portfolio to all industries that are not part of the regional portfolio.

According to NEFFKE et al. (2011a), a regional portfolio is considered to be cohesive if the average closeness of industries to the RPF industries is higher than to industries that are not part of the RPF (regions are considered cohesive if the solid line is above the dotted line). According to Fig. 3, regional portfolios are, on average, cohesive and stable over time. This stability seems somewhat at odds with the turnover of industries depicted in Fig. 2. It is thus useful to examine how the entry and exit of industries influences the technological cohesion of a regional portfolio. Entrants are defined as industries that entered over a five-year period, while exits are defined as industries that exited over a five-year period.[9] The average closeness of entrants to the portfolio of industries in regions they enter is represented by upward-pointing triangles, while the average closeness of exits is represented by diamonds. Entrants tend to be closer to the regional portfolio of industries than industries that remain outside the region, suggesting that regions diversify into industries that are related to the existing industrial base. But entrants are less related to the regional portfolio members than the incumbent portfolio members, suggesting that entrants are complementing rather than simply reproducing the existing industry structure. Entry weakens the technological cohesion of regional portfolios and may be important for regions to avoid negative lock-in (see also Table 4). Exits tend to be more closely related to the regional portfolio than industries that are not part of the regional portfolio, suggesting that they are not entirely unrelated to the regional portfolio of which they have been part. But exits are less close to the regional portfolio of industries than the industries remaining in the portfolio, which suggests that industries that are less close to their regional portfolio are less likely to benefit from knowledge spillovers and, hence, more likely to exit a region. Because the technological cohesion of exits is lower than the technological cohesion of the remaining regional portfolio industries, exit improves the overall cohesion of a region (see also Table 4). Notice that there is little difference in the technological cohesion of entrants and exits. While entrants are closer to the regional portfolio in 1977, exits are closer to the regional portfolio in 1992. The differences between the closeness values of entrants and exits are not statistically significant in 1982 and 1988 (Fig. 3). This is different from the Swedish case, where the

technological cohesion of entrants is considerably higher than the technological cohesion of exits and much closer to the technological cohesion of regional portfolio members. But overall, the results are similar despite the fact that relatedness is measured differently and the economic–geographic context differs for the two cases. More specifically, the three main sets of findings identified by NEFFKE et al. (2011a) are broadly substantiated: First, regional portfolios are technologically cohesive and remain so over time. Second, industries are more likely to enter a region if they are technologically related to the existing regional portfolio of industries. Third, industries that are less closely tied to the regional portfolio than other portfolio members are more likely to exit the industry. These three findings are examined in further detail below.

Membership, entry and exit can be formally defined as:

$$member_{ir}^t = I(i \in RPF(r, t)) \qquad (4)$$

$$entry_{ir}^{t+5} = I(i \notin RPF(r, t) \wedge i \in RPF(r, t+5)) \qquad (5)$$

$$exit_{ir}^t = I(i \in RPF(r, t) \wedge i \notin RPF(r, t+5)) \qquad (6)$$

The member variable takes on a value of 1 if industry i was part of regional portfolio RPF_r at time t and 0 if it was not part of RPF_r. The entry variable takes on a value of 1 if industry i was not part of regional portfolio RPF_r in year t and was part of RPF_r in year $t+5$. The exit variable takes on a value of 1 if industry i was part of regional portfolio RPF_r in year t and was no longer part of RPF_r in year $t+5$. Table 1 presents descriptive information of the dummy variables and the size of regions and industries. All tables are based on industry–metropolitan area observations pooled across four five-year periods resulting in 521 280 (352 industries × 360 metropolitan areas × 4 periods) observations for calculations involving the membership dummies. Because entry can only occur if industries were not present in a region in year t, the number of observations involving the entry dummy is reduced to a subsample of 356 454 industry–regions. These are the potential entry opportunities for industries. Because exit can only occur if industries were present in year t, the subsample for potential exit opportunities of 164 826 industry–regions was used for the calculation of descriptive statistics involving the exit dummy. Adding both subsamples results in the complete sample again.

Table 2 reveals the correlation coefficients between values for closeness and member, entry and exit dummies. While the relationship between closeness values and membership and entry dummies is positive, the correlation coefficient for exit is negative. Industries are more likely to be members of a regional portfolio and enter a metropolitan area if they are closely related to the existing portfolio while they are more

Table 1. Descriptive statistics

Variable	Number of observations	Mean	Standard deviation (SD)	Minimum	Maximum
Member	521 280	0.32	0.46	0.00	1.00
Entry	356 454	0.09	0.28	0.00	1.00
Exit	164 826	0.14	0.35	0.00	1.00
Closeness (PF_r)	521 280	13.83	15.96	0.00	273.00
Closeness (non-PF_r)	521 280	22.28	26.31	0.00	280.00
$\log_{10}[emp(r)]$	521 280	4.21	0.56	2.31	6.10
$\log_{10}[emp(i)]$	521 280	4.43	0.48	2.98	6.04

Note: Observations refer to industry–region combinations. Variables: *Member* = membership dummy variable; *Entry* = entry dummy variable; *Exit* = exit dummy variable; *Closeness (PF_r)* = number of closely related industries present in a metropolitan area; *Closeness (non-PF_r)* = number of closely related industries that are absent from the metropolitan area; $\log_{10}[emp(r)]$ = logarithm (base 10) of total employment in metropolitan area *r*; and $\log_{10}[emp(i)]$ = logarithm (base 10) of total employment in industry *i*; The values for the entry and exit dummies are based on restricted samples.

Table 2. Correlation between the values for closeness and the membership, entry and exit dummy variables

	Correlation	*p*-value	N
Member	0.3411	< 0.0001	521 280
Entry	0.1498	< 0.0001	356 454
Exit	−0.1271	< 0.0001	164 826

Note: The correlation coefficients for entry and exit are based on restricted samples.

likely to exit if they are less closely related to the portfolio. All correlation coefficients are statistically significant below the 0.0001 level.

In order to determine the economic importance of closeness, it is useful to examine how closeness affects the probabilities of membership, entry and exit. The probability of membership is 31.6% – the total number of industry–regions that exist in year *t* (164 826) divided by the total number of potential of industry–regions (521 280) – the probability of entry is 8.6% – the number of industry–region entrants (38 690) divided by the total number of potential entry opportunities (356 454) – and the probability of exit is 14.5% – the number of actual exits (31 407) divided by the number of potential exits (164 826). These probabilities can be calculated separately for different closeness values. Because of the large number of values that the closeness variable could assume, closeness values have been grouped into closeness classes with an interval width of five (for example, 0–4, 5–9, etc.). Figs 4a–c depict the probabilities of regional portfolio membership, entry and exit with increasing closeness values.

Figs 4a and 4b reveal that the probabilities of membership and entry are well below average membership and entry probabilities for low closeness values and end up far above them for high closeness values. The probability of regional portfolio membership is more than five times as high for closeness values of thirty or more compared with membership probability for closeness values of 0–4. The relative frequency of entry is close to five times higher for closeness values of thirty

or higher than the relative frequency for closeness values of 0–4. Fig. 4c depicts the probabilities of exit and demonstrates that exit probabilities decrease from 22.7% for closeness values of 0–4 to 7.7% for closeness values of thirty or higher.

In order to control for potential confounding variables, Table 3 presents the results of logistic regression analyses with membership (models 1a–c), entry (models 2a–c) and exit (models 3a–c) dummies as dependent variables. Logistic regression rather than ordinary least squares (OLS) is used because the dependent variables are binary variables (yes = 1; no = 0). Robust standard errors are reported in parentheses and odds ratios are reported in brackets. In Models 1a, 2a and 3a the closeness values of individual industries to the regional portfolio of industries are regressed on membership, entry and exit. Confirming the patterns from Figs 4a–c, closeness is positively related to membership and entry, but negatively related to exit. The odds ratios give an indication of how the odds of membership/entry/exit change after a unit change in the dependent variable (that is, one additional link). An odds ratio > 1 indicates an increase in the odds that the outcome is obtained, while an odds ratio < 1 indicates a decrease in the odds that an outcome is obtained when increasing the independent variable by 1 unit. Table 3 reveals that the odds of membership increase by 6.9%, the odds of entry by 3.7% and the odds of exit decrease by 3.1% if an industry's closeness to the regional portfolio increases by one additional link.

The membership, entry and exit dummies are likely to be influenced by the size of industries and regions. Large industries are more likely to be part of a regional portfolio and are more likely to enter a region and less likely to exit a region. Larger metropolitan areas are able to sustain more industries and are more likely to attract new and retain existing industries. In order to control for size effects, the logarithm of total metropolitan employment and the logarithm (both with base 10) of total national industry employment has been included in models 1b, 2b and 3b. Both variables have the expected signs in all models, but the parameter estimates for closeness declined. The size of industries and metropolitan areas

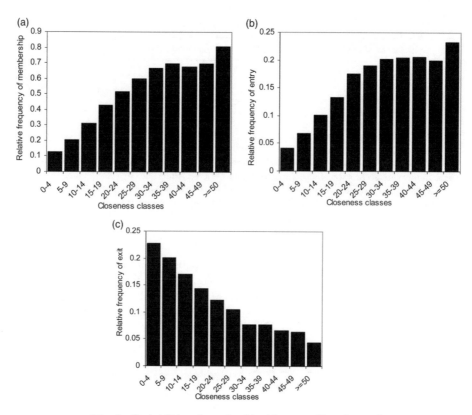

Fig. 4. Probabilities of membership (a), entry (b) and exit (c)

Table 3. Logistic regression analysis of the probabilities of membership, entry and exit

Dependent variables →	Membership			Entry			Exit		
Model	1a	1b	1c	2a	2b	2c	3a	3b	3c
Closeness (PF)	0.067*	0.016*	0.030*	0.037*	0.014*	0.025*	−0.031*	−0.008*	−0.012*
	(0.000)	(0.000)	(0.000)	(0.000)	(0.000)	(0.000)	(0.000)	(0.000)	(0.000)
	[1.069]	[1.016]	[1.031]	[1.037]	[1.014]	[1.026]	[0.969]	[0.992]	[0.988]
$\log_{10}[emp(r)]$		1.777*	1.462*		0.903*	0.658*		−0.952*	−0.861*
		(0.000)	(0.000)		(0.000)	(0.000)		(0.000)	(0.000)
		[5.911]	[4.315]		[2.468]	[1.931]		[0.386]	[0.423]
$\log_{10}[emp(i)]$		1.62*	1.740*		1.058*	1.164*		−0.928*	−0.976*
		(0.000)	(0.000)		(0.000)	(0.000)		(0.000)	(0.000)
		[5.079]	[5.697]		[2.879]	[3.204]		[0.395]	[0.377]
Closeness (non-PF)			−0.006*			−0.010*			0.004*
			(0.000)			(0.000)			(0.000)
			[0.989]			[0.990]			[1.004]
Constant	−1.700*	−15.914*	−15.024*	−2.786*	−10.940*	−10.696*	−1.219*	6.937*	6.643*
	(0.000)	(0.000)	(0.000)	(0.000)	(0.000)	(0.000)	(0.000)	(0.000)	(0.000)
Log-likelihood	−290054.9	−252124.2	−250133.1	−101949.9	−98174.1	−97761.4	−66163.7.5	−63545.9	−63485.2
Number of observations	521280	521280	521280	356454	356454	356454	164826	164826	164826

Note: Robust errors are shown in parentheses; and odds ratios are shown in brackets. Independent variables: *Closeness (PF)* = number of closely related industries in the region; $\log_{10}[emp(r)]$ = logarithm (base 10) of total manufacturing employment in a metropolitan area; $\log_{10}[emp(i)]$ = logarithm (base 10) of total US employment in the industry; and *Closeness (non-PF)* = number of closely related industries absent from regions. Dependent variables: *Membership* = 1 if an industry is found in the regional portfolio in year t; *Entry* = 1 if an industry is found in the regional portfolio in year $t + 5$ but not year t; and *Exit* = 1 if an industry is found in the regional portfolio in year t but not in year $t + 5$. $t = 1977$, 1982, 1988 and 1992. The year 1988 was chosen as the starting year for period 3 in order to avoid any remaining inconsistencies from changes in industry classifications between 1987 and 1988. However, using 1987 instead of 1988 did not alter the conclusions of the results.

will positively influence membership and entry independent of the relatedness of specific industries to the regional portfolio of industries. *Ceteris paribus*, they will also influence exit probabilities negatively. In order to

get an indication of the size of the effects, it is useful to look at the odds ratios again. The odds ratios for industry and metropolitan size are similar. Keeping the effects of other independent variables constant, a 1-unit increase in the size of a metropolitan area (equalling a tenfold employment increase), will increase the odds of membership by 5.9%, the odds of entry by 2.5% and decrease the odds of exit by 61.4%. Similarly, a 1 unit increase in the size of industry will increase the odds of membership by 5.1%, the odds of entry by 2.9% and decrease the odds of exit by 60.5%. On the other hand, a 1 unit change in the closeness variable would result in an increase in the odds of membership by 1.6% and the odds of entry by 1.4%, while it would decrease the odds of exit by 0.8%.

The probabilities of membership, entry and exit of an industry may also be influenced by its closeness to industry portfolios absent from the region as relatededness to industries in other regions may increase the probability of industries to exit from the regional portfolio and relocate to those regions. Models 1c, 2c and 3c thus add an industry's closeness to the portfolio of industries absent from the region to the model. This variable is negatively related to member and entry probabilities and positively related to exit probabilities. Under *ceteris paribus* conditions, if a large number of related industries is absent from a region, then membership and entry probabilities are lower and the probability of exit increases. Or, in other words, other regions that host related industries are more likely to host, attract and retain those industries. The signs of the parameter estimates for closeness (RPF), metropolitan and industry size do not change with the inclusion of this variable although the odds ratios for closeness (RPF) and industry size increase somewhat and the odds ratios for the size of metropolitan areas decreases. The odds ratio for the closeness to industries absent from a region is relatively small, lowering the odds of membership and entry by 1.1% and 1.0% and increasing the odds of exit by 0.4% with an additional link to industries absent from the region.

The analysis shows the membership, entry and exit probabilities of individual industries to regional portfolios but does not explain the contribution of industry entry and exit to changes in regional technological cohesion overall. While NEFFKE *et al.* (2011a) conceptualize regional evolution as creative destruction through entry and exit of related industries, they do not consider selection effects. Entry and exit are probably the driving forces of change in the long-run, but the differential growth of industries will contribute to changes in regional technological cohesion in the short and medium run. The next section thus offers a decomposition of aggregate changes in metropolitan technological cohesion into selection, entry and exit effects.

COMPONENTS OF CHANGE IN TECHNOLOGICAL COHESION OF METROPOLITAN AREAS

In order to account for selection in addition to entry and exit effects on changes in technological cohesion, an

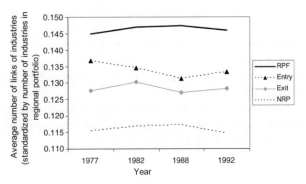

Fig. 5. *Evolution of standardized metropolitan technological cohesion*

Note: The vertical axis depicts the average number of links of an industry to regional portfolio members standardized by the number of industries in a regional portfolio (see equation 7) and averaged over all metropolitan areas; the solid line depicts the values for regional portfolio members; the dashed line depicts the closeness of absent industries to the regional portfolio members; the line with the upward-pointing triangles depicts the closeness of entrants; and the line with diamonds depicts the closeness of exits to the regional portfolio. All values are statistically significantly different from each other at the 0.01 level, with the exception of entry and exit in 1982 and 1988 where the difference is only significant at the 0.05 level

employment-weighted measure of technological cohesion is required. Rather than treating each industry equal as assumed in the previous analysis, the contribution of an industry to the technological cohesion of a metropolitan area depends not only on its closeness to the regional portfolio, but also on its metropolitan employment share. Furthermore, the closeness measure (see equation 2) is in part influenced by the size of a metropolitan area and is expected to be higher in large metropolitan areas than in small metropolitan areas, as larger areas tend to sustain a larger number of industries and, hence, the expected number of links of any single industry is higher in large metropolitan areas with a large number of industries with which to link.[10] Because the desire is to look at the relative effects of entry, exit and incumbents on technological cohesion, it is therefore useful to standardize the closeness of industry i to regional portfolio r by the number of industries in a region, N_r, to obtain the standardized closeness measure, SC_{ir}, where:

$$SC_{ir} = \frac{closeness_{ir}}{N_r} \qquad (7)$$

The value of this measure can be interpreted as the average number of links of industry i to all other regional portfolio members. Fig. 5 depicts the average of SC_{ir} for industries belonging to a regional portfolio (solid line), industries absent from the regional portfolio (dashed line), and entering (upward-pointing triangles) and exiting (diamonds) industries. While the result appears similar to the average closeness values depicted in Fig. 3, entrants exhibit considerably higher standardized closeness values than exits (the differences between entry and exit are statistically significant at the 0.01 level for the periods 1977 and 1992, and at the 0.05 level for the periods 1982 and 1988).

An employment-weighted measure of metropolitan technological cohesion of metropolitan area r and at time t, WTC_r^t, is then defined as:

$$WTC_r^t = \sum_i s_{ir}^t SC_{ir}^t \qquad (8)$$

where:

$$s_{ir}^t = \frac{emp_{ir}^t}{\sum_i emp_{ir}^t}$$

is the employment share of industry i in metropolitan area r at time t, divided by total manufacturing employment in the metropolitan area. Following the literature on productivity decomposition (FOSTER et al., 1998), the change in technological cohesion in metropolitan area r and between times t and $t+1$ is then:

$$WTC_r^{t+1} - WTC_r^t = \sum_{i \in INC} \left(SC_{ir}^{t+1} - SC_{ir}^t \right) s_{ir}^t$$
$$+ \sum_{i \in INC} \left(s_{ir}^{t+1} - s_{ir}^t \right) \left(SC_{ir}^t - WTC_r^t \right)$$
$$+ \sum_{i \in INC} \left(SC_{ir}^{t+1} - SC_{ir}^t \right) \left(s_{ir}^{t+1} - s_{ir}^t \right)$$
$$+ \sum_{i \in N} \left(SC_{ir}^{t+1} - WTC_r^t \right) s_{ir}^{t+1}$$
$$- \sum_{i \in X} \left(SC_{ir}^t - WTC_{ir}^t \right) s_{ir}^t \qquad (9)$$

The subscript INC denotes incumbent industries, industries that exist in t and $t+1$; N represents entering industries that exist in $t+1$ but were not in operation in year t; and X denotes exiting industries, industries that were part of the regional portfolio in year t but were no longer present in the region in year $t+1$.

Aggregate change in technological cohesion of a metropolitan area can then be understood as the sum of five components. The first three components in equation (9) represent changes relating to incumbent industries, while the fourth component represents changes attributed to entrants, and the fifth component represents changes attributed to exits. The first incumbent term measures the change in the standardized closeness values of incumbent industries assuming that employment shares of those industries remain constant. This term is usually interpreted as innovation effect in productivity studies, but here refers to the adaptation of the regional portfolio to the existing sets of industries. Because the relatedness between sectors, IOR_{ij} (see equation 1) was kept constant over time, SC_{ir} can only change if the composition of the regional portfolio changes. Thus, a positive 'portfolio effect' means that the regional industry portfolio has become more closely related to its incumbent industries, that is, the net effect of entry and exit results in a more coherent portfolio (assuming that the relative weight of incumbent industries is kept constant). The second term represents a selection effect. This term is positive if industries with standardized relatedness values higher than the value for the regional average (weighted technological cohesion) expand their employment shares relative to those with relatedness values lower than the regional average. The term is negative if less related industries expand market shares or if more related industries shrink. If industries do indeed benefit from their relatedness with other sectors in the metropolitan area, then selection would expected to be positive. The third term is a covariance term that is positive if industries for which the regional portfolio of industries has become more closely related also expand their market shares. From an evolutionary point of view, the selection effect is the most interesting and meaningful of the three incumbent effects and, as Table 4 illustrates, it is also the most important of the three incumbent effects to explain aggregate change in technological cohesion. The entry term is positive if entering industries are more closely related to the regional portfolio than average. The exit term is negative if industries more closely related to the regional portfolio than average exit the metropolitan area and positive if less

Table 4. *Components of change in employment-weighted metropolitan technological cohesion, 1977–1997*

Period		Change in metropolitan technological cohesion	'Portfolio'	Selection	Covariance	Entry	Exit
1977–1982	Δ	0.00525	0.00112	0.00256	0.00044	−0.00171	−0.00284
	%	(2.87)	(12.90)	(29.58)	(5.06)	(−19.73)	(−32.73)
1982–1987	Δ	0.00145	−0.00074	0.00165	0.00006	−0.00155	−0.00202
	%	(0.77)	(−12.23)	(27.49)	(1.05)	(−25.69)	(−33.54)
1988–1992	Δ	0.00325	−0.00119	0.00399	−0.00013	−0.00124	−0.00182
	%	(1.69)	(−14.20)	(47.63)	(−1.60)	(−14.80)	(−21.77)
1992–1997	Δ	0.00543	0.00112	0.00501	−0.00030	−0.00302	−0.00262
	%	(2.78)	(9.31)	(41.52)	(−2.47)	(−25.01)	(−21.69)

Note: Percentages for aggregate change represent rates of change for each period. Percentages for the individual components refer to the share of each component in the sum of the absolute values of each component.

closely related industries exit the industry (the exit of less related industries increases metropolitan technological cohesion).

Table 4 depicts the average contributions of each component to average change in metropolitan technological cohesion for each of the four periods. The percentages (in parentheses) are based on the share of each component on the sum of the absolute values of the five components.

The employment-weighted technological cohesion measure increased during all periods and growth was most pronounced in the periods 1977–1982 (2.87%) and 1992–1997 (2.78%). Although entry and exit contribute significantly to aggregate changes in technological cohesion in all periods (in particular up to the mid-1980s), selection effects are not negligible and selection was the most important effect from 1988 onwards. It is also noticeable that entry reduces technological cohesion, although the net effect of entry and exit results in an increase in cohesion save for the period 1992–1997. While industry entry and exit are important for shaping metropolitan technological cohesion, the decomposition analysis also demonstrates that selection operating on incumbent industries constitutes an important evolutionary force, at least in the short and medium run. The analysis also demonstrates that high contributions of selection and exit results in increasing employment concentrations in related industries.

CONCLUSION

This paper contributes to the conceptual and empirical development in evolutionary economic geography focusing on the emergence and path-dependent trajectory of technological and industrial variety (BOSCHMA and FRENKEN, 2006; BOSCHMA and MARTIN, 2010; ESSLETZBICHLER and RIGBY, 2010; ESSLETZBICHLER, 2012). More specifically, it complements and augments the literature on relatedness and the conceptualization of regional evolution as industrial branching process (FRENKEN and BOSCHMA, 2007; NEFFKE et al., 2011a). Rather than measuring relatedness through co-occurrence or exploiting information embedded in industry hierarchies, this paper attempted to corroborate the general findings of this literature with a relatedness measure based on the relative strength of input–output relations (FAN and LANG, 2000). One of the shortcomings of using a different relatedness measure is the inability to identify the sources of similarities and differences in results as they could arise from the properties of the respective relatedness measures or from differences in economic–geographic context (for example, differences in subsidies to keep unproductive industries alive, research and development (R&D) programmes to search actively for and attract new industries to a region, etc.).

Despite the differences in measurement and context, this paper confirms broadly the results of NEFFKE et al.'s (2011a) analysis of the Swedish manufacturing sector. First, the probabilities of metropolitan industry portfolio membership and entry to the portfolio are positively related to the closeness of those industries to their respective metropolitan industry portfolios, while exit probabilities increase with declining closeness to the metropolitan portfolio. Second, the average number of links of entrants and exits is smaller than the average number of links among metropolitan portfolio members. Thus, while entrants add technological variety and decrease technological cohesion, exits reduce technological variety and increase technological cohesion in a metropolitan area. Third, as a result of the combined entry and exit effects and despite considerable industry turnover, metropolitan technological cohesion remains relatively stable over time. While those results are broadly confirmed, the relative impact of relatedness on the probabilities of membership, entry and exit differs between the Swedish and US case. More systematic comparative research is necessary to examine the origin of those differences.

In a second step, the paper then examined the impact of different forces behind changes in technological cohesion including selection, entry and exit. For this purpose, an employment-weighted measure of technological cohesion was developed where not only relatedness, but also the relative size of sectors was taken into consideration. Changes in employment-weighted cohesion could then be decomposed into selection, entry and exit effects. While the entry/exit dynamic explains in part the evolution of metropolitan technological cohesion, selection effects are equally important in the US case. Cities become more cohesive because the positive effect of exit on technological cohesion is larger than the negative effect of entry and because those industries that are more closely related to the metropolitan industry portfolio expand their employment shares relative to those that are not. Because of the variety-reducing effects of selection and exit, entry is essential to inject novelty in metropolitan areas. The decomposition analysis demonstrates the importance of employment reallocation to related incumbent industries and the importance of entry to lower technological cohesion, but it does not answer the question whether technological cohesion, changes in cohesion or the contribution of individual components result in faster economic transformation or metropolitan growth.

The results point to a number of future research questions with important policy implications. First, while it is interesting to uncover the roots of path-dependent evolution in metropolitan areas, it is important to examine how the technological cohesion of metropolitan areas is linked to their performance including changes in employment and unemployment rates, productivity and output growth or the pace of technological change. Are regions that are more/less technologically cohesive expanding their market shares relative to those that are not?

Second, detailed historical industry case studies could help to examine the trajectories of individual metropolitan areas over time as performance is likely linked to particular metropolitan industry specializations (see also HIDALGO et al., 2007; POTTER and WATTS, 2012). Are areas with industries occupying central locations in product space more likely to diversify into new industries and, hence, rejuvenate their economies? Are those areas with industries occupying peripheral parts of the product space more likely to become locked into a declining regional trajectory and/or have less potential to create new evolutionary pathways?

Third, a more careful analysis of the components of change for individual metropolitan areas may help identify the main bottlenecks for future economic development. If incumbent industries dominate a metropolitan area, selection pressures may result in negative lock-in, while too much entry may result in technological incoherence and lack of knowledge spillovers between individual sectors.

Fourth, the focus on branching into related industries paints a picture of gradual metropolitan evolution. However, cities often go through phases of rapid transformation and surges of economic growth that are difficult to reconcile with this image of gradual change. Hence, the identification of threshold effects or minimum levels of relatedness could prove important

for regional path creation and needs to be investigated in future papers on regional evolution. Future work also requires an explicit analysis of the time frame over which change is measured as radical technological breakthrough will occur necessarily in one place or another over longer time frames. It certainly will require new methodological work as existing industry, product or skill classifications will be unable to shed light on radically new industries, products or skills not yet defined as such. Work also needs to take into consideration the fact that relatedness measures are based on actually observed and already-made links, but that they do exclude industry complementarities that are not yet exploited and hence detectable with those measures.[11]

In this sense, the analysis presented in this paper complements and adds to the rapidly growing theoretical and empirical literature in evolutionary economic geography on the role of relatedness for the creative destruction of regional and metropolitan economies. It points towards the need for theoretical refinement and systematic comparative empirical work to understand the influence of different relatedness measures, time frames and geographic context on the empirical findings.

Acknowledgement – The author would like to thank the three independent reviewers for their critical engagement with an earlier version of this paper and for excellent suggestions to improve it.

APPENDIX A

Table A1. *Logistic regression analysis of the probabilities of membership, entry and exit*

Dependent variables →	Membership			Entry			Exit		
Model	1a	1b	1c	2a	2b	2c	3a	3b	3c
Closeness (PF)	0.036*	0.011*	0.019*	0.022*	0.011*	0.017*	−0.017*	−0.005*	−0.008*
	(0.000)	(0.000)	(0.000)	(0.000)	(0.000)	(0.000)	(0.000)	(0.000)	(0.000)
	[1.037]	[1.011]	[1.019]	[1.023]	[1.011]	[1.017]	[0.983]	[0.995]	[0.992]
$\log_{10}[emp(r)]$		1.610*	1.133*		0.737*	0.416*		−0.880*	−0.697*
		(0.000)	(0.000)		(0.000)	(0.000)		(0.000)	(0.000)
		[5.002]	[3.105]		[2.089]	[1.516]		[0.415]	[0.498]
$\log_{10}[emp(i)]$		1.563*	1.758*		0.992*	1.132*		−0.904*	−1.005*
		(0.000)	(0.000)		(0.000)	(0.000)		(0.000)	(0.000)
		[4.772]	[5.801]		[2.697]	[3.102]		[0.404]	[0.366]
Closeness (non-PF)			−0.007*			−0.005*			0.003*
			(0.000)			(0.000)			(0.000)
			[0.993]			[0.995]			[1.003]
Constant	−2.024*	−15.086*	−13.746*	−3.006*	−10.124*	−9.261*	−1.013*	6.496*	6.084*
	(0.000)	(0.000)	(0.000)	(0.000)	(0.000)	(0.000)	(0.000)	(0.000)	(0.000)
Log-likelihood	−278651.23	−251027.0	−248271.8	−100541.6	−97774.6	−97345.9	−65482.8	−63500.6	−63362.3
Number of observations	521280	521280	521280	356454	356454	356454	164826	164826	164826

Note: Robust errors are shown in parentheses; and odds ratios are shown in brackets. Independent variables: *Closeness (PF)* = number of closely related industries in the region; $\log_{10}[emp(r)]$ = logarithm (base 10) of total manufacturing employment in a metropolitan area; $\log_{10}[emp(i)]$ = logarithm (base 10) of total US employment in the industry; and *Closeness (non-PF)* = number of closely related industries absent from regions. Dependent variables: *Membership* = 1 if an industry is found in the regional portfolio in year *t*; *Entry* = 1 if an industry is found in the regional portfolio in year *t* + 5 but not year *t*; *Exit* = 1 if an industry is found in the regional portfolio in year *t* but not in year *t* + 5. *t* = 1977, 1982, 1988 and 1992. The year 1988 was chosen as the starting year for period 3 in order to avoid any remaining inconsistencies from changes in industry classifications between 1987 and 1988. However, using 1987 instead of 1988 did not alter the conclusions of the results. Industries are considered related if $IOR_{ij} \geq 0.024$, such that the top 25% of industry pairs are considered to be related.

NOTES

1. SIC = Standard Industry Classification.
2. Exploring the existence of critical threshold effects to generate rapid regional transformations would be an interesting study of research and could point towards regional evolution as punctuated equilibria rather than gradual change.
3. As one of the reviewers pointed out, this paper contributes a novel empirical analysis to the existing set of studies on industrial branching, but is unable to offer a clear conclusion on the origin of diverging results from other studies as not only the measure of relatedness, but also the geographic and temporal contexts vary.
4. In this analysis industry relatedness is held constant over the whole period to facilitate the component-of-change analysis. Treating relatedness as a dynamic concept is left for future investigation.
5. For a complete list and definition of metropolitan areas, see http://www.census.gov/population/metro/data/

metrodef.html/. Metropolitan areas in Alaska, Hawaii and Puerto Rico were excluded from the analysis.
6. See http://www.nber.org/nberces/.
7. Substituting these relatedness values with the original IOR_{ij} values or a threshold value of 0.024, the 75th percentile, does not produce qualitatively different results from those presented here. The logistic regression results are presented in Table A1 in Appendix A.
8. The year 1988 rather than 1987 was chosen as the starting year of the third period in order to eliminate a potential impact of the industry reclassification on entry and exit rates.
9. Experiments with one-year periods did not alter the conclusions of the results.
10. This was addressed through the inclusion of metropolitan size as an independent variable in the regression analysis presented in Table 3.
11. The author thanks one of the reviewers who pointed this out as this is an important methodological question that will need addressing especially when examining change over long time frames.

REFERENCES

BALDWIN J. (1998) *The Dynamics of Industrial Competition. A North American Perspective.* Cambridge University Press, Cambridge.
BATHELT H., MALMBERG A. and MASKELL P. (2004) Clusters and knowledge: local buzz, global pipelines and the process of knowledge creation, *Progress in Human Geography* **28**, 31–56.
BEAUDRY C. and SCHIFFAUEROVA A. (2009) Who's right, Marshall or Jacobs? The localization versus urbanization debate, *Research Policy* **38**, 318–337.
BOSCHMA R., ERIKSSON R. and LINDGREN U. (2009) How does labour mobility affect the performance of plants? The importance of relatedness and geographical proximity, *Journal of Economic Geography* **9**, 169–190.
BOSCHMA R. and FRENKEN K. (2006) Why is economic geography not an evolutionary science? Towards and evolutionary economic geography, *Journal of Economic Geography* **6**, 273–302.
BOSCHMA R. and FRENKEN K. (2011) *Technological Relatedness and Regional Branching.* Working Paper Series Number 09.07, Papers in Evolutionary Economic Geography. Utrecht University, Utrecht.
BOSCHMA R. and IAMMARINO S. (2009) Related variety, trade linkages and regional growth, *Economic Geography* **85**, 289–311.
BOSCHMA R. and MARTIN R. (Eds) (2010) *The Handbook of Evolutionary Economic Geography.* Edward Elgar, Cheltenham.
BOSCHMA R., MINONDO A. and NAVARRO M. (2012) Related variety and regional growth in Spain, *Papers in Regional Science* **91**, 241–256.
BOSCHMA R., MINONDO A. and NAVARRO M. (2013) The emergence of new industries at the regional level in Spain: a proximity approach based on product relatedness, *Economic Geography* **89**, 29–51.
BOSCHMA R. and WENTING R. (2007) The spatial evolution of the british automobile industry. Does location matter?, *Industrial and Corporate Change* **16**, 213–238.
BRESCHI S., LISSONI F. and MALERBA F. (2003) Knowledge-relatedness in firm technological diversification, *Research Policy* **32**, 69–87.
DAVIS S., HALTIWANGER J. and SCHUH S. (1996) *Job Creation and Destruction.* MIT Press, Boston, MA.
DE GROOT H. L. F., POOT J. and SMIT M. J. (2009) Agglomeration externalities, innovation and regional growth: theoretical perspectives and meta-analysis, in CAPELLO R. and NIJKAMP P. (Eds) *Handbook of Regional Growth and Development Theories*, pp. 256–281. Edward Elgar, Northampton, MA.
DUMAIS G., ELLISON G. and GLAESER E. (1997) *Geographic Concentration as Dynamic Process.* NBER Working Paper Number 6270. National Bureau of Economic Research (NBER), Cambridge, MA.
DUNNE T., ROBERTS M. and SAMUELSON L. (1988) Patterns of firm entry and exit in U.S. manufacturing industries, *Rand Journal of Economics* **19**, 495–515.
DURANTON G. and PUGA D. (2001) Nursery cities: urban diversity, process innovation, and the life cycle of products, *American Economic Review* **91**, 1454–1477.
ESSLETZBICHLER J. (2004) The geography of job creation and destruction in the US manufacturing sector, 1967–1997, *Annals of the Association of American Geographers* **94**, 602–619.
ESSLETZBICHLER J. (2012) Generalized Darwinism, group selection and evolutionary economic geography, *Zeitschrift für Wirtschaftsgeographie* **56**, 129–146.
ESSLETZBICHLER J. and RIGBY D. L. (2002) The impact of industry mix, technological change, selection, and plant entry and exit on metropolitan labor productivity in the United States, *Urban Geography* **23**, 279–298.
ESSLETZBICHLER J. and RIGBY D. L. (2005) Competition, variety and the geography of technology evolution, *Tijdschrift voor Economische en Sociale Geografie* **95**, 48–62.

EVOLUTIONARY ECONOMIC GEOGRAPHY

ESSLETZBICHLER J. and RIGBY D. L. (2010) Generalized Darwinism and evolutionary economic geography, in BOSCHMA R. and MARTIN R. (Eds) *The Handbook of Evolutionary Economic Geography*, pp. 43–61. Edward Elgar, Cheltenham.

FAN J. P. H. and LANG L. H. P. (2000) The measurement of relatedness: an application to corporate diversification, *Journal of Business* **73**, 629–660.

FARJOUN M. (1994) Beyond industry boundaries: human expertise, diversification and resource related industry groups, *Organization Science* **5**, 185–199.

FESER E. (2003) What regions do rather than make: a proposed set of knowledge-based occupation clusters, *Urban Studies* **40**, 1937–1958.

FOSTER L., HALTIWANGER J. and KRIZAN C. (1998) *Aggregate Productivity Growth: Lessons from Microeconomic Evidence.* NBER Working Papers Number 6803. National Bureau of Economic Research (NBER), Cambridge, MA.

FRENKEN K. and BOSCHMA R. A. (2007) A theoretical framework for evolutionary economic geography: industrial dynamics and urban growth as a branching process, *Journal of Economic Geography* **7**, 635–649.

FRENKEN K., IZQUIERDO L. R. and ZEPPINI P. (2012) *Recombinant Innovation and Endogeneous Technological Transitions.* Working Paper Number 12.01. Eindhoven Centre for Innovation Studies, Eindhoven University of Technology, Eindhoven.

FRENKEN K., VAN OORT F. G. and VERBURG T. (2007) Related variety, unrelated variety and regional economic growth, *Regional Studies* **41**, 685–697.

GLAESER E., KALLAL H. D., SCHEINKMAN J. A. and SCHLEIFER A. (1992) Growth in cities, *Journal of Political Economy* **100**, 1126–1152.

GRABHER G. (1993) The weakness of strong ties – the lock-in of regional development in the Ruhr area, in GRABHER G. (Ed.) *The Embedded Firm*, pp. 255–277. Routledge, London.

HARTOG M., BOSCHMA R. and SOTARAUTA M. (2012) The impact of related variety on regional employment growth in Finland 1993–2006: high-tech versus medium/low-tech, *Industry and Innovation* **19**, 459–476.

HASSINK R. and SHIN D. H. (2005) Guest Editorial: The restructuring of old industrial areas in Europe and Asia, *Environment and Planning A* **37**, 635–356.

HAUSMANN R. and KLINGER B. (2007) *The Structure of the Product Space and the Evolution of Comparative Advantage.* Working Paper Number 146. Center for International Development, Harvard University, Cambridge, MA.

HENDERSON J. V., KUNCORO A. and TURNER M. (1995) Industrial development in cities, *Journal of Political Economy* **103**, 1067–1085.

HIDALGO C. A., KLINGER B., BARABASI A.-L. and HAUSMANN R. (2007) The product space conditions and the development of nations, *Science* **317**, 482–487.

ISSERMAN A. M. and WESTERVELT J. (2006) 1.5 million missing numbers: overcoming employment suppression in Country Business Patterns data, *International Regional Science Review* **29**, 311–335.

JACOBS J. (1969) *The Economy of Cities.* Vintage, New York, NY.

KLEPPER S. (2007) Disagreements, spinoffs, and the evolution of Detroit as the capital of the U.S. automobile industry, *Management Science* **53**, 616–631.

MARSHALL A. (1920) *The Principles of Economics*, 8th Edn. Macmillan, London.

MARTIN R. (2010) Rethinking regional path-dependence: beyond lock-in to evolution, *Economic Geography* **86**, 1–27.

MARTIN R. and SUNLEY P. (2006) Path dependence and regional economic evolution, *Journal of Economic Geography* **6**, 395–437.

NEFFKE F. and HENNING M. (2008) *Revealed Relatedness: Mapping Industry Space.* Working Paper Series Number 08.19. Papers in Evolutionary Economic Geography, Utrecht University, Utrecht.

NEFFKE F. and HENNING M. (2013) Skill relatedness and firm diversification, *Strategic Management Journal* **34**, 297–316.

NEFFKE F., HENNING M. and BOSCHMA R. (2011a) How do regions diversify over time? Industry relatedness and the development of new growth paths in regions, *Economic Geography* **87**, 237–265.

NEFFKE F., HENNING M., BOSCHMA R., LUNDQUIST K. J. and OLANDER L. O. (2011b) The dynamics of agglomeration externalities along the life cycle of industries, *Regional Studies* **45**, 49–65.

NOOTEBOOM B. (2000) *Learning and Innovation in Organizations and Economies.* Oxford University Press, Oxford.

POTTER A. and WATTS D. (2012) Revisiting Marshall's agglomeration economies: Technological relatedness and the evolution of the Sheffield metals cluster, *Regional Studies* doi: 10.1080/00343404.2012.667560.

QUATRARO F. (2010) Knowledge coherence, variety and economic growth: manufacturing evidence from Italian regions, *Research Policy* **39**, 1289–1302.

RIGBY D. L. (2012) *The Geography of Knowledge Relatedness and Technological Diversification in U.S. Cities.* Papers in Evolutionary Economic Geography (PEEG) Number 1218. Utrecht University, Utrecht.

RIGBY D. and ESSLETZBICHLER J. (2000) Impacts of industry mix, technological change, selection and plant entry/exit on regional productivity growth, *Regional Studies* **34**, 333–342.

RIGBY D. L. and ESSLETZBICHLER J. (2006) Technological variety, technological change and a variety of production techniques, *Journal of Economic Geography* **6**, 45–70.

ROSENTHAL S. and STRANGE W. (2004) Evidence on the nature and sources of agglomeration economies, in HENDERSON J. V. and THISSE J. F. (Eds) *Handbook of Regional and Urban Economics,* Vol. 4, pp. 2119–2171. Elsevier, New York, NY.

SCHUMPETER J. (1939) *Business Cycles.* McGraw-Hill, New York, NY.

STORPER M. and WALKER R. (1989) *The Capitalist Imperative.* Blackwell, New York, NY.

TÖDTLING F. and TRIPPL M. (2004) Like phoenix from the ashes: the renewal of clusters in old industrial areas, *Urban Studies* **41**, 1175–1195.

VON HIPPEL E. (1988) *Sources of Innovation.* Oxford University Press, Oxford.

Related Variety, Unrelated Variety and Technological Breakthroughs: An analysis of US State-Level Patenting

CAROLINA CASTALDI, KOEN FRENKEN and BART LOS

School of Innovation Sciences, Eindhoven University of Technology, the Netherlands.
Innovation Studies, Copernicus Institute of Sustainable Development, Utrecht University,
the Netherlands.
Faculty of Economics and Business, University of Groningen, the Netherlands.

CASTALDI C., FRENKEN K. and LOS B. Related variety, unrelated variety and technological breakthroughs: an analysis of US state-level patenting, *Regional Studies*. This paper investigates how variety affects the innovation output of a region. Borrowing arguments from theories of recombinant innovation, it is expected that related variety will enhance innovation as related technologies are more easily recombined into a new technology. However, it is also expected that unrelated variety enhances technological breakthroughs, since radical innovation often stems from connecting previously unrelated technologies opening up whole new functionalities and applications. Using patent data for US states in the period 1977–99 and associated citation data, evidence is found for both hypotheses. This study thus sheds a new and critical light on the related variety hypothesis in economic geography.

CASTALDI C., FRENKEN K. and LOS B. 相关多样性、非相关多样性与技术突破：美国州层级的专利授予分析，*区域研究*。本文探讨多样性如何影响一个区域的创意产出。本文借用重组式创新理论的主张，预期相关多样性将会增进创新，因为相关技术更容易重组成为新的技术。但本文同时预期，非相关多样性能够增进技术突破，因为突破性的创新经常源自于连结过去不相关的技术，并开启崭新的功能性与应用。本研究运用美国各州在1977年至1999年之间的专利数据和相关的引用数据，同时发现支持上述两项假说的证据。本研究因此对经济地理学中的相关多样性假说，提供了崭新且具批判性的洞见。

CASTALDI C., FRENKEN K. et LOS B. La variété reliée, la variété non reliée et les percées technologiques: une analyse de l'obtention de brevets au niveau des états aux É-U, *Regional Studies*. Cet article examine comment la variété influe sur l'innovation d'une région. S'appuyant sur les théories de l'innovation recombinante, on s'attend à ce que la variété reliée améliore l'innovation parce que l'on peut recombiner plus facilement les technologies reliées en nouvelle technologie. Cependant, on s'attend aussi à ce que la variété non reliée améliore les percées technologiques, étant donné que l'innovation radicale provient souvent du raccordement des technologies jusqu'alors sans rapport, ce qui offre des fonctionnalités et des applications tout nouvelles. À partir des données sur les brevets pour les états aux É-U pendant la période de 1977 à 1999 et des données de citation y associées, on a trouvé des preuves qui corroborent les deux hypothèses. Cette étude jette une lumière nouvelle et critique sur l'hypothèse de la variété reliée dans la géographie économique.

CASTALDI C., FRENKEN K. und LOS B. Verwandte Varietät, nichtverwandte Varietät und technologische Durchbrüche: eine Analyse der Patente auf US-Bundesstaatsebene, *Regional Studies*. In diesem Beitrag wird untersucht, wie sich Varietät auf die Innovationsleistung einer Region auswirkt. Unter Anlehnung an die Argumente der Theorien der rekombinanten Innovation gehen wir davon aus, dass verwandte Varietät die Innovation verbessert, da sich verwandte Technologien einfacher zu einer neuen Technologie kombinieren lassen. Allerdings gehen wir auch davon aus, dass nichtverwandte Varietät technologische

Durchbrüche verbessert, da radikale Innovation oft auf einer Kombination bisher nichtverwandter Technologien beruht, die völlig neue Funktionalitäten und Anwendungen ermöglicht. Anhand von Patentdaten für US-Bundesstaaten im Zeitraum von 1977 bis 1999 sowie mithilfe der zugehörigen Zitatdaten werden Belege für beide Hypothesen gefunden. Diese Studie lässt somit die Hypothese der verwandten Varietät in der Wirtschaftsgeografie in einem neuen und kritischen Licht erscheinen.

CASTALDI C., FRENKEN K. y LOS B. Variedad relacionada, variedad no relacionada y avances tecnológicos: un análisis de las patentes estatales en los Estados federales de EE.UU., *Regional Studies*. En este artículo investigamos qué efecto tiene la variedad en la capacidad innovadora de una región. Tomando prestados argumentos de teorías de la innovación recombinante, se prevé que la variedad relacionada aumente la innovación puesto que las tecnologías relacionadas se pueden volver a combinar más fácilmente en una nueva tecnología. Sin embargo, también se supone que con la variedad no relacionada aumenten los avances tecnológicos dado que la innovación radical muchas veces surge de combinar tecnologías no relacionadas previamente, descubriendo toda una serie de nuevas funcionalidades y aplicaciones. A partir de datos de patentes estatales de Estados Unidos durante el periodo de 1977 a 1999 y de datos de citación pertinentes, observamos evidencia de ambas hipótesis. Por consiguiente, este estudio aporta un enfoque nuevo y crítico a la hipótesis de la variedad relacionada en la geografía económica.

INTRODUCTION

Innovation is commonly held to be the key factor in regional development, underlying short-run productivity gains and long-run employment growth through new industry creation. Since innovation processes draw on knowledge that is often sourced locally (ALMEIDA and KOGUT, 1999; STUART and SORENSON, 2003; BRESCHI and LISSONI, 2009), regional development is essentially an endogenous process with strong path dependencies (IAMMARINO, 2005; RIGBY and ESSLETZBICHLER, 2006) akin to an evolutionary branching process (FRENKEN and BOSCHMA, 2007; NEFFKE et al., 2011).

In so far as knowledge is drawn from a variety of sectors, as in 'recombinant innovation' (WEITZMAN, 1998), the sectoral composition of a region will affect the rate and direction of technical change in regions (EJERMO, 2005). In this context, it has been argued that the more sectors are related, the more easily knowledge created in one sectoral context can be transferred to other sectoral contexts. Both NIGHTINGALE (1998) and NOOTEBOOM (2000) stress that decision-makers in firms have limited cognitive capabilities, limiting their abilities to identify potentially fruitful combinations of pieces of knowledge that seem unrelated to their existing knowledge bases and/or to each other. Hence, variety per se may not support innovation; rather it is 'related variety' (NOOTEBOOM, 2000; FRENKEN et al., 2007) that provides the basis for knowledge spillovers and recombinant innovation, spurring productivity and employment growth. The related variety hypothesis has motivated a large number of other empirical studies on the effect of related variety in sectoral composition on regional productivity and employment growth (ESSLETZBICHLER, 2007;

FRENKEN et al., 2007; BOSCHMA and IAMMARINO, 2009; BISHOP and GRIPAIOS, 2010; QUATRARO, 2010, 2011; ANTONIETTI and CAINELLI, 2011; BRACHERT et al., 2011; BOSCHMA et al., 2012; HARTOG et al., 2012; MAMELI et al., 2012). Results tend to show that related variety indeed supports productivity and employment growth at the regional level, though some studies suggest that the effects are sector-specific (BISHOP and GRIPAIOS, 2010; MAMELI et al., 2012).

In putting forward their hypothesis on related variety, FRENKEN et al. (2007) associated related variety as being supportive of knowledge spillovers and recombinant innovation, which in turn would support regional growth, particularly employment growth. In their analysis of the impact of related variety, however, they did not provide direct evidence on the relationship between related variety and innovation processes as such. Hence, the question remains open whether related variety supports innovation (TAVASSOLI and CARBONARA, 2014).[1] The present paper aims to develop further the notion of related variety and its effect on innovation. It does so within a theoretical framework that explicitly distinguishes between related and unrelated variety and predicts differential effects of the two types of variety on innovation processes. The authors take issue with the notion that related variety supports all kinds of innovation. Instead, it is argued that related variety is supportive of the bulk of innovations that incrementally build on established cognitive structures across 'related' technologies, while unrelated variety provides the building blocks for technological 'breakthroughs' stemming from combinations across unrelated knowledge domains. Since such radical innovations often stem from connecting previously unrelated technologies, these innovations lead to whole new functionalities and applications, and span new technological trajectories for their further improvement (Dosi 1982). As a result, the unrelated technologies lying at the root of the breakthrough innovations become more related over time.

This paper's new framework is not incompatible with the original related variety framework by FRENKEN *et al.* (2007), since related variety is still expected to support innovation in general. Hence, in so far innovations lead to employment growth, the original related variety hypothesis still holds. Additionally, it is also expected that unrelated variety supports breakthrough innovations. Potentially, breakthrough innovations may have much more impact on employment growth than innovations more generally, since whole new industries can emerge out of breakthrough innovations in the long run (SAVIOTTI and FRENKEN 2008). Nevertheless, the present additional hypothesis does not necessarily contradict previous findings that unrelated variety does not support employment growth, since earlier studies only analysed the short-term effect of variety on employment. What is more, the employment effects of technological breakthroughs need not be found in the region of origin, since the successful commercialization of a breakthrough technology may well take place in regions other than the region from which it originated (BOSCHMA 1997; MURMANN 2003).

Within this new theoretical framework, two hypotheses are tested. The first contends that related variety of the existing knowledge stock in a region enhances its overall innovation rate, while a high degree of unrelated variety does not have effects. The second states that unrelated variety of the regional knowledge base supports the rare breakthrough innovations, while related variety does not have such an effect.

A criterion based on the numbers of citations to a patent is used as included in subsequent patent documents (so-called forward citations) to operationalize the concepts of incremental innovation and breakthrough innovations (SILVERBERG and VERSPAGEN, 2007; CASTALDI and LOS, 2012). The dataset contains all utility patents granted by the US Patent and Trademark Office (USPTO) between 1977 and 1999, for which the first inventor resided in the United States. Information on the locations of first inventors is used to assign patents to US states. To construct variables regarding various types of variety of the regional knowledge base, technological classification schemes at different levels of aggregation were used, as designed by the USPTO. The actual construction of related- and unrelated variety variables is rooted in entropy statistics (FRENKEN *et al.*, 2007).

The results show a positive effect of related variety on regional innovation in general, and a positive effect of unrelated variety when looking at regions' capability to forge breakthrough innovations. This finding is shown to be robust for the inclusion of a spatially lagged research and development (R&D) variable, that is, the sum of R&D investments in neighbouring states.

The paper is structured as follows. The second section gives a brief overview of the theoretical concepts on the interplay of existing pieces of knowledge in recombinant innovation processes. The methods are introduced in the third section, which includes a discussion of the procedure adopted to distinguish between incremental innovations and breakthrough innovations. The fourth section shows how the numbers of produced breakthrough innovations vary across states and provides indications of differences in the variety of their knowledge bases, before testing the hypotheses using econometric estimation techniques. The fifth section concludes.

VARIETY, RECOMBINATION AND INNOVATION

Technological innovation is commonly understood to be a cumulative process in which most new artefacts are being invented by recombining existing technologies in a new manner (BASALLA, 1988; ARTHUR, 2007). The recombination is a novelty in itself, but could only emerge given the pre-existence of the technologies being recombined. As a recent and telling example, smart phones combine technologies related to batteries, chips, antennas, audio, video, display and the Internet. In this context, Schumpeter famously spoke of innovation as the bringing about of new combinations ('*Neue Kombinationen*'), an idea that continues to inspire evolutionary theorizing in economics (BECKER *et al.*, 2012). A more recent and very similar concept is that of 'recombinant innovation' defined as 'the way that old ideas can be reconfigured in new ways to make new ideas' (WEITZMAN, 1998, p. 333). This concept motivated new formal models of innovation within the evolutionary economics literature, including one on optimal variety in recombinant innovation (VAN DEN BERGH, 2008) and another on the role of recombinant innovation in technological transitions (FRENKEN *et al.*, 2012).

In a regional context, it follows from the notion of recombinant innovation that, to the extent that innovation processes draw on geographically localized knowledge, regions with a more diverse stock of knowledge would have a greater potential for innovation. This is in line with Jacobs' argument that cities hosting many different industries would experience more innovation as the exchange of knowledge by people with different backgrounds would lead to more new products and processes. As JACOBS (1969, p. 59) observed:

the greater the sheer numbers and varieties of divisions of labor already achieved in an economy, the greater the economy's inherent capacity for adding still more kinds of goods and services. Also the possibilities increase for combining the existing divisions of labor in new ways.

This mechanism was later labelled as Jacobs externalities, which refer to positive externalities arising from the co-location of different sectors (GLAESER *et al.*, 1992).

FRENKEN *et al.* (2007) added to Jacobs' argument that regions hosting related industries can more easily engage in recombinant innovation. Such related industries draw from different but not completely disconnected knowledge bases. In the words of FRENKEN *et al.* (2007, p. 687), related variety 'improves the opportunities to interact, copy, modify, and recombine ideas, practices and technologies across industries giving rise to Jacobs externalities'. One expects the related variety hypothesis to hold for innovation in general. However, it should be recognized that unrelated varieties can sometimes be combined successfully as well. Such innovations render pieces of knowledge that were previously unrelated to become related, in the form of an artefact or service exemplar that paves the way for future innovations to follow suit. Indeed, while recombinant innovation among previously unrelated domains is more likely to fail, such innovations, when successful, are also more likely to be of a radical nature as recombination across unrelated technologies can lead to complete new operational principles, functionalities and applications (FLEMING, 2001; SAVIOTTI and FRENKEN, 2008).

Turning to the regional level, one can expect regions with high levels of related variety to outperform regions with low levels of related variety in terms of the sheer number of inventions they produce. However, when it comes to breakthrough inventions, regions with high levels of unrelated variety are expected to outperform regions with low levels of unrelated variety. The following two hypotheses will guide the remainder of this study:

Hypothesis 1: Regional related variety is positively associated with regional inventive performance.

Hypothesis 2: Regional unrelated variety is positively associated with the regional ability to produce breakthrough inventions.

RESEARCH DESIGN

The hypotheses are tested using patent data. Their use to trace innovation is widespread and by now reasonably accepted. Patents have a number of attractive features with regard to the measurement and classification of inventive output. These particularly include the facts that formal novelty requirements have to be met to have a patent granted and that all patents are assigned to technological classes by independent and knowledgeable experts (SMITH, 2005). In a well-known early contribution to the literature, ACS *et al.* (1992) found evidence that patent counts are a noisy but useful indicator of innovative activity at the state level, by comparing patent counts to numbers of innovations identified in professional and trade journals.[2] Given that money

was invested in advertising these innovations, it is likely that these corresponded to patents with a perceived high value. A more debated issue is how to quantify success in producing breakthrough innovations in a systematic way. Can this also be attained using patent statistics? Recently, empirical research on innovation has offered a number of alternatives, all basically aimed at capturing the value of patents (VAN ZEEBROECK, 2011). Citations received by patents (forward citation numbers) are a common indicator for patent value, as suggested already by TRAJTENBERG (1990). Many researchers have measured breakthrough inventions by considering the top-cited patents in a given subpopulation (e.g., AHUJA and LAMPERT, 2001; SINGH and FLEMING, 2010). These subpopulations are often chosen as cohorts of patents in a technological field or subfield, to provide a fair comparison between patents of different age ('young' patents did not have much time to receive citations) and technological field (in the period of analysis, many more patents were granted in a category like Chemical than in Computers and Communications, as a consequence of which Chemical patents generally receive more citations than Computers and Communications patents (HALL *et al.*, 2002). This study uses a refined methodology proposed by CASTALDI and LOS (2012) to identify what they term 'superstar patents'. The basic idea behind this methodology is to derive endogenously the share of superstars in a subpopulation of patents by exploiting statistical properties of the frequency distribution of forward citation numbers, which are characterized by a fat tail. This approach is original, as most studies use exogenously fixed (identical across years and technologies) criteria to distinguish between breakthrough and regular innovations instead, by defining breakthroughs as the patents belonging to the top 5% or top 1% quantiles of the citations distributions.

The statistical properties that spurred the initial application of the method were highlighted by SILVERBERG and VERSPAGEN (2007). They showed that a lognormal distribution fits most of the forward citations distribution for patents quite well, except for the tail: the numbers of received citations of highly cited patents rather follow a Pareto distribution. This implies that there are a few patents for which the 'citations-generating' process is different. The technologies underlying such patents act as focusing devices for technological developments within new technological paradigms (DOSI, 1982). By estimating the number of citations needed by a patent to fall into the Pareto tail of the forward citations distribution, CASTALDI and LOS (2012) classify US patents registered at the USPTO as either superstars or not.[3] This estimation relies on a modified version of the estimation routine in SILVERBERG and VERSPAGEN (2007), based upon the so-called Hill estimator (for more details, see Appendix A). Additionally, it was ensured that only patents with the same application year and belonging to an identical technological subcategory were compared. USPTO patents have been classified by HALL *et al.* (2002) in six broad technological categories and 36 technological subcategories, each corresponding to 417 even more disaggregate patent classes (HALL *et al.*, 2002, pp. 41–42). The classification is part of the National Bureau of Economic Research (NBER) Patent Citation database and its updates and allows assigning each registered patent to one single category, one single subcategory and one single patent class.

For present purposes, the aim is to count patents and superstar patents across regions. US patents included in the NBER database can be assigned to the US state of the first inventor. The state will be the definition of a region in this study.[4] For each state and each year from 1976 to 1999, there are the number of total granted patents applied for in that year at the USPTO by inventors in that state and also estimates of how many of the total patents are superstar patents.[5] As the hypotheses relate to explaining regional innovative output, this paper works with two dependent variables for each state i:

- The total number of granted patents with application year t, as a proxy for the general innovation performance of a state ($NUMPATENTS_{it}$).
- The share of superstar patents in all patents of the state with application year t, as a proxy for the ability to produce breakthrough innovations ($SHARESUPER_{it}$).

It was chosen to consider shares of superstars rather than absolute numbers, since shares indicate something about the type of innovative activity: shares indicate revealed comparative (dis)advantages in breakthrough innovation.

CASTALDI and LOS (2012) analyse the geographical concentration of superstar patents across US states and find that the regional clustering of superstar patents is much higher than for non-superstar patents. Apparently, companies locate their search for breakthrough innovations in very specific places, while the production of regular innovations happens in many more places. Their descriptive results regarding this issue are in line with similar ones by EJERMO (2009) and indicate already that explaining regional performance in terms of breakthrough innovation requires different hypotheses than explaining regional innovative performance in more general terms.

The paper now turns to the explanatory variables. The key independent variables in the model will be measures of regional variety in innovative activity. Again, patent data are used, as patents indicate something about the technological fields in which states contribute innovations. In line with previous work, variety is measured with entropy indicators (GRUPP, 1990; FRENKEN, 2007). Entropy captures variety by measuring the 'uncertainty' of probability distributions. Let E_i stand for the event that a region is patenting in a

given technological field i; and let p_i be the probability of event E_i occurring, with $i = 1, \ldots, n$. The entropy level H is given by:

$$H = \sum_{i=1}^{n} p_i \ln\left(\frac{1}{p_i}\right) \quad (1)$$

with:

$$p_i \ln\left(\frac{1}{p_i}\right) = 0 \quad \text{if} \quad p_i = 0$$

The value of H is bounded from below by zero and has a maximum of $\ln(n)$. H is zero if $p_i = 1$ for a single value of i; and $p_i = 0$ for all other i. In the context of this study, such a situation would occur if a state were to have all its patents in a single patent class. If a patent were to be drawn from this state's patent portfolio, uncertainty about the patent class to which it belongs would be non-existent. The maximum value of $\ln(n)$ is attained if all p_i values are identical. In terms of the application, such a situation emerges if the shares of all patent classes in a state's patent portfolio are the same. If a patent were drawn at random from such a portfolio, the uncertainty about the patent class to which it belongs would be the largest.

Apart from its roots in information theory (THEIL, 1972), a very appealing feature of entropy statistics is that overall entropy can be decomposed in entropy measures at different levels of aggregation (FRENKEN, 2007). This allows one to construct variables that represent different levels of relatedness of variety in technological capabilities of states, as reflected in patent statistics. Assume that all events E_i ($i = 1, \ldots, n$) can be aggregated into a smaller number of sets of events $S_1, \ldots, S_G$ in such a way that each event exclusively falls in a single set S_g, where $g = 1, \ldots, G$. For the data, this corresponds to the situation that all 417 patent classes can be grouped into one of the 36 more aggregated technological subcategories constructed by HALL *et al.* (2002), or at an even higher level of aggregation to one of their six technological categories. The probability that event E_i in S_g occurs is obtained by summation:

$$P_g = \sum_{i \in S_g} p_i \quad (2)$$

The entropy at the level of sets of events is:

$$H_0 = \sum_{g=1}^{G} P_g \ln\left(\frac{1}{P_g}\right) \quad (3)$$

H_0 is called the 'between-group entropy'. Within the present context, it would give an indication of the extent to which a state has patents that are evenly distributed over broadly defined technological categories. The entropy decomposition theorem specifies the relationship between the between-group entropy H_0

at the level of sets and the entropy H at the level of events as defined in (1). As shown by THEIL (1972), one obtains:

$$H = H_0 + \sum_{g=1}^{G} P_g H_g \qquad (4)$$

The entropy at the level of events is thus equal to the entropy at the level of sets plus a weighted average of within-group entropy levels within the sets. For present purposes, (4) implies that one can consider technological variety at the lowest level of aggregation as the sum of technological variety within classes at a higher level of aggregation and variety between these classes.[6]

As mentioned above, the technological classification by HALL et al. (2002) is relied upon. Because CASTALDI and LOS (2012) focused on 31 subcategories (leaving out all patents in HALL et al.'s (2002) 'Miscellaneous' subcategories) in identifying superstar patents, one can only consider patents in six categories, 31 subcategories and 296 classes. Unrelated variety (UV) is measured as the entropy of the distribution of patents over one-digit categories, which states how diversified each state is across the six broad unrelated technological categories:

$$UV_{it} = \sum_{k=1}^{6} s_{k,it} \ln\left(\frac{1}{s_{k,it}}\right) \qquad (5)$$

where $s_{k,it}$ represents the share of patents in technological category k in all patents granted with the first inventor in state i and applied for in year t.

Next, semi-related variety (SRV) is defined as the weighted sum of two-digit entropies in each one-digit category. The decomposition theorem (4) implies that this is the difference between the entropy measure at the level of two-digit technological subcategories and UV itself:

$$SRV_{it} = \sum_{l=1}^{31} s_{l,it} \ln\left(\frac{1}{s_{l,it}}\right) - \sum_{k=1}^{6} s_{k,it} \ln\left(\frac{1}{s_{k,it}}\right) \qquad (6)$$

in which l indexes the technological subcategories.

Finally, related variety (RV) is the diversity of a state's patent portfolio at the most fine-grained classification. It is computed in a similar vein as SRV, but taking the difference between total entropy at the level of narrowly defined three-digit patent classes and two-digit technological subcategories:

$$RV_{it} = \sum_{m=1}^{296} s_{m,it} \ln\left(\frac{1}{s_{m,it}}\right) - \sum_{l=1}^{31} s_{l,it} \ln\left(\frac{1}{s_{l,it}}\right) \qquad (7)$$

The related variety and semi-related variety indicators measure the within-group variety components and

indicate how diversified a state is within the higher level categories.

It should be stressed that (semi-)related and unrelated variety are not opposites, but orthogonal in their meaning (FRENKEN et al., 2007). In principle, a state can be characterized by both high related and unrelated variety. These would be states that are diversified into unrelated technological categories while being diversified into many specific classes in each of these categories as well. Any other combination of above- and below-average levels of UV, SRV and RV is possible as well, at least theoretically, even if empirically related and unrelated variety tend to correlate positively (FRENKEN et al., 2007; QUATRARO, 2010, 2011; BOSCHMA et al., 2012; HARTOG et al., 2012).

Next to the entropy measures, one also takes into account each state's R&D expenditures (RD) as their key innovation input variable. R&D expenses give a measure of the scale of inventive efforts in each state. Historical R&D data are collected at the state level from NSF (2012). The figures cover total (company, federal and other) funds for industrial R&D performance by US state for the years 1963–98. Until 1995, data are available only for odd years since the R&D survey was administered every other year. The values for even years are estimated using linear interpolation. Next, the figures are expressed in constant 2005 US dollars using gross domestic product (GDP) deflators.

The observations are pooled across states and years and each of the two dependent variables is modelled as a function of one-year lag independent variables, namely the three entropy measures and R&D. The lag is there to account for the fact that inventive output is related to prior efforts, rather than happening simultaneously. These considerations are reflected in the two regression equations:

$$NUMPATENTS_{it} = \alpha^N + \beta_1^N UV_{i,t-1}$$
$$+ \beta_2^N SRV_{it-1} + \beta_3^N RV_{it-1}$$
$$+ \gamma^N RD_{it-1} + \delta^N \mathbf{d} + \varepsilon_{it} \qquad (8)$$

$$SHARESUPER_{it} = \alpha^S + \beta_1^S UV_{i,t-1}$$
$$+ \beta_2^S SRV_{it-1} + \beta_3^S RV_{it-1}$$
$$+ \gamma^S RD_{it-1} + \delta^S \mathbf{d} + \upsilon_{it} \qquad (9)$$

The vector $\mathbf{d}$ contains dummies to capture time-invariant state-specific effects and a variable to capture trends over time. Given that R&D data are available until 1998, the sample covers 51 US states for the years 1977–99. Missing values of the R&D variable (for a number of states these data are not available for periods of varying length) imply that there is a total of 877 observations.

The method relies on generalized linear model (GLM) regression methods to estimate (8) and (9). For

(8), a negative binomial model is estimated, given that NUMPATENTS is a count variable. For (9) a linear model can be estimated. Tests based on the model deviance (McCULLAGH and NELDER, 1989) are used to gauge the goodness of fit of the models and to compare the performance of nested models. Standardized coefficients are reported; for the case of the negative binomial model only the independent variables are standardized since the dependent one is a count.

RESULTS

Before turning to the tests of the hypotheses, it is important to give indications of the empirical importance of the differences being explained, and to give some ideas about statistical properties of the explanatory variables. Table 1 gives some descriptive statistics, computed over all 877 observations.

The output of patents (NUMPATENTS) varies strongly across states and years. In 1990, South Dakota only produced 12 patents, whereas California churned out as many as 15 404 in 1997. The average number of patents by state grew rather steadily from 567 in 1977 to 1169 in 1999. This modest growth in combination with the absence of wild swings implies that most of the variation in NUMPATENTS is in the 'across states' dimension. In 1977, the top-five patent producers in that year (California, New York, New Hampshire, Indiana and Pennsylvania) produced as much as 45% of all patents considered. In 1999, the share of the top five was also 45%, but the composition of the top five changed slightly (California, Texas, New York, Michigan and New Hampshire).

A lot of variation is also found with respect to the second dependent variable: the share of superstar patents in all patents (SHARESUPER). A substantial number of states almost never produce a superstar patent. Alaska, South Dakota, Wyoming and Nevada generated less than one superstar patent per year over the period 1977–99. At the other end of the spectrum, California managed to generate more than 11 500 superstar patents over this period. On average, California was not the state with the strongest specialization in the production of superstar patents,

however. Idaho and Minnesota averaged shares of 7.1% and 6.9%, while there are shares of 6.7%, 6.7% and 6.4% for California, New Mexico and Massachusetts, respectively.[7] At the bottom end are mainly found states that produced only a few patents in general, such as South Dakota (1.9%), Nevada (2.1%) and Arkansas (2.6%).

Unrelated variety (UV) remained relatively constant over time, at around 1.60. The maximum entropy for a situation with six technological categories is $\ln(6) = 1.79$, so 1.60 implies that most states had a very diversified patent production at this level of aggregation. In a few states, though, much less variety could be found. Alaska, Nevada and Wyoming are examples of states that did not generate many patents, and it could be expected that their patents could not cover the entire technological range to a substantial extent. The situation is different for Delaware and Idaho, however. These states produced as many as about 300 patents per year on average, but have average UV values of 1.30 and 1.39, respectively. Patents in Chemicals as a fraction of all patents over the period 1977–99 assigned to Delaware amounted for as much as 57% (mainly due to DuPont's activities), while patents in Electrical and Electronic accounted for almost 49% of all patents in Idaho (as a consequence of Micron's inventive capabilities). New York, Connecticut and Minnesota are the states with the highest average over years for UV, in the 1.74–1.75 range.

For SRV and RV, the maximum attainable values (given the numbers of technological subcategories and classes) are $\ln(31) - \ln(6) = 1.64$, and $\ln(296) - \ln(31) = 2.16$, respectively. As Table 1 reveals, the actual averages over states and years for these variables are 1.38 and 1.37. These averages were again relatively stable, with a slight decline in SRV over the last six to seven years of the period under investigation. The top three states in terms of average SRV were California (1.53), Colorado (1.50) and New York (1.49). New Hampshire is the prime example of a heavy producer of patents with little semi-related variety. With an average SRV of 1.29 it belongs to the bottom 15 of states, besides states that do not produce many patents, Delaware and Idaho. Turning to RV, a different top three is found: Indiana (1.83), Ohio (1.79) and

Table 1. Variables and descriptive statistics (N = 877)

Variable	Description	Minimum	Maximum	Mean	SD
NUMPATENTS	Total number of US Patent and Trademark Office (USPTO) patents applied in year t assigned to inventors located in the state	12	15 404	887.66	1402.37
SHARESUPER	Share (%) of superstar patents in total patents for year t and state i	0.00	12.21	4.34	1.95
UV	Entropy at the one–digit-level technological categories	0.79	1.78	1.61	0.13
SRV	Entropy at the two–digit-level subcategories minus entropy at the one-digit-level categories	0.61	1.64	1.38	0.14
RV	Entropy at the three–digit-level classes minus entropy at the two–digit-level subcategories	0.09	1.93	1.37	0.35
RD	Total research and development (R&D) expenditures (2005 US$, thousands)	2000	41 561 000	2 886 000	4 821 000

Michigan (1.75). Idaho (0.90), Rhode Island (0.98) and New Jersey (1.00) are examples of states that produce sizable numbers of patents, but with little related variety. These examples strengthen the impression conveyed by the last two columns of Table 1, which show that the coefficient of variation (standard deviation divided by mean) increases with the level of technological detail at which variety is measured.

R&D budgets went up over time. In the data, the average amount of R&D expenditures over states grew from about US$1.75 billion in 1977 to about US$3.75 billion in 1999 (all amounts converted to constant prices in 2005). The top five states in terms of average R&D funds were California (US$28.9 billion), Michigan (US$11.0 billion), New York (US$10.0 billion), New Jersey (US$8.7 billion) and Massachusetts (US$6.7 billion). States like Wyoming (US$0.014 billion), South Dakota (US$0.015 billion) and North Dakota (US$0.032 billion) appear at the bottom.

The previous section argued that the entropy decomposition theorem allows one to quantify UV, SRV and RV in a way that allows for complete statistical independence of these variety measures. Empirically, however, the entropy measures may still be correlated. Fig. 1 contains observations for all 51 states. The horizontal axis indicates the average value of UV over the entire period (including observations that had to be removed from the regression analysis as a consequence of missing data for RD), while the average values for states for RV are reflected by the vertical axis. The scatterplot shows that there is a clear positive relation between the two variables in line with previous findings (FRENKEN et al., 2007; QUATRARO, 2010, 2011; BOSCHMA et al., 2012; HARTOG et al., 2012). An increase of 0.1 in UV implies (on average) an increase of 0.22 in RV. This hardly changes if only the 30 states with the highest values of UV are taken into account (0.21). The explanatory power of a simple model of RV with UV and a constant intercept as independent variables is not extremely high, though ($R^2 = 0.58$).

Fig. 1 reveals some examples of states with similar average unrelated variety levels, but which had very different levels of related variety. Wyoming and Delaware are examples of such states with very low levels of UV, while Washington, DC, and Michigan show such differences in RV at higher levels of UV. An example from 1999 is illustrative. In that year, Iowa had an UV of 1.70 and Florida's UV amounted to 1.71, which indicates that these states were diversified to the same extent if the six technological categories are considered. Since the maximum attainable UV is 1.79, both states can be considered as having a fairly high degree of unrelated variety. Examining the 296 patent classes on which the RV variable is based, it is found that Florida had 1,999 patents in as many as 217 classes, whereas Iowa's patents were present in only 138 classes. Apparently, Iowa's patents were much more clustered in relatively few classes within the categories than Florida's, which is clearly reflected in the RVs for both states (Florida = 1.72, Iowa = 1.26).

The positive, but far from perfect, linear relationship between UV and RV, as depicted in Fig. 1, also shows up in Table 2, which gives the pairwise (Pearson) correlations between the variables that enter the regression equations (8) and (9). Table 2 indicates that positive relationships of about equal strength are also found for pairwise comparisons of UV and RV with SRV. Overall, the results indicate that almost all variables are weakly correlated with each other. The correlations for R&D clearly show that R&D efforts explain a large part of variation in total innovative output (NUMPATENTS), but have much less of an impact on the share of breakthrough innovations (SHARESUPER).

Table 3 reports the results of maximum likelihood estimates of the regression models (8) and (9). For each equation, three nested models are actually estimated. Model 1 is a baseline model including only the R&D variable and basically capturing the relation between R&D efforts as innovation inputs and patent counts as proxies for innovation outputs. Model 2 refines Model 1 by inserting state dummies and a time trend. Thereby one controls for state-specific fixed effects and a possible positive trend in the intensity of innovative activity. Finally, Model 3 is a complete model in which the entropy-based measures of variety are included. This last model allows one to test the two main hypotheses of this study.

For both equations, the Chi-square tests based on the difference of the models' deviance indicate that Model 2 significantly improves upon the goodness of fit of Model 1 and Model 3 significantly improves upon Model 2.

State-level inventive output measured by the total number of patents is positively related to R&D efforts in Model 1, as expected. When state dummies and a time trend are included, the significance of R&D vanishes. This is most probably due to the fact that R&D expenditures vary strongly in terms of levels across states and have grown rather steadily over time,

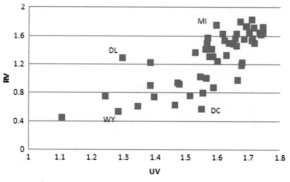

Fig. 1. Related variety (RV) versus unrelated variety (UV)
Note: Squares denote state averages for UV and RV over
1977–99

Table 2. Correlation analysis (N = 877)

	NUMPATENTS	SHARESUPER	RD_{t-1}	UV_{t-1}	SRV_{t-1}
SHARESUPER	0.286**				
RD_{t-1}	0.847**	0.251**			
UV_{t-1}	0.258**	0.238**	0.238**		
SRV_{t-1}	0.205**	−0.015	0.271**	0.429**	
RV_{t-1}	0.461**	0.144**	0.378**	0.571**	0.599**

Note: **Significant at 5%.

for virtually all states. As a result, the state dummies and the time trend already explain the major differences in R&D efforts and since state dummies and time trend are also strongly significantly related to patent performance, the residual effect of R&D is not significant.[8] Model 3 reveals a significant relation between total patents production NUMPATENTS and related variety RV, while the unrelated and semi-related variety variables UV and SRV are not significant. This evidence supports the first hypothesis that innovation in general benefits from diversification in related technologies.

If one looks at the estimates in the lower panel of Table 3, it can be seen that R&D is also strongly related to the shares of superstars in Model 1. The positive relation remains significant also in Models 2 and 3. Differences in the production of breakthroughs across states cannot be simply reduced to state-specific effects, such as size. The estimates for Model 3 indicate that both RD and UV help in explaining those differences. On average, states that are more specialized in breakthroughs are more diversified across unrelated technologies. The second hypothesis that states with higher unrelated variety would outperform states with

lower unrelated variety in terms of breakthrough innovation is thus confirmed. Semi-related variety is also found to be 'detrimental' for breakthroughs. If the recombination theory is applied, this would suggest that, conditional on a given level of unrelated variety, the more specialized the knowledge in selected subcategories within large technological categories, the more likely is recombination across categories. A lot of focused technological knowledge in diverse technology appears to enhance the specialization of states in producing relatively many breakthrough innovations. On the other hand, the semi-related variety measure is a measure that was included because of the properties of the data classification. Notice that the key results about related and unrelated variety remain valid even when leaving aside the semi-related variety measure in the model estimations (Model 4).

Regressions on spatial units of analysis can be subject to spatial dependence effects. To get an idea of the robustness of the results reported in Table 3, it was tested whether not only R&D efforts of the state itself but also of neighbouring states have played a role. An adjacency matrix was constructed where two states are defined as neighbours if they share a border. The

Table 3. Generalized linear model (GLM) regression results for the models explaining the total number of patents and the share of breakthrough innovations per state (standardized estimates)

	Model 1		Model 2		Model 3		Model 4	
	b	p-value	b	p-value	b	p-value	b	p-value
Dependent variable: NUMPATENTS								
RD_{t-1}	0.910	0.000	0.068	0.540	0.087	0.457	0.093	0.425
State dummies			Yes		Yes		Yes	
Time trend			0.301	0.000	0.298	0.000	0.303	0.000
UV_{t-1}					−0.084	0.330	−0.086	0.324
SRV_{t-1}					−0.046	0.529		
RV_{t-1}					0.325	0.022	0.322	0.023
Deviance	791		44		37		37	
d.f.	875		824		821		822	
Dependent variable: SHARESUPER								
RD_{t-1}	0.216	0.000	0.167	0.004	0.197	0.001	0.210	0.000
State dummies			Yes		Yes			
Time trend			0.378	0.000	0.334	0.000	0.345	0.000
UV_{t-1}					0.118	0.006	0.117	0.007
SRV_{t-1}					−0.103	0.005		
RV_{t-1}					0.085	0.233	0.078	0.275
Deviance	611		230		226		228	
d.f.	875		824		821		822	

Table 4. *Generalized linear model (GLM) regression results for the models including a spatial variable (R&D of neighbouring states). Coefficient estimates are standardized*

	Model 1		Model 2		Model 3		Model 4	
	b	p-value	b	p-value	b	p-value	b	p-value
Dependent variable: NUMPATENTS								
RD_{t-1}	0.820	0.000	0.084	0.511	0.101	0.455	0.109	0.421
$RDneighbours_{t-1}$			−0.014	0.904	0.005	0.964	0.013	0.914
State dummies			Yes		Yes		Yes	
Trend			0.281	0.000	0.272	0.000	0.273	0.000
UV_{t-1}					−0.061	0.522	−0.059	0.537
SRV_{t-1}					−0.046	0.576		
RV_{t-1}					0.309	0.065	0.311	0.063
Deviance	682		44		25		25	
d.f.	692		640		637		638	
Dependent variable: SHARESUPER								
RD_{t-1}	0.211	0.000	0.180	0.005	0.223	0.001	0.238	0.001
$RDneighbours_{t-1}$			0.061	0.263	0.048	0.379	0.064	0.379
State dummies			Yes		Yes		Yes	
Trend			0.342	0.000	0.290	0.000	0.293	0.000
UV_{t-1}					0.169	0.000	0.173	0.000
SRV_{t-1}					−0.095	0.014		
RV_{t-1}					0.023	0.774	0.027	0.736
Deviance	482		164		159		161	
d.f.	692		640		637		638	

variable *RDneighbors*, which equals the R&D efforts of all neighbouring states taken together, was then constructed. The results of the new estimates are reported in Table 4. The number of observations gets reduced to 693, since the missing values in the R&D variables translate into even more missing values for *RDneighbors*. The additional variable turns out to be not significant, while the other estimates do not change qualitatively, except for RV becoming marginally insignificant at 5% in the modified version of (8). All in all, the additional estimations are reassuring that spatial dependence effects are not relevant at the state level.

DISCUSSION

In many recent studies, empirical support has been established for positive relationships between the related variety present in a region and its economic performance. Implicitly, these studies assume that the two variables considered are linked to each other via innovation. Not much work has been done, however, on directly investigating the impact of technological variety on innovation performance. The theory of recombinant innovation provides a framework from which testable hypotheses in this respect can be derived. It was argued that breakthrough innovations will most likely depend on technological variety in a way that is different from innovation in general. To produce a breakthrough innovation, recombination of very different types of technological knowledge is needed, while more incremental innovation (along well-defined technological trajectories) would benefit

mainly from recombining knowledge about closely related topics.

This paper used patent data from the USPTO regarding inventions in US states and used statistical regularities in the numbers of citations that patents receive to distinguish between breakthrough innovations and more regular innovations. Having complete information on the classifications of these patents at three levels of technological aggregation, entropy statistics were used to construct variables reflecting unrelated variety, semi-related variety and related variety. By including these as independent variables in a regression framework, the hypotheses could be tested. It was found that a high degree of unrelated variety affects the share of breakthrough innovation in a state's total innovation output positively, while semi-related variety has a negative effect. As hypothesized, related variety does not influence breakthrough innovation, but has a clear positive effect on innovation output in general. The models include control variables, time trends and dummies to capture time-invariant state-specific effects. The results also appeared robust against inclusion of spatial effects.

A key conclusion from this study holds that the alleged opposition between related and unrelated variety can be misleading, since both types of variety can lead to innovation. Related variety would raise the likelihood of innovations in general, while unrelated variety would raise the likelihood of breakthrough innovations, which in itself are rare. It is precisely in this context that DESROCHERS and LEPPÄLÄ (2011, p. 859) proposed 'to consider the essence of innovation to be about making connections between previously unrelated things'. Following this reasoning, one can

EVOLUTIONARY ECONOMIC GEOGRAPHY

understand that the relatedness structure among technologies is evolving, albeit slowly, in a way that is driven by radical innovation that renders previously unrelated technologies to become related (Fig. 2).

The famous example of the car can help to illustrate the idea. In car technology various extant technologies were being recombined, notably engine technology, bicycle technology and carriage technology. These technologies were largely unrelated at the time the car technology was still in its infancy, but gradually became related through the development of the car. The reason why unrelated technologies can become related is that the new, recombinant technology provides a new context for extant technologies to be related, that is, to be recombined.

A dynamic view on related and unrelated variety would suggest a further research agenda on the topic. In particular, one would be interested to understand at what pace technological relatedness is indeed changing. Furthermore, one can investigate if recombinant innovations across unrelated technologies are indeed driving the fundamental changes in relatedness, and whether firms and regions pioneering such recombinant innovations also thrive economically in the long run. Indeed, further investigations in the mechanisms underlying the evolving nature of technological relatedness are considered to be among the most interesting and challenging research avenues for the future.

The new framework also has potential implications for regional policy initiatives. In particular, the role of variety in regional development is linked to the smart specialization strategy framework pursued by regions supported by the European Commission (FORAY *et al.*, 2009; MCCANN and ORTEGA-ARGILES, 2013). One important part of the smart specialization concept holds that regions should build on related variety to support regional development in the long run (FORAY, 2014). By combining knowledge and competences from related sectors or technologies, new activities can emerge in a continuous process of related diversification. Clearly, this is in line with past empirical research on the role of related sectoral variety on employment growth as well as the present study showing the role of related technological variety on patenting. However, this study also suggests that regions should also aim to exploit possible connections between sectors and technologies that are (currently)

unrelated in attempt to find innovations that would make them more related. A full discussion of policy instruments that can be helpful to exploit unrelated variety is, however, beyond the scope of the current paper.

It goes without saying that further studies are required to probe the validity of the findings regarding the differential effects of related variety and unrelated variety on the types of innovation processes they support. This can be done in at least four ways. First, future studies could replicate this study for regions in different countries. Second, given the limitations of patent data, one could attempt to test the theoretical framework by using other proxies for innovation, breakthrough innovation, and related and unrelated variety. Third, the links between variety and different types of innovation could be analysed at a lower level of geographical aggregation. As long as R&D data at the level of metropolitan statistical areas (MSAs) are not available, one would have to resort to alternative approaches that do not use knowledge production functions. Fourth, this type of research could be done for companies rather than for regions. If innovation is mainly seen as a firm-specific process in which externalities among regional clusters play a smaller role, the distinction between unrelated variety and related variety could be linked to TEECE's (1996) notion that different archetypes of companies are better at specific types of innovation than others. His 'multi-product integrated hierarchies', for example, will generally have firm-specific knowledge bases with a higher degree of unrelated variety than his 'high-flex Silicon Valley types'.

Acknowledgements – The authors thank the editors and anonymous referees for help in improving this paper. They also acknowledge the comments received at the Geography of Innovation Conference in Utrecht (January 2014), at the Science and Policy Research Unit (SPRU) research seminar series (March 2014), and at the European Regional Science Association (ERSA) conference in Palermo (August 2013).

APPENDIX A: USE OF HILL ESTIMATORS TO IDENTIFY SUPERSTAR PATENTS (BASED UPON CASTALDI AND LOS, 2012)

Empirical examination of patent data shows that Pareto distributions are superior at matching the observed frequency distributions in the right tail of the distribution of the 'value' of innovations (SCHERER *et al.*, 2000), also when the value is measured with the numbers of citations received by patents (SILVERBERG and VERSPAGEN, 2007).

To illustrate this with two technologies from the sample, Fig. A1 was generated by ordering all patents with application year 1976 assigned to subcategory 12 ('biotech'), according to the numbers of citations they received in the period 1976–2006 and similarly for subcategory 22 ('optics'). The numbers of citations are depicted along the horizontal axis. The numbers of

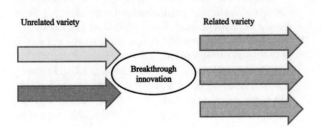

Fig. 2. Breakthrough innovation turning unrelated variety (UV) into related variety (RV)

73

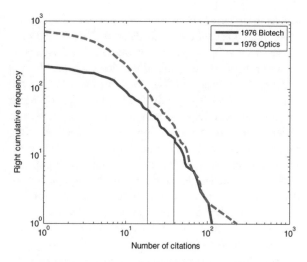

Fig. A1. Fat tails in numbers of forward citations
Source: Authors' computations on NBER Patent-Citations Datafile, citations received in 1976-2006. Estimated cutoff points between lognormal distributions and Pareto distributions (vertical lines) obtained by Drees-Kaufman-Lux procedure.

patents with an equal or higher number of citations than the value depicted on the horizontal axis are indicated along the vertical axis. Since both axes have a logarithmic scale, a Pareto distribution appears as a straight, downward sloping line. Exponential distributions (such as the lognormal) show curvature. For both technologies, a mixed distribution depicts indeed the observed frequencies in Fig. A1 more accurately than one type of distribution over the whole range. For less-cited patents, lognormal distributions fit the evermore steeply declining curves better. The rightmost parts of the curves are approximately linear, reflecting Pareto distributions.

Results from extreme value statistics (COLES, 2001) allow the numbers of citations that correspond to the cut-off point to be estimated. Given a comparable set of patents, i.e. applied in the same year and in the same technological field, CASTALDI and LOS (2012) call a patent a superstar patent if it received the cut-off point number of citations or more.

Following SILVERBERG and VERSPAGEN (2007), they estimate the cut-off point by using an estimator for the essential parameter of the Pareto distribution. If the tail follows this distribution $F(x) = 1 - x - \alpha$, a maximum likelihood estimator of the parameter α can be obtained using the Hill estimator (HILL, 1975). Given the rank-order statistics of the sample $X(1) \geq X(2) \geq \ldots \geq X(n)$, the Hill estimator of the inverse of α is obtained as:

$$\bar{\gamma} = \hat{\alpha}^{-1} = \left(\frac{1}{k}\right) \sum_{i=1}^{k} (\ln X_{(i)} - \ln X_{(k+1)})$$

Note that the parameter α reflects the magnitude of the negative slope of the straight line characterizing the Pareto distributions in Pareto-plots like Fig. A1.

The value of the Hill estimator is a function of k, the number of observations included in the tail. The slope parameter of the Pareto distribution is initially estimated for an extremely small subsample, which contains the most highly cited patents only. Next, the subsample is extended with the most cited patent that did not belong to the initial subsample and the Hill estimator is again computed. This procedure is repeated for a successively growing subsample of well-cited patents. As long as these growing subsamples remain drawn from a Pareto distribution indeed, the estimated slopes will remain relatively stable. This changes, however, as soon as patents are added that are well-cited, but belong to the lognormally distributed part of the set of patents. This can be easily visualized with the aid of a so-called Hill plot: the sequence of estimated slopes starts to show a saw-toothed pattern, and each added patent causes a swing in the estimated slopes. The Hill plot can be used to get an idea of the value at which the Hill estimates stabilizes. If the underlying distribution is Paretian, the Hill estimates will stabilize at a certain value. But if the distribution is not overall Paretian, including observations from the central part of the distribution will decrease the validity of the estimator. A method is then needed to estimate the 'optimal' value of the parameter k.

In the computationally convenient procedure adopted by DREES and KAUFMANN (1998), the length of the right tail is first set to one observation. Next, the most likely length is found by examining the fluctuations in the value of the Hill estimator when adding more observations to the tail. Such fluctuations emerge if Hill estimators are applied to distributions that are not Pareto. If a predetermined threshold value is exceeded by the fluctuation, an estimate for k is found. CASTALDI and LOS (2012) use a slightly modified version of this Drees–Kaufmann estimator, proposed by LUX (2001): in this version the stopping rule is modified with a higher threshold so that the tail includes fewer observations from the central part of the distribution.

NOTES

1. Actually, invention is the focus here since issues of successful commercialization are not addressed, but technological attainments are the sole focus. Throughout, the paper uses the terms 'innovation' and 'invention' interchangeably since the theory of recombinant innovation has been framed in terms of innovation rather than invention.

2. Subsequently, patent statistics have often served as a source of indicators for regional inventive activity (e.g. BOTTAZZI and PERI, 2003; FISCHER and VARGA, 2003; EJERMO, 2009). There are good arguments to study smaller geographical units than the state level. California, for example, contains a number of metropolitan areas (the Bay Area with San Francisco and Silicon Valley; the state capital Sacramento; and the Los Angeles agglomeration, among others). Most probably, these agglomerations are

geographically too distant from each other to allow for frequent knowledge spillovers (e.g., THOMPSON, 2006). Many other states, though, like Oregon, Illinois and Massachusetts, are dominated by a single large agglomeration. In such cases, the variety characteristics of the regional knowledge bases at the state level will be very similar to those of the dominant consolidated metropolitan statistical area (CMSA). In view of the fact that this analysis entails the estimation of augmented regional knowledge production functions, analyses for smaller geographical units cannot be done. Data on R&D expenditures, the most important inputs into knowledge production processes, are only available at the state and national levels.

3. An interesting alternative approach was chosen by DAHLIN and BEHRENS (2005). In identifying radical inventions in tennis racket technology, they focused not only on the numbers of citations the associated patents received, but also to what extent citations in these patents to prior art were dissimilar from existing patents. The identified patents were largely successfully confronted with expert opinions afterwards.

4. With state-level data, one can control for state-specific fixed effects such as institutions, including state regulations concerning products and the labour market. Compared with smaller spatial units of analysis, state-level analysis also has the advantage of having a substantial number of breakthrough innovations per state.

5. The original NBER Patent Citation database covers all patents granted at the USPTO in 1975–99. Bronwyn Hall updated the NBER database in 2002, and the NBER itself has published a new version with data until 2006. Since the latest update does not contain information about the location of inventors, the 2002 database is used.

6. As for the Herfindahl index, entropy values are biased for small numbers of patent counts (HALL, 2005).

7. The maximum SHARESUPER of 12.1% in the sample was recorded for New Mexico in 1992. Idaho (which produced a high number of superstar patents in semiconductor technology; CASTALDI and LOS, 2012) had an even higher SHARESUPER (16.4%) for 1992, but this observation could not be included in the sample since R&D data for this state were lacking for 1991–93.

8. Additional tests (available from the authors upon request) were performed by excluding the state dummies from the regressions. The two key hypotheses remain confirmed and the overall results do not change dramatically.

REFERENCES

ACS Z. J., AUDRETSCH D. B. and FELDMAN M. P. (1992) Real effects of academic research: comment, *American Economic Review* **82**, 363–367.

AHUJA G. and LAMPERT C. M. (2001) Entrepreneurship in the large corporation: a longitudinal study of how established firms create breakthrough inventions, *Strategic Management Journal* **22**, 521–543. doi:10.1002/smj.176

ALMEIDA P. and KOGUT B. (1999) Localisation of knowledge and the mobility of engineers in regional networks, *Management Science* **45**, 905–917. doi:10.1287/mnsc.45.7.905

ANTONIETTI R. and CAINELLI G. (2011) The role of spatial agglomeration in a structural model of innovation, productivity and export: a firm-level analysis, *Annals of Regional Science* **46**, 577–600. doi:10.1007/s00168-009-0359-7

ARTHUR W. B. (2007) The structure of invention, *Research Policy* **36**, 274–287. doi:10.1016/j.respol.2006.11.005

BASALLA G. (1988) *The Evolution of Technology*. Cambridge University Press, Cambridge.

BECKER M. C., KNUDSEN T. and SWEDBERG R. (2012) Schumpeter's theory of economic development: 100 years of development, *Journal of Evolutionary Economics* **22**, 917–933. doi:10.1007/s00191-012-0297-x

BISHOP P. and GRIPAIOS P. (2010) Spatial externalities, relatedness and sector employment growth in Great Britain, *Regional Studies* **44**, 443–454. doi:10.1080/00343400802508810

BOSCHMA R. A. (1997) New industries and windows of locational opportunity. A long-term analysis of Belgium, *Erdkunde* **51**, 12–22. doi:10.3112/erdkunde.1997.01.02

BOSCHMA R. A. and IAMMARINO S. (2009) Related variety, trade linkages and regional growth in Italy, *Economic Geography* **85**, 289–311. doi:10.1111/j.1944-8287.2009.01034.x

BOSCHMA R. A., MINONDO A. and NAVARRO M. (2012) Related variety and regional growth in Spain, *Papers in Regional Science* **91**, 241–256.

BOTTAZZI L. and PERI G. (2003) Innovation and spillovers in regions: evidence from European patent data, *European Economic Review* **47**, 687–710. doi:10.1016/S0014-2921(02)00307-0

BRACHERT M., KUBIS A. and TITZE M. (2011) *Related Variety, Unrelated Variety and Regional Functions: Identifying Sources of Regional Employment Growth in Germany from 2003 to 2008*. IWH-Diskussionspapiere No. 2011, 15. Halle Institute for Economic Research (IWH), Halle.

BRESCHI S. and LISSONI F. (2009) Mobility of skilled workers and co-invention networks: an anatomy of localized knowledge flows, *Journal of Economic Geography* **9**, 439–468. doi:10.1093/jeg/lbp008

CASTALDI C. and LOS B. (2012) Are new 'Silicon Valleys' emerging? The changing distribution of superstar patents across US states. Paper presented at the Danish Research Unit for Industrial Dynamics (DRUID) Summer Conference 2012.

COLES, S. (2001) *An Introduction to Statistical Modeling of Extreme Values*. Springer, London.

DAHLIN K. B. and BEHRENS D. M. (2005) When is an invention really radical?, *Research Policy* **34**, 717–737. doi:10.1016/j.respol.2005.03.009

DESROCHERS P. and LEPPÄLÄ S. (2011) Opening up the 'Jacobs spillovers' black box: local diversity, creativity and the processes underlying new combinations, *Journal of Economic Geography* **11**, 843–863. doi:10.1093/jeg/lbq028

DOSI G. (1982) Technological paradigms and technological trajectories, *Research Policy* **11**, 147–162. doi:10.1016/0048-7333(82)90016-6

DREES H. and KAUFMANN E. (1998) Selecting the optimal sample fraction in univariate extreme value estimation, *Stochastic Processes and their Applications* **75**, 149–172. doi:10.1016/S0304-4149(98)00017-9

EJERMO O. (2005) Technological diversity and Jacobs' externality hypothesis revisited, *Growth and Change* **36**, 167–195. doi:10.1111/j.1468-2257.2005.00273.x

EJERMO O. (2009) Regional innovation measured by patent data: does quality matter?, *Industry and Innovation* **16**, 141–165. doi:10.1080/13662710902764246

ESSLETZBICHLER J. (2007) Diversity, stability and regional growth in the United States 1975–2002, in FRENKEN K. (Ed.) *Applied Evolutionary Economics and Economic Geography*, pp. 203–229. Edward Edgar, Cheltenham.

FISCHER M. and VARGA A. (2003) Spatial knowledge spillovers and university research: evidence from Austria, *Annals of Regional Science* **37**, 303–322. doi:10.1007/s001680200115

FLEMING L. (2001) Recombinant uncertainty in technological space, *Management Science* **47**, 117–132. doi:10.1287/mnsc.47.1.117.10671

FORAY D. (2014) *Smart Specialisation*. Innovation for Growth (i4 g) Policy Brief No. 8. European Commission.

FORAY D., DAVID P. A. and HALL B. (2009) *Smart Specialisation – The Concept*. Knowledge Economists Policy Brief No. 9. European Commission.

FRENKEN K. (2007). Entropy statistics and information theory, in HANUSCH H. and PYKA A. (Eds) *The Elgar Companion to Neo-Schumpeterian Economics*, pp. 544–555. Edward Elgar, Cheltenham.

FRENKEN K. and BOSCHMA R. A. (2007) A theoretical framework for evolutionary economic geography: industrial dynamics and urban growth as a branching process, *Journal of Economic Geography* **7**, 635–649. doi:10.1093/jeg/lbm018

FRENKEN K., IZQUIERDO L. and ZEPPINI P. (2012) Branching innovation, recombinant innovation and endogenous technological transitions, *Environmental Innovation and Societal Transitions* **4**, 25–35. doi:10.1016/j.eist.2012.06.001

FRENKEN K., VAN OORT F. G. and VERBURG T. (2007) Related variety, unrelated variety and regional economic growth, *Regional Studies* **41**, 685–697. doi:10.1080/00343400601120296

GLAESER E., KALLAL H. D., SCHEINKMAN J. A. and SHLEIFER A. (1992) Growth in cities, *Journal of Political Economy* **100**, 1126–1152. doi:10.1086/261856

GRUPP H. (1990) The concept of entropy in scientometrics and innovation research. An indicator for institutional involvement in scientific and technological developments, *Scientometrics* **18**, 219–239. doi:10.1007/BF02017763

HALL B. H. (2005) A note on the bias in Herfindahl-type measures based on count data, *Revue d'Economie Industrielle* **110**, 149–156. doi:10.3406/rei.2005.3076

HALL B. H., JAFFE A. B. and TRAJTENBERG M. (2002) The NBER patent-citations data file: lessons, insights, and methodological tools, in JAFFE A. B. and TRAJTENBERG M. (Eds) *Patents, Citations & Innovations*, pp. 403–459. MIT Press, Cambridge, MA.

HARTOG M., BOSCHMA R. and SOTARAUTA M. (2012) The impact of related variety on regional employment growth in Finland 1993–2006: high-tech versus medium/low-tech, *Industry and Innovation* **19**, 459–476. doi:10.1080/13662716.2012.718874

HILL B. M. (1975) A simple general approach to inference about the tail of a distribution, *Annals of Statistics* **3**, 1163–1173. doi:10.1214/aos/1176343247

IAMMARINO S. (2005) An evolutionary integrated view of regional systems of innovation. Concepts, measures and historical perspectives, *European Planning Studies* **13**, 497–519. doi:10.1080/09654310500107084

JACOBS J. (1969) *The Economy of Cities*. Vintage, New York, NY.

LUX T. (2001) The limiting extremal behaviour of speculative returns: an analysis of intra-daily data from the Frankfurt Stock Exchange, *Applied Financial Economics* **11**, 299–315. doi:10.1080/096031001300138708

MAMELI F., IAMMARINO S. and BOSCHMA R. (2012) *Regional Variety and Employment Growth in Italian Labour Market Areas: Services Versus Manufacturing Industries*. Papers in Evolutionary Economic Geography No. 12.03. Utrecht University, Utrecht.

MCCANN P. and ORTEGA-ARGILES R. (2013) Transforming European regional policy: a results-driven agenda and smart specialization, *Oxford Review of Economic Policy* **29**, 405–431. doi:10.1093/oxrep/grt021

MCCULLAGH P. and NELDER J. A. (1989) *Generalized Linear Models*. Chapman & Hall, London.

MURMANN J. P. (2003) *Knowledge and Competitive Advantage. The Co-Evolution of Firms, Technology, and National Institutions*. Cambridge University Press, Cambridge.

NEFFKE F., HENNING M. and BOSCHMA R. (2011) How do regions diversify over time? Industry relatedness and the development of new growth paths in regions, *Economic Geography* **87**, 237–265. doi:10.1111/j.1944-8287.2011.01121.x

NIGHTINGALE P. (1998) A cognitive theory of innovation, *Research Policy* **27**, 689–709. doi:10.1016/S0048-7333(98)00078-X

NOOTEBOOM B. (2000) *Learning and Innovation in Organizations and Economies*. Oxford University Press, Oxford.

NSF (2012) *Industrial Research and Development Information System, Historical Data* (available at: http://www.nsf.gov/statistics/iris/excel-files/historical_tables/h-21.xls).

QUATRARO F. (2010) Knowledge coherence, variety and productivity growth: manufacturing evidence from Italian regions, *Research Policy* **39**, 1289–1302.

QUATRARO F. (2011) Knowledge structure and regional economic growth: the French case, in LIBECAP G. D. and HOSKINSON S. (Eds) *Entrepreneurship and Global Competitiveness in Regional Economies: Determinants and Policy Implications*, pp. 185–217. Emerald Group, Bingley.

RIGBY D. L. and ESSLETZBICHLER J. (2006) Technological variety, technological change and a geography of production techniques, *Journal of Economic Geography* **6**, 45–70. doi:10.1093/jeg/lbi015

SAVIOTTI P. P. and FRENKEN K. (2008) Trade variety and economic development of countries, *Journal of Evolutionary Economics* **18**, 201–218. doi:10.1007/s00191-007-0081-5

SCHERER F. M., HARHOFF D. and KUKIES J. (2000) Uncertainty and the size distribution of rewards from innovation, *Journal of Evolutionary Economics* **10**, 175–200. doi:10.1007/s001910050011

SILVERBERG G. and VERSPAGEN B. (2007) The size distribution of innovations revisited: an application of extreme value statistics to citation and value measures of patent significance, *Journal of Econometrics* **139**, 318–339. doi:10.1016/j.jeconom.2006.10.017

SINGH J. and FLEMING L. (2010) Lone inventors as sources of technological breakthroughs: myth or reality?, *Management Science* **56**, 41–56. doi:10.1287/mnsc.1090.1072

SMITH K. (2005) Measuring innovation, in FAGERBERG J., MOWERY D. C. and NELSON R. R. (Eds) *The Oxford Handbook of Innovation*, pp. 148–177. Oxford University Press, New York, NY.

STUART T. and SORENSON O. (2003) The geography of opportunity: spatial heterogeneity in founding rates and the performance of biotechnology firms, *Research Policy* **32**, 229–253. doi:10.1016/S0048-7333(02)00098-7

TAVASSOLI M. H. and CARBONARA N. (2014) The role of knowledge variety and intensity for regional innovation, *Small Business Economics*, 1–17.

TEECE J. D. (1996) Firm organization, industrial structure, and technological innovation, *Journal of Economic Behavior and Organization* **31**, 193–224. doi:10.1016/S0167-2681(96)00895-5

THEIL H. (1972) *Statistical Decomposition Analysis*. North-Holland, Amsterdam.

THOMPSON P. (2006) Patent citations and the geography of knowledge spillovers: evidence from inventor- and examiner-added citations, *Review of Economics and Statistics* **88**, 383–388. doi:10.1162/rest.88.2.383

TRAJTENBERG M. (1990) A penny for your quotes: patent citations and the value of innovations, *RAND Journal of Economics* **21**, 172–187. doi:10.2307/2555502

WEITZMAN M. L. (1998) Recombinant growth, *Quarterly Journal of Economics* **113**, 331–360. doi:10.1162/003355398555595

VAN DEN BERGH J. (2008) Optimal diversity: increasing returns versus recombinant innovation, *Journal of Economic Behavior and Organization* **68**, 565–580. doi:10.1016/j.jebo.2008.09.003

VAN ZEEBROECK N. (2011) The puzzle of patent value indicators, *Economics of Innovation and New Technology* **20**, 33–62. doi:10.1080/10438590903038256

The Role of External Linkages and Gatekeepers for the Renewal and Expansion of US Cities' Knowledge Base, 1990–2004

STEFANO BRESCHI and CAMILLA LENZI

Department of Management and Technology and CRIOS, Bocconi University, Milan, Italy.
Department of Architecture, Built Environment and Construction Engineering, Politecnico di Milano,
Piazza Leonardo da Vinci, Italy.

BRESCHI S. and LENZI C. The role of external linkages and gatekeepers for the renewal and expansion of US cities' knowledge base, 1990–2004, *Regional Studies*. This paper examines the role of external linkages and gatekeepers for the renewal and expansion of cities' knowledge base in US metropolitan co-invention networks. It is argued that the relative importance of direct external linkages and external relations mediated by gatekeepers varies according to specific local conditions. It is found that direct external relations, on average, contribute to broadening and rejuvenating the local knowledge base and outperform external links mediated by gatekeepers; the latter, however, are especially important in cities with a localized and specialized knowledge base, as they enable the trans-coding and absorption at the local level of externally sourced knowledge.

BRESCHI S. and LENZI C. 外部连结与把关人在美国城市知识基础的更新与扩张中的角色，1990 年至 2004 年，区域研究。本文检视美国大都会的共同创新网络中，城市知识基础更新与扩张的外部连结与把关人的角色。本文主张，直接的外部连结和把关人中介的外部关系的相对重要性，随着特定的在地条件而异。本研究发现，平均而言，直接外部关系导致在地知识基础的扩张与复苏，并胜过由把关人中介的外在连结；但把关人在具有在地化且专殊化的知识基础的城市中却特别重要，因为他们能将外来知识进行代码转换，并促进地方层级的吸收。

BRESCHI S. et LENZI C. Le rôle des liens externes et des gardiens quant au renouveau et à l'expansion de la base de connaissance des grandes villes aux E-U, de 1990 à 2004, *Regional Studies*. Cet article cherche à examiner le rôle dans les réseaux de coinvention métropolitains aux E-U des liens externes et des gardiens quant au renouveau et à l'expansion de la base de connaissance des grandes villes. On affirme que l'importance relative des liens externes directs et des relations externes facilités par des gardiens varient selon les conditions locales spécifiques. En moyenne, il s'avère que les relations externes contribuent à l'élargissement et au rajeunissement de la base de connaissance locale et font de meilleure figure que les liens externes facilités par des gardiens. Cependant, ces derniers revêtent une importance particulière dans les grandes villes dont la base de connaissance est localisée et spécialisée, parce qu'ils permettent de convertir et d'assimiler au niveau local la connaissance recherchée à l'extérieur.

BRESCHI S. und LENZI C. Die Rolle von externen Verknüpfungen und Gatekeepern für die Erneuerung und Erweiterung der Wissensbasis in Städten der USA, 1990–2004, *Regional Studies*. In diesem Beitrag wird die Rolle von externen Verknüpfungen und Gatekeepern für die Erneuerung und Erweiterung der Wissensbasis von Städten der USA in metropolitanen Netzwerken für gemeinsame Erfindungen untersucht. Wir argumentieren, dass die relative Wichtigkeit von direkten externen Verknüpfungen und von durch Gatekeeper vermittelten Außenbeziehungen je nach den spezifischen lokalen Bedingungen unterschiedlich ausfällt. Es stellt sich heraus, dass direkte Außenbeziehungen im Durchschnitt zur Erweiterung und Verjüngung der lokalen Wissensbasis beitragen und leistungsfähiger sind als durch Gatekeeper vermittelte externe Verknüpfungen; allerdings sind diese in Städten mit einer lokalisierten und spezialisierten Wissensbasis besonders wichtig, da sie die Transcodierung und Absorption auf der lokalen Ebene des extern beschafften Wissens ermöglichen.

BRESCHI S. y LENZI C. Papel de los vínculos externos y los guardianes para la renovación y la expansión de la base de conocimiento en las ciudades estadounidenses, 1990–2004, *Regional Studies*. En este artículo analizamos el papel de los vínculos externos y guardianes para la renovación y la expansión de la base de conocimiento en las ciudades estadounidenses en redes de coinvención metropolitana. Sostenemos que la importancia relativa de los vínculos externos directos y las relaciones externas mediadas por los guardianes varía en función de las condiciones locales específicas. Observamos que las relaciones externas directas contribuyen en general a ampliar y rejuvenecer la base de conocimiento local y superan a los vínculos externos mediados por los guardianes; sin embargo, estos últimos son especialmente importantes en las ciudades con una base de conocimiento localizada y especializada porque permiten la transcodificación y absorción en un ámbito local del conocimiento de origen externo.

INTRODUCTION

The role of social networks for the creation and spatial diffusion of scientific and technological knowledge has received a great deal of attention in the last decade. A rather wide consensus has emerged in the literature about the importance of social proximity within well-defined knowledge communities vis-à-vis spatial proximity to explain knowledge flows and their spatial reach (BOSCHMA, 2005; BRESCHI and LISSONI, 2001; CAPELLO, 2009). In addition, the debate on the most suitable network architecture to stimulate regional innovation has revealed the paramount importance not only of internal structural properties, but also of the embeddedness of local actors in broader networks (FLEMING *et al.*, 2007a; LOBO and STRUMSKY, 2008). Dense interactions at the local level (i.e. local buzz) combined with embeddedness in global knowledge networks (i.e. global pipelines) allow one to exploit the advantages deriving from trusted and repeated ties at the local level with non-redundant information deriving from external sources (BATHELT *et al.*, 2004; MORRISON *et al.*, 2013; STORPER and VENABLES, 2004), thereby leading to a superior innovative performance.

Building upon these insights, the most recent literature has thus focused on the roles played and the positions held by specific actors in local networks, by investigating their characteristics, attributes and performances. In this respect, *gatekeepers* have attracted much attention, especially in studies on industrial clusters, as they perform a crucial interfacing function between the local and the external knowledge systems, such as screening external sources, accessing them and conveying new knowledge to local actors (GIULIANI and BELL, 2005; GRAF, 2011; MUNARI *et al.*, 2012). However, most of the existing studies are small-scale investigations on single clusters, providing thus only limited evidence on the actual contribution of these actors to the overall innovative performance of the local contexts in which they are embedded.

This paper proposes an assessment of the importance of external relations and gatekeepers for inventive performance at the local level by introducing two important novelties with respect to the extant literature. At the conceptual level, it argues that external linkages, albeit important, are not all alike; rather, their value

and contribution to broadening and rejuvenating the local knowledge base can vary considerably according to specific local conditions. In particular, it distinguishes between direct external ties and external linkages mediated by gatekeepers and argues that gatekeepers play a more fundamental role in contexts characterized by a specific and localized knowledge base because of their ability to access, convey, trans-code external knowledge, and to make it accessible and meaningful to local actors. At the methodological level, the paper examines the impact of external linkages and gatekeepers by departing from the ego-network perspective, prevailing in the existing literature, which focuses on the attributes of single actors in the network and their performance. Rather, it aims at assessing the importance of connections to external sources of knowledge and the specific role of gatekeepers in a large-scale framework, by examining their impact on the inventiveness of the cities in which they are located. In other words, the paper analyses the meso-level outcomes, in terms of innovativeness, of micro-level knowledge exchanges among individuals. In so doing, it also provides a methodological contribution by explicitly modelling the structure of external relations and, accordingly, the channels through which external knowledge flows into a city.

The expectations are tested on a large data set of patents and their inventors in 196 US metropolitan statistical areas (MSAs) in the period 1990–2004.[1] The focus on urban settings particularly suits the study of the link between knowledge network structure and innovation, as invention in the United States has ever been and still is a predominantly metropolitan phenomenon (CARLINO *et al.*, 2007; FELLER, 1971; LAMOREAUX and SOKOLOFF, 2000; PRED, 1973).

The paper is structured as follows. The next section reviews the literature and elaborates the hypotheses to be tested. The paper then discusses the methodological issues related to the construction of appropriate indicators to capture the intensity of a city's external linkages and the identification of gatekeepers, and describes the data sources and the econometric framework. The results of the empirical analysis are then presented. The final section offers some concluding remarks and outlines directions for future research.

THE IMPORTANCE OF EXTERNAL LIN-KAGES AND GATEKEEPERS FOR THE RENEWAL AND EXPANSION OF CITIES' KNOWLEDGE BASE

The importance of external linkages as sources of innovation is a fertile research topic in management, innovation and regional studies. Broadly speaking, the recombination of diverse pieces of knowledge is at the heart of any knowledge creation and dynamics process (ANTONELLI, 1995; FLEMING, 2001; FLEMING and SORENSON, 2001; SAVIOTTI, 2007). Given the increasing complexity of technologies and knowledge, the creation of novel solutions relies increasingly upon the integration and recombination of different knowledge sources (BRESNAHAN et al., 2001; GITTELMAN, 2007; OWEN-SMITH and POWELL, 2004). Openness to external repositories of knowledge and embeddedness in knowledge networks reaching actors beyond local boundaries are therefore crucial and can provide some shelter to the risk of over-embeddedness, lock-in to obsolete sets of technologies and decrease in the variety of technological approaches and solutions by favouring a continuous expansion and rejuvenation of the existing knowledge base (UZZI, 1996, 1997).

At the regional level, the importance of connecting to spatially dispersed sources of knowledge has been emphasized in several studies. In particular, it has been pointed out that, given the highly localized nature of knowledge, knowledge exchanges among the same set of (co-located) actors may lose value over time as information becomes redundant and opportunities for recombination may fade out (BOSCHMA and FRENKEN, 2010). A disproportionate inward orientation in knowledge exchanges may crystallize the existing knowledge base and reduce technological heterogeneity and the potential for knowledge exploration and recombination, thus leading to decreases in creativity and possible losses of positions in the spatial ranking (BATHELT et al., 2004; GRAF, 2011; STORPER and VENABLES, 2004).

In this respect, the recent literature suggests that *gatekeepers* play a fundamental role as mediators of the knowledge exchanges between external and local actors (GIULIANI and BELL, 2005; MORRISON, 2008; MORRISON et al., 2013; MUNARI et al., 2012). Originally proposed by ALLEN and COHEN (1969) and ALLEN (1977), gatekeepers (also, and frequently interchangeably, termed 'boundary spanners') are individuals who guarantee access to external sources of knowledge by establishing unique linkages with outside actors and, more importantly, ensure knowledge absorption and diffusion within their proximate working and social environments. In the definition put forward by GOULD and FERNANDEZ (1989, p. 92), gatekeeping is a specific form of brokerage that corresponds to structural position in transaction networks in which 'an actor can selectively grant outsiders access to members of his

or her own group'. Likewise, in regional studies, gatekeepers are generally intended as individuals (and sometimes organizations) that enable knowledge transfer among different spatial units, i.e. industrial clusters, cities or regions (GIULIANI and BELL, 2005; GRAF, 2011; MORRISON et al., 2013).

Because of their key intermediation role, gatekeepers may be crucial to overcome any communication impedance that may occur in cross-boundary knowledge exchanges, regardless of how boundaries are defined (namely, in geographical, organizational or institutional terms). Knowledge and technologies, in fact, especially those related to specific artefacts, products and manufacturing processes tend to evolve in a cumulative, path-dependent and highly localized way, within defined technological, organizational and geographical spaces (ANTONELLI, 1995; BOSCHMA and FRENKEN, 2006; DOSI, 1982; FRENKEN and BOSCHMA, 2007). Specific coding schemes, standard concepts and technical jargons develop within and across firms located in a regional cluster (LISSONI, 2001). These *codebooks*, which are highly specific to the epistemic communities of engineers and technicians working in a given cluster, are instrumental to facilitate internal communication and information processing, but may also impose barriers to the exchange of knowledge across regional boundaries (COWAN et al., 2000). In other words, a highly localized and specialized knowledge base provides efficiency gains in internal knowledge exchanges within firms as well as within regions and clusters, whilst it may hinder cross-boundary exchanges due to mismatches in interpretation, cognitive mapping or, more simply, misunderstanding of contents (TUSHMAN and KATZ, 1980; TUSHMAN and SCANLAN, 1981). In this regard, gatekeepers not only may search for and collect relevant information outside their proximate professional and social environments, but also are able to trans-code this information and diffuse it within their organizations and geographical areas. In other terms, integrating the external knowledge into the local knowledge base requires the absorptive capacity to read the diverse external knowledge and create mental maps and codes to translate it at the local level. Gatekeepers are those best positioned to dispatch the externally sourced knowledge at the local level by framing, coding and separating it into pieces that can be easily understood, processed and used by others thanks to shared language and symbols. Differently, absent the intermediary role played by gatekeepers, individuals with 'the same specialized language and symbolic representations [...] will not be able to tap into diverse external knowledge sources even if the relevant pipelines are in place' (BATHELT et al., 2004, p. 45).

In order to perform this fundamental function, gatekeepers have to possess a number of key attributes, which distinguish them from other individuals. In general, they are more productive (BURT, 1992), more creative and capable to develop alternative solutions and original visions by framing problems from a different and fresh perspective (BURT, 2004; FLEMING et al., 2007b; HARGADON and SUTTON, 1997; OBSTFELD, 2005). Moreover, they also tend to occupy a highly central and influential position in the social structures in which they are embedded (FERNANDEZ and GOULD, 1994; PADGETT and ANSELL, 1993).

From the individual perspective, the uniqueness and importance of such gatekeeping positions do provide gatekeepers with competitive advantages with respect to other network members (BURT, 2008), which in turn can lead to higher (private) returns in terms of economic and innovative outcomes. However, the competitive advantages and superior performance of gatekeepers parallel their control power (and the relative rents they may accrue from) on the bridging ties and knowledge exchanges that they enable between internal and external actors (BURT, 2008; GOULD and FERNANDEZ, 1989). If social ties are channels for the exchange of knowledge or other resources, gatekeepers are therefore in the position to choose whether or not to grant access to information flows from outside. Whereas this power to restrict knowledge exchanges may have negligible effects on a single gatekeeper's performance (and possibly it may provide a sufficient basis for the generation of rents), it can have substantial impact when moving from the individual to the aggregate level of analysis, such as the firm or the regional one.

In fact, gatekeepers may not always be willing to share the valuable knowledge they source from outside with other actors nearby and frequently prefer to act as external stars rather than as true gatekeepers. Given their control power on external knowledge sources, gatekeepers can restrict strategically the diffusion and circulation of valuable knowledge. This is, for example, documented in the case of leading firms in industrial clusters that frequently play a significant role in facilitating the flow of outside information into the cluster (GIULIANI and BELL, 2005; MORRISON, 2008; MORRISON et al., 2013).

Moreover, gatekeepers may have trouble in managing and matching multiple external and internal connections due to increasing coordination costs, thus reducing the amount and efficiency of information flows (WHITTINGTON et al., 2009). Similarly, the larger the number of external sources managed by each gatekeeper, the more complex becomes to process, code, interpret and absorb information; too much information can be harmful by decreasing the efficiency of knowledge exchanges (DAHLANDER and FREDERIKSEN, 2012). More generally, social structures where external linkages (and the associated knowledge flows) are predominantly mediated by gatekeepers, are more exposed to the disruption of such links than social structures in which external ties are mostly direct, and possibly redundant. In addition to this, direct links could be generally preferable than indirect links as they allow faster knowledge diffusion (i.e. in a shorter number of steps), possibly with fewer knowledge leakages and risks of distortion of the message contents because of a lower number of intermediaries (TUSHMAN and SCANLAN, 1981).

In brief, though external ties look crucial for the renewal and expansion of the local knowledge base and, more generally, for innovation and creativity, the importance of gatekeepers for mediating the access to external sources of knowledge cannot be considered uncontroversial at an aggregate level of analysis such as the regional or urban one. On the one hand, direct external links may outperform gatekeeper-mediated links as they allow faster and less noisy access to external knowledge. On the other hand, gatekeepers are more open-minded, creative thinking, innovative and influential than other actors and, even more importantly, they perform the translation and trans-coding of external information, which may be necessary for successfully transfer and apply the externally sourced knowledge at the local level. Thus, under what conditions, are gatekeepers a more effective way to link local actors to external sources of knowledge?

As argued by TUSHMAN and KATZ (1980), the answer to this question depends on the nature of the tasks and activities performed and, accordingly, the characteristics of the knowledge base. In fact, similar problems may be approached with very different solutions, also by firms operating in the same industry, as a result of the evolution of the different knowledge bases and coding schemes (TUSHMAN and KATZ, 1980; TUSHMAN and SCANLAN, 1981). Therefore, communication impedance and barriers in knowledge exchanges and learning are likely to be more frequent the greater the insularity, localism and dissimilarity between the knowledge base of internal firms and external counterparts (LISSONI, 2001; COWAN et al., 2000). Especially in these contexts, gatekeepers can improve knowledge transfer by translating the external knowledge into meaningful and useful knowledge for local actors (GRAF, 2011). On the other hand, knowledge flows are less likely to find major impedance when trading partners share similar cognitive maps, notions and languages; in these case, the trans-coding role of gatekeepers is less valuable and single actors can rely on their own direct contacts to access external knowledge.

Therefore, although external ties are, on average, important to sustain the expansion and renewal of the existing knowledge base, they are not all alike but rather they may have different impact according to specific-context conditions, namely the nature of the local knowledge base. By extending the argument by TUSHMAN and KATZ (1980) into a spatial perspective, the role of gatekeepers is likely to be more important in regions and cities with a more *localized* and, thus, specialized knowledge base as gatekeepers can ensure the translation and circulation of external knowledge at the local level. Differently, regions and cities with a more *general* and diversified knowledge base are more likely to possess the coding schemes and technical languages needed to interpret external knowledge, having developed approaches and solutions more similar to externally located actors. In these cases, the trans-coding function of gatekeepers becomes less valuable and direct connections can be more efficient in accessing external knowledge in faster and a less noisy fashion.

Accordingly, it is posited that:

Hypothesis 1: The intensity of external linkages is positively associated with the renewal and expansion of the local knowledge base in a city.

Hypothesis 2: External linkages mediated by gatekeepers are relatively more important in cities with a localized and specialized knowledge base, whereas external direct connections play a more significant role in cities with a general and diversified knowledge base.

MEASURING EXTERNAL RELATIONS AND IDENTIFYING GATEKEEPERS

The use of patents as relational data has made amenable the study of the impact of social networks and personal interactions on innovation and creative processes through the tools of social network analysis and graph theory (BRESCHI and LISSONI, 2004, 2009; SINGH, 2005; TER WAL and BOSCHMA, 2009). In such a framework, the nodes of the network are inventors and the edges of the network link co-inventors listed on the same patent document, i.e. any two inventors are connected if they are designated together as inventors in one or more patent documents.

This study extracted data on all patent applications made by US organizations at the European Patent Office (EPO) in 1990–2004,[2] using the CRIOS-PATSTAT database. As the proper application of social network analysis techniques depends on the correct identification of individual inventors (i.e. nodes), their names and addresses were thoroughly cleaned and standardized.[3] The reported addresses were used to assign each inventor to one of the 370 US MSAs, using the definition files available on the US Census Bureau website.[4]

The basic assumption behind the use of patents as relational data is that co-invention ties work as pipes through which knowledge is transmitted. As the effectiveness with which a pipe performs this function is likely to decay with its age, the current practice was followed and a five-year moving window was adopted to construct the co-invention network (FLEMING *et al.*, 2007a; LOBO and STRUMSKY, 2008; SCHILLING and PHELPS, 2007). In other words, the network observed at any time *t* is built using the co-invention ties formed during the time period $[t-1, t-5]$ and excluding older ties. Adopting

different time windows did not substantively change the results.

To measure the extent to which metropolitan inventors are connected with inventors external to the city, the *average distance-weighted external reach* between inventors located in a given city and all other inventors located in all other cities was computed. This index captures the proximity between inventors in the global network. In particular, for an individual inventor *i*, it is defined as the sum of the reciprocal distances to all other inventors she can reach in the global US co-invention network.[5] Accordingly, the average distance-weighted external reach of city *c* is the distance-weighted external reach averaged across all inventors located in the city.

Formally, this index is defined as follows:

$$(\text{Average distance} - \text{weighted external reach})_c$$
$$= \frac{\sum_{i=1}^{n_c} \sum_{j=1}^{n_h} \frac{1}{d_{ij}}}{n_c}$$

where n_c denotes the number of inventors located in city *c*; n_h denotes the number of inventors located in other cities (i.e. not located in city *c*); and d_{ij} denotes the geodesic distance (i.e. shortest path) in the global co-invention network between inventor *i* (located in city *c*) and inventor *j* (not located in city *c*).[6]

The index takes a minimum value of 0 (i.e. all inventors in city *c* are not connected to any external inventor). In the (theoretical) case in which every inventor in city *c* directly collaborates with every other inventor in every other city (i.e. when every node is connected by a path length of one to all other nodes in the network), the numerator of the index takes value $(n_c n_h)$ and thus the theoretical maximum value of the index is n_h. Higher values of the external reach index imply that a city has faster access to a larger pool of external knowledge and resources.

This index shows several desirable features for modelling a city's external ties with respect to the measures used in previous studies, such as the number of co-inventors external to the city (FLEMING *et al.*, 2007a; LOBO and STRUMSKY, 2008) or centrality indexes (GIULIANI and BELL, 2005). First, it captures both a network's size and connectivity simultaneously, as both aspects matter in explaining knowledge flows across cities and their impact on a city's creative potential. Higher values of the external reach index imply that a city's inventors are socially close to many inventors located in other cities (i.e. they are separated by a low number of intermediaries) and thus have *faster* access to a *larger* pool of external knowledge and resources, with less noise. Second, it enables one to consider not only first-order ties (i.e. external inventors directly connected to a city's inventors because of joint patents), but also second-order and higher-order co-invention links, and thus the overall scope of a city's external ties. The amount of external knowledge that a city can reach is likely to depend not only on the number of external direct ties but also on the number of external indirect ties, though the value and impact of the knowledge received is also likely to decay with the social distance between sender and receiver (AHUJA, 2000). Third, contrary to other studies that adopt an ego-network approach and focus on the performance of individual actors, a meso-level perspective focusing on the overall network structural properties and their impact upon regional performance is adopted.

Following the discussion above, it was expected that external reach has a positive impact on the expansion and renewal of a city's knowledge base. Yet, given that the importance of external ties is likely to decay quite rapidly with the *social* distance among nodes, the external reach index was computed by considering only inventor pairs for which $d_{ij} \leq 4$ (BRESCHI and LISSONI, 2004; SINGH, 2005).[7] Fuller details on the computation of this index are available in the Appendix to this paper.

It is important to point out that external reach comprises different types of relationships between local and external inventors. In particular, external linkages can be either *direct*, whenever a local inventor is directly connected to an external inventor, or *indirect*, whenever a local inventor needs the intermediation of another co-localized inventor to reach external inventors.

In this second case, external reach is mediated by specific actors, i.e. gatekeepers, that occupy distinctive positions in the US global co-invention network by establishing bridges across cities. In this paper, the identification of gatekeepers is based on the work of GOULD and FERNANDEZ (1989), who elaborate on the original definition proposed by ALLEN (1977) and TUSHMAN and KATZ (1980). Accordingly, an inventor i located in city c is defined as a gatekeeper when the shortest path leading from any other inventor j in city c to any other inventor h in city d (different from c) passes through i.

In order to account for the importance of gatekeepers in mediating external linkages, the share of the overall distance weighted external reach, which is mediated by gatekeepers, is computed. This corresponds to how much the external reachability would decrease for local inventors, should one remove all gatekeepers from the city (BORGATTI, 2006; VALENTE and FUJIMOTO, 2010). Higher values of the index correspond to cities in which external linkages mostly rely upon gatekeepers. On the other hand, lower values of the index imply that most of the linkages with externally located inventors are direct and do not need any intermediation (i.e. removing the gatekeepers would not diminish substantially the external reachability).

The index shows some attractive features for capturing the importance of gatekeepers in mediating knowledge flows across cities. First, it refines and improves on

centrality-based indexes or ratios between internal and external linkages used in previous spatial analyses (GIULIANI and BELL, 2005; GRAF, 2011; MORRISON, 2008). In fact, these measures either do not define gatekeepers as the necessary and single bridge able to link actors in two different spatial units or neglect the inflation bias that may arise in co-invention networks due to inventors listed in the same patent document or both. More interestingly, it provides a measure of the relative contribution of direct versus indirect (i.e. gatekeeper-mediated) relations to the total external reach of a city and how much its external relations are robust to the removal of the links established by gatekeepers (i.e. how much gatekeepers control the flows of knowledge across cities).

Following the discussion above, it is expected that external reach mediated by gatekeepers has a positive effect on the expansion and renewal of the knowledge base in cities with a localized and specialized knowledge base.

DATA AND ESTIMATION FRAMEWORK

Dependent variable: definition and measurement

To account for the renewal and expansion of a city's knowledge base, information on the technological classification of patent documents is exploited. In fact, patents can be described as a bundle of different technologies, defined by the technological codes in which each patent is classified; accordingly, a city's knowledge base can be decomposed and portrayed through the technology fields, and their possible combinations, associated with the locally produced patents (STRUMSKY et al., 2012).

Following the conceptual discussion, the dependent variable is defined as the number of *new pairs of technological codes* introduced in a city at time t, in which either one or both technological codes are new to the city, i.e. no local patent before time t had been classified in one or both of those fields. It is worth stressing that, differently from other studies (e.g. FLEMING et al., 2007b), the new pairs of technological classes that are purely recombination of existing knowledge (i.e. technological classes) are excluded and a city's knowledge base is not expanded.[8] As shown in the next section, however, the results are robust to alternative measurements of the dependent variable. Importantly, this variable not only improves on measures such as the count of new combinations in a city, but also is preferable to other (simpler) indicators such as the number of patents introducing a new technical field or the simple count of the newly introduced codes, as it emphasizes the intrinsic recombinatorial nature of technical change and inventive processes (FLEMING, 2001; FLEMING et al., 2007b; KATILA and AHUJA, 2002).

As patenting activities may show erratic patterns on a short time basis and the dependent variable can take on a positive value only in cities with a number of patents greater than 0, the analysis has been carried out on a subsample of US cities (196 out of 370) showing persistent inventive activity (i.e. with a positive number of patents for each year in the period 1990–2004).

The identification of the most appropriate level of technological aggregation is quite an important issue in such a definition of the dependent variable. Following STRUMSKY et al. (2012) and FLEMING et al. (2007b), patents were classified at the *group* level, as it corresponds to the lowest hierarchical level in the International Patent Classification (IPC) adopted at the EPO. As will be shown below, however, the results are robust to the use of a more aggregated technological classification.[9] Looking at the distribution of the 504 400 patents in the sample, it is observed that around 20% of them are classified in only one IPC technological group. By definition, those patents do not enter into the calculation of the dependent variable. Moreover, 95% of all patents in the sample are classified in fewer than or equal to eight technological groups, and 99% in fewer than or equal to 15 groups. The remaining 1% of all patents (4702 observations) represent outliers classified in a number of technological groups going from 15 to 63. As the presence of such extreme observations may bias the count of new *combinations* observed in a city, in the construction of the dependent variable it was chosen to limit the attention to patents classified in fewer than or equal to eight groups.[10] Yet, robustness checks carried out by also including in the computation patents classified in a greater number of technological groups show that the basic findings hold and are qualitatively similar.

Finally, for the construction of the dependent variable, patents were considered in which *only* inventors located in the focal MSA were reported in the document. By excluding new combinations that are the outcome of cross-city collaborative patents, this variable not only mitigates possible endogeneity concerns with reference to the external reach and gatekeeping indicators, but also can be considered as a measure of a city's autonomous recombinatorial and inventive capabilities.

Explanatory variables

The empirical model was designed to assess the importance of external linkages and gatekeepers, while controlling for other factors affecting the renewal and expansion of a city's knowledge base, namely:

- the importance of agglomeration economies (DURANTON and PUGA, 2004; ELLISON et al., 2010; GLAESER, 1999);
- the nature of the local knowledge base (FRENKEN and BOSCHMA, 2007; FRENKEN et al., 2007;

NEFFKE et al., 2011; Ó HUALLACHÁIN and LEE, 2011); and
- the structure of the co-invention network within the city (BETTENCOURT et al., 2007; FLEMING et al., 2007a; LOBO and STRUMSKY, 2008).

In terms of agglomeration, the empirical model includes two variables to measure the scale of inventive inputs and the relevance of agglomeration economies. First, the number of *internal patents* in the city at time t (i.e. by excluding patents with inventors external to the city) captures both the scale effect associated with the agglomeration of inventive activities at the city level, as suggested by BETTENCOURT et al. (2007) and LOBO and STRUMSKY (2008), and the potential for technological recombination.[11] Second, the degree of *concentration* of inventive activities among firms was also controlled for by computing the Herfindahl index at the level of patent assignees. This accounts for the local market structure and captures whether more competitive cities enable greater knowledge creation and recombination (BEAUDRY and SCHIFFAUEROVA, 2009).

Several variables were included to capture the nature of the knowledge base in the city. First, the Herfindahl index was computed for each city and for each year by using the share of patents made in IPC four-digit (i.e. subclass) technological fields. This is an index of *absolute* specialization. It captures to what extent a city is specialized into a narrow set of fields, thereby controlling for the presence of externalities arising from technological specialization (FELDMAN and AUDRETSCH, 1999).[12] Second, the average number of *citations to the non-patent literature* (NPL) made by a city's internal patents was also computed. This variable captures the scientific orientation and generality of the local knowledge base. On the one hand, it might be argued that a more generic and science-based knowledge base could sustain higher opportunities of technological recombination; more universal notions are more likely to find multiple applications at the junction of different technological domains (FLEMING and SORENSON, 2001, 2004). On the other hand, it might also be argued that science-based knowledge is more distant from technological applications, with a negative effect on the recombinatorial capabilities of a city.

Whereas the Herfindahl index captures the *absolute* technological specialization of a city, the main hypothesis on the role of the local knowledge base refers to the similarity across cities in the profile of technological specialization. To this purpose, included in the model was an index of *relative* technological specialization between the technological profile of city c and all the other cities with which inventors of city c have collaborative linkages. In particular, the so-called Krugman index (KI) was computed at the level of technological *groups* in which a city's patents are classified. For each

EVOLUTIONARY ECONOMIC GEOGRAPHY

city c a time t, the following index was computed:

$$KI_c = \sum_{i=1}^{n} \left| \frac{P_{ci}}{P_c} - \frac{P_i}{P} \right|$$

where P_{ci} is the number of patents of city c in technological field i; P_c is the total number of patents of city c; P_i is the total number of patents made by all US cities (excluding city c) in technological field i, weighted by the frequency of co-inventing links between inventors of city c and inventors of city d; and P is the total number of patents made by all US cities (except city c), weighted by the frequency of co-inventing links between inventors of city c and inventors of city d.[13] The index ranges from 0 to 2, taking value 0 for cities whose technological profile is perfectly identical to the average technological profile of the other cities with which it has external linkages, and taking value 2 in cities which are specialized in completely different fields. It is expected that the more specialized and dissimilar the knowledge base in a city (i.e. its technological specialization profile) from the average knowledge base of all other cities with which it has linkages, the more the recombination of internal and external knowledge may be hindered by communication and learning impedances in knowledge exchanges. In this case, the mediating role of gatekeepers can be especially important to access, code and transfer the external knowledge into the city.

As far as the network variables are concerned, in addition to the variables capturing the importance of external linkages and gatekeepers, two further controls for other structural properties of the co-invention network *within* a city (by considering only ties among inventors located in the same city) were included.

First, the fraction of a city's inventors in the *largest connected component* is the ratio between the number of inventors that are in the largest component of the network and the total number of metropolitan inventors. It ranges from 0 (all inventors are isolates) to 1 (all inventors are directly or indirectly connected). Previous studies used this indicator to capture the size and

degree of internal connectivity in the co-invention network (e.g. LOBO and STRUMSKY, 2008). Second, the *clustering coefficient* captures the extent to which the partners of an inventor, within the city, are also partners with each other. This index ranges from 0 to 1, with higher values indicating that the internal city network is composed of dense cliques of collaboration.[14] As argued by some authors, cliquishness can cause isolation and localism, reduce exposure to alternative ideas, limit the access, absorption and recombination of externally sourced, and ultimately recombination opportunities (UZZI and SPIRO, 2007).

All explanatory variables (with the exclusion of internal patents) are computed on a five-year moving window and are one-year lagged (i.e. computed over the period $t - 1$, $t - 5$) with respect to the dependent variable to mitigate endogeneity concerns. Summary statistics for all variables are available in Table 1 and the correlation matrix is reported in the Appendix. In order to reduce concerns about collinearity among variables and to facilitate interpretation of results, all dependent variables were mean-centred.[15]

Estimation framework

To account for the integer and over-dispersed nature of the dependent variable, a conditional negative binomial framework with fixed effects was used by controlling for time effects, as done in similar studies (FLEMING *et al.*, 2007a, 2007b; SCHILLING and PHELPS, 2007). Since the conditional fixed-effects negative binomial model has been recently criticized for not being a 'true fixed-effect' model (ALLISON and WATERMAN, 2002), the robustness of the results was tested by using alternative estimation models. Moreover, the possibility of spatial dependence in the dependent variable, i.e. correlation in the dependent variable among neighbouring cities, was checked. To this purpose, the Moran I index was computed for each year by using a continuous row-standardized distance matrix. Moran I is generally very small and never statistically significant, supporting the null hypothesis of zero spatial correlation in the dependent variable. As an additional control, the Moran I index

Table 1. Summary statistics

Variable	Mean	SD	Minimum	Maximum
Number of new combinations	98.454	119.686	0	727
Number of internal patents	136.245	309.367	1	2916
Herfindahl (firms)	0.129	0.147	0.004	0.914
Herfindahl (technologies; IPC four-digit)	0.068	0.057	0.012	0.488
Average number of citations to NPL	1.278	1.070	0.000	6.263
Krugman index (KI)	1.381	0.344	0.370	1.971
Fraction of inventors in the largest component	12.223	10.351	1.005	67.262
Clustering coefficient	0.245	0.227	0.000	1.000
Average (distance-weighted) external reach ($d_{ij} \leq 4$)	7.302	10.105	0.071	162.995
Share of external reach mediated by gatekeepers ($d_{ij} \leq 4$)	0.235	0.201	0.000	0.862

Note: There are 2940 observations (196 MSA × 15 years). NPL, non-patent literature.

on the regression residuals was also computed for each year and for each model. Also in this case, Moran I is generally very small and largely not statistically significant.

RESULTS

The results of regression estimates are reported in Table 2. The first two columns report estimates of models, which include only the variables of interest, plus the total number of internal patents. The third column instead reports the full model, which also includes the control variables. All models report estimated coefficients transformed to incidence rate ratios (IRR), defined as $\exp(\hat{\beta})$.[16] Starting with the control variables, the coefficient of the number of internal patents shows, as expected, that the scale of experimentation matters. More specifically, estimates indicate that, all else being equal, a unit increase in the (log) number of internal patents is associated with a doubling in the number of new combinations of technological groups introduced in a city. Regarding the other control variables, an IRR < 1 on the Herfindahl index at the level of IPC four-digits suggests that *absolute* specialization on a narrow set of technological fields is associated with a decreased ability to recombine existing technologies

with new ones and to expand the knowledge base. Similarly, the coefficients on the fraction of inventors in the largest component and on the clustering coefficient seem to suggest that in cities characterized by dense cliques of collaborators, knowledge may circulate rapidly within cliques, but it may also be highly redundant, which is detrimental for recombination opportunities. Furthermore, the value of the coefficient on the KI signals that a city with a technological profile dissimilar from that of the other cities with which it exchanges knowledge is more likely to expand and renew its knowledge base, possibly because the lower cognitive overlapping enhances the opportunities for learning.

Turning attention to the main hypotheses, it is first observed that the average external reach presents a larger than 1 and statistically significant IRR, thereby confirming Hypothesis 1, even though the magnitude of the effect is not extremely large: keeping all other variables constant, a standard deviation increase in the average external reach (for $d_{ij} \leq 4$, see above) brings around 6.4% (= $[\exp(0.0061317 \times 10.105) - 1] \times 100$) more new combinations in a city.[17] In addition to this, the coefficient of the interaction between KI and the share of external reachability mediated by gatekeepers provides support to Hypothesis 2: the more similar (dissimilar) the technological profile of a city to

Table 2. *Determinants of knowledge base renewal and expansion in US cities, 1990–2004. Dependent variable: Number of new combinations of IPC technological groups*

Variables	(1)	(2)	(3)
Number of internal patents (log)	2.152**	2.176**	2.158**
	(0.037)	(0.037)	(0.037)
Herfindahl index (firm level)			0.853
			(0.127)
Herfindahl index (technology level)			0.199**
			(0.081)
Average number of citations to NPL			0.984
			(0.020)
Fraction of inventors in largest component			0.994**
			(0.002)
Clustering coefficient			0.979
			(0.041)
Average external reach	1.002†	1.004**	1.006**
	(0.001)	(0.001)	(0.001)
External reachability mediated by gatekeepers	0.573**	0.655**	0.878
	(0.041)	(0.048)	(0.074)
Krugman index (KI)	1.271**	1.192*	1.307**
	(0.091)	(0.085)	(0.097)
External reachability mediated by gatekeepers × KI		2.706**	3.153**
		(0.375)	(0.445)
Constant	5.852**	6.142**	6.207**
	(0.229)	(0.240)	(0.244)
Number of observations (196 cities × 15 years)	2940	2940	2940
Log-likelihood	−12136.4	−12110.7	−12085.6
χ^2	3150.8	3147.9	3204.7

Notes: $^{\dagger}p < 0.10$, $^{*}p < 0.05$, $^{**}p < 0.01$. Year dummies are included. The table reports the estimated coefficients transformed to incidence rate ratios (IRR) defined as $\exp(\hat{\beta})$. Standard errors are given in parentheses. NPL, non-patent literature.

the other cities with which it exchanges knowledge, the smaller (greater) the importance of gatekeepers to access external information and, in parallel, the greater (smaller) the importance of direct linkages. This result is broadly consistent with the view that gatekeepers not only perform a bridging function, but also transcode and diffuse the external knowledge at the local level. In order to appreciate the magnitude of this effect, it may be useful to consider two polar cases: on the one hand, a city with a technological profile relatively similar to the other cities (i.e. with KI = 25th percentile) and, on the other hand, a city with a relatively dissimilar technological profile (i.e. KI = 75th percentile). For each city, one can compute the effect of a similar increase in the share of external reach mediated by gatekeepers on the expected number of new technological combinations. In particular, the estimates show that when the share of external reachability mediated by gatekeepers goes from 6% to 36%,[18] the expected number of new combinations *decreases* by 11% for a city with a relatively similar profile, whereas the same variation *increases* the expected number of new combinations by 5.8% for a city with a relatively dissimilar profile.

As these results might depend on the assumptions made to construct the dependent and independent variables, several robustness checks were carried out. In the first place, the robustness of results with respect to alternative estimation methods was tested. The model in Table 2 was estimated using both Poisson fixed effects and unconditional negative binomial regression (GUIMARÃES, 2008). Results (not reported for brevity) were remarkably stable. Secondly, the extent to which the results might depend on the assumptions made to build the measures of gatekeeping was tested.[19] In particular, Model 1 in Table 3 considers only pairs of inventors at $d_{ij} \leq 2$ in order to construct the external reach indicator and the share of it mediated by gatekeepers, while Model 2 in Table 3 considers only pairs of inventors at $d_{ij} \leq 3$. All major results are again confirmed. Interestingly, the estimates indicate that the impact of external reach decreases as the social distance between internal and external inventors increases. If one compares the coefficient of the external reach variable in Tables 2 and 3 (Models 1 and 2), it is observed that its value decreases as the threshold value for d_{ij} increases, thus suggesting that socially closer interactions are more valuable for broadening the existing

Table 3. Estimates for different thresholds of distance (Models 1 and 2) and for different definitions of the dependent variable (Models 3 and 4)

	(1) Threshold distance $d_{ij} \leq 2$	(2) Threshold distance $d_{ij} \leq 3$	(3) Completely new combinations of IPC groups	(4) New combinations of IPC subclasses (four-digit)
Number of internal patents (log)	2.172**	2.161**	1.931**	1.884**
	(0.037)	(0.037)	(0.042)	(0.042)
Herfindahl index (firm level)	0.888	0.869	0.669*	0.709[†]
	(0.132)	(0.130)	(0.127)	(0.139)
Herfindahl index (technology level)	0.188**	0.195**	0.157**	0.608
	(0.077)	(0.080)	(0.078)	(0.321)
Average number of citations to NPL	0.986	0.985	0.991	1.016
	(0.020)	(0.020)	(0.024)	(0.026)
Fraction of inventors in largest component	0.995**	0.995**	0.996[†]	0.991**
	(0.002)	(0.002)	(0.002)	(0.002)
Clustering coefficient	0.975	0.978	0.944	0.886[†]
	(0.041)	(0.041)	(0.057)	(0.055)
Average external reach	1.034**	1.011**	1.009**	1.007**
	(0.007)	(0.002)	(0.002)	(0.002)
External reachability mediated by gatekeepers	0.632**	0.814*	0.777*	0.808[†]
	(0.093)	(0.083)	(0.091)	(0.096)
Krugman index (KI)	1.362**	1.328**	1.567**	1.441**
	(0.101)	(0.098)	(0.147)	(0.146)
External reachability mediated by gatekeepers × KI	5.858**	3.640**	3.428**	4.338**
	(1.429)	(0.609)	(0.704)	(1.091)
Constant	6.226**	6.178**	3.649**	4.027**
	(0.247)	(0.244)	(0.174)	(0.214)
Number of observations (196 cities × 15 years)	2940	2940	2940	2940
Log-likelihood	−12086.0	−12087.3	−10397.5	−8709.3
χ^2	3205.6	3202.4	1470.7	1082.1

Notes: [†]$p < 0.10$, *$p < 0.05$, **$p < 0.01$. The table reports the estimated coefficients transformed to incidence rate ratios (IRR) defined as $\exp(\hat{\beta})$. Standard errors are given in parentheses. Year dummies are included. Model 1 includes only pairs of inventors at distance $d_{ij} \leq 2$ in order to calculate the external reach variable and the share of it mediated by gatekeepers. Model 2 includes only pairs of inventors at distance $d_{ij} \leq 3$. Model 3 defines the dependent variable as the count of new combinations of IPC technological groups, in which both groups are new to the city (i.e. they represent completely new technological combinations). Model 4 defines the dependent variable as the count of new combinations of IPC technological subclasses (IPC four-digit). NPL, non-patent literature.

knowledge base, as knowledge passes through a lower number of intermediaries and it is thus more trusted and less distorted. The third set of robustness checks concerned the dependent variable. To this purpose, alternative and more restrictive measures of the dependent variable were tested. Specifically, Model 3 in Table 3 estimates a model in which the dependent variable is defined as the number of new pairs of technological *groups*, in which *both* groups in the pair were never used previously in the city (i.e. the number of totally new technological combinations is counted). In addition, as the results might be affected by the highly disaggregated technological level used to build the dependent variable and to measure the dissimilarity in the technological specialization profile, these two variables (i.e. the number of new combinations introduced in a city and KI) were recomputed by using a higher level of aggregation (i.e. so-called IPC four-digit technological *subclasses*) (Model 4 in Table 3). In both cases, the key findings are largely confirmed.

CONCLUSIONS

This paper aimed at assessing the importance of external sources of knowledge and gatekeepers for the expansion and renewal of a city's knowledge base. Differently from most of the literature on the subject, this paper has adopted a meso-level perspective and discussed under what local conditions gatekeepers are more likely to generate positive returns on the innovative outcomes (measured through the introduction of new and previously uncombined technology pairs) of the geographical contexts in which they are embedded. Interestingly, the results indicate that although external relations and their structure play a pivotal role to renew, expand and regenerate a city's knowledge base, not all types of relations are alike. Importantly, albeit considered as more imaginative, inspired and open to novelties and radical innovation, gatekeepers per se do not necessarily contribute to enrich the knowledge base of the cities in which they are located. It is argued that, at an aggregate level of analysis, such as the urban level, the control power that gatekeepers can exert on the knowledge flows they govern can more than offset the benefits accruing from their superior inventive performance. Still, given their ability to interpret and trans-code externally sourced knowledge into locally meaningful information, gatekeepers can have quite a substantial role in spurring the expansion and renewal of the knowledge base in cities characterized by a highly localized and specialized knowledge base, dissimilar from the average technological specialization profile of the other cities, with which it exchanges knowledge. These cities, in fact, require an interface to access, absorb and use external knowledge. On the other hand, those cities that have a more general and universal knowledge base prefer to rely on direct connections (and thus less

noisy information exchanges) to source knowledge from outside the city boundaries.

The paper adds two main contributions to the extant literature. On conceptual grounds, it helps to qualify the role and function of gatekeepers. Gatekeepers have been often invoked as the most important means to access and exploit external knowledge. In this perspective, strategy and policy recommendations have been drawn that aim at increasing their number and importance in mediating knowledge flows both across organizational and geographical boundaries. Not only does this paper question this view, but also it shows that on average direct linkages outperform connections mediated by gatekeepers by allowing faster, more trusted and less noisy knowledge exchanges. On methodological grounds, the paper proposes an operational method to quantify the importance of gatekeepers in brokering knowledge flows across cities that emphasizes the meso-level effects (i.e. on the metropolitan knowledge base) of individual behaviour and interactions (i.e. knowledge exchanges and gatekeeping roles) and that, hopefully, will be useful and deployed in future research.

Some cautionary words should be finally mentioned. First, patent data capture only a subset of the links relevant to knowledge exchanges within and across cities, albeit it should also be noted that the network of collaborators is the most immediate and influential environment from which inventors draw ideas and information. In this respect, the authors believe that the work is supplying rather conservative estimates on the impact of external linkages on a city's knowledge base. Second, in order to corroborate and boost confidence about the findings on the role of external linkages and gatekeepers for the rejuvenation and expansion of the knowledge base, the meso-level approach adopted in this paper should be complemented by empirical work at a different level of analysis, such as the firm or the inventive team level. In particular, the analysis at the team level would enable the technological profile of potential gatekeepers to be linked directly to the inventive output and recombinatorial capabilities of the team with whom she is collaborating, whereas the analysis at the metropolitan level captures not only this direct effect but also the indirect effects that gatekeepers may exert on the recombinatorial capabilities of the other inventors in the city, although they might not be direct team-workers. Finally, the dependent variable used in this paper does not take into account the degree of relatedness between different technologies and thus the ease of recombination between them, nor does it distinguish the newly introduced combinations according to the their radical versus incremental nature. In this sense, it is believed that the contribution of this paper is complementary to the most recent studies exploring the role of knowledge relatedness for the dynamics of technological specialization in cities. Overall, the three limitations above represent equally promising avenues for further research.

APPENDIX

This appendix illustrates in detail the construction of the measures used in the paper to capture the intensity of external linkages and the role gatekeepers play in mediating the access to the external sources of knowledge. To this end, the example reported in Fig. A1 is used. The example illustrates the hypothetical case of a city, in which eight inventors are located (denoted in Fig. A1 by the small letters from a to h). Outside the boundaries of the hypothetical city there are 17 inventors (denoted by the capital letters from I to Z).

If one takes inventor a located in the hypothetical city c, it takes two steps to reach inventor J outside her city, three steps to reach inventor L, four steps to reach inventor P, five steps to reach inventor Q, and so on. Her distance-weighted external reach equals the sum of the reciprocal distances to all other external inventors she can reach, as follows:

$$\text{DWR}_{a,c} = \sum_{j=I}^{Z} \frac{1}{d_{aj}} = \frac{1}{2} + \frac{1}{2} + \frac{1}{3} + \frac{1}{3} + \frac{1}{2} + \frac{1}{3} + \frac{1}{4}$$

$$= 2.75$$

Note that since $d_{aQ} = 5 > 4$, we set $1/d_{aQ} = 0$.[20] The average distance-weighted external reach (ADWR) for the hypothetical city is easily obtained by computing the DWR for each inventor located in that city and then taking the average across all inventors. In the

example, this becomes:

$$\text{ADWR}_c = \frac{1}{8}(\text{DWR}_{a,c} + \text{DWR}_{b,c} + \text{DWR}_{c,c}$$

$$+ \text{DWR}_{d,c} + \text{DWR}_{e,c} + \text{DWR}_{f,c}$$

$$+ \text{DWR}_{g,c} + \text{DWR}_{h,c})$$

$$= \frac{1}{8}(2.75 + 5.08 + 0.83 + 1.16 + 2 + 1.5$$

$$+ 2 + 1)$$

$$= 2.04$$

The above calculation assumes that indirect linkages whose distance is greater than 4 do not convey any knowledge flow. This threshold is somewhat arbitrary, though it has been shown that it corresponds to the distance at which knowledge flows start decaying very rapidly (BRESCHI and LISSONI, 2004; SINGH, 2005). In order to test the robustness of results, the ADWR index can be recalculated by assuming a faster rate of depreciation of knowledge with respect to social distance. For example, it can easily be checked that, assuming a threshold at distance 3, the ADWR index in the example takes a value of 1.98.

As far as gatekeepers are concerned, the definition given by GOULD and FERNANDEZ (1989) is adapted. Informally, they are actors that mediate the access to externally located inventors for local inventors. Formally, an inventor i located in city c is defined as a gatekeeper when the shortest path

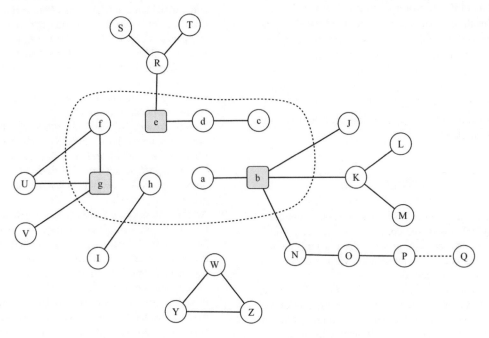

Fig. A1. External linkages and gatekeepers

Note: Small letters from a to h denote inventors located in a city, whose boundaries are defined by the dashed line. Capital letters from I to Z denote inventors located outside the boundaries of the city. Rounded square, yellow nodes denote gatekeepers, namely inventors located in the city that mediate the access to externally located inventors for other co-located inventors

leading from any other inventor j in city c to any other inventor h in city d (different from c) passes through i. Following this definition, there are three gatekeepers in the hypothetical city illustrated in Fig. A1. They are identified by the rounded square, yellow nodes. For example, the shortest path from node f to node V is through node g, even though f can directly reach node U. Similarly, the shortest paths from node a to nodes N, O and P pass through node b. On the other hand, inventor h does not need any intermediation to reach the external inventor I.

Given the above definition of gatekeepers, one way to measure the relative importance of gatekeepers versus direct external linkages in mediating the access to external sources of knowledge is by computing to what extent the average distance-weighted external reach would decrease, should one remove them from the city (BORGATTI, 2006; VALENTE and FUJIMOTO, 2010). To this purpose, simply computed for each city is the share of total distance-weighted external reachability, which is mediated by gatekeepers.

With reference to the example above, the (distance-weighted) external reachability of inventor a is entirely mediated by node b. Similarly, inventors c and d can reach other externally located inventors only through node e. As far as inventor f is concerned, she can reach inventor U in a direct way, so that g does not perform any gatekeeping role.[21] Yet, inventor f needs to pass through inventor g in order to reach inventor V. Given that the total external reachability of inventor f is equal to $1 + 0.5 = 1.5$, the share of it that is mediated by gatekeepers is $0.5/1.5 = 1/3$. In other words, the external reachability of node f would decrease by 0.5 (or 1/3 of the total) should one remove all gatekeepers from the city. If one applies the same logic to all inventors in the hypothetical city, it can be easily checked that the share of total external reachability that is mediated by gatekeepers is equal to $5.25/16.32 = 0.32$. In other words, 32% of the total external reachability in the city is accounted for by indirect linkages, which are mediated by gatekeepers.

NOTES

1. MSAs are defined by the US Office of Management and Budget (OMB) as urban core areas of at least 50 000 people, plus adjacent counties that have a high degree of social and economic integration with the core, as measured by commuting ties.
2. The US Patent and Trademark Office (USPTO) patent data might appear a more natural choice for a study on invention in US cities. However, the average quality of USPTO patents has declined considerably in the period under consideration due to a series of concomitant factors. Because of these trends, patents of insufficient quality or with inadequate search of prior art were issued more often (HALL et al., 2004; JAFFE and LERNER, 2004). The use of EPO data reduces this noise as only more valuable patents are extended to Europe. Patents are dated by using their priority year, i. e. the first date at which the patent was applied for anywhere in the world as this date is closest to the actual time of the invention.
3. Fuller details on the routine implemented for data cleaning and standardization are provided by LISSONI et al. (2006).
4. The June 2003 definition of MSAs issued by OMB was used. For details and maps, see http://www.census. gov/population/www/metroareas/metrodef.html/.
5. Note that the adjectives 'internal' and 'external' used to characterize the network ties only refer to the spatial boundaries delimiting a city. Thus, a co-invention tie between two inventors located within the same city is internal to that city, whereas a co-invention tie between two inventors located in different cities is external to them, regardless of the organizational affiliation of the two inventors. In particular, in the case of firms with plants located in different cities, the external reach indicator considers also those links that may arise between inventor i working in city c for applicant a and all inventors working for applicant a in every other US city. Although one may question that such types of links are more likely to be established (and possibly mediated by firm-level practices and strategies), from a spatial perspective they do not differ from the links established by inventor i working in city c for applicant a with all the other inventors in any other US city and working for other firms than a.
6. For disconnected (i.e. not reachable) pairs of inventors, $d_{ij} = \infty$ and, therefore, $1/d_{ij}$ is equal to $1/\infty$, which reduces to 0.
7. Precisely, for pairs of inventors (ij), where $d_{ij} > 4$, $1/d_{ij}$ is set equal to 0. Namely, it was assumed that no knowledge flow is taking place for a distance above that threshold.
8. To be more specific, consider two technological classes i and j in which a city's patents before time t have been classified, but which were not combined together in any patent. Suppose that a patent at time t is co-classified in i and j. This patent introduces a new combination of technologies. Yet, this recombination does not expand or renew the existing knowledge base of a city. For this reason, it is not included in the computation of new pairs of technological codes.
9. Groups are next divided into subgroups; however, subgroups are nested into groups (i.e. their hierarchical level varies across groups) and therefore cannot be exploited in a study such as this one. For further details, see http://www.wipo.int/export/sites/www/classifications/ipc/en/guide/guide_ipc.pdf/.
10. An illustrative case of the problems that may arise from the inclusion of these outliers is that of patent EP1632470, which has been applied for by NPS Pharmaceuticals, located in Salt Lake City, Utah. This patent, with priority year 1991, is classified in 40 different technological groups. Of the 780 combinations of technological groups associated to this patent, 702 were new to Salt Lake City in 1991. Given that in the same year this company applied for other three patents classified in a similarly large number of different technological groups, the total number of new combinations introduced in Salt Lake City in 1991 was 2978, which is an order of magnitude higher than the number of new combinations in 1990 (210) and 1992 (212).

11. The authors also tried to include in the analysis the total number of technological groups in which the internal patents made in a city in the period $(t-1, t-5)$ are classified. Yet, we were forced to exclude it because of problems of multicollinearity with the other independent variables. The authors thank two anonymous referee for raising this issue.

12. Although the adoption of a relatively aggregated technological classification level may not allow the details about the technological content of patent data to be exploited fully, the measurement of this variable is based on technological subclasses (i.e. four-digit IPC) and not technological groups (i.e. the lower technological aggregation level), as the use of groups would disproportionately and artificially inflate its value.

13. More formally, P_i is defined as:

$$P_i = \sum_{d \neq c} w_{dc} P_{di}$$

where P_{di} is the number of patents that city d has made in technological field I; and w_{dc} is the weight of city d on all external collaborative links between inventors of city c and inventors in all other cities. This implies that cities with which inventors of city c have more collaborative links (and thus exchange knowledge) weight more in the computation of the Krugman index of city c. Similarly, only cities with which inventors of city c have external linkages enter into the computation of the index.

14. In affiliation networks as co-invention networks, this coefficient tends to increase with the number of inventors per patent (NEWMAN, 2010). In fact, any three inventors listed in the same patent document by construction form a triangle, i.e. all paths of length two are automatically closed. By extension, the greater the number of patents with more than two inventors, the greater the coefficient. To correct for this possible bias and inflationary mechanism, the generalized version of the clustering coefficient proposed by OPSAHL (2013) was computed, which excludes those triples of inventors connected because of a joint patent and only counts the number of triples (i.e. closed paths of length two) that are the outcome of independent interactions between pairs of inventors.

15. Diagnostic tests tend to exclude serious risks of collinearity. The variance inflation ratio (VIF) is below 2.5 for all variables, with the exception of the (log) of internal patents (3.52), the share of external reach mediated by the gatekeepers (3.12), and the Krugman index (2.56). However, even for these variables, VIF is well below 10, which is the rule of thumb value usually considered in order to detect serious problems of multicollinearity.

16. For a unit change in x_k, the expected count in the dependent variable changes by a factor of $\exp(\hat{\beta}_k)$, holding all other variables constant. For a standard deviation change in x_k, the expected count changes by a factor of $\exp(\hat{\beta}_k \times s_k)$. Alternatively, IRR can be interpreted in terms of percentage change in the expected count. Thus, for a unit change in x_k, the percentage change in the expected count is given by $[\exp(\hat{\beta}_k \times 1) - 1] \times 100$.

17. Note that $\exp(0.0061317) = 1.0061505$ is the IRR associated with the average external reach.

18. The two values correspond, respectively, to the 25th and 75th percentiles of the empirical distribution of the variable. In this way, one can simulate what happens to the expected number of new combinations when the share of external reach mediated by the gatekeepers increase from small to large values.

19. See note 7.

20. See note 7.

21. To put it in a different way, the shortest path from f to U does not pass through g. More generally, there are cases in which an inventor reaches an external inventor through both direct connections and indirect links, mediated by other inventors. As indirect links imply, by definition, a greater distance than direct links, these triples are obviously excluded from the computation of the external reach mediated by gatekeepers. This happens particularly in the case of patents with more than two inventors, one of whom is located outside the boundaries of the city.

REFERENCES

AHUJA G. (2000) Collaboration networks, structural holes, and innovation: a longitudinal study, *Administrative Science Quarterly* **45**, 425–455.

ALLEN T. J. (1977) *Managing the Flow of Technology*. MIT Press, Cambridge, MA.

ALLEN T. J. and COHEN S. I. (1969) Information flow in research and development laboratories, *Administrative Science Quarterly* **14**, 12–19. doi:10.2307/2391357

ALLISON P. D. and WATERMAN R. P. (2002) Fixed-effects negative binomial regression models, *Sociological Methodology* **32**, 247–265. doi:10.1111/1467-9531.00117

ANTONELLI C. (1995) *The Economics of Localized Technological Change and Industrial Dynamics*. Kluwer, Dordrecht.

BATHELT H., MALMBERG A. and MASKELL P. (2004) Clusters and knowledge: local buzz, global pipelines and the process of knowledge creation, *Progress in Human Geography* **28**, 31–56.

BEAUDRY C. and SCHIFFAUEROVA A. (2009) Who's right, Marshall or Jacobs? The localization versus urbanization debate, *Research Policy* **38**, 318–337.

BETTENCOURT L. M. A., LOBO J. and STRUMSKY D. (2007) Invention in the city: increasing returns to patenting as a scaling function of metropolitan size, *Research Policy* **36**, 107–120. doi:10.1016/j.respol.2006.09.026

BORGATTI S. P. (2006) Identifying sets of key players in a social network, *Computational and Mathematical Organization Theory* **12**, 21–34. doi:10.1007/s10588-006-7084-x

BOSCHMA R. (2005) Proximity and innovation: a critical assessment, *Regional Studies* **39**, 61–74. doi:10.1080/0034340052000320887

Boschma R. A. and Frenken K. (2006) Why is economic geography not an evolutionary science? Towards an evolutionary economic geography, *Journal of Economic Geography* **6**, 273–302. doi:10.1093/jeg/lbi022

Boschma R. and Frenken K. (2010) The spatial evolution of innovation networks. A proximity perspective, in Boschma R. and Martin R. (Eds) *Handbook of Evolutionary Economic Geography*, pp. 120–135. Edward Elgar, Cheltenham.

Breschi S. and Lissoni F. (2001) Knowledge spillovers and local innovation systems: a critical survey, *Industrial and Corporate Change* **10**, 975–1005. doi:10.1093/icc/10.4.975

Breschi S. and Lissoni F. (2004) Knowledge networks from patent data: methodological issues and research targets, in Glanzel W., Moed H. and Schmoch U. (Eds) *Handbook of Quantitative S&T Research: The Use of Publication and Patent Statistics in Studies of S&T Systems*, pp. 613–643. Springer, Berlin.

Breschi S. and Lissoni F. (2009) Mobility of skilled workers and co-invention networks: an anatomy of localized knowledge flows, *Journal of Economic Geography* **9**, 439–468. doi:10.1093/jeg/lbp008

Bresnahan T., Gambardella A. and Saxenian A. (2001) 'Old economy' inputs for 'new economy' outcomes: cluster formation in the new silicon valleys, *Industrial and Corporate Change* **10**, 835–860. doi:10.1093/icc/10.4.835

Burt R. S. (1992) *Structural Holes: The Social Structure of Competition*. Harvard University Press, Cambridge, MA.

Burt R. (2004) Structural holes and good ideas, *American Journal of Sociology* **110**, 349–399. doi:10.1086/421787

Burt R. S. (2008) Information and structural holes: comment on Reagans and Zuckerman, *Industrial and Corporate Change* **17**, 953–969. doi:10.1093/icc/dtn033

Capello R. (2009) Indivisibilities, synergy and proximity: the need for an integrated approach to agglomeration economies, *Tijds-chrift voor Economische en Sociale Geografie* **100**, 145–159.

Carlino G. A., Chatterjee S. and Hunt R. M. (2007) Urban density and the rate of invention, *Journal of Urban Economics* **61**, 389–419. doi:10.1016/j.jue.2006.08.003

Cowan R., David P. A. and Foray D. (2000) The explicit economics of knowledge codification and tacitness, *Industrial and Corporate Change* **9**, 211–253. doi:10.1093/icc/9.2.211

Dahlander L. and Frederiksen L. (2012) The core and cosmopolitans: a relational view of innovation in user communities, *Organization Science* **23**, 988–1007. doi:10.1287/orsc.1110.0673

Dosi G. (1982) Technological paradigms and technological trajectories: a suggested interpretation of the determinants and directions of technical change, *Research Policy* **11**, 147–162. doi:10.1016/0048-7333(82)90016-6

Duranton G. and Puga D. (2004) Micro-foundations of urban agglomeration economies, in Henderson J. V. and Thisse J. F. (Eds) *Handbook of Regional and Urban Economics*, pp. 2063–2117. Elsevier, Amsterdam.

Ellison G., Glaeser E. and Kerr W. (2010) What causes industry agglomeration? Evidence from coagglomeration patterns, *American Economic Review* **100**, 1195–1213. doi:10.1257/aer.100.3.1195

Feldman M. P. and Audretsch D. B. (1999) Innovation in cities: science-based diversity, specialization and localized competition, *European Economic Review* **43**, 409–429.

Feller I. (1971) The urban location of United States invention, 1860–1910, *Explorations in Economic History* **8**, 285–303. doi:10.1016/0014-4983(71)90010-6

Fernandez R. M. and Gould R. V. (1994) A dilemma of state power: brokerage and influence in the national health policy domain, *American Journal of Sociology* **99**, 1455–1491. doi:10.1086/230451

Fleming L. (2001) Recombinant uncertainty in technological search, *Management Science* **47**, 117–132. doi:10.1287/mnsc.47.1.117.10671

Fleming L., King C. and Juda A. I. (2007a) Small worlds and regional innovation, *Organization Science* **18**, 938–954. doi:10.1287/orsc.1070.0289

Fleming L., Mingo S. and Chen D. (2007b) Collaborative brokerage, generative creativity, and creative success, *Administrative Science Quarterly* **52**, 443–475.

Fleming L. and Sorenson O. (2001) Technology as a complex adaptive system: evidence from patent data, *Research Policy* **30**, 1019–1039. doi:10.1016/S0048-7333(00)00135-9

Fleming L. and Sorenson O. (2004) Science as a map in technological search, *Strategic Management Journal* **25**, 909–928. doi:10.1002/smj.384

Frenken K. and Boschma R. A. (2007) A theoretical framework for evolutionary economic geography: industrial dynamics and urban growth as a branching process, *Journal of Economic Geography* **7**, 635–649. doi:10.1093/jeg/lbm018

Frenken K., van Oort F. and Verburg T. (2007) Related variety, unrelated variety and regional economic growth, *Regional Studies* **41**, 685–697.

Gittelman M. (2007) Does geography matter for science-based firms? Epistemic communities and the geography of research and patenting in biotechnology, *Organization Science* **18**, 724–741. doi:10.1287/orsc.1070.0249

Giuliani E. and Bell M. (2005) The micro-determinants of meso-level learning and innovation: evidence from a Chilean wine cluster, *Research Policy* **34**, 47–68. doi:10.1016/j.respol.2004.10.008

Glaeser E. L. (1999) Learning in cities, *Journal of Urban Economics* **46**, 254–277. doi:10.1006/juec.1998.2121

Gould R. V. and Fernandez R. M. (1989) Structures of mediation: a formal approach to brokerage in transaction networks, *Sociological Methodology* **19**, 89–126. doi:10.2307/270949

Graf H. (2011) Gatekeepers in regional networks of innovators, *Cambridge Journal of Economics* **35**, 173–198. doi:10.1093/cje/beq001

Guimarães P. (2008) The fixed effects negative binomial model revisited, *Economics Letters* **99**, 63–66. doi:10.1016/j.econlet.2007.05.030

Hall B. H., Graham S., Harhoff D. and Mowery D. C. (2004) Prospects for improving U.S. patent quality via postgrant opposition, *Innovation Policy and the Economy* **4**, 115–143.

HARGADON A. and SUTTON R. I. (1997) Technology brokering and innovation in a product development firm, *Administrative Science Quarterly* **42**, 716–749. doi:10.2307/2393655

JAFFE A. B. and LERNER J. (2004) *Innovation and its Discontents: How Our Broken Patent System is Endangering Innovation and Progress, and What To Do About It.* Princeton University Press, Princeton, NJ.

KATILA R. and AHUJA G. (2002) Something old, something new: a longitudinal study of search behavior and new product introduction, *Academy of Management Journal* **45**, 1183–1194.

LAMOREAUX N. R. and SOKOLOFF K. L. (2000) The geography of invention in the American glass industry, 1870–1925, *Journal of Economic History* **60**, 700–729. doi:10.1017/S0022050700025730

LISSONI F. (2001) Knowledge codification and the geography of innovation: the case of Brescia mechanical cluster, *Research Policy* **30**, 1479–1500. doi:10.1016/S0048-7333(01)00163-9

LISSONI F., SANDITOV B. and TARASCONI G. (2006) *The Keins Database on Academic Inventors: Methodology and Contents.* CESPRI Working Papers No. 181. Centro di Ricerca sui Processi di Innovazione e Internazionalizzazione (CESPRI), Bocconi University, Milan.

LOBO J. and STRUMSKY D. (2008) Metropolitan patenting, inventor agglomeration and social networks: a tale of two effects, *Journal of Urban Economics* **63**, 871–884.

MORRISON A. (2008) Gatekeepers of knowledge within industrial districts: who they are, how they interact, *Regional Studies* **42**, 817–835. doi:10.1080/00343400701654178

MORRISON A., RABELLOTTI R. and ZIRULIA L. (2013) When do global pipelines enhance the diffusion of knowledge in clusters?, *Economic Geography* **89**, 77–96. doi:10.1111/j.1944-8287.2012.01167.x

MUNARI F., SOBRERO M. and MALIPIERO A. (2012) Absorptive capacity and localized spillovers: focal firms as technological gatekeepers in industrial districts, *Industrial and Corporate Change* **21**, 429–462. doi:10.1093/icc/dtr053

NEFFKE F., HENNING M. and BOSCHMA R. (2011) How do regions diversify over time? Industry relatedness and the development of new growth paths in regions, *Economic Geography* **87**, 237–265. doi:10.1111/j.1944-8287.2011.01121.x

NEWMAN M. (2010) *Networks: An Introduction.* Oxford University Press, New York, NY.

Ó HUALLACHÁIN B. and LEE D.-S. (2011) Technological specialization and variety in urban invention, *Regional Studies* **45**, 67–88. doi:10.1080/00343404.2010.486783

OBSTFELD D. (2005) Social networks, the *tertius iungens* orientation, and involvement in innovation, *Administrative Science Quarterly* **50**, 100–130.

OPSAHL T. (2013) Triadic closure in two-mode networks: redefining the global and local clustering coefficients, *Social Networks* **35**, 159–167.

OWEN-SMITH J. and POWELL W. W. (2004) Knowledge networks as channels and conduits: The effects of spillovers in the Boston biotechnology community, *Organization Science* **15**, 5–21. doi:10.1287/orsc.1030.0054

PADGETT J. F. and ANSELL C. K. (1993) Robust action and the rise of the Medici, 1400–1434, *American Journal of Sociology* **98**, 1259–1319. doi:10.1086/230190

PRED A. R. (1973) *Urban Growth and the Circulation of Information: The United States System of Cities, 1790–1840.* Harvard University Press, Cambridge, MA.

SAVIOTTI P. P. (2007) On the dynamics of generation and utilisation of knowledge: the local character of knowledge, *Structural Change and Economic Dynamics* **18**, 387–408.

SCHILLING M. A. and PHELPS C. C. (2007) Interfirm collaboration networks: the impact of large-scale network structure on firm innovation, *Management Science* **53**, 1113–1126. doi:10.1287/mnsc.1060.0624

SINGH J. (2005) Collaborative networks as determinants of knowledge diffusion patterns, *Management Science* **51**, 756–770. doi:10.1287/mnsc.1040.0349

STORPER M. and VENABLES A. J. (2004) Buzz: face-to-face contact and the urban economy, *Journal of Economic Geography* **4**, 351–370. doi:10.1093/jnlecg/lbh027

STRUMSKY D., LOBO J. and VAN DER LEEUW S. (2012) Using patent technology codes to study technological change, *Economics of Innovation and New Technology* **21**, 267–286. doi:10.1080/10438599.2011.578709

TER WAL A. and BOSCHMA R. (2009) Applying social network analysis in economic geography: framing some key analytic issues, *Annals of Regional Science* **43**, 739–756. doi:10.1007/s00168-008-0258-3

TUSHMAN M. L. and KATZ R. (1980) External communication and project performance: an investigation into the role of gatekeepers, *Management Science* **26**, 1071–1085. doi:10.1287/mnsc.26.11.1071

TUSHMAN M. L. and SCANLAN T. J. (1981) Boundary spanning individuals: their role in information transfer and their antecedents, *Academy of Management Journal* **24**, 289–305.

UZZI B. (1996) The sources and consequences of embeddedness for the economic performance of organizations: the network effect, *American Sociological Review* **61**, 674–698. doi:10.2307/2096399

UZZI B. (1997) Social structure and competition in interfirm networks: the paradox of embeddedness, *Administrative Science Quarterly* **42**, 35–67. doi:10.2307/2393808

UZZI B. and SPIRO J. (2007) Collaboration and creativity: the small world problem, *American Journal of Sociology* **111**, 447–504. doi:10.1086/432782

VALENTE T. W. and FUJIMOTO K. (2010) Bridging: locating critical connectors in a network, *Social Networks* **32**, 212–220. doi:10.1016/j.socnet.2010.03.003

WHITTINGTON K., OWEN-SMITH J. and POWELL W. (2009) Networks, propinquity, and innovation in knowledge-intensive industries, *Administrative Science Quarterly* **54**, 90–122.

rKnowledge: The Spatial Diffusion and Adoption of rDNA Methods

MARYANN P. FELDMAN, DIETER F. KOGLER and DAVID L. RIGBY

Department of Public Policy, University of North Carolina, Chapel Hill, USA.
School of Geography, Planning & Environmental Policy, University College Dublin, Dublin, Ireland.
Department of Geography, University of California, Los Angeles, USA.

FELDMAN M. P., KOGLER D. F. and RIGBY D. L. rKnowledge: the spatial diffusion and adoption of rDNA methods, *Regional Studies*. The 1980 patent granted to Stanley Cohen and Herbert Boyer for their development of rDNA technology played a critical role in the establishment of the modern biotechnology industry. From the birth of this general-purpose technology in the San Francisco Bay area, rDNA-related knowledge diffused across sectors and regions of the US economy. Patent data are used here to track the geography and timing of rDNA technology adoption in US metropolitan areas. Using event history and fixed effects conditional logit models, it is shown how the diffusion of rDNA techniques was influenced by cognitive, geographical and social proximity.

FELDMAN M. P., KOGLER D. F. and RIGBY D. L. r知识：rDNA方法的空间散佈与採用，区域研究。1980年授予史丹尼．科恩（Stanley Cohen）与赫博．玻伊尔（Herbert Boyer）所研发的rDNA技术之专利，在现代生物科技产业的发展中，扮演了关键的角色。从此一通用技术在加州湾区诞生开始，rDNA 的相关知识便扩散至美国经济的各部门及区域。我们运用专利数据，追溯美国大都会地区採用rDNA技术的地理与时间。本文运用事件历史与固定效应条件逻辑特模型，显示 rDNA 技术的散佈如何受到认知、地理与社会邻近性所影响。

FELDMAN M. P., KOGLER D. F. et RIGBY D. L. La connaissance-r: la diffusion et l'adoption spatiales des méthodes ADNr, *Regional Studies*. Le brevet de 1980 délivré à Stanley Cohen et à Herbert Boyer en reconnaissance du développement de la technologie ADNr a joué un rôle essentiel dans l'établissement de l'industrie biotechnologique moderne. Depuis la naissance de cette technologie universelle dans la baie de San Francisco, la connaissance liée à l'ADNr s'est diffusée à travers des secteurs et des régions de l'économie des É-U. On emploie ici les données sur les brevets pour découvrir la géographie et le calendrier de l'adoption de la technologie ADNr dans les zones métropolitaines des É-U. Se servant de l'historique des événements et des modèles logit conditionnels à effets fixes, on montre comment la diffusion des techniques ADNr a été influée par la proximité cognitive, géographique et sociale.

FELDMAN M. P., KOGLER D. F. und RIGBY D. L. rWissen: räumliche Diffusion und Einführung von rDNA-Methoden, *Regional Studies*. Für die Gründung der modernen Biotechnologiebranche spielte das Patent, das Stanley Cohen und Herbert Boyer 1980 für ihre Entwicklung der rDNA-Technik erhielten, eine entscheidende Rolle. Nach der Geburt dieser Basistechnologie in der San Francisco Bay Area diffundierte das Wissen über rDNA in verschiedene Sektoren und Regionen der gesamten US-Wirtschaft. In diesem Beitrag werden die Geografie und Zeitpunkte der Einführung von rDNA-Technik in den Ballungsgebieten der USA anhand von Patentdaten nachverfolgt. Mithilfe von Ereignisverlaufs- und konditionalen Festeffekt-Logitmodellen wird gezeigt, wie die Diffusion von rDNA-Techniken von kognitiver, geografischer und sozialer Nähe beeinflusst wurde.

FELDMAN M. P., KOGLER D. F. y RIGBY D. L. Conocimiento-r: la difusión espacial y la adopción de los métodos ADNr, *Regional Studies*. La patente concedida en 1980 a Stanley Cohen y Herbert Boyer por su desarrollo de la tecnología de ADN recombinante desempeñó un papel fundamental en el establecimiento de la industria de la biotecnología moderna. Desde el nacimiento de esta tecnología básica en la región de la Bahía de San Francisco, el conocimiento relacionado con la ADNr se difundió en todos los sectores y regiones de la economía estadounidense. En este estudio utilizamos los datos de patentes para rastrear la geografía y el momento de la adopción de la tecnología ADNr en las zonas metropolitanas de los Estados Unidos. Con ayuda de modelos logit condicionales sobre acontecimientos de la historia y efectos fijos, mostramos cómo influyó la proximidad cognitiva, geográfica y social en la difusión de las técnicas de ADNr.

INTRODUCTION

In December 1980, the United States Patent and Trademark Office (USPTO) issued a patent entitled *Process for Producing Biologically Functional Chimeras* (number 4237224). The patent covered the recombinant DNA (rDNA) technique developed by Dr Stanley Cohen of Stanford University and Dr Herbert Boyer of the University of California – San Francisco. In later evaluation of the Cohen–Boyer patent, the USPTO introduced a new category (435/69.1) to its classification system, a relatively rare occurrence signalling the birth of a new type of technology. While most technological innovation is incremental, certain discoveries provide fundamental breakthroughs that revolutionize industrial activity and provide a platform for increased productivity throughout the economy. The rDNA patent represented this kind of transformative general purpose technology laying the foundations for the growth of the modern biotechnology industry (FELDMAN and YOON, 2012).

From its conception in the Bay Area of California, knowledge of the Cohen–Boyer discovery spread rapidly to select cities across the country, stimulating the development of nascent clusters of biotechnology production. The diffusion of rDNA technology might have followed many different trajectories, but only one historical geography played itself out. This paper seeks to understand the forces shaping this geography in the characteristics of different metropolitan areas, in the knowledge structure of different cities, in the social ties that bind cities to one another through inventor collaborations, and in terms of the friction of distance.

Theory argues that innovative activity tends to cluster in regions where resources relevant to the performance and survival of knowledge-based firms are most abundant (FELDMAN, 1994), including the presence of skilled workers and labour market flexibility (SAXENIAN, 1994; GLAESER, 2000), proximity to markets and input suppliers (STORPER and CHRISTOPHERSON, 1987; BAUM and HAVEMAN, 1997), the presence of universities and research organizations (ZUCKER et al., 1998), and cultural and institutional supports for entrepreneurial activity (SAXENIAN, 1994; SORENSON and AUDIA, 2000). Yet, the ways in which radical technological breakthroughs diffuse through space and the

ways in which new scientific discoveries are adopted and incorporated with existing expertise have not been considered in a systematic way. We appeal for some guidance in this regard to the classical literature on the spatial diffusion of innovations (HAGERSTRAND, 1953; GRILICHES, 1957; BROWN, 1981) updated with more recent claims on the different dimensions of proximity (NOOTEBOOM, 2000; BOSCHMA, 2005), on absorptive capacity (COHEN and LEVINTHAL, 1990), and the importance of social relationships to knowledge flow (BRESCHI et al., 2003; SORENSON, 2003; COWAN and JONARD, 2004).

Armed with such, this paper aims to shed some empirical light on the emergence of innovative, technology-driven industrial clusters. This is done by examining a specific technology and its diffusion over time and across space. That space takes different forms in this work: it is always geographical, but it is also constituted through sets of social relationships and the shifting character of regional knowledge bases. The focus is on Cohen–Boyer's rDNA technology because the boundaries of this new knowledge subset are relatively well defined by USPTO class 435/69.1 and because the geographical movement and adoption of rDNA technologies are captured in approximately 9000 patents distributed across US metropolitan areas. Working from an evolutionary economic geography framework, the influence of cognitive proximity, geographical proximity and social proximity on the diffusion and adoption of rDNA knowledge across US cities is explored. The analysis employs event history models to examine the timing of a city's first rDNA patent and the more general class of fixed effect panel models to explore the determinants of repeated rDNA technology adoption across the US urban system. Results show that the diffusion and adoption of the Cohen–Boyer technology was directed mainly by social contacts developed among co-inventors and by the absorptive capacity of host cities, measured through the structure of their knowledge cores and the cognitive proximity of those cores to knowledge in technology class 435/69.1. The initial diffusion of rDNA technology followed a hierarchical pattern jumping between relatively large and distant urban areas. A subsequent phase of diffusion sees rDNA technology radiating out from these larger cities exhibiting a classic distance–decay-type pattern. The results highlighted here appear robust to variations in model structure and to concerns with endogeneity.

The paper is organized in five sections. The second section offers a brief review of theory that links key ideas in evolutionary economic change to the diffusion and adoption of new technological knowledge. The third section provides more historical detail about the Cohen–Boyer patent along with a note on the structure of the USPTO classification system. The fourth section turns attention to the geographical and sectoral diffusion of rDNA technology after 1980 to a simple model specification, and to descriptive information about key independent variables in that model. The fifth section presents results from a Cox hazard model of rDNA technology diffusion extended to incorporate time-varying independent variables, along with output from a more general fixed effects logit model. The latter model is the platform for a series of robustness checks of the basic hypotheses. The sixth section offers some brief discussion and conclusions.

TECHNOLOGY EVOLUTION AND ADOPTION IN AN EVOLUTIONARY FRAMEWORK

The economic landscape is in constant flux, pushed and pulled by processes of competition that both trap capital, labour and routines within some sectors and regions while encouraging experimentation and discovery in others. Evolutionary economic geography offers a broad, though still contested, framework that has at its core the production and destruction of novelty in space and the links between novelty and regional economic fortunes (BOSCHMA and MARTIN, 2010). The creation of technological knowledge, its movement and recombination within different regional ensembles of economic agents and institutions plays only one, but nonetheless critical, role in the evolution of the space-economy (RIGBY and ESSLETZBICHLER, 1997).

It has become convention to characterize the history of technological change as comprising long periods of more or less constant incremental improvement punctuated by a periodic bursts of basic discovery, the creative gales of innovation that usher in new knowledge systems and that shift parts of the economy to new planes of development (SCHUMPETER, 1942; NELSON and WINTER, 1982). The temporal lumpiness of basic innovation (MENSCH, 1975) is mirrored by its uneven geography, with islands of innovation emerging from the economic landscape, sometimes remote and sometimes connected via heterogeneous social and economic networks, that bloom and wither as economic agents compete within, and simultaneously shape the evolution of, the capitalist space economy (ESSLETZBICHLER and RIGBY, 2007).

Over the course of history there have been many attempts to identify and define technologies that are

radical and to separate them from innovations that are more incremental in nature (SAHAL, 1981; DOSI, 1982; NELSON and WINTER, 1982; ABERNATHY and CLARK, 1985; CLARK, 1985). Recent research on the importance of inventions focuses on valuations of patents through forward citations (TRAJTENBERG, 1990a; HALL et al., 2005, 2007; GAMBARDELLA et al., 2008), though some are highly critical of this approach (BESSEN, 2008; ABRAMS et al., 2013). Interest in breakthrough inventions focuses on their role in creating private wealth (HARHOFF et al., 1999) while at the same time generating social benefits (TRAJTENBERG, 1990b), but more fundamentally in the way in which they hold the potential to transform the economic landscape (CHRISTENSEN, 1997). HELPMAN (1998) and LIPSEY et al. (2005) argue that these transformative powers reside in the broad applicability of many breakthrough innovations that they characterize as general purpose technologies (GPTs). Although the history of development of some GPTs is well-known (e.g. FOGEL, 1964; FISHLOW, 1965), isolating the introduction of a GPT to the economy and studying its subsequent adoption across the economy has proven difficult (PHENE et al., 2006; KERR, 2010). FELDMAN and YOON (2012) argue that the Cohen–Boyer class of patents provides an example of a GPT. To date, the factors that influenced the patterns of adoption of this breakthrough technology remain largely unexplored.

How does one explain the inconstant geography and history of technological advance? A starting point is acknowledging the difficulty of knowledge adoption. Ideas and knowledge are complex goods and Edison's aphorism aside, a precise recipe for their production is unknown. However, with the advent of intellectual property rights protection, knowledge production has become increasingly commodified (LAMOREAUX and SOKOLOFF, 1996), and a critical dimension of competition (LICHTENBERG and PHILIPSON, 2002). Nonetheless, the risk of working with new and uncertain knowledge and the attendant high cost of cultivating absorptive capacity cannot be borne by all firms. The search for new technology is highly specialized reflecting the resources and knowledge capabilities of individual economic agents and their partners (WENERFELT, 1984; BARNEY, 1991; KOGUT and ZANDER, 1992), the maturity of the industries within which they compete (ABERNATHY and UTTERBACK, 1978; KLEPPER, 1997), and the broader ecology of the places where they are located (COOKE et al., 1997; MORGAN, 1997; STORPER, 1997; GERTLER, 2003; ASHEIM and GERTLER, 2005).

Spatial variations in the creation of knowledge and competitive advantage are well known (FELDMAN, 1994; MASKELL and MALMBERG, 1999, FELDMAN and KOGLER, 2010). This heterogeneity reflects the pool of private assets and capabilities created by distinct assemblages of firms, workers and institutions in different locations, and by the capacity of these assemblages to develop localized forms of social capital (SAXENIAN, 1994; STORPER, 1997; FELDMAN and ZOLLER, 2012). In relatively thin geographical extensions of these claims the region is viewed as little more than the spatial analogue of the strategic firm partnership. More robust geographical models examine the ways in which spatial proximity increases the flow of tacit knowledge directly through face-to-face contact (MALMBERG and MASKELL, 2002; ASHEIM and GERTLER, 2005), and indirectly through enhancing other forms of proximity within localized clusters of economic actors (GERTLER, 2003).

Arguments about spatial proximity have long played a role in the diffusion of knowledge within geography (HÄGERSTRAND, 1953; BROWN, 1981) and beyond (GRILICHES, 1957). Empirical evidence of the localization of knowledge flows by JAFFE et al. (1993), MAURSETH and VERSPAGEN (2002) and SONN and STORPER (2008) reinforce those earlier claims. At the same time, growing recognition of different forms of proximity and relatedness (NOOTEBOOM, 2000; BOSCHMA, 2005; BOSCHMA and FRENKEN, 2010) has raised questions about the role of distance in regulating both the creation and the flow of knowledge. Attention is increasingly directed at the role of social proximity and cognitive proximity in the use and adoption of knowledge (HUBER, 2012).

Social proximity refers to the strength of interpersonal relationships that exist between individual actors (BOSCHMA, 2005). These relationships may take a variety of forms, though they tend to cohere around the concept of trust borne by repeated interaction in common workplaces, industrial organizations or related institutions. AUTANT-BERNARD et al. (2007) also note that social proximity can be developed among actors well beyond the local scale often through work-related collaboration, regular meetings, through conferences and trade fairs. Once trust-based social relationships are in place, it is much more likely that actors will engage in interactive learning processes and knowledge sharing, guided by an open attitude towards communicative rationality rather than purely market-driven considerations (LUNDVALL, 1992). Social proximity is much more likely to develop when actors are connected through short social chains. Formal collaboration among individuals, as in the case of co-inventorship, or common employment with the same company, adds to the development of such short chains, that in turn enhances the strength of social proximity (BRESCHI and LISSONI, 2009).

Cognitive proximity focuses upon the extent to which different actors, or in aggregate industries and regions, share common knowledge structures. High cognitive proximity implies greater correspondence between knowledge sets, skills, routines and institutions of knowledge creation and sharing and, thus, a higher potential for absorptive capacity (COHEN and LEVINTHAL, 1990; NOOTEBOOM, 2000). Higher levels of cognitive proximity also lead to enhanced collaboration as well as knowledge sharing. In a similar fashion, recombinant models of technological progress rest on the cognitive proximity of technological subsets and of the economic agents that shape their integration (WEITZMAN, 1998; FLEMING and SORENSON, 2001). KOGLER et al. (2013) and RIGBY (2013) extend these arguments in an explicitly spatial framework.

These different forms of proximity are finding purchase in a variety of empirical applications. Thus, BRESCHI and LISSONI (2001, 2004) express a good deal of scepticism regarding the measurement of localized knowledge spillovers, suggesting that empirical estimates are unreliable, at least in part, because they do not separate social from spatial proximity. MAGGIONI et al. (2007) develop econometric models exploring knowledge production and co-patenting within and across European regions and show that geographical proximity is always more important than social networks measured by participation within the European Union Fifth Framework Program and European Patent Office (EPO) co-patent applications. Using similar data, AUTANT-BERNARD et al. (2007) find strong evidence of spatial and social proximity in research and development (R&D) cooperation across Europe. FISCHER et al. (2006) examine patent citations across European regions in an extended gravity model, revealing that spatial and cognitive proximity regulate knowledge flows. In the United States, AGRAWAL et al. (2008) use the knowledge production function to explore how spatial proximity and social proximity influence access to knowledge. Using patent citations structured by metropolitan statistical area (MSA) and the co-ethnicity of inventors, they show that the two forms of proximity are statistically significant and that they act as substitutes. STRUMSKY and LOBO (2008) report that the agglomeration of inventors is more important than inventor networks in regulating the pace of invention in metropolitan areas. RIGBY and VAN DER WOUDEN (2013) find that cognitive proximity trumps both spatial and sectoral proximity in this regard. HUBER (2012) provides an excellent summary of much of this work and reports a more nuanced set of results regarding the importance of the different measures of proximity operating within the Cambridge technology cluster.

THE COHEN–BOYER rDNA PATENTS AND THE CREATION OF A NEW SUBCLASS

The Cohen–Boyer discovery builds upon a series of prior technological advances in biochemistry and genetics (FELDMAN et al., 2008). The patent was controversial when filed in 1974 and it was subject to three continuations and a six-year delay. Three factors delayed the granting of the patent (FELDMAN and YOON, 2012). First, academic patents were rare at the time and ownership for discoveries under federally funded research was not automatically assigned to universities until passage of the Bayh–Dole Act. Second, it was unclear whether genetically modified organisms could be patented. This question was answered in the affirmative by the Supreme Court in its ruling on the Diamond–Chakrabarty case. Third, rDNA was highly controversial (SMITH HUGHES, 2001). At the Asilomar Conference organized by Nobel Laureate Paul Berg, the scientific community agreed to a voluntary moratorium on rDNA research until its safety could be investigated.

The original Cohen–Boyer patent application claimed both the process of making rDNA and any products that resulted from using that method. When the USPTO initially denied the product claims, Stanford University divided the original patent application into two divisional product applications, one that claimed rDNA products produced in prokaryotic cells and the other that claimed rDNA products produced in eukaryotic cells[1] along with the process patent. The process patent (USPTO patent number 4237224) is the focus of the present study. The Cohen–Boyer patent has an application date of 1979 and a grant year date of 1980.

Upon granting, every patent is placed into one or more distinct technology classes that are designed to reflect the technological characteristics of the underlying knowledge base that they embody. At the time the Cohen–Boyer patent was granted in 1980, subclass 435/69.1 did not exist. On 5 December 1989, the USPTO issued Classification Order Number 1316, which created a new patent class 435/69.1 – Chemistry: Molecular Biology and Microbiology/rDNA technique that included the method of making a protein or polypeptide. When the set of technology codes is revised, as in this example, the USPTO reviews all granted patents and reclassifies those meeting the criteria of the new codes. At this time, the Cohen–Boyer patent, and all existing patents that made similar knowledge claims, were listed as belonging, at least in part, to class 435/69.1. The USPTO reclassification process provides the researcher with a continuously updated and consistent set of all patents that use specific technologies. STRUMSKY et al. (2012) review the use of patent technology codes to study technological change and point to their usefulness in tasks that relate to the identification of technological capabilities, the definition of technology spaces or as an indicator of the arrival of technological novelty.

The data used in this analysis are patent records made available through the USPTO. Patents have become an analytic staple for scholars interested in the geography and history of knowledge production (LAMOREAUX and SOKOLOFF, 1996; Ó HUALLACHÁIN, 1999; JAFFE and TRAJTENBERG, 2002; Ó HUALLACHÁIN and LEE, 2011), on the various types of technical knowledge produced as indicated by patent classes (HALL et al., 2001; STRUMSKY et al., 2012), and on the factors that regulate knowledge flow (JAFFE et al., 1993; BRESCHI

and LISSONI, 2001; SONN and STORPER, 2008). The popularity of patent data is related to their ready availability and to the wealth of information they provide. At the same time, the disadvantages of patents as overall measures of economic and inventive activity are well known (PAVITT, 1985; GRILICHES, 1990). It is clear that patents do not represent all forms of knowledge production within the economy and that they do not capture all produced knowledge. Patents, however, do provide insights into the organizations actively engaged in inventive activity in technologies, like rDNA, where the protection of intellectual property is important.

This paper focuses on patents that make knowledge claims in USPTO class 435/69.1, regardless of whether 435/69.1 is the primary class or not.[2] In total, there are 8947 patents used in this analysis. All patents in the sample contain at least one inventor residing in a US MSA.[3] Patents are allocated to the metropolitan areas within which the inventors on those patents are located. If a single patent has two inventors located in different MSAs, then both MSAs are regarded as having knowledge of rDNA technology. Inventors located outside the United States or not located within one of the 366 US metropolitan areas are dropped from the data. Inventors responsible for the production of rDNA patents are identified within USPTO data files using the inventor disambiguation routines of Ronald Lai and colleagues at Harvard (LAI et al., 2011).

The start of the study is 1976, the year of the first USPTO patent application in USPTO class 435/69.1. Three patents predate the application of the rDNA patent (number 4237224) in 1978 because their knowledge claims were adjudicated to belong to class 435/69.1 in a process of reclassification. This paper focuses on the year of application rather than on patent grant year to capture the time of invention. Because many patents are not granted for several years after application, the analysis is ended in 2005 to dampen the impact of right censoring in the data.[4]

THE SPATIAL DIFFUSION OF rDNA

Diffusion of rDNA technology can be traced by 'mapping' the distribution of patents in technology class 435/69.1 across time and space. Fig. 1 shows the growth of rDNA knowledge claims over time, recording the annual count of rDNA patents and the number of metropolitan areas where inventors using rDNA technology resided. The number of patents associated with class 435/69.1 increased rapidly through the late 1980s and early 1990s, following the classic 'S'-shaped diffusion curve. The counts of rDNA patents remain level throughout the late 1990s at around 800 applications per year, although some significant fluctuations are visible. The number of patent

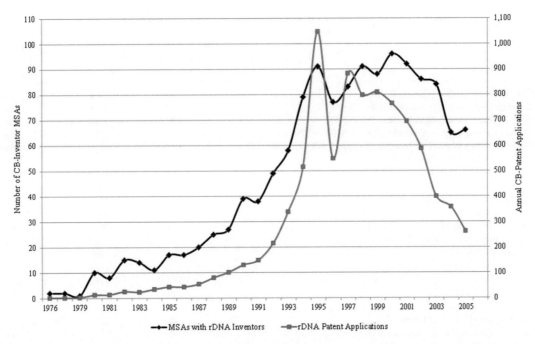

Fig. 1. Annual number of rDNA patent applications and corresponding count of metropolitan statistical areas (MSAs) where their respective inventors reside, 1976–2005

Note: The analysis is based on rDNA patents developed by inventors residing in one of the 366 MSAs) in the United States

applications that make knowledge claims in class 435/69.1 has subsequently levelled off, falling below 300 in 2005, the final year of the investigation.

Few cities were engaged in the production of rDNA inventions before the mid-1980s. By 1987, 11 years after the initial rDNA patent application, only 20 MSAs were producing patents in this technology field. Over the following ten years geographic diffusion accelerated with a little over 90 MSAs developing rDNA technologies in the early 1990s. After stabilizing at this number for about five years, the number of MSAs participating in rDNA invention activities started to decline in 2001. In the final two years observed, 2004 and 2005, the number of MSAs where rDNA invention took place was around 65. Note, however, that right censoring in the data series likely means this number is somewhat higher.

The geographical spread of rDNA technology is further detailed in Table 1 which lists the year of the first rDNA patent in each of the metropolitan areas listed and the year when rDNA-related inventions in each city reached ten patents. The cities listed are well-known centres of invention associated with academic research and subsequently the biotechnology industry. The first ranked city on this list, based on the total number of rDNA-related patent applications from 1976 to 2005, is the metropolitan area around San Francisco (California). Home to Stan Cohen and Herbert Boyer, the two initial inventors of the rDNA technology, this is certainly no surprise. Within San Francisco there is evidence of rapid adoption as a

number of different inventors there produced ten patents within three years of the development of rDNA applications. From this initial lead, the city developed a well-known centre of biotechnology research and commercialization activities. The Boston–Cambridge–Quincy (Massachusetts–New Hampshire) metropolitan area, which is also considered one of the key biotechnology centres in the nation, runs a close second to San Francisco, with the same year of initial rDNA patent application but a longer lag of six years to achieve ten patent applications. Total application counts start slightly later in the metropolitan areas of Philadelphia (Pennsylvania), Washington (DC), New York (New York) and San Diego (California).

As awareness of rDNA techniques expanded over space and time, this knowledge subset found broader application as an input to invention across related patent classes. Fig. 2 illustrates the patent classes that have been most frequently combined with the rDNA technology over three year periods running from 1976 to 2005. Technology in class 435/69.1 is most closely associated with its parent class 435: Chemistry: Molecular Biology and Microbiology. While USPC 930: Peptide or Protein Sequence is frequently combined with the rDNA technology in the initial time periods, its significance rapidly declines over time. Moving counter to this, USPC 424: Drug, Bio-Affecting and Body Treating Compositions appears to become increasingly linked to rDNA technology over time, as measured by its co-classification share in patent applications. Over time, the combinations of other

Table 1. Key places (metropolitan statistical areas – MSAs) of rDNA invention

MSA		rDNA patent applications, 1976–2005	Year of first rDNA patent application	Year when MSAs reached ten applications
1	San Francisco–Oakland–Fremont, CA	1133	1978	1981
2	Boston–Cambridge–Quincy, MA–NH	990	1978	1984
3	Philadelphia–Camden–Wilmington, PA–NJ–DE–MD	691	1981	1988
4	Washington–Arlington–Alexandria, DC–VA–MD–WV	639	1980	1986
5	New York–Northern New Jersey–Long Island, NY–NJ–PA	617	1980	1985
6	San Diego–Carlsbad–San Marcos, CA	585	1982	1985
7	San Jose–Sunnyvale–Santa Clara, CA	483	1985	1990
8	Seattle–Tacoma–Bellevue, WA	400	1981	1988
9	Los Angeles–Long Beach–Santa Ana, CA	260	1982	1989
10	St. Louis, MO–IL	150	1976	1989
11	Chicago–Joliet–Naperville, IL–IN–WI	147	1980	1990
12	Sacramento–Arden–Arcade–Roseville, CA	127	1987	1992
13	Baltimore–Towson, MD	126	1988	1993
14	Houston–Sugar Land–Baytown, TX	123	1983	1992
15	Madison, WI	122	1982	1987
16	Indianapolis–Carmel, IN	116	1981	1984
17	Durham–Chapel Hill, NC	113	1984	1992
18	Des Moines–West Des Moines, IA	97	1989	1995
19	Oxnard–Thousand Oaks–Ventura, CA	90	1985	1994
20	Dallas–Fort Worth–Arlington, TX	79	1983	1992

technologies used with USPC 435/69.1 expand. In addition to USPCs 536: Organic Compounds, 530: Chemistry: Natural Resins or Derivatives; Peptides or Proteins, 424: Drug, Bio-Affecting and Body Treating Compositions, 800: Multicellular Living Organisms and Unmodified Parts Thereof and Related Processes, and 514: Drug, Bio-Affecting and Body Treating Compositions, which represent the largest shares of

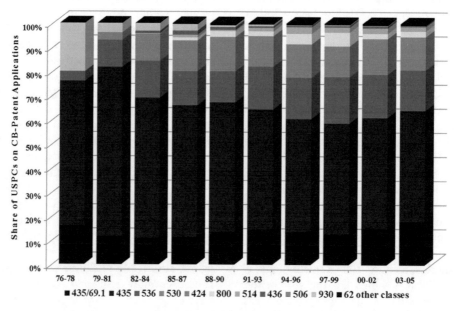

Fig. 2. Distribution of US patent classes (USPC) listed on rDNA-related patent documents; three-year shares based on application year, 1976–2005

Note: 435/69.1 = rDNA USPC 435/69.1, 435 = Chemistry: Molecular Biology and Microbiology, 536 = Organic Compounds, 530 = Chemistry: Natural Resins or Derivatives; Peptides or Proteins, 424 = Drug, Bio-Affecting and Body Treating Compositions, 800 = Multicellular Living Organisms and Unmodified Parts Thereof and Related Processes, 514 = Drug, Bio-Affecting and Body Treating Compositions, 436 = Chemistry: Analytical and Immunological Testing, 506 = Combinatorial Chemistry Technology: Method, Library, Apparatus, and 930 = Peptide or Protein Sequence. The '62 other classes' refers to USPCs that are either rarely combined with class 435/69.1 or to classes that only have been combined with the rDNA technology in more recent time periods, including USPCs 510 (Cleaning Compositions), 977 (Nanotechnology), 426 (Food and Edible Material), and 702 (Data Processing); USPC 514 is an integral part of class 424 combined patent classes, more recently rDNA technology is connected with such diverse technology fields as cleaning compositions (USPC 510), nanotechnology (USPC 977), and data processing (USPC 702).

The primary aim in this paper is to examine the determinants of the spatial diffusion of rDNA technology across US cities. Combining arguments from early research on the diffusion of technology (SILVERBERG, 1991; GEROSKI, 2000; KELLER, 2004) with more recent claims about different forms of proximity (BOSCHMA, 2005) and technological diversification (HAUSMANN and KLINGER, 2007; BOSCHMA et al., 2014; RIGBY 2013) prompts exploration of the following simple model:

$$Y_{ct} = \beta_1 GP_{ct} + \beta_2 CP_{ct} + \beta_3 SP_{ct} + \beta X_{ct}$$

where the dependent variable is binary, indicating whether city (MSA) c develops an rDNA patent in year t; and the three key independent variables represent geographical proximity of a city to rDNA technology (GP), cognitive proximity of a city's knowledge base to rDNA technology (CP) and the social proximity of the city to knowledge about rDNA (SP). The final term in the model captures the influence of a number of covariates that might impact the development of rDNA technology. The interest in these arguments also is related to research examining the relative strength of social proximity and spatial proximity in mediating knowledge flows (JAFFE et al., 1993; BRESCHI and LISSONI, 2001). Analysis of this model takes different forms that are detailed below. First the paper turns to development of the key measures of proximity.

Spatial proximity of rDNA

Invention incorporating rDNA technology depends upon access to knowledge of rDNA. Codified rDNA information may be broadly available, but tacit knowledge of rDNA technology depends upon the ability of a set of potential adopters who have the relevant absorptive capacity. The role of geographical proximity in constraining the flow of rDNA knowledge between US metropolitan areas is operationalized in two ways. First, data on the latitude and longitude of each MSA determine the Euclidean distance between each pair of metropolitan areas. For each city, the average distance to all other 365 metro areas is calculated. A simple hypothesis is that, *ceteris paribus*, metropolitan areas on average closer to all other MSAs are more likely to develop rDNA related capacity in the form of inventions in class 435/69.1. This physical measure of MSA geography is fixed over time. A second measure of geographical proximity combines the distance from city i to all other cities j that have already generated an rDNA patent in class 435/69.1. From this information, two alternative variables capture the changing access of individual cities to the techniques developed by Cohen and Boyer. The first

of these variables is the average distance from a city to all other cities that possess knowledge of rDNA technology. The second of the two variables is the distance from each city to its nearest neighbour that has patented in the rDNA technology class. Both variables change over time as the set of MSAs that invent rDNA patents evolves. Theory does not clearly help to differentiate between the alternatives and so both were tried in early empirical work. The minimum distance measure of geographical proximity was much more consistent in the models examined and so the option was for that measure. It is hypothesized that the smaller this minimum distance, the greater the likelihood of a city generating an rDNA patent in a subsequent year. For empirical analysis all independent variables are lagged one year.

Descriptive statistics on this time-varying measure of geographical proximity (minimum distance to rDNA) are reported in Table 2. The minimum distances of zero indicate that a number of cities developed rDNA class patents in the prior year. Those cities that did not develop an rDNA patent in the given year but that are closest to cities that did develop such patents are the top-ranked cities listed at the bottom of Table 2. The maximum value identifies the city that is most remote in terms of having the maximum nearest-neighbour distance to a city that has developed a patent in class 435/69.1. The maximum and mean values of spatial proximity decline over time as expected as the number of cities developing rDNA patents increase through the mid-1990s. Thereafter, these values increase once more, though the mean value of geographical proximity rises only modestly as the set of cities developing rDNA technologies declines late in the study period.

Table 2. Descriptive statistics for city geographical proximity (minimum distance) to knowledge of rDNA

Year	1985	1995	2005
Minimum	0	0	0
Maximum	39.298	6.949	38.825
Mean	3.263	1.111	1.462
SD	3.587	1.190	3.139
Top-ranked cities	Raleigh	State College	Allentown
	Vallejo	Anacortes	Vallejo
	Stockton	Detroit[a]	Salinas
	Providence	Ogden	Daytona Beach[a]
	Ocala	Joplin	Salt Lake City[a]

Note: The distances between cities are Euclidean and based on the geographical coordinates of the centroids of each metropolitan statistical area (MSA). The minimum distances on which the values are based are the distances from each city to its nearest neighbour that developed a patent in class 435/69.1 in the previous year. The top-ranked cities are those without an rDNA patent in the specified year but closest to a city that has. [a]Those cities that developed an rDNA patent the following year.

Social proximity of rDNA

While geographical proximity might represent one measure of relative city access to a certain pool of knowledge, it says nothing about the extent of the interaction that actually occurs between any pair of metropolitan areas. The interaction of particular interest is the potential flow of rDNA-related knowledge. An attempt is made to capture this flow better using information on the spatial distribution of the inventors of rDNA patents and all their collaborators. This measure is operationalized in the following way. First, a city social proximity matrix with dimension 366×366 is constructed. All cells in this matrix are coded zero. Second, all inventors of rDNA patents with an application year t are identified. A single inventor of an rDNA patent results in a 1 being added to the city social proximity matrix in the cell of the principal diagonal indicating the city where that inventor resides. Co-inventors on a single rDNA patent who live in two cities i and j result in the value 1 being added to cells (i,j) and (j,i) of the city social proximity matrix that is symmetrical. Next, all non-rDNA patents that the rDNA inventors of year t have developed over the previous five years are identified. Cross-city collaborations on these non-rDNA inventors result in the value 0.5 being added to the corresponding city-by-city cells of the social proximity matrix. The value 0.5 reflects a discounting of knowledge exchange regarding rDNA that might be present in non-rDNA collaboration. It is to be admitted that this discounting is rather ad hoc and that additional empirical work in this area is warranted. The length of the paper means that such investigation must be reserved for another time. The focus here is on prior co-inventor collaborations for it is anticipated that the knowledge development process takes time and during this development period some knowledge about rDNA might flow to non-rDNA collaborators of rDNA inventors and the former might pass this information to interested parties in their place of residence. The city social proximity matrices are built up annually for the period 1980–2005. Each of these matrices is examined in UCINET and a measure of eigenvector centrality recorded for each city in each year corresponding to the social proximity of the metropolitan area (BORGATTI *et al.*, 2002). Note that the social proximity centrality measures are lagged one year in the models below.

Over the first few years after the introduction of the patent for rDNA, the city with the highest social proximity to this technology was Bridgeport (Connecticut), home of Yale University (1980), then Chicago (Illinois) (1981) and then San Francisco (1982). Unsurprisingly, perhaps, San Francisco, the location of the original Cohen–Boyer patent, has the highest measure of social proximity by 1985 and maintains the top-ranked position over the next 20 years. After 1985, larger MSAs, most known for their biotechnology industry clusters, fill out the remaining top ranks of the social proximity measure.

Table 3. Descriptive statistics for city social proximity to rDNA inventors

Year	1985	1995	2005
Minimum	0	0	0
Maximum	50.787	34.786	36.163
Mean	2.214	3.485	3.460
SD	7.063	6.528	6.541
Top-ranked cities	San Francisco	San Francisco	San Francisco
	New York	San Diego	San Jose
	Chicago	New York	San Diego
	Cleveland	Boston	Boston
	Boston	San Jose	Philadelphia

Note: Values are centrality measures from UCINET (BORGATTI *et al.*, 2002).

Descriptive statistics on the rDNA metropolitan social proximity measure are reported in Table 3 for three time periods. The relatively high maximum value of social proximity in 1985 indicates the concentration of this technology in patent class 435/69.1, soon after its development. Thereafter, the increase over time in the mean social proximity measure for US metropolitan areas, together with a decline in the maximum value, is evidence of the spatial diffusion of knowledge regarding the Cohen–Boyer technology. The data in Table 3 suggest that between 1995 and 2005 there is little change in the geographical spread of rDNA knowledge.

Cognitive proximity of rDNA

By cognitive or technological knowledge subsets of knowledge are referred to which are associated with particular classes of inventions, technologies or even industries. The proximity of a region to such knowledge subsets refers to local facility or expertise with specific technologies or to how close, in a technological sense, the economic agents of a region are to having such expertise. The knowledge subset of most interest is that circumscribed by patent class 435/69.1. While rDNA patents are a subset of the broader class 435, the subclass is separated in what follows and it is mapped in technology space as a distinct set of knowledge along with 438 other unique primary patent classes.

In order to construct a US knowledge space information is needed on the number of patents in each technology class along with measures of cognitive proximity, the technological distance, between each pair of classes. Co-class information on individual patents is employed to measure the cognitive distance between each pair of technology classes, following the earlier work of JAFFE (1986), ENGELSMAN and VAN RAAN (1994), VERSPAGEN (1997), BRESCHI *et al.* (2003), and NESTA and SAVIOTTI (2005). The number of primary patent classes of focus here is considerably larger than that employed in most prior studies and thus the technology space outlined below is of higher resolution than those reported to date.

To measure the cognitive proximity, or knowledge relatedness, between patent technology classes in a single year the following method is employed. Let P indicate the total number of patent applications in the chosen year. Then, let $F_{ip} = 1$ if patent record p lists the classification code i, otherwise $F_{ip} = 0$. Note that i represents one of the 438 primary technology classes into which the new knowledge contained in patents is classified, plus an additional class identified as 435/69.1. In a given year, the total number of patents that list technology class i is given by $N_i = \sum_p F_{ip}$. In a similar fashion, the number of individual patents that list the pair of co-classes i and j is identified by the count $N_{ij} = \sum_p F_{ip}F_{jp}$. Repeating this co-class count for all pairs of 439 patent classes yields the (439 × 439) symmetric technology class co-occurrence matrix C, the elements of which are the co-class counts N_{ij}. The co-class counts measure the technological proximity of all patent class pairs, but they also are influenced by the number of patents found within each individual patent class N_i. Thus, the elements of the co-occurrence matrix are standardized by the square root of the product of the number of patents in the row and column classes of each element, or:

$$S_{ij} = \frac{N_{ij}}{\sqrt{N_i * N_j}}$$

where S_{ij} is an element of the standardized co-occurrence matrix (S) that indicates the technological proximity, or knowledge relatedness, between all pairs of patent classes in a given year. The elements on the principal diagonal of S are set to 1. Alternative forms of standardization are discussed by VAN ECK and WALTMAN (2009) and JOO and KIM (2010).

With the aid of UCINET (BORGATTI et al., 2002), the network of technological relatedness across the 438 primary patent classes and class 435/69.1 is mapped. The technological relatedness network is generated with the Gower-scaling metric, itself derived to examine patterns of similarity across network nodes (GOWER, 1971). The nodes in the network correspond to each of the 438 distinct technological classes within the USPTO, and class 435/69.1. The relative positions of the nodes are fixed by the standardized co-occurrence class counts (S_{ij}). Note that the standardized co-occurrence matrix (S) is symmetric. The principal diagonal plays no role in the relative locations of the nodes.

The knowledge relatedness networks for 1975–2005 are shown in Fig. 3. The node colours represent the aggregate technology (six class) grouping of HALL et al. (2001): black = Chemicals (1), green = Computers and Communications (2), yellow = Drugs and Medical (3), red = Electronics (4), blue = Mechanical (5), and grey = Miscellaneous (6). There is clear evidence of the clustering of individual patent categories within most of these classes, indicating that the technological proximity or relatedness measure is capturing what may be considered as a common knowledge base within these more aggregate technology groupings. The size of each node illustrates the number of patents in that technology class in the given year. Node sizes have been scaled to allow comparison over time. rDNA patents in class 435/69.1 are illustrated with the small, yellow triangle in each of the slides of Fig. 3. In early years, rDNA patents are closely linked in the knowledge space with chemicals and with drugs and medical patent classes.

In order to measure the cognitive proximity of the knowledge base of a metropolitan area to the rDNA patent class the average relatedness of a city's patents to class 435/69.1 is found. In technology space, nodes that are close together have a high relatedness score. These are the technology classes that tend to co-occur with relatively high frequency on individual patents. In terms of rDNA, the average relatedness value for metropolitan area m in year t is calculated as:

$$AR^{mt} = \frac{\sum_j S^t_{CBj} * D^{mt}_j}{N^{mt}}$$

where S^t_{CBj} represents the technological relatedness between rDNA (class 435/69.1) patents and patents in all other 439 technology classes j, where the vector j includes class 435/69.1. This term is the (row or column) vector of the standardized co-occurrence matrix noted above for the rDNA technology class. D^{mt}_j is the count of the number of patents in technology class j in metro area m in year t; and N^{mt} is a count of the total number of patents in city m in year t.

The measure of cognitive proximity captures the mass of invention that occurs in a particular city and the overall relatedness of that inventive effort to technology class 435/69.1. In general it would be good if the cognitive proximity variable could indicate something about the distribution of a city's inventive efforts in knowledge space along with an index of how close those efforts are to the technology of interest. The chosen term is not ideal, however, for it cannot readily discriminate between small cities that generate few patents that are an average distance away from class 435/69.1 and large cities that generate many patents some close and some far away from class 435/69.1. In this example, whether the small or large city has an advantage in terms of developing rDNA technologies is unclear.

Table 4 presents descriptive statistics for metropolitan area cognitive proximity to the rDNA patent class. The mean average relatedness value of patents in general to the rDNA class of patents within US metropolitan areas was approximately three times higher in 2005 than in 1985, indicating broader use of rDNA and closely related technologies. The metro areas with the highest cognitive proximity values to patent class 435/69.1 are, perhaps, not those that might have been

Fig. 3. The U.S. technology space incorporating rDNA (USPC 435/69.1)

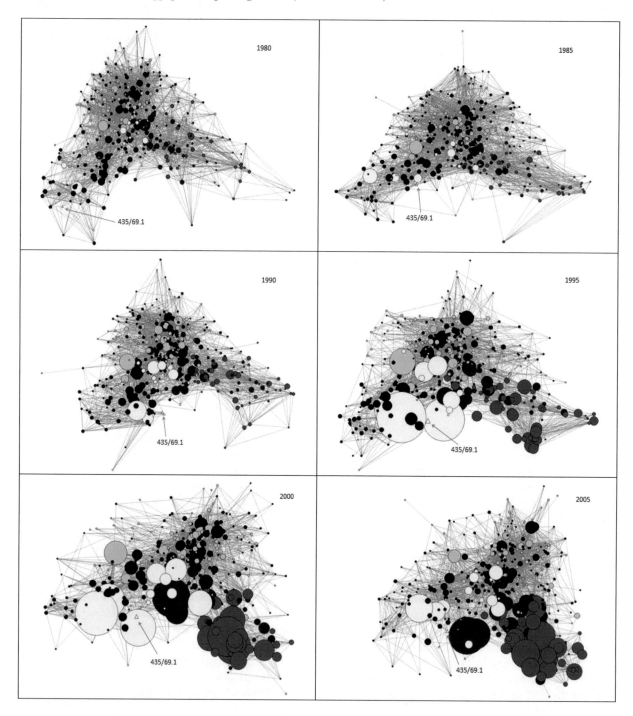

Note: Patent class 435/69.1 is depicted by the triangle in the lower left of the technology space. The nodes represent all 438 primary classes of utility patents and node sizes reflect the number of patents in each class, scaled for comparability over the years 1980, 1985, 1990, 1995, 2000 and 2005. The various greyscales of the nodes represent the six aggregate technology classes of Hall et al. (2001). From light to dark these are: Drugs & Medical, Miscellaneous, Electronics, Computers & Communications, Mechanical, Chemicals.

Table 4. *Descriptive statistics for cognitive proximity of metropolitan areas to rDNA*

Year	1985	1995	2005
Minimum	0	0	0
Maximum	0.0241	0.0449	0.1160
Mean	0.0016	0.0055	0.0046
SD	0.0029	0.0083	0.0094
Top-ranked cities	Madison	Honolulu	Flagler
	Kennewick	Shreveport	Athens
	Elkhart	Durham–Chapel Hill	Auburn
	College Station	Madison	Iowa City
	Charleston	Blacksburg	Decatur

expected. Most metro areas listed in Table 4 have relatively small numbers of patents, but those patents are in patent class 435/69.1 or close to it in the technology space of Fig. 3. Indeed, Madison (Wisconsin), Kennewick (Washington), Durham–Chapel Hill (North Carolina), Blacksburg (Virginia), Flagler (Florida), Athens (Georgia), and Iowa City (Iowa) are all university towns and sites of rDNA inventions over the period investigated. All the metropolitan areas listed in Table 1 as key centres of rDNA invention have average cognitive proximity values that are greater than average for US cities. It is hypothesized that metropolitan areas with higher levels of cognitive proximity to Cohen–Boyer technology are more likely to develop patents that make knowledge claims in class 435/69.1.

MODEL AND ESTIMATION RESULTS

The primary research question focuses on the probability of a metropolitan area generating an rDNA patent in class 435/69.1. There are time-series panel data available for 366 MSAs over 26 years (1980–2005). The limited (binary) nature of the dependent variable suggests use of a logit or probit regression model. There is also a right-censoring issue in the data that may generate significant bias in estimated coefficients (ALLISON, 1984). Armed with repeated observations on the same set of metropolitan areas over time enables exploration of a fixed effects panel model to deal with potential problems of unobserved heterogeneity. Another possibility that does not control for unobserved heterogeneity, but that more explicitly handles censored data, is the event history model. Both possibilities are explored below using the Cox non-proportional (extended) hazard model, incorporating time-varying covariates, to examine the date of a first rDNA invention within a metropolitan area, while the panel form of the logit model us used to examine the probability of repeated invention in patent class 435/69.1 across all years in the study period.

Time-varying independent variables are lagged by one year in all models employed to generate the results discussed below. There is no clear theoretical rationale for employing a lag of only one period, the aim is only to ensure that the spatial distribution of rDNA patents in year t do not influence the value of independent variables constructed for the same year. While one-period lags might dampen some concerns with endogeneity, this is a more serious issue that is returned to below. Attention is first turned to the event history model and at attempts to identify the date at which a metropolitan area first develops a patent in class 435/69.1. The patent data by city are not left-censored for the data series start with the introduction of the first rDNA patent in 1980. However, there are right-censoring issues with the data, as a number of metropolitan areas, 165 out of 366, do not develop a Cohen–Boyer invention by 2005 when the study period ends. In standard regression models that incorporate cross-sectional and time-series data, cross-sectional units that exhibit no variance over time in the dependent variable, are omitted from the model. However, such observations may provide valuable information. For example, a city might never develop a Cohen–Boyer patent because it is geographically remote and inventors in that city might have weak social connections with Cohen–Boyer inventors elsewhere. The authors sought to keep this information in the data set by employing event history techniques. The Cox semi-parametric survival model is the most widely used of the family of hazard models, largely because it does not assume a particular form of probability distribution for survival times. The cost of this flexibility is the assumption of the proportionality of hazards, an assumption that is violated because of the time-varying covariates that enter the model. Thus, the extended Cox model is made use of (BLOSSFELD et al., 2007).

In all the statistical analysis reported below, the paper controls for a number of other covariates that likely influence the spatial diffusion of rDNA technology in addition to the influence of geographical, social and cognitive proximity. The number of patents generated in each metropolitan area provides a proxy for city size/inventiveness. Insofar as patenting in a specialized field of biotechnology is likely associated with basic research in universities and hospitals, typically though not always found in larger urban areas, it is hypothesized that patent counts in general will be positively related to the probability of a city patenting in class 435/69.1. Note that the city-size variable is positively correlated with the social proximity variable, as might be expected. However, that correlation is not cause for undue concern as collinearity renders estimators inefficient rather than biased. Levels of biomedical research funding in universities and in industry were also constructed from National Institute of Health (NIH) awards for each city across the period under study. Higher levels of biomedical research are expected to increase the probability of patenting in rDNA. These

Table 5. Estimating the influence of different forms of proximity on the likelihood of a city inventing a first Cohen–Boyer patent in relation to the baseline hazard (single failure estimated with the extended Cox semi-parametric hazard model with time-varying covariates)

Time-fixed covariates	Hazard ratios		
	Model 1: Full sample	Model 2: Low-patent cities (< 10 patents)	Model 3: High-patent cities (> 90 patents)
Average Distance to Other Cities	1.03451***	1.01377***	1.02711***
	(0.0107)	(0.0484)	(0.0248)
Time-varying covariates			
Lag Geographic Proximity	0.99059	1.05948	0.99897
	(0.0146)	(0.0456)	(0.0243)
Lag Social Proximity	1.03280***	1.29740***	1.00837
	(0.0095)	(0.0916)	(0.0099)
Lag Cognitive Proximity	1.01147***	1.00282	1.04668*
	(0.00243)	(0.0048)	(0.0269)
Lag Patent Count	1.00157***	1.02773	1.00096***
	(0.0002)	(0.0186)	(0.0002)
Lag University R&D	0.99999**	0.99999	0.99999*
	(2.47E–07)	(8.18E–07)	(4.03E–07)
Lag Industry R&D	1.00000***	1.00000	1.00000
	(2.31E–06)	(9.38E–06)	(5.93E–06)
	$n = 6573$	$n = 2397$	$n = 740$
	Failures = 201	Failures = 17	Failures = 87
	LL = –1048.071	LL = –65.944	LL = –292.007
	Prob > Chi^2 = 0.000	Prob > Chi^2 = 0.000	Prob > Chi^2 = 0.000

Notes: All time-varying covariates are lagged one period and are interacted with log(time). The Breslow method is used for ties. Robust standard errors reported in parentheses.

***Significant at the 0.01 level, **significant at the 0.05 level and *significant at the 0.1 level.

LL, log pseudo-likelihood and the overall significance of the model is given by the *p*-value in the Chi^2 test shown at the bottom of the table. Converting the hazard ratios to a regression coefficient by logging and then dividing by the standard error yields the usual *p*-scores.

covariates also are lagged one year in all estimations. Finally, also identified in the data were those inventors of rDNA patents who moved cities through the period of investigation and thus took knowledge of Cohen–Boyer technology with them. In only ten (of 201) cases was an inventor move associated with the first year of rDNA invention across all US cities. Omitting these observations in the hazard model resulted in no significant differences in the results discussed below.

Table 5 presents estimation results of the extended Cox hazard model for the patent data against the time-varying covariates. The dependent variable in this model is the number of years after 1980 when a city introduces its first rDNA patent, the hazard. The dependent variable is binary with values of zero representing years prior to the first rDNA patent within a city. The base model is first run and then a series of questions in extensions of the initial specification are examined. Model 1 presents results for all 366 metropolitan areas over all 26 years of the analysis. Two measures of geographical proximity are employed in this first model: the time-fixed measure of the average distance of each city to all its 365 neighbours and the time-varying measure of spatial proximity (minimum distance to rDNA knowledge) defined above. The hazard ratio for the time-fixed measure of the average distance of a city to its neighbours in

model 1 is greater than 1 and significant. This means that across all years, MSAs that are on average further from one another have a greater likelihood of developing an rDNA patent. This finding is somewhat unexpected and runs counter to the usual assumptions that information flows more readily over shorter distances rather than long. Turning to the time-varying measure of geographical proximity, the distance of a city to its nearest neighbour that has already developed a patent in class 435/69.1, the hazard ratio is less than 1, consistent with expectations, though it is statistically insignificant. The hazard ratios for social proximity and cognitive proximity are both in line with hypothesized values and are statistically significant. A one-unit increase in social proximity raises the probability that a metropolitan area will generate a first rDNA patent over the baseline hazard by 3.3%. Cognitive proximity raises the hazard ratio by a little more than 1% for every one-unit increase in this variable. Thus, cities that have strong social ties to inventors who have knowledge of rDNA technologies, and cities that have a knowledge base that is relatively close to rDNA technologies are more likely to develop rDNA patents than cities that do not have such characteristics. Examining the other covariates in model 1, large cities, those that patent more in general, tend to develop rDNA patents before smaller cities, and

EVOLUTIONARY ECONOMIC GEOGRAPHY

this effect is significant. Similarly, cities with more industrial R&D in the biomedical area develop rDNA patents earlier, though cities with more university R&D are less likely to develop rDNA technologies than others. Even though the effects of R&D spending in the biomedical area have a small influence on the hazard ratio, the negative impact of university R&D spending is puzzling.

Note that metropolitan patent counts are highly correlated with social proximity (Pearson coefficient = 0.6) as might be expected. As the number of patents increase within a metropolitan area, the social proximity of the city also increases. Removing the patent count variable from the Cox model doubles the size of the hazard ratio for social proximity, while leaving all other covariates essentially unchanged.

Models 2 and 3 in Table 5 provide results from the extended Cox model for small cities with relatively few patents and for large cities with relatively high patent counts, respectively. These two groups fall just inside the interquartile range of the distribution of metropolitan areas by patent count, corresponding to the 30th and 70th percentiles. (Trying to estimate the model for the lower quartile generated a very small number of failures (patents in class 435/69.1) and no model convergence.) Cities in the bottom quartile of metro areas by patent count generated only 17 of the 201 total first-time patents examined in the Cox model. Cities in the top quartile were responsible for 87 Cohen–Boyer patents. The key differences between these two subsamples are found in the values of the hazard ratios for social and cognitive proximity. On the one hand, for small cities, the hazard ratio for social proximity is very large, indicating that a one-unit increase in the connectedness of the city's inventors to inventors of rDNA patents raises the probability of patenting in class 435/69.1 by about 30% over the baseline rate. Cognitive proximity has no significant influence on the hazard ratio in small cities. On the other hand, in large cities, social proximity has no significant influence on the hazard ratio, while cognitive proximity exerts a significant, positive effect. It is suspected that cities over a certain size threshold have a sufficient level of social proximity to generate rDNA technologies and that further increases in social proximity make little difference to the probability of such events. In large cities, whether the knowledge base is closely related to rDNA technology is a much more important predictor of increases in the hazard ratio.

The unexpected results on the measures of geographical proximity in Table 5 prompted additional exploration of the spread of rDNA technology across US metropolitan areas. The early years of diffusion seem to dominate the results in Table 5 when rDNA technology jumped between larger cities such as San Francisco, Boston, Philadelphia, Washington, New York, St. Louis (Missouri) and San Diego. This appears to be a process more reflective of hierarchical

Table 6. Estimating the Cox extended hazard model for different time periods

Time-fixed covariates	Hazard ratios	
	Model 4: For years before 1995	Model 5: For 1995 and later years
Average Distance to Other Cities	1.04523***	0.99659
	(0.0110)	(0.0209)
Time-varying covariates		
Lag Geographic Proximity	0.99338	0.91656*
	(0.0129)	(0.0450)
Lag Social Proximity	1.02815***	1.05739***
	(0.0105)	(0.0223)
Lag Cognitive Proximity	1.02582***	1.00896***
	(0.0062)	(0.0028)
Lag Patent Count	1.00166***	1.00160***
	(0.0002)	(0.0003)
Lag University R&D	0.99999	0.99999
	(2.95E–07)	(5.50E–07)
Lag Industry R&D	1.00000	1.00000
	(3.50E–06)	(3.65E–06)
	n = 4398	n = 2175
	Failures = 127	Failures = 74
	LL = –670.296	LL = –369.168
	Prob > Chi^2 = 0.000	Prob > Chi^2 = 0.000

Notes: All time-varying covariates are lagged one period and are interacted with log(time). The Breslow method is used for ties. Robust standard errors reported in parentheses.

***Significant at the 0.01 level, **significant at the 0.05 level and *significant at the 0.1 level.

LL, log pseudo-likelihood and the overall significance of the model is given by the *p*-value in the Chi^2 test shown at the bottom of the table. Converting the hazard ratios to a regression coefficient by logging and then dividing by the standard error yields the usual *p*-scores.

diffusion rather than the standard epidemic model. Only later in the study period is there more growth of rDNA invention in smaller cities that are somewhat closer to one another than the large cities that dominate the early years. To examine this argument further, the extended Cox model is rerun for two different time periods, before and after 1994. The results are displayed in Table 6.

Table 6 confirms the intuition. Model 4 is restricted to the years up to 1994, while Model 5 runs over the years since 1994. Note that the significance of the time-fixed measure of geographical proximity disappears in the second time-period while the time-varying measure of geographical proximity becomes significant with the expected negative sign (hazard ratio < 1). Thus, after 1994 (see Model 5), a one-unit increase in the distance of cities to their nearest neighbours with knowledge of rDNA is associated with an 8.5% reduction of the baseline hazard ratio, the likelihood of developing an rDNA patent. Since the mid-1990s, the historical geography of rDNA patenting appears to have shifted, leading to a pattern of geographical infilling, with production of patents in

107

Table 7. Estimating the influence of different forms of proximity on the probability of a city inventing an rDNA patent (repeated events estimated with fixed effects panel models)

Independent variables	Model 1: Fixed effects panel logit log odds	Model 2: Linear probability model instrumental variables (GMM2S)
Lag Geog Proximity	0.00974	−0.13351***
	(0.0169)	(0.0451)
Lag Social Proximity	0.04570***	0.14152***
	(0.0122)	(0.0204)
Lag Cognitive Proximity	0.00767**	0.14572***
	(3.1092)	(0.0271)
Lag Patent Count	0.00032	−0.01033
	(0.0004)	(0.0172)
Lag University R&D	−1.17E–06**	−0.01507**
	(4.93E–07)	(0.0068)
Lag Industry R&D	0.00001**	0.02217***
	(6.47E–06)	(0.0086)
	$n = 4975$	$n = 8418$
	Log likelihood = −1207.355	$R^2 = 0.0972$
	Prob > Chi^2 = 0.000	Root MSE = 0.2731
Under-identification test		
Kleibergen–Paap LM-statistic		
(Chi^2 *p*-value)		173.929 (0.000)
Weak Identification test		
Cragg–Donald Wald *F*-statistic		27.827
Kleibergen–Paap Wald *F*-statistic		19.566
Over-identification test		
Hansen *J*-statistic		
(Chi^2 *p*-value)		8.834 (0.1831)

Note: All independent variables are lagged one period. ***Significant at the 0.01 level, **significant at the 0.05 level and *significant at the 0.1 level. Year fixed effects included but not reported. A total of 167 cities (4175 observations) are dropped by the conditional logit (Model 1) because of no change in the dependent variable. In Model 2 all independent variables are log transformed and assumed to be endogenous. The instrumental variables used in this model are two-, three- and four-year time-lags of the full set of independent variables. Model 2 is estimated using generalized methods of moments techniques with Newey–West standard errors that are robust to arbitrary serial autocorrelation and heteroskedasticity. Standard errors are shown in parentheses. In tests of under-identification and weak identification.

technology class 435/69.1 increasingly found in cities that are closer together than in the period before 1994. While the roles of social and cognitive proximity along with city size remain similar over the whole time period, it is noteworthy that the impact of university R&D spending on rDNA patent production is insignificant over both time periods in Table 6.

Table 7 shifts the analysis to a fixed effects logit model (Model 1) that allows one to control for unobserved heterogeneity, though at the expense of concerns regarding the right-censoring in the data. The key finding is that the results are broadly consistent with those already reported for the event history model. One marked difference between the Cox extended hazard model and the logistic model is that the probability of repeated rDNA patenting over time is examined in the latter model, while in the former the focus was only on the time to the first rDNA patent. The fixed-time measure of average distance between cities also drops out of the fixed effects model. In the fixed effects logit model of Table 7 is included time fixed effects, though they are not reported. Note also that the conditional form of the fixed effects logit model

eliminates 167 cities from analysis because the value of the dependent variable in these cities is unchanged. In almost all these cases the metropolitan areas in question never develop an rDNA patent. (This is the obvious cost of right-censoring.)

The partial logistic regression coefficients reported in Model 1 of Table 7 are log odds ratios, reporting how a one-unit increase in the independent variable influences a change in the log odds of the dependent variable. For all years, the lagged value of geographic proximity, distance to the nearest city that has generated a Cohen–Boyer patent, has no significant influence on the log odds of a patent in class 435/69.1. Social proximity and cognitive proximity have a significant effect on the log odds ratio and both exhibit the anticipated positive sign. For example, a one-unit increase in social proximity raises the log odds of an rDNA patent being invented in a metropolitan area by 0.0457. This is an increase in the odds ratio of a Cohen–Boyer patent of 1.046, after transforming the coefficient. City size, as proxied by the sum of patent counts, has no significant influence on the log odds ratio. Removing the patent count variable yields no change on the social proximity measure in this model. Research and development in the university and in industry significantly influence the log odds ratio, though again in different directions. Industry R&D increases those odds, while university R&D reduces the log odds of an rDNA patent, suggesting that further work might consider the technology transfer orientation and operations at different institutions. While the Bayh–Dole Act passed in 1980, it was not until the later 1990s that the majority of research universities had established tech-licensing offices. Attitudes towards technology transfer were even slower to change to encourage active patenting. Note that marginal effects are not reliably produced for the panel form of the fixed effects logit model.

Model 2 in Table 7 returns to some robustness issues. First, this paper deals with potential concerns regarding the distribution of independent variables by logging them all. It then moves to the more difficult problem of endogeneity. With MSA-level data, no obvious instruments are available to exploit and thus this paper resorts to a series of two-, three- and four-period lags of all independent variables to serve as instruments. Experimenting with additional lags had little impact on the results, except for the significance of the university R&D variable that tended to become insignificant with longer lags. Kleibergen–Paap statistics reveal that the instrumental-variables model is identified and that lagged values of the independent variables are not weak instruments. The Hansen J-statistic suggests that the instruments (collectively) may be regarded as exogenous. Concerns with persistence in the data are dampened using Newey–West standard errors that are robust to arbitrary serial correlation and heteroskedasticity. Given all these caveats, the results in Model 2 lend general support to the key claims, though there are one or two notable changes. First, and most important perhaps, the geographical proximity variable is now significant and consistent with the theoretical claims. When the distance from a city to its nearest neighbour with knowledge of rDNA technology falls, then the probability that the city will develop a patent in class 435/69.1 increases. Second, the city-size (patent count) effect remains insignificant in the fixed effects models of Table 7, unlike in the hazard models presented above.

REFLECTIVE CONCLUSIONS AND SUGGESTIONS FOR FUTURE RESEARCH

This paper traces changes in the geography of adoption of a significant new technology, rDNA, as represented by knowledge creation in USPTO patent class 435/69.1. Between 1980 and 2005 multiple rDNA patents were developed in approximately 200 US metropolitan areas (counting the location of all co-inventors on these patents). The geographical spread of rDNA technology proceeded slowly at first hitting an inflection point in

1990 when both the number of rDNA patent applications and the number of inventing cities increased rapidly. As rDNA technology matured, perhaps around the year 2000, the number of patent applications began to slow down and a shakeout occurred in the number of cities with active rDNA inventors.

The primary interest was in the factors that regulated the spatial spread of this new knowledge class and, in particular, the relative roles of geographical proximity, social proximity and cognitive proximity. This paper follows a tradition in the literature that seeks to understand the relative importance of these different forms of proximity and that illustrates the mechanisms by which knowledge is transmitted and new technology put to use. Overall, the results suggest that social connections were most important in the diffusion of rDNA technologies. Social proximity, measured by the network of rDNA co-inventors within the United States, played a positive and significant role in the spread of rDNA technology. Inventors associated with patents in technology class 435/69.1 passed information on this new knowledge set to their co-inventors located in the same city or in different cities across the country. This suggests that co-inventing relationships provided a mechanism for the diffusion of the technology: individuals learn about new techniques through inventive work with others and then adopt these new technologies in their subsequent work.

Adoption of this new technological information was not automatic, however, and also depended on cognitive proximity, the technological profile of knowledge in a city and the closeness of that profile to the knowledge base of rDNA. The specialization of rDNA technology appears to have limited adoption in early years to those few metropolitan areas with strong concentrations of biotechnology-related activity. Cognitive proximity to rDNA technology appears to have been the critical dimension of absorptive capacity in those cities exposed to this new technology through their social networks.

rDNA techniques spread from San Francisco to a number of relatively large metropolitan areas and to a few small cities around the country. At least initially, these areas were relatively far from one another and thus little evidence was found to support the role of spatial proximity in facilitating the flow of rDNA-related knowledge. After the mid-1990s, however, the pattern of spatial diffusion shifted to one that was significantly influenced by geographical proximity to rDNA knowledge. Analysis of repeated rDNA invention in the fixed effects logit model, after instrumenting for endogeneity, showed that social, cognitive and geographical proximity all played a significant role in the spread of this technology across US metropolitan areas.

Extensions of the event history model revealed that in smaller, less inventive US cities where cognitive proximity to rDNA technology had little overall effect, social proximity played the critical role in the adoption of knowledge in patent class 435/69.1. This indicates that technology adoption within a city can be enhanced by attracting a few key individuals who have strong social ties to inventors elsewhere. This finding supports the logic of state and local promotion of programmes to hire eminent scholars and star scientists (FELDMAN et al., 2014). Conversely, in larger, more inventive cities, where it might be assumed that social proximity is always relatively high, absorptive capacity appears to hinge on cognitive proximity, on familiarity with related technologies.

Industry and university R&D spending had mixed roles in accounting for the spread of rDNA technology. The negative influence of university R&D is inconsistent with the theoretical priors. Perhaps the use of NIH awards to university research is not capturing the basic rDNA analysis that was anticipated. Additional work is clearly required on this question.

The aim in this paper was to extend empirical research in evolutionary economic geography through an exploration of different dimensions of proximity and the way in which those dimensions influence the spatial diffusion of a particular technology. Related measures may be employed to examine patterns of diffusion for other technologies. It seems reasonable to assume that patterns of technology diffusion will vary across industries, regions and time periods and for incremental rather than for radical technological breakthroughs. The findings question the extent to which different forms of proximity are substitutes for one another. It is shown that once an idea is patented it is codified and that, at least initially, it follows a pattern of diffusion predicated on social relationships. Overall, though, the results presented here surely raise more questions than they answer:

- How do different technologies travel?
- How are technologies reshaped as they move from one region to another?
- How do the impacts of new technologies vary over space as they interact with existing knowledge systems.

- What are the characteristics of those new technologies that dramatically shift the trajectories of innovation within and across regions?
- How does the diffusion of technology alter knowledge variety within regions, the fundamental building block, perhaps, of evolution within the space-economy?

Acknowledgements – The authors thank Ron Boschma and two anonymous reviewers for insightful comments. The participants at the 'Evolutionary Economic Geography Special Sessions' at the 2012 (New York) and 2013 (Los Angeles) Annual Meetings of the Association of American Geographers also provided useful suggestions on earlier versions of the paper. The authors of this paper are listed alphabetically.

Funding – Financial support for part of this research, which is gratefully acknowledged, was provided by the Regional Studies Association through the Early Career Grant Scheme [grant number R13455 – D. F. Kogler].

NOTES

1. A prokaryotic cell is one without a contained nucleus. The Prokaryotic patent is US 4468464, issued on 28 August 1984. A eukaryotic cell has a contained nucleus. The Eukaryotic patent is US 4740470, issued on 26 April 1988.
2. When rDNA or Cohen–Boyer patents are referred to, one is explicitly referring to patents that make claims to producing or using knowledge in class 435/69.1.
3. For a detailed list and definitions of MSAs, see OFFICE OF MANAGEMENT AND BUDGET (OMB) (2009).
4. The average time-lag between the application year and grant year of patents that make a knowledge claim in USPTO class 435/69.1 is about 2.5 years in the early 1980s, rising to just over 3.5 years by the end of the period studied. The database utilized in this study provides data for USPTO patents granted up to the end of 2010 (LAI et al., 2011), and therefore right-censoring the data in 2005 is considered a conservative approach.

REFERENCES

ABERNATHY W. J. and CLARK K. B. (1985) Innovation: mapping the winds of creative destruction, *Research Policy* **14**, 3–22. doi:10.1016/0048-7333(85)90021-6

ABERNATHY W. J. and UTTERBACK J. M. (1978) Patterns of industrial innovation, *Technology Review* **80**, 40–47.

ABRAMS D., AKCIGIT U. and POPADAK J. (2013) *Patent Value and Citations: Creative Destruction or Strategic Disruption?* Penn Institute for Economic Research Working Paper No. 13–065. University of Pennsylvania, Philadelphia, PA.

AGRAWAL A., KAPUR D. and MCHALE J. (2008) How do spatial and social proximity influence knowledge flows? Evidence from patent data, *Journal of Urban Economics* **64**, 258–269. doi:10.1016/j.jue.2008.01.003

ALLISON P. (1984) *Event History Analysis: Regression for Longitudinal Event Data.* Sage, Newbury Park, CA.

ASHEIM B. and GERTLER M. S. (2005) The geography of innovation: regional innovation systems, in FAGERBERG J., MOWERY D. and NELSON R. (Eds) *The Oxford Handbook of Innovation*, pp. 291–317. Oxford University Press, Oxford.

AUTANT-BERNARD C., MAIRESSE J. and MASSARD N. (2007) Spatial knowledge diffusion through collaborative networks, *Papers in Regional Science* **86**, 341–350. doi:10.1111/j.1435-5957.2007.00134.x

BARNEY J. B. (1991) Firm resources and sustained competitive advantage, *Journal of Management* **17**, 99–120. doi:10.1177/014920639101700108

BAUM J. and HAVEMAN H. (1997) Love they neighbor: differentiation and agglomeration in the Manhattan hotel industry, 1898–1990, *Administrative Science Quarterly* 42, 304–338. doi:10.2307/2393922

BESSEN J. (2008) The value of U.S. patents by owner and patent characteristics, *Research Policy* 37, 932–945. doi:10.1016/j.respol.2008.02.005

BLOSSFELD H.-P., GOLSCH K. and ROHWER G. (2007) *Event History Analysis with STATA*. Lawrence Erlbaum Associates, Mahwah, NJ.

BORGATTI S., EVERETT M. and FREEMAN L. (2002) *UCINET for Windows: Software for Social Network Analysis*. Analytic Technologies, Harvard, MA.

BOSCHMA R. A. (2005) Proximity and innovation: a critical assessment, *Regional Studies* 39, 61–74. doi:10.1080/0034340052000320887

BOSCHMA R. A., BALLAND P. A. and KOGLER D. F. (2014) Relatedness and technological change in cities: the rise and fall of technological knowledge in U.S. metropolitan areas from 1981 to 2010, *Industrial and Corporate Change*. doi:10.1093/icc/dtu012

BOSCHMA R. A. and FRENKEN K. (2010) The spatial evolution of innovation networks: a proximity perspective, in BOSCHMA R. and MARTIN R. (Eds) *The Handbook of Evolutionary Economic Geography*, pp. 120–135. Edward Elgar, Cheltenham.

BOSCHMA R. A. and MARTIN R. (2010) The aims and scope of evolutionary economic geography, in BOSCHMA R. and MARTIN R. (Eds) *The Handbook of Evolutionary Economic Geography*, pp. 3–39. Edward Elgar, Cheltenham.

BRESCHI S. and LISSONI F. (2001) Knowledge spillovers and local innovation systems: a critical survey, *Industrial and Corporate Change* 10, 975–1005. doi:10.1093/icc/10.4.975

BRESCHI S. and LISSONI F. (2004) *Knowledge Networks from Patent Data: Methodological Issues and Research Targets*. KITeS Working Paper No. 150. KITeS, Centre for Knowledge, Internationalization and Technology Studies, Università Bocconi, Milan.

BRESCHI S. and LISSONI F. (2009) Mobility of skilled workers and co-invention networks: an anatomy of localized knowledge flows, *Journal of Economic Geography* 9, 439–468. doi:10.1093/jeg/lbp008

BRESCHI S., LISSONI F. and MALERBA F. (2003) Knowledge-relatedness in firm technological diversification, *Research Policy* 32, 69–87. doi:10.1016/S0048-7333(02)00004-5

BROWN L. A. (1981) *Innovation Diffusion*. Methuen, London.

CHRISTENSEN C. M. (1997) *The Innovator's Dilemma*. Harvard Business School Press, Boston, MA.

CLARK K. B. (1985) The interaction of design hierarchies and market concepts in technological evolution, *Research Policy* 14, 235–251. doi:10.1016/0048-7333(85)90007-1

COHEN W. M. and LEVINTHAL D. A. (1990) Absorptive capacity: a new perspective on learning and innovation, *Administrative Science Quarterly* 35, 128–152. doi:10.2307/2393553

COOKE P., URANGA M. and ETXEBARRIA G. (1997) Regional innovation systems: institutional and organizational dimensions, *Research Policy* 26, 475–491. doi:10.1016/S0048-7333(97)00025-5

COWAN R. and JONARD N. (2004) Network structure and the diffusion of knowledge, *Journal of Economic Dynamics and Control* 28, 1557–1575. doi:10.1016/j.jedc.2003.04.002

DOSI G. (1982) Technological paradigms and technological trajectories: a suggested interpretation of the determinants and directions of technical change, *Research Policy* 11, 147–162. doi:10.1016/0048-7333(82)90016-6

ENGELSMAN E. C. and VAN RAAN A. F. J. (1994) A patent-based cartography of technology, *Research Policy* 23, 1–26. doi:10.1016/0048-7333(94)90024-8

ESSLETZBICHLER J. and RIGBY D. L. (2007) Exploring evolutionary economic geographies, *Journal of Economic Geography* 7, 549–571. doi:10.1093/jeg/lbm022

FELDMAN M. P. (1994) *The Geography of Innovation*. Kluwer, Dordrecht.

FELDMAN M. P., COLAIANNI A. and LIU C. K. (2008) Chapter D, 17.22: Lessons from the commercialization of the Cohen–Boyer patents: the Stanford University licensing program, in KRATTIGER A., MAHONEY R. T., NELSEN U., THOMPSON J. A., BENNETT A. B., SATYANARAYANA K., GRAFF G. D., FERNANDEZ C. and KOWALSKI S. P. (Eds) *Intellectual Property Management in Health and Agricultural Innovation: A Handbook of Best Practices, Vol. 1*, pp. 1797–1808. MIHR, Oxford; PIPRA, Davis, CA; Oswaldo Cruz Foundation, Brazil; and *bio*Developments – International Institute, Ithaca, NY.

FELDMAN M. P. and KOGLER D. F. (2010) Stylized facts in the geography of innovation, in HALL B. and ROSENBERG N. (Eds) *Handbook of the Economics of Innovation*, pp. 381–410. Elsevier, Oxford.

FELDMAN M. P., LANAHAN L. and LENDEL I. V. (2014) Experiments in the laboratories of democracy: state scientific capacity building, *Economic Development Quarterly* 28, 107–131.

FELDMAN M. P. and YOON J. W. (2012) An empirical test for general purpose technology: an examination of the Cohen–Boyer rDNA technology, *Industrial and Corporate Change* 21, 249–275. doi:10.1093/icc/dtr040

FELDMAN M. P. and ZOLLER T. D. (2012) Dealmakers in place: social capital connections in regional entrepreneurial economies, *Regional Studies* 46, 23–37. doi:10.1080/00343404.2011.607808

FISCHER M., SCHERNGELL T. and JANSENBERGER E. (2006) The geography of knowledge spillovers between high-technology firms in Europe: evidence from a spatial interaction modeling perspective, *Geographical Analysis* 38, 288–309. doi:10.1111/j.1538-4632.2006.00687.x

FISHLOW A. (1965) *American Railroads and the Transformation of the Ante-Bellum Economy*. Harvard University Press, Cambridge, MA.

FLEMING L. and SORENSON O. (2001) Technology as a complex adaptive system: evidence from patent data, *Research Policy* 30, 1019–1039. doi:10.1016/S0048-7333(00)00135-9

FOGEL R. (1964) *Railroads and American Economic Growth: Essays in Econometric History*. Johns Hopkins University Press, Baltimore, MD.

GAMBARDELLA A., HARHOFF D. and VERSPAGEN B. (2008) The value of European patents, *European Management Review* **5**, 69–84. doi:10.1057/emr.2008.10

GEROSKI P. A. (2000) Models of technology diffusion, *Research Policy* **29**, 603–625. doi:10.1016/S0048-7333(99)00092-X

GERTLER M. S. (2003) Tacit knowledge and the economic geography of context, or the undefinable tacitness of being (there), *Journal of Economic Geography* **3**, 75–99. doi:10.1093/jeg/3.1.75

GLAESER E. (2000) The new economics of urban and regional growth, in CLARK G. L., FELDMAN M. P. and GERTLER M. S. (Eds) *The Oxford Handbook of Economic Geography*, pp. 83–93. Oxford University Press, Oxford.

GOWER J. C. (1971) A general coefficient of similarity and some of its properties, *Biometrics* **27**, 857–871. doi:10.2307/2528823

GRILICHES Z. (1957) Hybrid corn: an exploration in the economics of technological change, *Econometrica* **25**, 501–522. doi:10.2307/1905380

GRILICHES Z. (1990) Patent statistics as economic indicators: a survey, *Journal of Economic Literature* **28**, 1661–1707.

HÄGERSTRAND T. (1953) *Innovation Diffusion as a Spatial Process*. University of Lund, Lund.

HALL B. H., JAFFE A. B. and TRAJTENBERG M. (2001) *The NBER Patent Citations Data File: Lessons, Insights and Methodology Tools*. National Bureau of Economic Research (NBER) Working Paper No. 8498. NBER, Cambridge, MA.

HALL B. H., JAFFE A. B. and TRAJTENBERG M. (2005) Market value and patent citations, *Rand Journal of Economics* **36**, 16–38.

HALL B., THOMA G. and TORRISI S. (2007) *The Market Value of Patents and R&D: Evidence from European Firms*. National Bureau of Economic Research (NBER) Working Paper No. 13426. NBER, Cambridge, MA.

HARHOFF D., NARIN F., SCHERER M. and VOPEL K. (1999) Citation frequency and the value of patented inventions, *Review of Economics and Statistics* **81**, 511–515. doi:10.1162/003465399558265

HAUSMANN R. and KLINGER B. (2007) *The Structure of the Product Space and the Evolution of Comparative advantage*. CID Working Paper No. 146. Center for International Development (CID), Harvard University, Cambridge, MA.

HELPMAN E. (1998) Introduction, in HELPMAN E. (Ed.) *General Purpose Technologies and Economic Growth*, pp. 1–14. MIT Press, Cambridge, MA.

HUBER F. (2012) On the role and interrelationship of spatial, social and cognitive proximity: personal knowledge relationships of R&D workers in the Cambridge information technology cluster, *Regional Studies* **46**, 1169–1182. doi:10.1080/00343404.2011.569539

JAFFE A. (1986) Technological opportunity and spillovers of R&D, *American Economic Review* **76**, 984–1001.

JAFFE A. and TRAJTENBERG M. (Eds) (2002) *Patents, Citations, and Innovations: A Window on the Knowledge Economy*. MIT Press, Cambridge, MA.

JAFFE A., TRAJTENBERG M. and HENDERSON R. (1993) Geographic localization of knowledge spillovers as evidenced by patent citations, *Quarterly Journal of Economics* **108**, 577–598. doi:10.2307/2118401

JOO S. H. and KIM Y. (2010) Measuring relatedness between technological fields, *Scientometrics* **83**, 435–454. doi:10.1007/s11192-009-0108-9

KELLER W. (2004) International technology diffusion, *Journal of Economic Literature* **42**, 752–782. doi:10.1257/0022051042177685

KERR W. R. (2010) Breakthrough inventions and migrating clusters of innovation, *Journal of Urban Economics* **67**, 46–60. doi:10.1016/j.jue.2009.09.006

KLEPPER S. (1997) Industry life cycles, *Industrial and Corporate Change* **6**, 145–182. doi:10.1093/icc/6.1.145

KOGLER D. F., RIGBY D. L. and TUCKER I. (2013) Mapping knowledge space and technological relatedness in U.S. cities, *European Planning Studies* **21**, 1374–1391. doi:10.1080/09654313.2012.755832

KOGUT B. and ZANDER U. (1992) Knowledge of the firm, combinative capabilities, and the replication of technologies, *Organization Science* **3**, 383–397. doi:10.1287/orsc.3.3.383

LAI R. D., AMOUR A., YU A., SUN Y. and FLEMING L. (2011) *Disambiguation and Co-authorship Networks of the U.S. Patent Inventor Database (1975–2010)*. Working Paper. Harvard University, Cambridge, MA.

LAMOREAUX N. and SOKOLOFF K. (1996) Long-term change in the organization of inventive activity, *Proceedings of the National Academy of Sciences, USA* **93**, 12686–12692. doi:10.1073/pnas.93.23.12686

LICHTENBERG F. R. and PHILIPSON T. J. (2002) *The Dual Effects of Intellectual Property Regulations: Within- and Between-Patent Competition in the US Pharmaceuticals Industry*. National Bureau of Economic Research (NBER) Working Paper No. 9303. NBER, Cambridge, MA.

LIPSEY R. G., CARLAW K. and BEKAR C. T. (2005) *Economic Transformations: General Purpose Technologies and Long Term Economic Growth*. Oxford University Press, Oxford.

LUNDVALL B. Å. (1992) *National Systems of Innovation: Towards a Theory of Innovation and Interactive Learning*. Pinter, London.

MAGGIONI M., NOSVELLI M. and UBERTI T. (2007) Space versus networks in the geography of innovation: a European analysis, *Papers in Regional Science* **86**, 471–493. doi:10.1111/j.1435-5957.2007.00130.x

MALMBERG A. and MASKELL P. (2002) The elusive concept of localization economies: towards a knowledge-based theory of spatial clustering, *Environment and Planning A* **34**, 429–449. doi:10.1068/a3457

MASKELL P. and MALMBERG A. (1999) The competitiveness of firms and regions: 'ubiquitification' and the importance of localized learning, *European Urban and Regional Planning Studies* **6**, 9–25. doi:10.1177/096977649900600102

MAURSETH P.-B. and VERSPAGEN B. (2002) Knowledge spillovers in Europe: a patent citations analysis, *Scandinavian Journal of Economics* **104**, 531–545. doi:10.1111/1467-9442.00300

MENSCH G. (1975) *Das Technologische Patt: Innovation Überwinden die Depression, Frankfurt, Umschau*; English edn (1979) *Stalemate in Technology: Innovations Overcome Depression*. Ballinger, New York, NY.

MORGAN K. (1997) The learning region: institutions, innovation and regional renewal, *Regional Studies* **31**, 491–503. doi:10.1080/00343409750132289

NELSON R. R. and WINTER S. G. (1982) *An Evolutionary Theory of Economic Change*. Belknap, Cambridge.

NESTA L. and SAVIOTTI P. P. (2005) Coherence of the knowledge base and the firm's innovative performance: evidence from the U.S. pharmaceutical industry, *Journal of Industrial Economics* **53**, 123–142. doi:10.1111/j.0022-1821.2005.00248.x

NOOTEBOOM B. (2000) *Learning and Innovation in Organizations and Economies*. Oxford University Press, Oxford.

Ó HUALLACHÁIN B. (1999) Patent places: size matters, *Journal of Regional Science* **39**, 613–636. doi:10.1111/0022-4146.00152

Ó HUALLACHÁIN B. and LEE D. (2011) Technological variety and specialization in urban invention, *Regional Studies* **45**, 67–88. doi:10.1080/00343404.2010.486783

OFFICE OF MANAGEMENT AND BUDGET (OMB) (2009) *OMB Bulletin No. 10–02: Update of Statistical Area Definitions and Guidance on Their Uses*. OMB, Washington, DC.

PAVITT K. (1985) Patent statistics as indicators of innovative activities: possibilities and problems, *Scientometrics* **7**, 77–99. doi:10.1007/BF02020142

PHENE A., FLADMOE-LINDQUIST K. and MARSH L. (2006) Breakthrough innovations in the U.S. biotechnology industry: the effects of technological space and geographic origin, *Strategic Management Journal* **27**, 369–388. doi:10.1002/smj.522

RIGBY D. L. (2013) Technological relatedness and knowledge space: entry and exit of US cities from patent classes, *Regional Studies*. doi:10.1080/00343404.2013.854878

RIGBY, D. L. and ESSLETZBICHLER, J. (1997) Evolution, process variety, and regional trajectories of technological change, *Economic Geography* **73**, 269–284. doi:10.2307/144484

RIGBY D. L. and VAN DER WOUDEN F. (2013) *Abandoning the Herfindahl: Knowledge Relatedness and the Rate of Invention in U.S. Cities*. Department of Geography, UCLA, Los Angeles, CA. [paper available from the authors upon request]

SAHAL D. (1981) *Patterns of Technological Innovation*. Addison Wesley, Reading, MA.

SAXENIAN A. (1994) *Regional Advantage: Culture and Competition in Silicon Valley and Route 128*. Harvard University Press, Cambridge, MA.

SCHUMPETER J. A. (1942) *Capitalism, Socialism and Democracy*. Harper, New York, NY.

SILVERBERG G. (1991) Adoption and diffusion of technology as a collective evolutionary process, in NAKIENOVIC N. and GRUBLER A. (Eds) *Diffusion of Technologies and Social Behavior*, pp. 209–229. IIASA/Springer, Berlin.

SMITH HUGHES S. (2001) Making dollars out of DNA: the first major patent in biotechnology and the commercialization of molecular biology, 1974–1980, *Isis* **92**, 541–575. doi:10.1086/385281

SONN J. W. and STORPER M. (2008) The increasing importance of geographical proximity in knowledge production: an analysis of US patent citations, 1975–1997, *Environment and Planning A* **40**, 1020–1039. doi:10.1068/a3930

SORENSON O. (2003) Social networks and industrial geography, *Journal of Evolutionary Economics* **13**, 513–527. doi:10.1007/s00191-003-0165-9

SORENSON O. and AUDIA P. G. (2000) The social structure of entrepreneurial activity: footwear production in the United States, 1940–1989, *American Journal of Sociology* **106**, 424–462. doi:10.1086/316962

STORPER M. (1997) *The Regional World: Territorial Development in a Global Economy*. Guilford, New York, NY.

STORPER M. and CHRISTOPHERSON S. (1987) Flexible specialization and regional agglomerations: the case of the U.S. motion picture industry, *Annals of the Association of American Geographers* **77**, 104–117. doi:10.1111/j.1467-8306.1987.tb00148.x

STRUMSKY D. and LOBO J. (2008) Metropolitan patenting, inventor agglomeration and social networks: a tale of two effects, *Journal of Urban Economics* **63**, 871–884. doi:10.1016/j.jue.2007.07.005

STRUMSKY D., LOBO J. and VAN DER LEEUW S. (2012) Using patent technology codes to study technological change, *Economics of Innovation and New Technology* **21**, 267–286. doi:10.1080/10438599.2011.578709

TRAJTENBERG M. (1990a) A penny for your quotes: patent citations and the value of innovations, *Rand Journal of Economics* **21**, 172–187. doi:10.2307/2555502

TRAJTENBERG M. (1990b) *Economic Analysis of Product Innovation: The Case of CT Scanners*. Harvard University Press, Cambridge, MA.

VAN ECK N. and WALTMAN L. (2009) How to normalize co-occurrence data? An analysis of some well-known similarity measures, *Journal of the American Society for Information Science and Technology* **60**, 1635–1651. doi:10.1002/asi.21075

VERSPAGEN B. (1997) Measuring intersectoral technology spillovers: estimates from the European and US Patent Office databases, *Economic Systems Research* **9**, 47–65. doi:10.1080/09535319700000004

WEITZMAN M. (1998) Recombinant growth, *Quarterly Journal of Economics* **113**, 331–360. doi:10.1162/003355398555595

WENERFELT B. (1984) A resource based view of the firm, *Strategic Management* **5**, 171–180. doi:10.1002/smj.4250050207

ZUCKER L. G., DARBY M. R. and BREWER M. B. (1998) Intellectual human capital and the birth of U.S. biotechnology enterprises, *American Economic Review* **88**, 290–306.

Interaction and Innovation across Different Sectors: Findings from Norwegian City-Regions

RUNE DAHL FITJAR and ANDRÉS RODRÍGUEZ-POSE

UiS Business School, University of Stavanger, Stavanger, Norway.
Department of Geography and Environment, London School of Economics, London, UK.

FITJAR R. D. and RODRÍGUEZ-POSE A. Interaction and innovation across different sectors: findings from Norwegian city-regions, *Regional Studies*. This article examines how different types of interaction are related to the capacity of firms to innovate in different sectors. Using a sample of 1604 Norwegian firms with more than ten employees, it analyses how interactions within the business group, with industry partners, and with research institutions and consultancies impinge on the probability of innovation for firms in six different economic sectors – manufacturing; construction; retail; accommodation and food; transport; and professional and business services – and six sector-by-skill categories – high- and low-skilled manufacturing, construction, and services. The results of ordinal regression analyses for product and process innovation show that the drivers of innovation differ widely across sectors. While exchanges internal to the firm tend to be disconnected from innovation across the board, those with scientific and industrial partners prove to be important drivers of innovation not only for firms in sectors, such as manufacturing, traditionally deemed to benefit from these partnerships, but also for sectors regarded as less innovative, such as construction. This pattern even holds for low-skilled firms in the manufacturing and construction sectors.

FITJAR R. D. and RODRÍGUEZ-POSE A. 不同部门之间的互动与创新：挪威城市区域的研究发现，*区域研究*。本文检视不同的互动类型，如何与不同部门的厂商创新能力有关。本研究运用一千六百零四家员工数超过十人的挪威厂商样本，分析在商业团体中、与产业伙伴、研究机构和顾问之间的互动，如何影响六个不同经济部门——製造、营建、零售、餐饮旅馆、交通、专业及商业服务，以及六个依照技术范畴区分的部门——高技术与低技术製造业、营建业和服务业中的厂商创新之可能性。对产品及製成创新的有序迴归分析结果，显示出创新的驱力，在各部门中有大幅的差异。厂商内部的交换，倾向与理事会的创新分离，但具有科学与产业伙伴者，却被证实不仅对传统上被认为得利于这些伙伴关係的经济部门中的产业创新而言，是重要的驱力，例如製造业，亦同时是被认为较不具创新性的部门的重要创新驱力，例如营建业。此一模型，甚至对製造和营建部门中的低技术厂商而言亦适用。

FITJAR R. D. et RODRÍGUEZ-POSE A. L'interaction et l'innovation à travers les différents secteurs: des résultats provenant des cités-régions norvégiennes, *Regional Studies*. Ce présent article examine comment les différents types d'interaction se rapportent à la capacité des entreprises d'innover dans divers secteurs. À partir d'un échantillon auprès de 1.604 entreprises norvégiennes, des entreprises de plus de dix employés, on analyse comment les interactions au sein du groupe d'entreprises, avec des partenariats industriels, et avec des instituts de recherches et des cabinets de conseil, influent sur la probabilité de l'innovation pour ce qui est des entreprises dans six secteurs différents de l'économie – à savoir, la fabrication; la construction; le commerce de détail; le logement et l'alimentation; le transport; les services aux entreprises et les services professionnels – et six catégories de secteurs déterminés en fonction du niveau des compétences – à savoir, la fabrication, la construction et les services à la fois hautement et peu qualifiés. Les résultats d'une régression ordinale pour l'innovation de produits et l'innovation de procédés montre que les forces motrices de l'innovation varient sensiblement par secteur. Alors que les échanges intérieurs à l'entreprise ont tendance à être déconnectés de l'innovation de manière généralisée, ceux qui jouissent des partenariats scientifique et industriel s'avèrent d'importantes forces motrices de l'innovation non seulement pour les entreprises des secteurs qui, de l'avis général, bénéficient de ces partenariats, tels la fabrication, mais aussi pour les secteurs considérés moins innovateurs, tels la construction. Cette distribution est valable même pour les entreprises où l'emploi dans la fabrication et la construction est peu qualifié.

FITJAR R. D. und RODRÍGUEZ-POSE A. Wechselwirkungen und Innovation in verschiedenen Sektoren: Ergebnisse aus norwegischen Stadtregionen, *Regional Studies*. In diesem Beitrag wird untersucht, in welchem Zusammenhang verschiedene Arten von Wechselwirkungen mit der Innovationskapazität von Firmen in verschiedenen Sektoren stehen. Anhand einer Stichprobe von 1604 norwegischen Firmen mit mehr als zehn Angestellten wird analysiert, wie sich die Wechselwirkungen innerhalb des Konzerns, mit Branchenpartnern sowie mit Forschungsinstitutionen und Beratungsfirmen auf die Wahrscheinlichkeit von Innovationen durch Firmen in sechs verschiedenen Wirtschaftssektoren – Produktion, Bauwesen, Einzelhandel, Hotelwesen und Gastronomie, Verkehr sowie professionelle und Geschäftsdienste – sowie in sechs sektor- bzw. qualifikationsspezifischen Kategorien – hoch und gering qualifizierte Produktionstätigkeit, Bauwesen und Dienstleistungen – auswirken. Aus den Ergebnissen der ordinalen Regressionsanalysen für Produkt- und Verfahrensinnovation geht hervor, dass die Faktoren der Innovation je nach Sektor hochgradig unterschiedlich ausfallen. Ein Austausch innerhalb der Firma ist zwar in der Regel vom generellen Innovationsprozess abgekoppelt, doch Firmen mit wissenschaftlichen und Branchenpartnern erweisen sich als wichtige Faktoren der Innovation – nicht nur in Sektoren wie der Produktion, von denen traditionell angenommen wird, dass sie von diesen Partnerschaften profitieren, sondern auch für Sektoren wie das Bauwesen, die als weniger innovativ gelten. Dieses Muster gilt sogar für Firmen mit gering qualifizierten Arbeitnehmern im Produktionssektor und Bauwesen.

FITJAR R. D. y RODRÍGUEZ-POSE A. Interacción e innovación en diferentes sectores: resultados de las regiones metropolitanas noruegas, *Regional Studies*. En este artículo se examina cómo se relacionan los diferentes tipos de interacciones con la capacidad de las empresas para innovar en distintos sectores. Partiendo de una muestra de 1604 empresas noruegas de más de diez empleados, analizamos cómo influyen las interacciones dentro del grupo de empresas, con socios industriales y con instituciones de investigación y firmas consultoras en la probabilidad de innovación en seis sectores económicos distintos –manufacturas; construcción; venta minorista; alojamiento y alimentación; y servicios profesionales y comerciales– así como en seis categorías de sectores, de acuerdo al grado de formación –construcción, servicios y manufactura de alto y bajo nivel de formación. Los resultados de los análisis de regresión ordinal para innovaciones de producto y de proceso ponen de manifiesto que los motores de la innovación difieren radicalmente entre sectores. Mientras que la interacción en el interior de la empresa no está particularmente ligada a la innovación independientemente del sector, los intercambios con socios en centros industriales y de investigación son importantes para la innovación en sectores, como el manufacturero, donde tradicionalmente se puede esperar que estos intercambios den frutos, pero también en sectores considerados menos innovadores, como la construcción. Este patrón se mantiene incluso para las empresas en sectores de bajo nivel de cualificación tanto en el sector manufacturero como en la construcción.

INTRODUCTION

Cooperation and interaction have been at the heart of evolutionary economic geography (MACKINNON et al., 2009). Firms – which are the fundamental object of analysis of this strand of research – adjust and adapt to changing socioeconomic conditions. This can be achieved through two types of mechanisms: either by innovation through in-house research or, as suggested by ASHEIM and GERTLER (2005), as a result of 'a dynamic interplay between, and transformation of, tacit and codified forms of knowledge as well as a strong interaction of people within organizations and between them' (p. 294). The internal structure, configuration, procedures and, more importantly for this article, the interaction between firms determine how individual firms evolve. Much of this interaction leading to the formation of partnerships and networks is a consequence of exchanges with sources external to the firm, such as customers, suppliers and competitors, on the one hand, and centres generating knowledge, such as universities, research centres and consultancies, on the other. The importance of internal versus external sources of innovation and the specific influence of diverse knowledge-generating partnerships have been the object of constant scrutiny, especially in determining

how innovation is achieved in manufacturing firms or in specific subsectors within manufacturing. These studies have tended to highlight different sectoral patterns in the importance of different sources of innovation, even within manufacturing industries (PAVITT, 1984). Recent research has also paid attention to services, in particular knowledge-intensive business services and other highly innovative subsectors (e.g. ASLESEN and ISAKSEN, 2007; DOLOREUX and SHEARMUR, 2012). Less attention has been paid to the analysis of how each of these sources affects innovation across a wide range of different sectors and whether the sources of innovation vary widely across industries (CASTELLACCI, 2008). Yet, as MALERBA (2005, p. 380) notes, 'innovation greatly differs across sectors in terms of characteristics, sources, actors involved, the boundaries of the process, and the organization of innovative activities'. Innovation in firms or sectors with varying production and market conditions and skills structures demands different approaches and different types of knowledge inputs, being the consequence of different forms of interaction across diverse types of industries. If this hypothesis is correct, variation across sectors in terms of the use of different types of partners, as well as in how closely these different types of collaboration are associated with innovation outcomes, can be expected. Hence, the understanding of how interaction affects firm adaptation and evolution remains somewhat limited.

This paper, which is part of a special issue on evolutionary economic geography, aims to make a contribution to filling this gap by understanding how different forms of interaction shape the genesis of new knowledge and innovation in firms working in different sectors. It will examine the role of interaction within the firm and with industrial and scientific partners in stimulating firm product and process innovation in six different Norwegian industries: manufacturing; construction; trade and retail; food and accommodation services; transport, storage, information and communications; and professional, scientific, technical and business services (hereafter professional services). Furthermore, it distinguishes between knowledge-intensive and low-skilled firms and compares the role of interaction across the two types of firms in manufacturing, construction and services industries. The research draws on a survey of 1604 firms across the five largest city-regions of Norway in order to probe through a series of ordered logit regression analyses the relative roles of cooperation internal to the firm, and with industrial (suppliers, customers and competitors) and scientific (universities, research institutes and consultancies) partners in shaping the probability of innovating among firms within each of these industries.[1] The objective is thus to draw a more complete picture than earlier studies – which have frequently been limited to the sources of innovation within a single industry (e.g. POWELL et al., 1996; MOODYSSON et al., 2008; STRAMBACH, 2008) or across industries regardless of sectors (e.g. TETHER, 2002; JENSEN et al., 2007; FITJAR and RODRÍGUEZ-POSE, 2013) – on what determines firm-level innovation.

The results of the analysis show that the drivers of innovation differ widely across sectors. While exchanges internal to the firm tend to have a limited association with innovation across the board, firm innovation relies on sector-specific combinations of interactions with scientific and industrial partners. Scientific partners prove to be closely connected with innovation not only for firms in sectors, such as manufacturing, that are traditionally deemed to benefit from interaction with universities, research institutes and consultancy firms, but also for sectors normally regarded as less innovative and research and development (R&D) intensive, such as construction. Even among low-skilled construction firms, those firms that collaborate with universities are significantly more likely to innovate. Similarly, industry-type interaction is, as expected, closely associated with innovation in a wide range of sectors, but while interaction with suppliers is important in the service sector, interaction with customers matters more for product innovation in manufacturing.

The paper is structured as follows. The next section discusses how different types of knowledge exchange may affect innovation across different sectors. The third section introduces the research design and the

methodology used in the analysis. The results of the empirical analysis are presented in the fourth section. Finally, the conclusions and some preliminary policy implications are included in the fifth section.

KNOWLEDGE EXCHANGE AND INNOVATION ACROSS DIFFERENT SECTORS

Traditionally, the scholarly literature looking at innovation has tended to identify three potential sources of innovation. First, innovation may be the result of sources internal to the firm. Firms frequently conduct scientific research which leads, directly or indirectly, to innovation (BUSH, 1945; MACLAURIN, 1953). In particular, larger firms and those with a greater capacity to invest in R&D in-house have been deemed to be more capable of innovating than those which, due to their limited dimensions or sector, lack the same capacity to invest in R&D, making firm size one of the key factors behind innovation. Firm sector is another (PAVITT, 1984; LAURSEN and SALTER, 2006). The structure of certain industrial sectors demands the need to invest heavily in R&D in order either to benefit from significant economies of scale or to maximize the appropriation of the returns to innovation and to the generation of new knowledge. This is, for example, the case of aeronautics or of firms in the aerospatial sectors and, to a lesser extent, of oil and gas. For this type of innovation to take place, the majority of the exchanges leading to knowledge generation will happen in-house, either within the same plant or across units within the same organization and/or firm.

In other sectors, however, in-house research is either impractical or conducive to lower levels of new knowledge generation. Firms in these sectors may also lack the scale to host large R&D projects in-house. Hence, in order for these firms to innovate they have to rely on a second source of innovation: interaction with outside sources, ranging from other firms which may act as suppliers or customers to scientific partners and consultancies. In particular, exchanges with centres generating new knowledge, such as universities or research centres (KEEBLE et al., 1999; LAWTON SMITH, 2007), or with external consultants (FOLEY and WATTS, 1996; LAWTON SMITH et al., 2001) represent a rich source of additional knowledge. The more firms interact, either formally or informally, with these scientific institutions and consultancies, the greater the chance for firms to innovate (AUDRETSCH and FELDMAN, 1996; CANTWELL and IAMMARINO, 1998; SONN and STORPER, 2008). This interaction can take on various forms, e.g. contract research, technical assistance, technology transfer, joint projects, etc., and serve different purposes. These sort of exchanges all fall in the category of what JENSEN et al. (2007) have denominated as the 'science, technology and innovation' (STI) mode of innovation. In the STI mode of innovation, external scientific knowledge is heavily used as the fundamental source of new knowledge in product and process innovation. The interaction leading to new knowledge generation tends to be dominated by formal exchanges and to rely heavily on formal investment in science and technology by the organizations external to the firm (JENSEN et al., 2007, p. 681) as the fundamental driver of new knowledge.

A third key source of new knowledge generation for innovation is related to the presence of incremental and networked innovation processes that emerge through frequent relations between firms and their suppliers and customers, often through informal networks and in geographically limited industrial districts (BECATTINI, 1987) or innovation systems (LUNDVALL, 1992). Repeated exchanges with suppliers, clients, and competitors represent a conveyor belt for the transmission of codified and tacit knowledge (LUNDVALL, 1992; STORPER and VENABLES, 2004), resulting in what JENSEN et al. (2007) referred to as the 'doing, using and interacting' (DUI) mode of innovation. In this mode, firms generate or acquire new knowledge by solving specific problems through exchanges of experience and know-how, without necessarily involving additional formal research in the process (JENSEN et al., 2007). DUI-type innovation is generally not R&D intensive – apart from applied R&D aimed at addressing practical issues – and is contingent on experience, skills and the sharing of these factors between workers. Once more, the interaction can take on different forms, e.g. development projects, focus groups, joint ventures, strategic alliances, etc.

These three fundamental sources of innovation can then be combined with the role of government to form triple helix-type systems of innovation (ETZKOWITZ and LEYDESDORFF, 2000; LEYDESDORFF, 2000; RANGA and ETZKOWITZ, 2013), creating complex networks of knowledge exchange, with firms at the heart of these systems benefiting from a greater capacity to innovate.

The ability to utilize any of these three sources of innovation crucially depends on factors such as the type of management and ownership of the firm, its size and, perhaps even more importantly, on the industrial sector. Different sectors will resort to each of the three sources of knowledge to different degrees in order to generate new ideas and product and process innovations. Of course, the definition of sectors can be done at various levels of aggregation, depending on the objectives of the analysis. Even within fairly specific sectors, the heterogeneity across subsectors may be great, e.g. between hardware and software producers in the information technology (IT) industry, or between platform developers and specialized producers within software, which nowadays also includes software-as-a-service providers (MALERBA, 2005).

This paper employs a high level of aggregation with the aim of generalizing across a large number of firms. It distinguishes between manufacturing and service industries, which is one of the most fundamental divisions in the economy. Innovation in services has been the subject of increasing attention in the literature on innovation, which for many years remained focused almost exclusively on manufacturing (GALLOUJ and WEINSTEIN, 1997; MILES, 2005; CHESBROUGH, 2011). Within services, two further distinctions are made. Firstly, according to the type of service provided, noting that there is a great deal of diversity across different service providers depending on the activities that they deliver. Secondly, according to the level of knowledge intensity, as the service sector encompasses both high-technology and routine activities. The same can be said for manufacturing, where the same distinction is employed.

How are the drivers of innovation expected to vary across different industries? PAVITT's (1984) taxonomy remains the classic treatment of this topic. In his taxonomy, Pavitt distinguishes between sectors which are scale intensive, science based and supplier dominated. This division maps onto the distinction made above between in-house sources of innovation, scientific/ STI-type interaction, and industrial/DUI-type interaction, respectively. In addition, Pavitt includes a category of specialized suppliers, which rely heavily on interaction with customers.

Pavitt's taxonomy mainly applies to manufacturing industrie, while services are only included within the category of supplier-dominated industries. In these industries, the sources of innovation tend to be external to the firm and are fundamentally developed by suppliers for application by the focal firm. However, other authors have discussed more thoroughly the question of how manufacturing and services industries differ in terms of the sources of innovation. MILES (2005) notes that service provision is a highly interactive activity, where the service is often customized to individual customers. This puts great emphasis on interaction with users. Customers could thus be expected to play a larger role for innovation in services than in manufacturing. On the flipside, service firms are often poorly connected to universities and other producers of scientific knowledge, as they are often less technology-intensive, although consultancies may play a greater role. Survey data tend to confirm this pattern (TETHER, 2005; TETHER and TAJAR, 2008).

Within the service sector, MIOZZO and SOETE (2001) have extended the Pavitt taxonomy to classify different services into the same categories. They note that personal services (such as hotels and restaurants) and public services are supplier dominated and mainly deliver minor process innovations. Transport and wholesale are scale-intensive services, while communications are network-intensive services, with a general reliance on in-house R&D and input from suppliers. Software and specialized business services are science-based and specialized suppliers, with close links to scientific knowledge producers and knowledge being produced within the sector.

Another key distinction involves the degree of knowledge-intensity involved. The service sector encompasses subsectors ranging from knowledge-intensive services and high-technology IT firms to mainly low-skilled retailers and personal service providers. A similar range can be found in manufacturing, from nanotechnology and biotechnology firms to routine industrial production of simple products. The conventional approach to analysing these differences, in policy as well as in academia, has been to classify sectors as high- or low-tech. However, as VON TUNZELMANN and ACHA (2005) indicate, technology content is hard to measure and may also vary a lot across firms and national contexts within individual sectors. On this basis, they suggest placing more emphasis on the knowledge intensity of industries. This approach recognizes that knowledge inputs to innovation processes may take other forms than basic or applied research and development of technologies. For instance, many service industries have low inputs of technology, but rely heavily on the application of workers' cognitive capacities to providing value-added for the customer. This is reflected in the large number of highly educated workers in these industries.

Less knowledge-intensive firms may be expected to rely more on learning by doing and using than on research and interaction with scientific partners in their innovation processes. Due to their lower absorptive capacity, collaboration with partners – in particular,

science-based ones – may be expected to have a smaller effect on innovation in these firms.

RESEARCH DESIGN AND METHODOLOGY

In order to test the above assumptions and predictions, the analysis is based on a survey of firms across six different sectors of the Norwegian economy: manufacturing; construction; wholesale and retail trade; accommodation and food services; transport, storage, information and communications; and professional services. A random sample of firms with more than ten employees, located in the five largest urban areas of Norway (Oslo, Bergen, Stavanger, Trondheim and Kristiansand) and operating in any sector of the economy, was drawn from the Norwegian Register of Business Enterprises, where all firms are required to register. More than 5800 firms were approached, with a response rate of 27.2%. The final sample includes 1604 firms. This response rate is similar to that of other surveys which have targeted top-level managers and included many small and medium-sized firms. For instance, BARTHOLOMEW and SMITH (2006, p. 85) report an average response rate of 27% for surveys published in two leading entrepreneurship and small business journals between 1998 and 2004, with a declining trend over time. The division of the firms sampled into sectors is as follows: 296 manufacturing firms, 258 construction firms, 276 trade and retail firms, 129 hotels and restaurants, 124 transport and communications firms, and 432 professional service firms.[2] Descriptive data on the sample in each industry are provided in Table 1.

In order to assess the risk of non-response bias, a non-response analysis was conducted. The aim of this is to assess whether those who responded to the survey

Table 1. Descriptive data on the sample

	Manufacturing	Construction	Trade	Hotels and restaurants	Transport and communications	Professional services
Number of employees						
0–19	38.2	52.5	47.5	42.6	32.3	38.9
20–49	31.4	31.5	34.1	34.1	33.1	33.8
50–99	14.9	11.7	9.8	12.4	10.5	13.4
100–999	14.2	4.3	8.7	8.5	22.6	13.9
1000 or more	1.4	0.0	0.0	1.6	1.6	0.0
N	296	257	276	129	124	432
Ownership						
Fully foreign owned	7.1	1.2	20.7	3.9	13.7	10.4
Partly foreign owned	3.0	1.1	3.9	0.0	3.4	7.2
Fully Norwegian owned	89.9	97.7	75.4	96.1	83.9	82.4
N	296	258	276	129	124	432
Region						
Oslo	15.5	15.1	42.4	23.3	19.4	30.1
Bergen	28.0	31.0	22.1	22.5	32.3	20.1
Stavanger	31.1	26.4	17.0	28.7	19.4	24.3
Trondheim	17.9	21.7	12.7	18.6	18.6	21.3
Kristiansand	7.4	5.8	5.8	7.0	10.5	4.2
N	296	258	276	129	124	432

differ in any systematic way from those who did not respond (BARUCH and HOLTOM, 2008, p. 1155). This typically involves as the first step to examine whether there are any systematic differences between the respondents and non-respondents on variables where the value is known for the entire population. In the database, the variables that satisfy this criterion are the location, size and industry of each firm. By design, the sample overrepresents firms in the four smaller city-regions and underrepresents firms in Oslo and the sample will thus not be representative of the population in terms of location. As regions have different industry structures and size profiles, the sample cannot be compared directly with the national population for the other two variables. Instead, the composition of the sample must be compared with the five regional sampling populations, i.e. the share of firms with more than ten employees belonging to different industries and size bands within each region.

Table 2 shows the share of firms in the sample compared with the sampling population within each region by sector and firm size, which is helpful in assessing the risk of non-response bias. As shown, the sample is broadly representative of the population in terms of sector, with some overrepresentation of manufacturing and professional services firms, and an underrepresentation of hotels and restaurants. Consequently, the survey is likely to be somewhat more representative of the population in the former sectors, and somewhat less representative in the latter. Larger firms are also overrepresented. Firms with more than 50 employees make up 26.1% of firms in the sample compared with 18.8% in the region-weighted sampling population.

A second step in non-response analysis is to assess the impact of non-response on the results (ROGELBERG and STANTON, 2007). In this case, the share of innovative firms is higher in the sectors where the response rates are higher (manufacturing and professional services), as the analysis later in the paper will show

(Table 3). Rates of collaboration also tend to be higher in these industries. The aggregate shares of innovative firms and collaborating firms may thus overestimate the shares in the overall population. A pressing question arising from this is whether the likelihood of non-response was affected mainly by the sector, or by the firms' innovation and collaboration activities. However, the latter seems less likely, as neither innovation nor collaboration was mentioned in the presentation of the survey to interviewees. Rather, the survey was presented as a study of management, value generation and business development. The differences in response rates across industries are also fairly minor compared to the differences in innovation levels and collaboration patterns.

The differences across sectors may also have been driven by underlying differences in firm size, which seems to have a larger impact on response rate. In this case, the impact of non-response is lower, as firm size only has a significant impact on innovation in a few industries, as the regression analyses below will show. The non-response bias on this variable should therefore not have a major impact on the results. Size is furthermore controlled for in the final analysis to further reduce the risk of bias.

A final step in non-response analysis is to assess the reasons for non-response. In this case, the majority of non-responding firms – 2366 firms – could not be contacted by the interviewers. This group consists completely of passive non-respondents, reducing the risk of bias (ROGELBERG and STANTON, 2007). Difficulty in contacting firms could partly account for the lower response among smaller firms, who have smaller administrative capacity and may be more likely to have contact details that are not up to date.[3] Another 1917 firms refused to participate in the survey, making for a response rate of 45.6% among firms that were actually contacted by the interviewers. This group includes both passive (e.g. those who did not have time) and

Table 2. Non-response analysis: share of the sampling population included in sample, by sector and size

Region	Manufacturing (%)	Construction (%)	Trade (%)	Hotels and restaurants (%)	Transport and communications (%)	Professional services (%)	Total (%)
Oslo	9.5	5.8	10.4	6.3	6.1	8.6	8.2
Bergen	37.6	31.1	36.7	23.2	36.7	30.9	33.1
Stavanger	33.3	29.8	31.3	26.8	26.7	35.8	31.2
Trondheim	39.0	31.8	32.1	18.3	31.5	39.3	33.2
Kristiansand	22.0	13.9	23.2	17.3	26.5	25.0	21.3
Total	24.3	17.8	17.0	14.0	17.4	18.1	18.3

Region	< 24 employees (%)	25–49 employees (%)	> 50 employees (%)	Total (%)
Oslo	7.5	8.2	10.1	8.2
Bergen	29.7	33.2	46.0	33.1
Stavanger	26.5	32.1	43.7	31.2
Trondheim	27.4	34.6	54.2	33.2
Kristiansand	17.3	25.0	30.8	21.3
Total	16.2	19.1	23.6	18.3

Table 3. Per cent of firms reporting incremental and radical innovation, by sector

	Manufacturing	Construction	Trade	Hotels and restaurants	Transport and communications	Professional services
Product innovation						
No innovation	35.8	71.7	39.1	55.8	49.2	40.7
Incremental innovation	21.3	16.3	24.6	25.6	24.2	24.5
Radical innovation	43.9	12.0	36.2	18.6	2.6	34.7
Process innovation						
No innovation	37.5	62.4	65.2	62.8	63.7	43.5
Incremental innovation	39.2	20.9	24.6	32.6	20.2	29.6
Radical innovation	23.3	16.7	10.1	4.7	16.1	26.9
N	296	258	276	129	124	432
	Low-skill manufacturing	High-skill manufacturing	Low-skill construction	High-skill construction	Low-skill services	High-skill services
Product innovation						
No innovation	47.9	33.5	73.8	69.9	46.5	41.6
Incremental innovation	17.0	20.6	16.4	16.2	24.9	26.1
Radical innovation	35.1	45.9	9.8	14.0	28.6	32.3
Process innovation						
No innovation	40.4	38.6	65.6	59.6	63.7	52.5
Incremental innovation	37.2	36.9	22.1	19.9	26.5	27.6
Radical innovation	22.3	24.5	12.3	20.6	9.8	20.0
N	94	233	122	136	245	762

active non-respondents, and thus carries a greater risk of bias. As discussed above, the survey was not introduced as a survey of innovation to avoid generating active non-response among non-innovative firms. The relatively small differences between innovative and less innovative sectors also does not appear to suggest that this has been the case.

A further distinction is made between high- and low-skilled firms, employing the education level of the firm's manager as a proxy. The firms with university-educated managers are classified as high skilled and firms with non-university-educated managers as low skilled. This is admittedly an imperfect proxy, as there will necessarily be several low-skilled firms with educated managers, as well as possibly some high-skilled firms with non-educated managers. However, as a general pattern, it is reasonable to expect university-educated managers to be more prevalent in high-skilled firms. Despite large firms being overrepresented, the majority of the firms included in the sample remain fairly small: the median size is 22 employees. Most firms below this size will not have a professional (e.g. business school educated) manager, but rather be run by an entrepreneur with a background in the field in which the business specializes (e.g. a plumber running a plumbing firm or a lawyer running a law firm). In this context, the education level of the manager can be expected reasonably to reflect whether or not the firm operates in a sector where university education is common or required.

In order to achieve a reasonable sample size, and to simplify comparison, the firms are reclassified when employing this distinction. In this analysis, firms are therefore divided into 2 × 3 categories, depending on their manager's education level and their inclusion in the three broad categories manufacturing (now also including mining), construction,[4] and services (trade, hotels/restaurants, transport/communications, financial services, and professional services). The firms are classified either as low-skilled manufacturing (94 firms), high-skilled manufacturing (233 firms), low-skilled construction (122 firms), high-skilled construction (136 firms), low-skilled services (245 firms), or high-skilled services firms (762 firms).

Data on innovation activities were collected through telephone interviews with the manager or chief executive officer (CEO) of each firm, conducted by the professional market research firm Synovate (later renamed Ipsos) in the spring of 2010. The questions were derived from Community Innovation Survey indicators, which were adjusted by the authors to fit the needs of the present analysis and supplemented with a range of additional questions concerning both the characteristics of the firm and of its manager or CEO.

For the dependent variables, managers were asked whether their firm had introduced any new and/or significantly improved goods or services during the preceding three years (*product innovation*), and also whether they had introduced any new and/or significantly improved methods or processes for production or delivery of products during the same time frame (*process innovation*). Successful innovators were asked whether any of the products were new to the market (*radical product innovation*) or only new to the firm (*incremental product innovation*), and, equivalently for process innovation,

EVOLUTIONARY ECONOMIC GEOGRAPHY

whether any of the processes were new to the industry (*radical process innovation*) or only new to the firm (*incremental process innovation*). The responses to the two questions on innovation versus no innovation and radical versus incremental innovation are combined into two ordinal variables, one for product innovation and another for process innovation, each with the three categories 'no innovation', 'incremental innovation' and 'radical innovation'.

Table 3 shows the distribution of responses to these four questions in each of the six sectors included in the analysis. In line with earlier findings of lower levels of innovation in services (MILES, 2005; TETHER and TAJAR, 2008), the manufacturing sector has the highest share of innovative firms for both product and process innovation, as well as for radical product innovation. However, the professional services sector has the highest share of firms reporting radical process innovation, which is also in line with expectations of high levels of innovation in this sector, particularly in terms of processes (ASLESEN and ISAKSEN, 2007; DOLOREUX and SHEARMUR, 2012). There is more variety at the other end of the scale, with construction firms reporting the lowest level of product innovation, while transport/storage/information/communications has the lowest

share of radical product innovation. For process innovation, it is the hotel/restaurants sector that performs worst. Hence, physical services tend to be, as expected, less innovative, although types of innovation vary across different physical services. Distinguishing by skill structure, high-skilled firms display higher levels of both product and process innovation, as well as of radical innovation, than low-skilled firms in the same sector, which is also as expected. Furthermore, manufacturing firms display higher levels of all types of innovation than services and construction firms of the same skill level.

In order to examine the relationship between collaboration with external agents and firms' potential for innovation, managers were asked whether the firm had collaborated with any of seven different types of partners, representing either in-house collaboration (other units in the conglomerate), DUI mode interaction (suppliers, customers and competitors), or STI mode exchanges (consultancies, universities and research institutes) during the preceding three years. Fig. 1 shows the distribution of responses to this question for each sector. For DUI type collaboration, there is not much difference between the sectors. The share of firms that collaborate with suppliers and customers

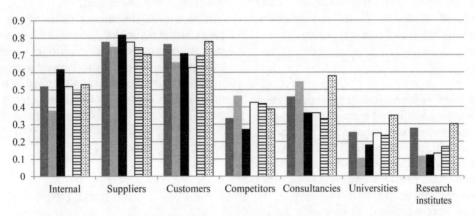

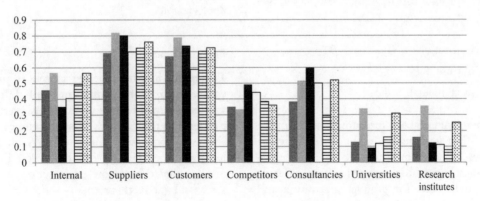

Fig. 1. Proportion of firms that collaborate with outside agents, by sector

is high across all industries. In manufacturing and to some extent in services, collaboration levels tend to be higher among high-skilled firms, while the situation is reversed in construction. There is more variation in the level of cooperation between competitors (with low-skilled firms tending to collaborate more), as well as for STI type collaboration. In the latter case, collaboration is particularly common in professional services for all three types of partners, and also quite common among manufacturing firms, while construction firms collaborate least frequently with universities and research institutes, although a high share (55%) of them collaborate with consultancies. This conforms to expectations of more science-based innovation approaches in manufacturing and professional services. In manufacturing and services, there is also a sharp difference between high- and low-skilled firms in STI collaboration levels. However, the difference is much smaller and not significant in construction. In-house collaboration between different plants is most common in retail trade and least common in construction. It is also more common among high-skilled firms.

It is also worth noting that DUI type interaction – in particular, with customers and suppliers – is by far the most common type of interaction in all industries. This is followed by in-house exchanges, while the more formal STI type of interaction is the least frequent, especially with universities and research centres.

Model specification

In order to test whether innovation in firms in different sectors is associated with different types of interaction, a series of ordinal regression analyses are conducted, examining how collaboration with different types of partners – specifically with scientific and research communities and with other firms – is connected to a firm's ability to innovate. Particular attention is paid to whether these impacts vary across sectors with diverse knowledge bases and core activities. The analytical model used to test the main hypothesis adopts the following form:

$$\text{logit}\left[\Pr\left(\text{Innovation}_i > j\right)\right] = \alpha_j + \beta\,\text{Partners}_i$$
$$+ \gamma\,\text{Controls}_i + \varepsilon_i$$
$$j = \{\text{incremental, radical}\}$$

where the dependent variable is measured in terms of the probability of firm i belonging to the jth category or higher on the trichotomous measure of innovation, rather than to any lower-order categories. Two different models are fitted – one for product innovation and another for process innovation – for each of the six sectors, as well as for each sector-by-skill category: a total of 24 regression analyses. The innovation outcome is hypothesized to depend on the firm's

values on two different vectors. First, a vector of the partners (*Partners*) with which the firm has collaborated during the same time frame, estimated through a set of seven dichotomous variables indicating whether the firm has interacted with a partner of the relevant type. Second, a vector of controls (*Controls*) that may affect both the firm's use of partners and its innovation outcome, the contents of which are further specified below. The model also includes two intercepts α_j, one for each of the j categories,[5] and an idiosyncratic error ε.

A set of six different control variables are applied. These concern the characteristics of the firms and of their managers. Regarding the characteristics of the firm, the paper first controls for the size of the firm, measured in terms of its number of employees, to which a base-e logarithmic transformation is applied, due to the skewness of the variable and the expectation that the impact of additional employees will decline with increasing size. Second, the proportion of shares held by foreign owners is included in the analysis, measured on a continuous scale from 0 to 1. Third, the region in which the firm is located is included in the analysis, measured by a set of dummy variables representing the five different city-regions, as region-specific characteristics may affect the probability of innovation in a given firm.

Concerning the characteristics of the manager, the paper first looks at his/her level of education by measuring the highest level of education completed by the manager in number of years beyond compulsory schooling.[6] The manager's age and personal network in other firms is also controlled for. The latter is measured in terms of the number of directorships held on boards of other firms and log transformed for the reasons stated above for company size.

RESULTS

Table 4 shows the results of the generalized ordinal regression analyses for product innovation as the dependent variable.

Product innovation

The results indicate that the sources of product innovation – proxied by partnerships with different actors – vary considerably across sectors. However, the types of partnerships more closely related to innovation are not always as expected. Collaboration with STI partners has the largest impact on innovation for firms in a mainly low-tech sector: construction. In this sector, the most basic R&D partners – universities and research institutes – are associated with a significantly higher likelihood of introducing new products. It is worth noting that this sector is also where these types of partners are used the least. STI partners tend to be less important

Table 4. Ordinal regression analysis of product innovation, by sector

	Manufacturing	Construction	Trade	Hotels and restaurants	Transport and communications	Professional services
Partner types						
Within the conglomerate	0.11	0.27	0.39	0.30	0.55	0.26
	(0.25)	(0.32)	(0.27)	(0.40)	(0.43)	(0.20)
Suppliers	0.16	0.74	−0.34	0.79	0.38	0.57**
	(0.30)	(0.46)	(0.33)	(0.56)	(0.55)	(0.23)
Customers	0.66**	−0.01	0.39	−0.32	−0.11	0.94***
	(0.30)	(0.38)	(0.28)	(0.43)	(0.43)	(0.26)
Competitors	0.01	−0.32	−0.83***	−0.39	−0.39	−0.52***
	(0.27)	(0.33)	(0.29)	(0.43)	(0.42)	(0.20)
Consultancies	0.30	−0.06	−0.04	0.63	1.11**	−0.03
	(0.25)	(0.35)	(0.27)	(0.43)	(0.47)	(0.20)
Universities	0.88***	1.02**	0.90**	−0.05	0.09	0.15
	(0.32)	(0.51)	(0.37)	(0.49)	(0.50)	(0.25)
Research institutes	0.16	1.09**	−0.12	0.73	−0.13	0.08
	(0.30)	(0.46)	(0.41)	(0.62)	(0.66)	(0.26)
Control variables						
Education	0.03	0.04	0.02	−0.19**	−0.10	0.03
	(0.05)	(0.06)	(0.05)	(0.09)	(0.08)	(0.05)
Manager's age	−0.01	−0.01	−0.00	−0.01	−0.04**	0.00
	(0.01)	(0.02)	(0.01)	(0.02)	(0.02)	(0.01)
Company directorships	0.07	−0.28	0.08	0.68**	0.54**	0.27**
	(0.18)	(0.21)	(0.17)	(0.35)	(0.26)	(0.14)
ln Employees	0.18	0.39**	0.31**	0.07	−0.07	0.01
	(0.14)	(0.20)	(0.16)	(0.22)	(0.19)	(0.10)
Foreign owned	0.10	0.35	0.76**	−0.23	0.49	0.74**
	(0.50)	(1.21)	(0.33)	(1.25)	(0.70)	(0.32)
Region	Controlled**	Controlled*	Controlled	Controlled	Controlled	Controlled
Constant$_{incremental}$	−0.18	3.73***	0.94	−0.31	−2.07	1.44*
	(0.92)	(1.50)	(0.99)	(1.21)	(1.46)	(0.86)
Constant$_{radical}$	0.84	4.96**	2.11**	1.08	−0.83	2.57**
	(0.92)	(1.51)	(0.99)	(1.21)	(1.46)	(0.86)
N	296	257	276	129	124	432
Pseudo-R^2	0.08	0.11	0.09	0.08	0.10	0.06

Notes: Values are the coefficient (standard error).

*$p < 0.10$, **$p < 0.05$, ***$p < 0.01$.

for innovation in the service industries, in line with findings in other surveys (MILES, 2005; TETHER and TAJAR, 2008). This even holds for the professional services sector, which displays the highest level of collaboration with each of the STI partner types, but in which none is significantly connected to product innovation.

The results are more mixed when it comes to collaboration with DUI partners. Collaboration with DUI partners seems to be most important for firms in the professional services sector, where both suppliers and customers are positively associated with innovation. Customers also have a significant positive effect in manufacturing. Conversely, the relationship with collaboration with competitors is negative in most industries, significantly so in trade/retail and professional services. Finally, the association between innovation and in-house collaboration across plants is weak across the board.

As for the control variables, it is worth noting that the effect of company size is mainly important in

construction and trade/retail, which appear to be more scale-intensive than the other service-oriented sectors, partly confirming MIOZZO and SOETE's (2001) classification. Foreign ownership is also significantly related to innovation in trade/retail and professional services. In manufacturing and construction, location in particular city-regions significantly affects innovation. This suggests a pattern where global pipelines through the presence of multinational enterprises are important for innovation in some sectors, whereas in others, firms rely more on their location in a particular regional environment.

Table 5 shows the same analysis for the six sector-by-skill categories. In manufacturing, there is not a lot of difference between low- and high-skilled firms in terms of which partner types are important. In both cases, universities have a significant positive association, with a stronger coefficient (but also a higher standard error) for low-skilled firms. In addition, cooperation with customers has a significant positive connection for high-skilled firms, but not for low-skilled firms,

Table 5. *Ordinal regression analysis of product innovation, by sector-by-skill category*

	Low-skilled manufacturing	High-skilled manufacturing	Low-skilled construction	High-skilled construction	Low-skilled services	High-skilled services
Partner types						
Within the conglomerate	0.22	0.15	0.96*	−0.17	0.53*	0.25*
	(0.53)	(0.29)	(0.52)	(0.46)	(0.28)	(0.15)
Suppliers	0.10	0.22	0.47	0.69	0.60*	0.30*
	(0.58)	(0.36)	(0.75)	(0.61)	(0.32)	(0.18)
Customers	0.88	0.70**	0.29	−0.07	0.06	0.61***
	(0.54)	(0.35)	(0.66)	(0.52)	(0.31)	(0.17)
Competitors	0.02	0.05	−1.05**	0.15	−0.74***	−0.56***
	(0.53)	(0.30)	(0.53)	(0.47)	(0.29)	(0.15)
Consultancies	0.63	−0.13	−0.41	0.44	0.36	0.22
	(0.50)	(0.28)	(0.53)	(0.50)	(0.31)	(0.15)
Universities	1.69**	0.55*	1.29*	0.39	−0.39	0.41**
	(0.76)	(0.33)	(0.74)	(0.80)	(0.42)	(0.18)
Research institutes	0.01	0.30	0.18	2.29***	0.81	0.01
	(0.68)	(0.32)	(0.68)	(0.76)	(0.55)	(0.19)
Control variables						
Manager's age	−0.03	−0.02	−0.00	−0.02	−0.03**	0.01
	(0.02)	(0.02)	(0.03)	(0.03)	(0.01)	(0.01)
Company directorships	−0.31	0.17	−0.09	−0.48	0.62***	0.18*
	(0.38)	(0.20)	(0.35)	(0.32)	(0.20)	(0.10)
ln Employees	0.45	0.18	0.19	0.61**	0.18	0.05
	(0.31)	(0.13)	(0.33)	(0.29)	(0.17)	(0.07)
Foreign owned	0.05	−0.22	Dropped[a]	0.32	0.94*	0.81***
	(1.04)	(0.44)		(1.30)	(0.53)	(0.21)
Region	Controlled**	Controlled	Controlled	Controlled*	Controlled	Controlled
Constant$_{incremental}$	−0.52	−0.39	2.78	4.17*	−0.17	0.35**
	(1.57)	(1.08)	(2.09)	(2.36)	(0.98)	(0.53)
Constant$_{radical}$	0.38	0.56	4.18*	5.43**	−0.42	2.54***
	(1.57)	(1.08)	(2.11)	(2.38)	(0.58)	(0.54)
N	94	233	122	135	245	762
Pseudo-R^2	0.14	0.06	0.13	0.18	0.08	0.05

Notes: [a]Only two firms were partly foreign owned in this category, and none was fully foreign owned. This created limited variability in the variable, which was therefore dropped from analysis.

Values are the coefficient (standard error).

*p < 0.10, **p < 0.05, ***p < 0.01.

although the coefficient is equally strong for the latter category, which comprises fewer firms. In construction, in-house collaboration has a significant positive association for low-skilled firms, while cooperation with competitors has a significant negative association. In this sector, STI collaboration is also important for both low- and high-skilled firms, with low-skilled firms seeming to benefit from interactions with universities, while high-skilled ones derive a particular premium from collaborating with research institutes. Again, this is somewhat at odds with the common perception of these firms as having low absorptive capacity (REICHSTEIN *et al.*, 2005).

External interaction tends to be most important in the services sector for both high- and low-skilled firms, but the types of partners that matter differ depending on skill level. Innovation in low-skilled firms tend to be more closely related to collaboration within the conglomerate and with suppliers, although both of these partner types are also positively associated with innovation for high-skilled firms. However, the most important partners for high-skilled service firms tend to be customers and universities, neither of which makes any difference for innovation in low-skilled firms. This conforms to expectations of high-skilled firms having a more science-based approach to innovation. Finally, cooperation with competitors is significantly negatively connected to innovation for both types of service firms.

Process innovation

Table 6 shows the results of the ordinal regression analyses for process innovation as the dependent variable.

The benefits of collaborating with STI partners are spread more evenly across industries for process innovation than what was the case in the analysis of product innovation above. In four of the sectors, at least one STI type partner is significantly positively associated with the likelihood of process innovation. In the DUI mode, it is mainly cooperation with

Table 6. Ordinal regression analysis of process innovation, by sector

	Manufacturing	Construction	Trade	Hotels and restaurants	Transport and communications	Professional services
Partner types						
Within the conglomerate	−0.30	0.01	0.24	0.66	0.10	0.00
	(0.25)	(0.29)	(0.32)	(0.44)	(0.47)	(0.20)
Suppliers	0.56*	1.26***	0.36	0.44	0.70	0.66***
	(0.31)	(0.42)	(0.38)	(0.58)	(0.62)	(0.23)
Customers	0.25	−0.63*	0.07	0.42	−0.41	0.48*
	(0.30)	(0.33)	(0.31)	(0.47)	(0.47)	(0.25)
Competitors	0.09	0.35	−0.86**	−1.01**	−0.22	−0.17
	(0.26)	(0.30)	(0.34)	(0.48)	(0.46)	(0.20)
Consultancies	0.31	−0.36	0.45	0.89*	0.23	−0.10
	(0.24)	(0.31)	(0.30)	(0.48)	(0.46)	(0.20)
Universities	0.22	0.18	0.81**	0.58	−0.69	0.04
	(0.30)	(0.49)	(0.37)	(0.52)	(0.55)	(0.24)
Research institutes	0.56*	1.37***	0.29	−0.01	0.83	0.39
	(0.30)	(0.44)	(0.41)	(0.65)	(0.73)	(0.26)
Control variables						
Education	−0.08*	0.14	−0.05	−0.12	0.12	0.06
	(0.05)	(0.19)	(0.06)	(0.10)	(0.08)	(0.05)
Manager's age	0.01	−0.00	−0.02	0.02	−0.01	0.01
	(0.01)	(0.02)	(0.01)	(0.02)	(0.02)	(0.01)
Company directorships	0.10	0.35**	−0.26	0.26	−0.24	−0.07
	(0.17)	(0.18)	(0.20)	(0.37)	(0.29)	(0.13)
ln Employees	0.31**	0.14	0.52***	0.02	−0.04	0.17*
	(0.13)	(0.19)	(0.17)	(0.23)	(0.20)	(0.10)
Foreign owned	0.26	−0.85	0.04	1.20	0.32	−0.05
	(0.47)	(1.17)	(0.37)	(1.21)	(0.69)	(0.31)
Region	Controlled**	Controlled	Controlled	Controlled	Controlled	Controlled
Constant$_{incremental}$	0.55	2.11*	1.84*	1.13	0.75	2.10**
	(0.93)	(1.21)	(1.10)	(1.32)	(1.57)	(0.83)
Constant$_{radical}$	2.45***	3.37**	3.61***	3.92***	−1.95	−3.45***
	(0.94)	(1.22)	(1.12)	(1.38)	(1.58)	(0.84)
N	296	257	276	129	124	432
Pseudo-R^2	0.07	0.09	0.09	0.10	0.07	0.04

Note: Values are the coefficient (standard error).
$*p < 0.10, **p < 0.05, ***p < 0.01.$

suppliers, rather than with customers or competitors, that is beneficial to process innovation. Collaboration with suppliers has a positive sign in all six industries, significantly so in three of them. Collaboration with customers has a significant positive sign only in professional services – and a significant *negative* association in construction. Once more, collaborating with competitors is also significantly negatively connected to innovation in two of the industries. As in the case of product innovation, collaboration in-house is the least conducive to process innovation of the three broad sources of innovation. Collaboration within the conglomerate is not significantly related to process innovation in any of the sectors considered.

When it comes to the control variables, company size seems to be important in a larger number of industries for process innovation than for product innovation. Conversely, personal networks in other firms are less important, having a significant effect only in the construction sector. Region and foreign ownership are generally also less important for process innovation. Region

has a significant effect only in manufacturing, whereas foreign ownership does not have a significant effect in any of the industries.

Table 7 shows the same analyses for the six sector-by-skill categories. The association with STI partners follow a distinct pattern across different skill levels: For research institutes, the connection is positive and significant for all high-skilled sectors, whereas the association is weaker and not significant in any of the low-skilled sectors, supporting the hypothesis that innovation is more science-based in high-skilled firms. Conversely, consultancies have a significant relationship in all the low-skilled sectors – positive in manufacturing and services, but negative in construction. Here, the association is weaker in the high-skilled sectors and only significant in services. Collaboration with universities is not significant in any of the categories.

For the DUI partners, the connection between collaboration with suppliers and innovation also tends to depend on skill level: it is significant and positive for all of the high-skilled sectors, but not significant in any of

Table 7. Ordinal regression analysis of process innovation, by sector-by-skill category

	Low-skilled manufacturing	High-skilled manufacturing	Low-skilled construct	High-skilled construct	Low-skilled services	High-skilled services
Partner types						
Within the conglomerate	−0.44	−0.48*	0.73	−0.74*	−0.05	0.15
	(0.51)	(0.28)	(0.45)	(0.44)	(0.30)	(0.15)
Suppliers	0.30	0.79**	0.31	1.87***	0.45	0.34*
	(0.54)	(0.38)	(0.68)	(0.58)	(0.35)	(0.19)
Customers	0.14	0.40	0.73	−1.43***	0.24	0.29*
	(0.52)	(0.36)	(0.60)	(0.47)	(0.33)	(0.18)
Competitors	0.42	0.12	0.48	0.30	−0.70**	−0.20
	(0.50)	(0.29)	(0.47)	(0.42)	(0.31)	(0.15)
Consultancies	0.85*	−0.06	−0.87*	0.21	0.63*	0.31**
	(0.49)	(0.27)	(0.48)	(0.45)	(0.32)	(0.15)
Universities	−0.02	0.15	0.19	−0.35	0.16	0.25
	(0.64)	(0.32)	(0.73)	(0.84)	(0.42)	(0.18)
Research institutes	−0.04	0.58*	0.58	2.35***	0.28	0.48**
	(0.64)	(0.32)	(0.61)	(0.78)	(0.56)	(0.19)
Control variables						
Manager's age	0.02	−0.01	0.00	−0.02	−0.01	0.00
	(0.02)	(0.02)	(0.03)	(0.02)	(0.01)	(0.01)
Company directorships	0.13	0.17	1.00***	−0.07	−0.33	0.01
	(0.34)	(0.19)	(0.31)	(0.27)	(0.22)	(0.10)
ln Employees	0.68**	0.21*	−0.05	0.30	0.24	0.17***
	(0.31)	(0.13)	(0.34)	(0.26)	(0.18)	(0.07)
Foreign owned	−0.32	0.40	Dropped[a]	−0.49	0.53	−0.03
	(1.00)	(0.44)		(1.23)	(0.56)	(0.21)
Region	Controlled	Controlled*	Controlled	Controlled	Controlled	Controlled
Constant$_{incremental}$	2.71	0.44	2.68	1.03	1.49	1.91***
	(1.65)	(1.08)	(1.91)	(1.87)	(1.13)	(0.54)
Constant$_{radical}$	4.64***	2.20**	4.24**	2.31	3.28***	3.29***
	(1.70)	(1.09)	(1.93)	(1.88)	(1.15)	(0.55)
N	94	233	122	135	245	762
Pseudo-R^2	0.10	0.06	0.12	0.16	0.06	0.04

Notes: [a]Only two firms were partly foreign owned in this category, and none was fully foreign owned. This created limited variability in the variable, which was therefore dropped from analysis.

Values are the coefficient (standard error).

*p < 0.10, **p < 0.05, ***p < 0.01.

the low-skilled ones. Collaboration with customers has a significant positive association only in high-skilled services, while it has a significant negative sign in high-skilled construction. Thus, high-skilled firms appear better placed also when it comes to industrial collaboration, whereas low-skilled firms lack the absorptive capacity to exploit external knowledge inputs. Collaboration with competitors is negatively associated with innovation mainly in the service sector, significantly so for low-skilled firms. In-house collaboration also has a negative association in two of the high-skilled sectors: manufacturing and construction.

CONCLUSIONS

This paper has looked at whether the sources of innovation of firms vary according to the sector to which the firm belongs. The hypothesis was that innovations would be linked to different types of interactions in services and manufacturing industries, and in knowledge-

intensive and low-skilled firms. Services industries were expected to rely more on industrial interactions and have less scientific inputs than manufacturing firms, in particular in personal services, such as construction, trade and hotels/restaurants. Low-skilled firms were expected to benefit less from interaction in general due to their lower absorptive capacity, and in particular from interaction with scientific knowledge producers.

These expectations were largely confirmed when it comes to firms' use of different types of partners. Manufacturing and professional services firms tend to collaborate more with scientific knowledge producers, while other types of service firms interact mainly with industrial partners. Similarly, high-skilled firms interact more than low-skilled firms with scientific partners. While there is substantial variation across sectors in interaction with scientific partners, there is little variation when it comes to industrial partners, in particular suppliers and customers, which is high across all sectors.

While the use of partners conforms to theoretical expectations, the pattern changes when looking at the association between collaboration and innovation outcomes. The types of interactions driving innovation in each sector are not necessarily those predicted by the theory. First, interaction with universities and research institutes – what has been dubbed as STI interaction – is closely connected with both product and process innovation, not just in manufacturing, but also in construction and retail firms, where innovation was expected to be driven mainly by DUI-type interactions. Even low-skilled construction firms seem to benefit from interaction with universities. Even though interaction with scientific partners is significantly less common in construction and retail, STI-type exchanges seem to be important for several types of innovation. This possibly underlines that many firms in the construction and retail sectors have an unrealized potential for innovation, which can surface through greater interaction with universities and scientists, rather than through the more traditional exchanges with clients and suppliers. In the three other service sectors examined, interaction with scientific partners is, however, not associated with significantly higher levels of innovation. In fact, greater collaboration with universities and research centres does not, depending on the sectors, always necessarily result in greater innovation. For firms in professional services, the sector in which links to universities and research institutes are most common, collaboration with suppliers and customers remains the most important source of both product and process innovation. However, the pattern is different for high-skilled firms in these sectors, which tend to benefit from interaction with STI partners in terms of increased likelihood of both product and process innovation.

Most DUI-type interactions – fundamentally supplier and customer relations – tend to be significantly associated with innovation also among manufacturing firms. However, other DUI-type interactions, such as exchanges with competitors, do not improve the likelihood of innovation in any industry. This type of interactions display a negative relationship to innovation both in the trade and retail and in the professional services sector. Frequent in-house interaction across different plants also has a much weaker impact than expected. In fact, interaction within the conglomerate rarely leads to significant innovation in the Norwegian case. However, the data do not address the impact of interaction *within* each plant, which may still be an important driver of innovation.

The contrasts between the empirical findings and the theoretical expectations provide some food for thought and potentially have implications for both research and policy on innovation. The results of the analysis indicate that interaction with universities and other scientific partners is not only important for firms in manufacturing and professional services, which tend to use these types of partners the most. Rather, firms in industries where interaction with research communities is relatively uncommon, such as construction and retail, may significantly improve their potential for innovation by developing closer relations to universities. However, the results also indicate that promoting STI interaction must not necessarily come at the expense of DUI-type interaction. In other service sector industries, it may be more important to encourage firms further to develop relations to suppliers and customers that allow the exchange of product information and more tacit knowledge. In general, the results underline the complexity of the sources of innovation across sectors and highlight that no two sectors follow the same path or rely on the same sources of innovation. Different combinations of exchanges with outside agents lead to different innovation dynamics across industries and factors considered to be the most common or adequate sources of innovation for a particular sector do not always reveal themselves as the most appropriate or prone to generating new products and processes. Hence, further research is needed in order to get a deeper understanding of the potential role of how sources of innovation which have so far attracted relatively little attention in certain industries may play or may potentially play a greater role in stimulating innovation than hitherto considered.

Acknowledgements – The authors are grateful to the numerous referees and the Editors of *Regional Studies* for the constructive comments made on previous revisions of this paper. They are also indebted to the participants at seminars and presentations in New York, London and Stavanger, whose comments helped shape this paper.

Disclosure statement – No potential conflict of interest was reported by the authors.

Funding – The financial support from the Research Council of Norway under the programmes Demosreg [project number 209761/H20] and FORFI [project number 212275/D00], and of the European Research Council (ERC) under the European Union's Seventh Framework Programme [(FP7/2007-2013)/ERC Grant Agreement Number 269868] is also gratefully acknowledged.

NOTES

1. This type of approach, relying on a single survey, can only identify associations and not whether these are the result of causal relationships, However, the analysis can probe whether there are differences in the association between collaboration and innovation for firms in different sectors, and, if so, whether these different levels of association conform to what would be expected, given the theoretical predictions of different drivers of innovation in the sectors. This is a necessary first step towards empirically assessing the claims made about sector differences in the literature.

2. The sample also included 88 firms in the sectors mining and quarrying; electricity, gas and water supplies; and financial and insurance activities. In each of these three sectors, the number of units was below 50, which was deemed too few to allow robust hypothesis tests of the model. These 88 firms were therefore excluded from the first part of the analysis.

3. Unfortunately, no data on the sector and size of firms that refused compared with those who could not be contacted are available.

4. Construction is a service industry, but its innovation processes and activities are often quite different from other industries (REICHSTEIN et al., 2005), and it is therefore often treated separately in industrial classifications (e.g. in the European Union's Structural Business Statistics, which uses three categories: Industry, Construction, and Distributive Trades and Services).

5. The model was also run using a generalized ordinal specification (WILLIAMS, 2006), in which the slope coefficients β_j and γ_j were allowed to depend on the category j of interest if the hypothesis that $\beta_{incremental} = \beta_{radical}$ at $p = 0.05$ is rejected. For most coefficients, the hypothesis could not be rejected and the model simplified to an ordinal regression. In the cases where there were differences, the results were compatible with the findings from the ordinal regression, with somewhat higher explanatory power due to the less parsimonious model.

6. In the analyses by sector-by-skill category, the education variable is used to define the different categories and is therefore not used as a control variable in the model.

REFERENCES

ASHEIM B. and GERTLER M. (2005) The geography of innovation: regional innovation systems, in FAGERBERG J., MOWERY D. and NELSON R. R. (Eds) Oxford Handbook of Innovation, pp. 291–317. Oxford University Press, Oxford.

ASLESEN H. W. and ISAKSEN A. (2007) New perspectives on knowledge-intensive services and innovation, Geografiska Annaler: Series B, Human Geography 89(Suppl. 1), 45–58. doi:10.1111/j.1468-0467.2007.00259.x

AUDRETSCH D. and FELDMAN M. P. (1996) R&D spillovers and the geography of innovation and production, American Economic Review 86, 630–640.

BARTHOLOMEW S. and SMITH A. D. (2006) Improving survey response rates from chief executive officers in small firms: the importance of social networks, Entrepreneurship Theory and Practice 30, 83–96. doi:10.1111/j.1540-6520.2006.00111.x

BARUCH Y. and HOLTOM B. C. (2008) Survey response rate levels and trends in organizational research, Human Relations 61, 1139–1160. doi:10.1177/0018726708094863

BECATTINI G. (1987) Mercato e forze locali: Il distretto industriale. Il Mulino, Bologna.

BUSH V. (1945) Science: The Endless Frontier. Ayer, North Stratford.

CANTWELL J. and IAMMARINO S. (1998) MNCs, technological innovation and the regional systems in the EU: some evidence in the Italian case, International Journal of the Economics of Business 5, 383–408. doi:10.1080/13571519884459

CASTELLACCI F. (2008) Technological paradigms, regimes and trajectories: manufacturing and service industries in a new taxonomy of sectoral patterns of innovation, Research Policy 37, 978–994. doi:10.1016/j.respol.2008.03.011

CHESBROUGH H. (2011) Open Services Innovation: Rethinking Your Business to Grow and Compete in a New Era. Jossey-Bass, San Francisco, CA.

DOLOREUX D. and SHEARMUR R. (2012) Collaboration, information and the geography of innovation in knowledge intensive business services, Journal of Economic Geography 12, 79–105. doi:10.1093/jeg/lbr003

ETZKOWITZ E. and LEYDESDORFF L. (2000) The dynamics of innovation: from national systems and 'Mode 2' to a triple helix of university–industry–government relations, Research Policy 29, 109–123. doi:10.1016/S0048-7333(99)00055-4

FITJAR R. D. and RODRÍGUEZ-POSE A. (2013) Firm collaboration and modes of innovation in Norway, Research Policy 42, 128–138. doi:10.1016/j.respol.2012.05.009

FOLEY P. and WATTS H. D. (1996) Production site R&D in a mature industrial region, Tijdschrift voor Economische en Sociale Geografie 87, 136–145. doi:10.1111/j.1467-9663.1998.tb01544.x

GALLOUJ F. and WEINSTEIN O. (1997) Innovation in services, Research Policy 26, 537–556. doi:10.1016/S0048-7333(97)00030-9

JENSEN M. B., JOHNSON B., LORENZ E. and LUNDVALL B.-Å. (2007) Forms of knowledge and modes of innovation, Research Policy 36, 680–693. doi:10.1016/j.respol.2007.01.006

KEEBLE D., LAWSON C., MOORE B. and WILKINSON F. (1999) Collective learning processes, networking and 'institutional thickness' in the Cambridge region, Regional Studies 33, 319–332. doi:10.1080/713693557

LAURSEN K. and SALTER A. (2006) Open for innovation: the role of openness in explaining innovation performance among U.K. manufacturing firms, Strategic Management Journal 27, 131–150. doi:10.1002/smj.507

LAWTON SMITH H. (2007) Universities, innovation, and territorial development: a review of the evidence, Environment and Planning C: Government and Policy 25, 98–114. doi:10.1068/c0561

LAWTON SMITH H., KEEBLE D., LAWSON C., MOORE B. and WILKINSON F. (2001) University–business interaction in the Oxford and Cambridge regions, Tijdschrift voor Economische en Sociale Geografie 92, 88–99. doi:10.1111/1467-9663.00141

LEYDESDORFF L. (2000) The triple helix: an evolutionary model of innovations, Research Policy 29, 243–255. doi:10.1016/S0048-7333(99)00063-3

LUNDVALL B.-Å. (1992) National Systems of Innovation: Towards a Theory of Innovation and Interactive Learning. Pinter, London.

MACKINNON D., CUMBERS A., PIKE A., BIRCH K. and MCMASTER R. (2009) Evolution in economic geography: institutions, political economy, and adaptation, Economic Geography 85, 129–150. doi:10.1111/j.1944-8287.2009.01017.x

MACLAURIN W. R. (1953) The sequence from invention to innovation and its relation to economic growth, Quarterly Journal of Economics 67, 97–111. doi:10.2307/1884150

MALERBA F. (2005) Sectoral systems: how and why innovation differs across sectors, in FAGERBERG J., MOWERY D. and NELSON R. R. (Eds) *Oxford Handbook of Innovation*, pp. 380–406. Oxford University Press, Oxford.

MILES I. (2005) Innovation in services, in FAGERBERG J., MOWERY D. and NELSON R. R. (Eds) *Oxford Handbook of Innovation*, pp. 433–458. Oxford University Press, Oxford.

MIOZZO M. and SOETE L. (2001) Internationalization of services: a technological perspective, *Technological Forecasting and Social Change* **67**, 159–185. doi:10.1016/S0040-1625(00)00091-3

MOODYSSON J., COENEN L. and ASHEIM B. (2008) Explaining spatial patterns of innovation: analytical and synthetic modes of knowledge creation in the Medicon Valley life-science cluster, *Environment and Planning A* **40**, 1040–1056. doi:10.1068/a39110

PAVITT K. (1984) Sectoral patterns of technical change: towards a taxonomy and a theory, *Research Policy* **13**, 343–373. doi:10.1016/0048-7333(84)90018-0

POWELL W. W., KOPUT K. W. and SMITH-DOERR L. (1996) Interorganizational collaboration and the locus of innovation: networks of learning in biotechnology, *Administrative Science Quarterly* **41**, 116–145. doi:10.2307/2393988

RANGA M. and ETZKOWITZ H. (2013) Triple helix systems: an analytical framework for innovation policy and practice in the knowledge society, *Industry and Higher Education* **27**, 237–262. doi:10.5367/ihe.2013.0165

REICHSTEIN T., SALTER A. J. and GANN D. M. (2005) Last among equals: a comparison of innovation in construction, services and manufacturing in the UK, *Construction Management and Economics* **23**, 631–644. doi:10.1080/01446190500126940

ROGELBERG S. G. and STANTON J. M. (2007) Introduction: Understanding and dealing with organizational survey non-response, *Organizational Research Methods* **10**, 195–209. doi:10.1177/1094428106294693

SONN J. W. and STORPER M. (2008) The increasing importance of geographical proximity in technological innovation: an analysis of US patent citations, 1975–1997, *Environment and Planning A* **40**, 1020–1039. doi:10.1068/a3930

STORPER M. and VENABLES A. J. (2004) Buzz: face-to-face contact and the urban economy, *Journal of Economic Geography* **4**, 351–370. doi:10.1093/jnlecg/lbh027

STRAMBACH S. (2008) Knowledge-intensive business services (KIBS) as drivers of multilevel knowledge dynamics, *International Journal of Services Technology and Management* **10**, 152–174. doi:10.1504/IJSTM.2008.022117

TETHER B. S. (2002) Who co-operates for innovation, and why: an empirical analysis, *Research Policy* **31**, 947–967. doi:10.1016/S0048-7333(01)00172-X

TETHER B. S. (2005) Do services innovate (differently)? Insights from the European innobarometer survey, *Industry and Innovation* **12**, 153–184. doi:10.1080/13662710500087891

TETHER B. S. and TAJAR A. (2008) Beyond industry–university links: sourcing knowledge for innovation from consultants, private research organisations and the public science-base, *Research Policy* **37**, 1079–1095. doi:10.1016/j.respol.2008.04.003

VON TUNZELMANN N. and ACHA V. (2005) Innovation in 'low-tech' industries, in FAGERBERG J., MOWERY D. and NELSON R. R. (Eds) *Oxford Handbook of Innovation*, pp. 407–432. Oxford University Press, Oxford.

WILLIAMS R. (2006) Generalized ordered logit/partial proportional odds models for ordinal dependent variables, *Stata Journal* **6**, 58–82.

What Makes Clusters Decline? A Study on Disruption and Evolution of a High-Tech Cluster in Denmark

CHRISTIAN RICHTER ØSTERGAARD ⓘ and EUNKYUNG PARK

Department of Business and Management, Aalborg University, Fibigerstraede 11, Denmark.

ØSTERGAARD C. R. and PARK E. What makes clusters decline? A study on disruption and evolution of a high-tech cluster in Denmark, *Regional Studies*. Most studies on regional clusters focus on identifying factors and processes that make clusters grow. However, sometimes technologies and market conditions suddenly shift, and clusters decline. This paper analyses the process of decline of the wireless communication cluster in Denmark. The longitudinal study on the high-tech cluster reveals that technological lock-in and exit of key firms have contributed to decline. Entrepreneurship has a positive effect on the cluster's adaptive capabilities, while multinational companies have contradicting effects by bringing in new resources to the cluster but being quick to withdraw in times of crisis.

ØSTERGAARD C. R. and PARK E. 导致集群衰落的原因？丹麦一个高科技集群的断裂和演化之研究，区域研究。区域集群的研究，多半聚焦于指认造成集群成长的因素和过程。但有时技术和市场条件会突然转变，致使集群衰落。本文分析丹麦一个无线通信集群的衰落过程。对高科技集群进行的纵贯性研究，揭露了关键厂商的技术锁定与离开，导致了集群的衰落。创业精神，对集群的调适能力有正面影响；跨国公司则为集群带入新的资源、但在危机时刻却快速抽离，因而具有矛盾的影响。

ØSTERGAARD C. R. et PARK E. Qu'est-ce qui explique le déclin des clusters? Une étude de la dégradation et de l'évolution d'un cluster à la pointe de la technologie au Danemark, *Regional Studies*. La plupart des études au sujet des clusters régionaux cherchent principalement à identifier les facteurs et les processus qui pilotent la croissance des clusters. Cependant, quelquefois les technologies et les conditions du marché se modifient rapidement, et les clusters se dégradent. Cet article analyse le processus de déclin en ce qui concerne le cluster de la communication sans fil au Danemark. L'étude longitudinale du cluster à la pointe de la technologie laisse voir que l'enclavement et la sortie technologiques des entreprises clés ont contribué au déclin. L'esprit d'entreprise a un effet positif sur les capacités d'adaptation du cluster, tandis que les sociétés multinationales ont des effets contraires en apportant de nouvelles ressources au cluster mais également n'hesitant pas à s'en retirer en temps de crise.

ØSTERGAARD C. R. und PARK E. Was führt zum Niedergang von Clustern? Studie über die Störung und Evolution eines Hightech-Clusters in Dänemark, *Regional Studies*. Im Mittelpunkt der meisten Studien über regionale Cluster stehen die identifizierenden Faktoren und Prozesse, die Cluster wachsen lassen. Allerdings können sich die technischen und Marktbedingungen manchmal plötzlich ändern, was zum Niedergang von Clustern führt. In diesem Beitrag wird der Prozess des Niedergangs eines Mobilfunk-Clusters in Dänemark analysiert. Aus der Longitudinalstudie des Hightech-Clusters geht hervor, dass der technologische Lock-in-Effekt und die Schließung wichtiger Firmen zum Niedergang beigetragen haben. Das Unternehmertum wirkt sich positiv auf die Anpassungsfähigkeit des Clusters aus, während multinationale Unternehmen mit widersprüchlichen Auswirkungen verbunden sind, da sie neue Ressourcen in den Cluster einbringen, sich aber in Krisenzeiten auch wieder schnell zurückziehen.

ØSTERGAARD C. R. y PARK E. ¿Qué provoca el declive de las aglomeraciones? Un estudio sobre la disrupción y evolución de una aglomeración de alta tecnología en Dinamarca, *Regional Studies*. La mayoría de los estudios sobre aglomeraciones regionales se centran en identificar factores y procesos que hacen crecer las aglomeraciones. Sin embargo, a veces las tecnologías y condiciones del mercado cambian de golpe causando el declive de las aglomeraciones. En este artículo analizamos el proceso de declive de una aglomeración de comunicación inalámbrica en Dinamarca. El estudio longitudinal sobre la aglomeración de alta tecnología indica que la dependencia tecnológica y la salida de empresas principales han contribuido a este declive. El empresariado tiene un efecto positivo en las capacidades de adaptación de la aglomeración, mientras que las empresas multinacionales tienen efectos contradictorios porque aunque aportan nuevos recursos a la aglomeración se dan prisa por desaparecer en tiempos de crisis.

INTRODUCTION

Regional clusters have gained much attention from scholars and practitioners over the last 20 years. One of the aspects investigated intensively in cluster research is the emergence and growth of clusters. In contrast, relatively little is known about how clusters evolve over time and why some clusters decline. The survival of clusters is of great interest for policy-makers, as decline will cause turmoil in regional economies. Detailed empirical studies on cluster decline are thus crucial in order to reveal patterns in how clusters decline.

It is commonly observed that disruptions, which often come from sudden changes in the industry, key technologies and the market, pose threat to clusters. The seminal work by GRABHER (1993) on the decline of the Ruhr district describes how the cluster started to decline after a disruption in demand. He argues that firms were not able to adapt to the disruption because of lock-in. Examples of Silicon Valley and Route 128 also show how disruptions affect clusters. Both clusters experienced disruption in the 1980s: Silicon Valley faced fierce competition from Japanese chipmakers and had to give up the random access memory (RAM) module market, while Route 128 lost its customers as they shifted from mini-computers to workstations and personal computers (LANGLOIS and STEINMUELLER, 1999; BEST, 2001). Both clusters survived the threats, but in other cases clusters start to decline after disruptions. The lack of capabilities to make changes to overcome internal and external disruptions – adaptive capabilities (MARTIN and SUNLEY, 2006; HERVÁS-OLIVER and ALBORS-GARRIGÓS, 2007) – appears to be a key issue in explaining cluster decline.

Clusters are often defined as 'geographic concentrations of interconnected companies, specialized suppliers, service providers, firms in related industries, and associated institutions in a particular field, linked by commonalities and complementarities' (PORTER, 1998, p. 199). The adaptive capabilities and the evolution of clusters need to be studied in consideration of the interaction among these various economic actors, taking into account the developments in industry, technology, and institution and the heterogeneity in actions

of firms. As evolutionary economic geography (EEG) is concerned with the processes by which the spatial organization of economic activities is transformed over time with attention to micro-behaviours of economic agents (BOSCHMA and MARTIN, 2007), it provides an important research framework for studies of evolution of clusters (MENZEL and FORNAHL, 2010; MARTIN and SUNLEY, 2011) and evolutionary processes of regional economic development (MARTIN and SUNLEY, 2006; BOSCHMA and FRENKEN, 2006; BOSCHMA and MARTIN, 2007).

This paper investigates the process of cluster decline. The conclusions derived are based on a detailed case study of the wireless communication cluster in North Jutland, Denmark. The high-tech cluster emerged in the 1980s and grew quickly during the 1990s; however, it showed signs of decline around 2004. In its history, the cluster experienced three disruption periods. The cluster survived the first technological disruption in the late 1980s. When the second disruption period, with a technological disruption and an economic recession, hit the cluster in the early 2000s, entry of new firms stopped, while exits increased. This process of decline was enhanced in 2009, when the third technological disruption and another economic recession came, and the two largest research and development (R&D) firms closed down within a few months.

The paper contributes to the literature in the following ways. Firstly, it provides a detailed longitudinal study on cluster decline, which is rather scarce in the literature. The data that span the whole history of the cluster allowed the analysis of the decline in light of the development path that the cluster has experienced. Secondly, the explanation for cluster decline with attention to disruptions and lock-in contributes to the discussion in EEG. The paper argues that clusters are often exposed to disruptions and they start to decline when the cluster's adaptive capabilities are limited in the time of disruptions. Firm-level dynamics including the relations among the firms and the joint action in the cluster can shed light on how adaptive capabilities change. Lastly, unlike other decline studies focusing on the industries that are in decline itself, this paper studies a cluster in a growing high-tech industry.

The analysis reveals that technological and cognitive 'lock-in' and the exit of focal firms in the cluster was the major force that hampered the adaptive capabilities of the cluster. Innovation and new firm formation are identified as the factors that increase the cluster's ability to overcome threats, while the presence of foreign multinational corporations (MNCs) is found to have two contradicting effects. On the one hand, foreign MNCs increase the employment level and bring investments and new knowledge into the cluster, but on the other hand, they are ultimately footloose and will quickly withdraw from the cluster in times of crisis.

The paper is structured as follows. Theories of cluster decline are presented in the second section. The third section describes the methodology. The case is described in the fourth section. The conclusions and discussion follow in the fifth section.

THEORIES OF CLUSTER DECLINE

Cluster decline and life cycle

The cluster literature has focused on the positive effects that lead to clustering, such as Marshallian externalities, explaining that firms benefit from co-location in a cluster through economies of specialization, economies of labour pooling and localized knowledge spillovers. However, most of these positive factors also have a negative side. When many related firms are co-located, the congestion effects raise prices and wages. Labour pooling increases competition for specific skills and thus raises wages. It is also easier for employees to change jobs within a cluster, which means that companies can lose valuable knowledge to potential competitors. In addition, the localized knowledge spillovers also lead to the loss of information that could weaken firms' performance. The attraction of other firms to the cluster might therefore hamper the incumbent firms' growth (FALCK et al., 2013). SORENSON and AUDIA (2000) find both a higher start-up rate and a higher exit rate in clusters, which indicates the existence of negative externalities. These negative externalities might hamper the development of the cluster and even be the cause of decline.

In the literature, there has been a tendency to link cluster evolution with industry life cycle. KLEPPER's (2010) theory on the origin and growth of industrial clusters implies that the growth in the industry gives opportunity for clusters to grow through spinoff activities. TER WAL and BOSCHMA (2011) explain how clusters co-evolve with the industry and its technological properties at the macro-level, with the firms at the micro-level, and with the knowledge network of firms in the industry. As the industry matures, it experiences shakeout, during which less-competent firms end up exiting the cluster (KLEPPER and SIMONS, 2005; KLEPPER, 2010). At the same time, the variety of firm capabilities decreases and

the network of firms become more stable, which might lead to cognitive lock-in and interfere with future learning. On the other hand, some studies suggest that cluster life cycles are different from industry life cycles. MENZEL and FORNAHL (2010) argue that different growth paths of the computer industry in Boston and Silicon Valley indicate that the cluster life cycle is not the local representation of the industry. Instead, they suggest a four-staged cluster life cycle – going from emergence, growth, sustainment and decline – and argue that the diversity and the heterogeneity of knowledge within the cluster provide foundation for the cluster's development. According to them, clusters decline when the heterogeneity cannot be sustained.

The critics of the life cycle approach claim that the concept implies a deterministic and smooth evolution that does not fit with empirics (MARTIN and SUNLEY, 2011). The emergence or growth of a potential cluster might be stopped and turn into decline at any point of the life cycle. MARTIN and SUNLEY (2011) therefore suggest a modified 'adaptive cycle model' in conceptualizing cluster evolution. This model recognizes that there exist two-way interactions between a cluster and its external environment and posits that there are numerous development trajectories for cluster evolution, based on the four basic phases of the adaptive cycle model: exploitation, reorganization, conservation and release. Among the trajectories, non-generative decline and cluster disappearance, which correspond to the decline in the standard life cycle terminology, is found to be the outcome of high internal connectivity and rigidity. High internal connectivity and rigidity may indicate poor adaptive capability, which is considered one of the important characteristics of a cluster that changes over the phases in the adaptive cycle model.

Therefore, to understand cluster decline, it is necessary to look at the cluster's adaptive capabilities in relation to shocks, such as economic recessions, environmental disasters, market disruptions and technological disruptions. Technological disruptions in particular change the underlying knowledge base for an industry and can easily lead to decline if the cluster firms are not able to move into the new technology (STORPER and WALKER, 1989; CHRISTENSEN, 1997; DALUM et al., 2005; KLEPPER, 2010). The disruptions could also be linked to changes in the industry life cycle during an industry shakeout. During the shakeout phase, exogenous innovations (JOVANOVIC and MACDONALD, 1994) or endogenous innovations (KLEPPER and SIMONS, 2005) create less space for new firms and increase the exit of technology laggard firms, which change the industry structure and leave room for fewer clusters.

Cluster decline, identity and adaptation

Cluster decline does not necessarily lead to the disappearance of all activities within a thematic field, but is linked to a loss of identity. The identity can be understood as the regional industrial identity, suggested by ROMANELLI and KHESSINA (2005), that emerges from the shared perception of internal and external audience about the features of the industrial activity in a certain region. Internally, clustered firms share the sense of community that is often tied to specific technology and product characteristics, e.g. a software cluster or a wireless communications cluster (STABER and SAUTTER, 2011). MENZEL and FORNAHL (2010) state that a declining cluster can transform itself by moving into a completely new field. Similarly, MARTIN and SUNLEY (2011) suggest that when a cluster reorganizes itself, it can either renew itself and start a new cycle of growth or it can be replaced with a new one, with a new identity and a new function. However, when the replacement or transformation happens, it cannot be considered the same cluster afterwards due to the change in the identity.

A cluster is a population-level concept. It is important to remember that a cluster consists of many firms and organizations that have different strategies. The only way the cluster can change is through the actions of individuals, firms and other organizations, all of which may react very differently to the same change. However, the reaction of a cluster as a whole appears to be more than the combined effect of reaction of individual actors because of the interconnections among them. SCHMITZ (1995) argues that the joint action of clustered firms can be an important element in overcoming challenges. Therefore, it is necessary to investigate the actions of different actors and the joint action among them at the same time when studying cluster evolution. The adaptive capabilities of the cluster depend on various factors, such as the rate of new firm creation, the innovativeness of incumbents and the willingness of the firms to move into new fields (BEST, 2001; HERVÁS-OLIVER and ALBORS-GARRIGÓS, 2007; MENZEL and FORNAHL, 2010; MARTIN and SUNLEY, 2011; HOLM and ØSTERGAARD, 2015). On the other hand, the lack of these factors will affect the evolution of the cluster negatively. The rest of this section will now discuss the key factors that influence cluster evolution.

Lock-in. According to GRABHER (1993), lock-in consists of factors that diminish a cluster's ability to recognize and make adjustments to sudden changes. Grabher identifies three kinds of lock-ins: the first is a functional lock-in, which refers to hierarchical inter-firm relationships that hinder suppliers from developing critical functions such as marketing and R&D. Cognitive lock-in means that clustered firms share a common worldview or mindset that makes it hard for them to respond to outside changes. Political lock-in concerns institutional effort to maintain existing industry structures which might damage the development of creativity.

The case of the Ruhr area shows that lock-in affects cluster evolution negatively (GRABHER, 1993). The Ruhr area faced disruptions stemming from falling demand and rising competition as early as in the 1960s. However, the functional lock-in led to lack of innovation among suppliers, which were suffering from 'dependent supplier syndrome', and the group-think from the cognitive lock-in made the firms believe that the worrying demand trend was only a short-term disruption. The firms were thus not able to respond in a timely manner to the changes in the environment. Cognitive lock-in is a fundamental problem for cluster firms in reacting to external changes. POUDER and ST. JOHN (1996) assert that the managers in the clustered firms have similar mental models because they have similar industry experience and educational training within a certain field. Through the origination and convergence phase of cluster, the existence of similar mental models and the proximity among the clustered firms induce groupthink as managers direct attention mostly towards the other cluster firms rather than firms outside the cluster and create narrow focus on their strategies. The clustered firms will eventually act differently than non-clustered firms and can miss out signals from outside the cluster, which can be critical for the continuity of the cluster.

Cognitive and functional lock-in can also lead to technological lock-in, if the firms are too focused on the current products and technologies or if the firms have not developed sufficient innovative competences. Then, they are less attentive to developing new technologies and products, which will also lead to a low level of entrepreneurship within firms (intra-preneurship). All in all, lock-in in incumbents leads to lack of innovation and intra-preneurship, which in turn makes the cluster less adaptive when the technologies shift in the specific field.

Lack of new firm creation. When clusters experience lock-in and show a tendency to decline, new firms can be a source of revitalization. The Ruhr case described by GRABHER (1993) proves that new firms contributed to the eventual reorganization of the industrial district that followed the decline. During the last half of the 1980s, some firms moved headquarters and R&D departments to other regions. Steel firms changed their strategic direction and began to focus more on 'processing of steel', diversifying into plant engineering, environmental technology, mechanical engineering and electronics. A new industrial complex in environmental technology was formed, comprised mainly of newly established firms. Thus, entrepreneurship was one of the forces that drove the renewal of the old industrial district.

Similarly, SAXENIAN (1990) found that the high rate of new-firm formation in Silicon Valley fostered industrial adaptation in the 1980s, when semiconductor producers were challenged by Japanese competitors. Unlike the established companies in the region, these new firms began to specialize in certain areas of expertise, such as chip design and fabrication processes, and contributed to strengthening the competitiveness of the region as a whole. SIMMIE and MARTIN (2010) argue that the Cambridge high-tech cluster recovered from the early 1990s' recession by continuously branching out into sub-clusters based on a strong knowledge platform in advanced mathematics and computing. New firms played an important role in this process. On the contrary, lack of new firms could lead a cluster to a declining phase. As is illustrated in the cases above, new firms provide an opportunity for a cluster to move into related areas of expertise. When clusters experience shocks and need to adapt to the change, new firms can be the driver for the change.

Among the different types of entrants into clusters, spinoffs are found to be especially important for cluster evolution (BUENSTORF and KLEPPER, 2009; DAHL and SORENSON, 2009). Spinoffs, defined as firms established by entrepreneurs with experience from existing firms in the same industry, tend to locate close to the 'parent' companies and perform better than other entrants, thereby driving the formation of clusters. However, some firms are better training grounds for entrepreneurs and create more spinoffs than others, while some companies never produce a single spinoff (KLEPPER, 2010). If the first type of company closes down, it limits the cluster's adaptability through entrepreneurship.

Role of foreign multinational corporations (MNCs). MNCs are increasingly basing their knowledge-intensive activities in clusters, 'affecting both the nature and intertemporal evolution of local innovative activities' (MUDAMBI and SWIFT, 2012, p. 1). The knowledge activities by the MNCs will depend on their motives for entering the cluster and their roles in the MNC knowledge networks.

CANTWELL and MUDAMBI (2005) distinguish the subsidiaries with a competence-creating mandate from the ones with a competence-exploiting mandate, using the analogies of exploration and exploitation in organizational learning theory. As the subsidiaries with a competence-creating mandate invest in R&D activities that are qualitatively different from the 'locally adaptive' R&D activities of the subsidiaries with competence-exploiting mandates, this kind of subsidiary will be more active in innovation activities and therefore will have a positive influence for a cluster's adaptive capabilities. However, when competence-creating subsidiaries are located in a highly concentrated industry, they become more like an outsider in the inter-firm network in the host country and therefore are inhibited in terms of knowledge inflows from the local innovation systems (CANTWELL and MUDAMBI, 2011).

DE PROPRIS and DRIFFIELD (2006) found a positive spillover effect of foreign direct investment in clusters.

This demonstrates that MNCs can have a positive influence on the cluster's adaptive capabilities by enhancing other cluster firms' competitiveness. The knowledge acquired via the global pipelines can be beneficial not only for the firms directly connected to the pipeline, but also for the other firms in the cluster through the spillover effect (BATHELT *et al.*, 2004). The connection outside the cluster also contributes to increasing the heterogeneity of knowledge, which makes the cluster sustainable over a longer period of time (MENZEL and FORNAHL, 2010).

The existence of foreign MNCs in the cluster can also have some negative sides. BIRKINSHAW and HOOD (2000) found that a high level of foreign ownership in a cluster is negatively related to cluster dynamism, which may indicate that clusters with high foreign ownership are less sustainable in the long run. High foreign ownership was also negatively associated with subsidiary autonomy and capabilities in this analysis. Moreover, foreign-owned firms are less-committed than indigenous ones. Foreign firms are more likely to restructure, relocate, sell and close down units in times of economic downturn (GÖRG and STROBL, 2003). The effect of foreign MNCs on the cluster's adaptive capabilities is thus a double-edged sword, as these companies bring knowledge and resources to the cluster, but might also leave quickly and hamper the dynamics within the cluster. If the MNCs are not embedded in the local knowledge network and do not participate in the joint action when it is needed, they can affect the cluster evolution negatively.

METHODS

Data collection

The wireless communication cluster in North Jutland is a relatively small and young cluster in a high-tech industry that emerged in the 1980s and began to decline in the mid-2000s. Despite its small size and relative short history, firms from the cluster were important players in the early growth phase of the mobile communications industry. In addition, several important innovations, such as the embedded mobile phone antenna, were developed in the cluster. This well-studied cluster makes it possible to follow the cluster's evolution closely and to study how the firms and institutions in the cluster reacted to three periods of disruption. The case resembles a critical case, and therefore it can be argued that what makes this high-tech cluster decline can also lead other clusters to decline (FLYVBJERG, 2006).

The data were collected in the following ways. First of all, the archives from earlier studies were used to identify cluster firms and the early history. This includes newspaper clippings, company reports, interview transcripts, draft papers and cluster association material. The list of all cluster firms until 2003 had been compiled by DAHL *et al.* (2003) with the founding and exit year, the names of founders and their previous workplaces, and the main events in the history of the firm. Then, new entrants from 2003 onwards were identified by consulting the cluster association's archive on member companies and searching various online databases for newspaper articles, media reports and corporate information. With the updated list of firms, the founders of the new companies and their former employers were investigated from similar sources. Each firm has been researched thoroughly for main events including ownership changes and close-downs, mainly using online sources, but also by formal and informal interviews.

The next step was to collect data on the number of employees of each firm for the last two decades. The early employment data until 2002 came from earlier work on the cluster (DALUM, 1993, 1995, 1998; DALUM et al., 1999, 2002; PEDERSEN, 2001). The recent numbers are collected from diverse corporate databases, but since not all firms are covered by those databases, newspaper articles and media reports were used to find the numbers that are missing.

The genealogy of the cluster

The genealogy of the wireless communication cluster until 2011 summarizes the development of the cluster (Fig. 1). Fine arrows between firms show that one or more employees from existing firms established spinoff firms. Dotted arrows represent parent spinoffs where the management have come from local firms. Bold arrows show change in the original structure of the company, including acquisition by another firm and reconstruction after financial difficulties. Firms with a dotted box have exited.

THE WIRELESS COMMUNICATION CLUSTER IN NORTH JUTLAND

The cluster includes firms in the field of maritime communication and navigation, telecom and land-based satellite communications equipment, and mobile and cordless communication. In 2011, it consists of 45 firms, 2294 employees, a university and a cluster association.[1]

In the early years of development, the relations among the firms could be explained by competition and 'production-chain-like-character' (REINAU, 2011, p. 296). Later on frequent job change within the cluster and the technical educations provided by local university encouraged the engineers to build personal relationships with former colleagues and fellow students, which then induced a high level of knowledge diffusion via the informal networks (DAHL and PEDERSEN, 2004). The university also played a role in promoting interaction among employees and firms by organizing research projects that helped build relationships and trust between the participants, which then contributed

to informal knowledge sharing afterwards (ØSTERGAARD, 2009). Lastly, the firms were also interconnected through the cluster association. The cluster association created a platform for dialogue and collective actions among the cluster firms and the university.

The cluster has experienced three periods of major external disruptions: (1) from 1988 to 1992, following the shift of the mobile communications standard from the Nordic standard for mobile telephony (Nordic Mobile Telephone – NMT) to the European global system for mobile communications (GSM) standard; (2) from 2000 to 2003, when the European standard shifted to a world communications standard, and the telecommunications industry was in turmoil following the 3G spectrum auctions and the dot.com crisis; and (3) from 2007 to 2009 during the financial crisis, the new standards, and the introduction of Apple's iPhone and the Android smart phones and new business models. The shifts in standards were not unexpected disruptions, but they were an immense technological and market challenge that disrupted the cluster and the entire industry (see Table 1 for more details). The next subsection investigates in more detail how the disruptions affected the cluster and how the firms reacted, while the following subsections analyse the evolution of the number of firms and employees in the cluster.

Disruptions of the cluster in its history

The emergence of the wireless communication cluster (1960–80s). The history of the cluster (named NorCOM) started with the success of the leading producer of maritime communication equipment, S.P. Radio located in a peripheral region with 0.5 million inhabitants that was characterized by traditional industries, such as agriculture, food, fishery, tourism, textiles, tobacco and metal manufacturing. The company started producing radio communication equipment for maritime use for small and medium-sized vessels in the early 1960s with huge success. A couple of successful local spinoffs sprang up from S.P. Radio in the 1970s. In 1973, three engineers from S.P. Radio established the first spinoff company, Dancom. It also produced maritime communication equipment, and competed with S.P. Radio in the same markets. A few years later, two engineers from Dancom started Shipmate, which also produced radiophones for maritime use.

In the 1980s, a range of next-generation spinoffs came from Dancom (restructured and renamed Dancall Radio in 1983) and Shipmate. These companies diversified into the related area of mobile communication equipment, which was led by the introduction of the common NMT.[2] Inheriting capabilities from the parent companies, the spinoffs were well-equipped for this diversification. One example of next-generation spinoff is Cetelco, which was established as a parent spinoff by Shipmate. Cetelco developed its first NMT phone in 1986, and began to produce mobile phones

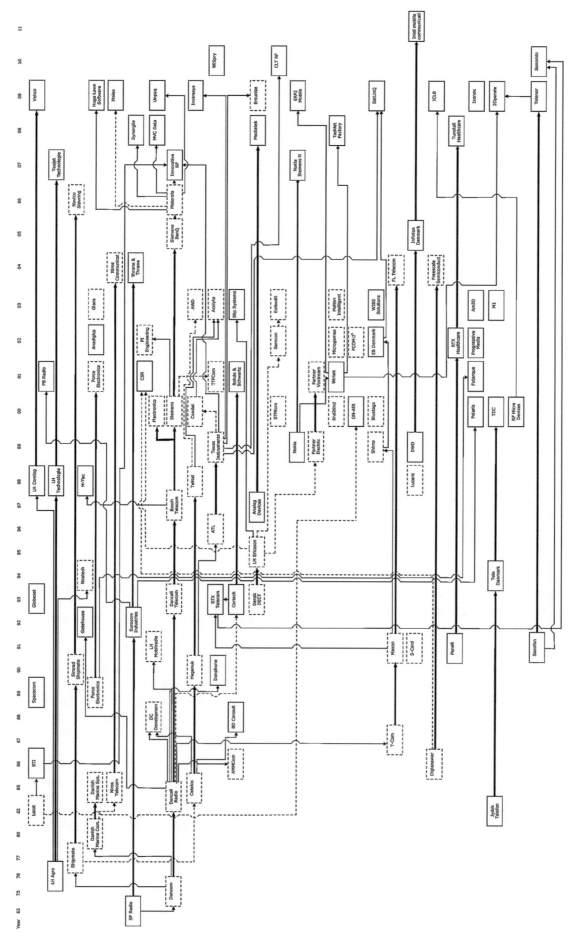

Fig. 1. Genealogy of the cluster

Table 1. Major disruptions in the cluster and change after each disruption

	1988–1992	2000–03	2007–09
External disruptions/ threats	*Technological disruption* New standard: 1G (NMT) to 2G (GSM) • From analogue to digital • From Nordic to European • Increasing complexity	*Technological disruption* New standard: 2G (GSM) to 3G (WCDMA/UTMS) • From European to worldwide standards • Increasing complexity • Tele service providers and 3G spectrum auctions *Economic recession* Dot.com crisis	*Technological disruption* New standard: 3G (WCDMA/UTMS) to 4G (LTE): importance of data transmission Introduction of smartphones: convergence with the computer industry *Economic recession* Financial crisis
Industry dynamics: demand, competition, structure, technology	Larger market spanning the whole of Europe Increasing demand Increasing competition Entry by large electronics firms Large-scale production Intense technology development Shorter product life cycle	Larger market spanning the whole world Increasing demand Mega competition Alliance between incumbents (e.g. Sony Ericsson) Entry of MNCs from other industries Large-scale production Intense technology development Shorter product life cycle Increasing modularization	New entry: Apple, Google and Microsoft New operating systems Increasing importance of software products New path in technology development Decline of old incumbents such as Nokia, Motorola and Sony Emergence of new leaders, e.g. Apple, Samsung Emergence of new markets, e.g. China, India
Cluster dynamics: structure, strategies, policy	Around 15 firms in the cluster Joint venture by Dancall and Cetelco to develop basic 2G technologies Some firms continued with 1G phones (e.g. Maxon) Science park NOVI providing an entrepreneurial environment to firms Collaboration with Aalborg University and the National Telecom Agency	Around 45 firms and 4000 employees in the cluster Increasing number of MNCs Specialization in different components of mobile phones CTIF established at Aalborg University to focus on 4G technologies Seedbed firms exited Fragmented strategies of firms led to lack of 3G competences in the cluster Attempt on collaboration on 3G failed Others did not move into 3G Ericsson with 3G competence closed down Siemens started offshore outsourcing	Around 40 firms and 2200 employees in the cluster Increasing number of software firms MNCs in crisis Exit of some major firms Diversification among firms Aalborg University focusing on 4G technologies Entry by spinoffs from exiting firms
Result: evolution	Increasing number of firms Troubled firms acquired by MNCs Laid-off employees were hired by other firms in the cluster Adaptive capabilities were strong and the cluster was still in the growing phase	Number of firms and employees started to decrease in 2004 No entry between 2004 and 2006 Adaptive capabilities were weakened and the cluster showed signs of decline	Decrease in the number of employees seems to be stabilized while the number of firms increased with new spinoffs from exiting firms Limited adaptive capabilities Firms that generated many spinoffs closed down Survival of new firms is also in doubt Cluster decline

Note: G, generation (e.g., 1G = first-generation technology system); GSM, Global System for Mobile Communications; LTE, Long Term Evolution; MNCs, multinational corporations; NMT, Nordic Mobile Telephone; UMTS, Universal Mobile Telecommunications System; WCDMA, Wideband Code Division Multiple Access.

for several European and East Asian countries. At the end of the 1980s, there were 15 firms in the cluster, and the majority of those were spinoffs.

The first disruption (1988–92) and the result (1990s). In the late 1980s, the European telecommunication operators decided to create a pan-European system (GSM) based on digital technology. This new generation (2G) became the first technological disruption that the cluster faced. The GSM networks allowed for semi-global roaming, which created a larger market, but also attracted new entrants. Thus, the cluster firms faced both increased technological complexity and international competition. To overcome this disruption, Dancall and Cetelco formed a joint venture company, DC Development, to develop the basic modules of a GSM phone together with Aalborg University. DC Development succeeded and its parent companies were among the first to produce a GSM phone. Other firms in the cluster followed other strategies; for example, Maxon decided to continue to make 1G phones and then moved into 2G later on when the technology had matured slightly.

In the 1990s, more spinoffs were founded based on GSM technologies, producing mobile phones, chips and other supporting technologies. This development, however, was not smooth, since several companies in the cluster faced severe financial and technological problems following the shift from 1G to 2G. Most of the troubled companies and laid-off employees were taken over by other companies in the cluster, which shows that the cluster was resilient in this period. For example, Cetelco, suffering from financial constraints, was acquired by Hagenuk in 1990. Dancall also experienced financial trouble, as their newly developed GSM phone was not competitive because of its high price. Furthermore, the export of NMT phones suffered from the growing GSM phone market and the closing of the markets in the Middle East during the Iraq War. Consequently, Dancall was acquired by Amstrad in 1993.

Despite these financial difficulties, the total employment in the cluster increased constantly from 1992. By the end of the 1990s, the number of firms in the cluster had more than doubled, mainly due to entry by spinoffs. Among the 20 entrants in the cluster, seven were entrepreneurial spinoffs and six were parent spinoffs of foreign companies such as Analog Devices, Lucent, Infineon and Nokia. In this period, the ownership structure of the cluster changed significantly, as many foreign MNCs entered the cluster to access the competencies of local development engineers (LORENZEN and MAHNKE, 2002).

In Denmark, the wireless communications industry was mainly located in North Jutland and in Copenhagen, where the latter mainly consisted of a very large R&D unit of Nokia (employing more than 1200 people) and a series of smaller firms. In North Jutland,

the firms and the local university had formed a cluster association in 1997 and were increasingly visible. The cluster accounted for approximately 2.6% of the total regional private sector employment in 2000, but it had become an important part of the regional identity. The location quotient of manufacturing of telecommunications equipment in North Jutland was more than five in the year 2000 (PEDERSEN, 2005).

The second period of disruptions (2000–03) – economic recession and technological disruption. The cluster experienced an external shock in the early 2000s when the telecommunication sector was hit by stagnating sales after the burst of the dot.com bubble. After this economic shock, the foreign MNCs in the cluster changed their strategies and either collected R&D units in the home country, or reduced R&D expenses in the subsidiaries. Consequently, many of the MNCs downsized and sacked local engineers. Some existing and new firms were able to absorb the released work force from the foreign MNCs, and some engineers even established their own companies. When Telital closed down in 2002, some employees joined new parent spinoffs established by two foreign companies. Nokia decided to move its R&D unit to Copenhagen in 2001, and former employees established Wirtek. Some local firms were also affected by this crisis and closed down. Despite the downsizing and exits, the number of companies grew, as there were many new companies entering the cluster. In terms of the wider economy, the economy was in a recession in the beginning of 2001, followed by slow growth in 2002 that increased the regional unemployment rate by less than 0.5 percentage points. The information and communication technology (ICT) sector employment also decreased slightly from 8700 to 8200 from 2000 to 2002. The cluster accounted for half of the employment in the regional ICT sector.

In a report from 2002, some of the managers for foreign MNCs complained about the lack of local decision-making power in deciding R&D strategies (DALUM and PEDERSEN, 2002). Others feared that distance to end-users and lack of knowledge related to production might become a problem. Many of the foreign MNC subsidiaries were dependent on single customers or on internal sales. The shift from 2G to 3G, the technological disruption, also posed a threat to the cluster. The standardization process for 3G had become global planning to create a global standard, bringing about intense global competition. The complexity of the technologies and the pressure on time to market had also increased. The firms in the cluster had various strategies. Some firms were initially active in 3G research (e.g. L.M. Ericsson, which closed down the unit in the cluster in 2003), and others decided to adopt a wait-and-see approach to the development. Some firms tried to cooperate with others in developing the new technologies, but failed (DALUM *et al.*, 2005). As a result, the cluster was not very active in the new technology, which affected its adaptive capabilities negatively.

The impact of the second wave of disruptions started to show in 2004 as many firms closed down or downsized, while there were no new entries. One of the big companies, Flextronics, closed down with 500 employees in 2004. The headquarters in Singapore decided to move the production to lower-cost locations. The close-down was considered a tragic event and marked the end of mobile phone manufacturing in Denmark, but the overall R&D employment was stable in the cluster, as the main layoffs were of low-skilled production workers.

The third period of disruption (2007–09) – technological disruption and economic recession. The introduction of the iPhone and Android-based smart phones in 2007 disrupted the industry and resulted in a significantly decreased demand for traditional mobile phones. These innovations, coming from the computer software industry, initiated a JOVANOVIC and MACDONALD (1994)-type of industry shakeout that completely changed the industry and led to the demise of the dominant firms like Nokia, Motorola and SonyEricsson that accounted for 60% of the market in 2007. In addition, the financial crisis from the second half of 2008 and the following economic crisis decreased the general demand. From 2008 to 2010, the Danish gross domestic product shrank with almost 8% and the unemployment rate doubled from 3% to 6%. The effect on North Jutland region was similar to that on the rest of the country.

These technological and economic disruptions posed serious threats to the cluster. As a result, two central players in the cluster, Motorola and Texas Instruments (TI), ceased their activities in the cluster in 2009. The entry of Apple and other new competitors made Motorola's market share drop from 14.3% in 2007 to 4.8% in 2009. Motorola's Aalborg division had focused on development of new mobile telephones and production planning until the headquarters reduced the number of newly developed models, and eventually closed its European mobile-phone divisions. TI suffered from focusing on chipsets for 2G phones instead of 3G phones, and ended up closing most of its European divisions. Motorola and TI had to lay off 275 and 75 employees respectively, consisting mainly of highly skilled R&D engineers. Unlike former instances in which foreign MNCs had laid off many engineers, this time the cluster could not take in all the released talent. This resulted in workforce migration to other regions and to other industries. It seems that the cluster was not able to adapt to this major crisis.

The role and actions of the local university and the cluster association

Aalborg University has been very influential for the development of the cluster. Since the university was established in 1974, its main role has been to supply highly skilled graduates. Although the indirect transfer of knowledge via graduates has been the most substantial role of Aalborg University, direct research transfer also occurred. The Center for Personal Communication (CPK), established in 1993 and supported by the Danish Council for Technical Scientific Research, played an important role in this type of knowledge transfer as this centre was established to focus on basic research in radiocommunications technology and speech recognition. CPK had several research projects involving both the researchers at the university and the employees in the cluster. The research effort in the field was followed by the establishment of the large research unit Centre for TeleInFrastructure (CTIF) in 2004.

During the first disruption, the university contributed to the development of GSM competences, when DC development was established. Since the establishment of CPK, the centre organized research projects aiming at developing other related technologies together with the cluster firms and the leading foreign firms in the industry. However, when the technology shift from 2G to 3G took place, the fundamental technologies for this new system were mainly developed in the other parts of the world. 3G research has been conducted at the university, but it did not have the same impact in the cluster as previously. One could argue that, during the second disruption, the university, as a source of new knowledge, failed to provide timely input for firm innovation. Realizing the need to develop new competences for the next generation of wireless communication technologies, CTIF has since initiated research projects for the upcoming 4G technologies with the participation from local firms and leading firms located abroad.

The cluster association, NorCOM, started in early 1997 as a club of firms and knowledge institutions and was formally founded as association with a board of directors in January 2000. The mission of NorCOM was to improve and expand the scope of business opportunities, technological development and innovation in the cluster. Internally, NorCOM provided a meeting place for the cluster firms to discuss some issues within the cluster and to network with other firms. Externally, it placed effort in promoting the cluster so it is visible to the external environment as a cluster with strong expertise in wireless communication. More specifically, NorCOM organized industry-specific activities such as symposia, recruiting events and plenary sessions.

As more foreign MNCs located their subsidiaries in the cluster by acquiring local firms, the share of foreign firms in the cluster increased, but they were not as keen on keeping the membership in the association as local firms (REINAU, 2011). The local firms were small in size and therefore needed the brand of NorCOM in doing their business. On the other hand, foreign MNCs did not see the necessity to be a part of the association as they already have strong brands. Additionally, some MNCs in the cluster were direct competitors to each other, which made them reluctant to participate in the joint action, especially on technology development. Therefore, the membership in the association decreased over time and the formal linkage of firms through association has weakened as well. The changed dynamics among firms in the association over time could have inhibited them to pursue efficient joint action during the crises. The decline of the cluster also affected NorCOM. It could not keep its specialized profile and it merged in January 2009 with the local industry association for the broader ICT sector.

Overview of the cluster in growth, sustainment and decline

The effects of the disruptions are also present in the data on employment and number of firms. Fig. 2 shows the change in the population and the number of entries and exits. The number of firms had increased steadily until 2003, as there were very few exits before then, and plenty of entries. Then, after the second disruption, between 2004 and 2006, the cluster started to show signs of decline; there was no entry at all, while firms continued to exit. There are several acquisitions and reconstructions in this period which are not counted as new entry. A decrease in new-firm formation is also observed in the Cambridge cluster in its declining phase around 2005–06 (STAM and GARNSEY, 2009). In 2009, entries peaked, as ten new firms were established. The majority of these were founded by former Motorola and TI employees. However, the survival of these entrants is questionable. Among eight spinoffs, four have founders with a regular job other than the

start-up. Moreover, the majority of the new firms have no employees except the founders and most of them do not show employment growth.

Fig. 3 shows the change in the number of employees in the cluster. The declining trend is apparent from 2004. Following the second disruption, total employment decreased slightly from 2000 to 2002, but increased again in 2003. From 2003, the number decreased drastically until 2005, as many firms downsized and exited in this period. Except for 2006, the number of employees continued to decline until 2010, when the number increased by merely 24. Figs 2 and 3 reveal the cluster life cycle with a long emergence phase followed by a growth phase and a short sustainment phase (2000–03 in the employment data). It could be argued that the sustainment period last until 2007 despite the decline in the number of firms and employees, because the qualitative description of the cluster suggest that it is during the third period of disruptions that the large companies close down, the technological heterogeneity and diversity shrinks, R&D employees leave to non-cluster industries and the identity as a wireless communications cluster is being challenged.

What changed the adaptive capabilities of the cluster and made the cluster decline?

The decline of the cluster is clearly linked to the lack of adaptability in the third period of disruptions. Table 1 shows the three periods of disruptions that the cluster faced, the dynamics within the industry and cluster at the time of disruptions, the impact of the disruptions, and the change observed after the disruptions.

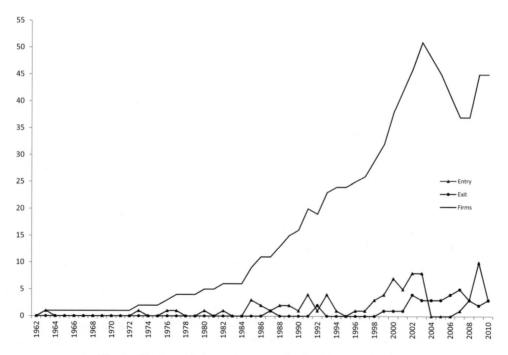

Fig. 2. Total population and entry and exit of firms in the cluster

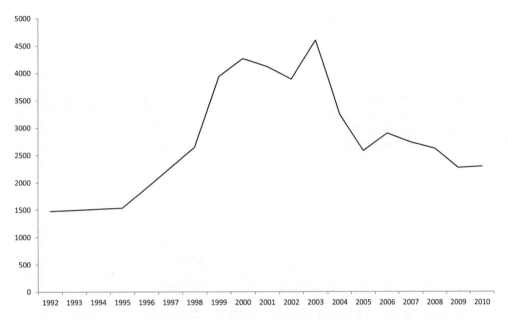

Fig. 3. Employment in the cluster

The most important factor that changed was the presence of relevant technological competence at the time of transition from one generation of system to another. During the first transition, two firms formed a successful joint venture in order to develop the new technologies. The technological heterogeneity broadened as some companies founded a joint venture to focus on cordless phones while others went into related fields. This broadening of the market and knowledge base must have increased the cluster's adaptive capabilities during the growth phase as suggested by MENZEL and FORNAHL (2010).

However, when 3G emerged, the development of basic technologies did not take place in the cluster to the same degree as with previous standards. Collaboration efforts initiated by some firms did not succeed. Furthermore, MNCs decided that R&D in 3G technologies should take place elsewhere. When TI acquired a cluster firm in 2002, it simply closed the 3G technology division. The 3G technology, which became a major disruption, was vastly more complex than 2G and required huge investments in R&D that only large companies could afford. The rise in innovations thus increased the entry barriers and put pressure on less efficient innovators (KLEPPER and SIMONS, 2005). Consequently, the technological competencies within 3G were mainly developed in other parts of the world. This technological lock-in was initially not a problem, because 3G had a slow start and initially seemed unsuccessful, while 2G products still sold well. A few years later, smart phones boosted 3G sales. Facing this disruption, the lack of 3G competencies became a major problem. In addition, the innovations introduced by Apple and Google disrupted the entire industry and increased the pressure for firms to innovate or implement the disruptive innovation (e. g. switch to the Android system) or simply exit.

The technological lock-in did not only lower the opportunities for new firms to emerge when the technology standard shifted, but it also deteriorated the competitiveness of incumbents by limiting intra-preneurial opportunities within firms, which eventually led to the exit of some important players in the cluster.

Another factor that might have affected the adaptive capabilities after the second disruption is the exit of firms that had created many spinoffs. Looking at the change in the population of firms by entry type (Fig. 4), it can be seen that entrepreneurial spinoffs largely account for the development of the cluster over the whole time period. The spinoff process was especially important in the emergent phase, which is also seen in other studies (KLEPPER, 2010).

These companies became seedbeds for many spinoffs later on, and were crucial for further development of the cluster as these function as training grounds for entrepreneurs who gain relevant capabilities and routines from the parent companies. The exit of these firms possibly affects the level and quality of entrepreneurship in the cluster in the future. This might explain the low level of entry from 2004 to 2010.

The next factor that changed was the concentration of foreign MNCs in the cluster. After the first disruption, some local companies were acquired by foreign firms due to financial problems. Moreover, more foreign MNCs entered the cluster in the 1990s, as they were attracted to its competence level. Initially, this increased the heterogeneity, creating global links and financial strength. However, the high concentration of foreign firms proved to be a weakness during the times of crisis. Many subsidiaries did not have much influence on strategic decisions made by the MNCs' headquarters and were also limited in their search for innovation (REINAU, 2011). Furthermore, when the

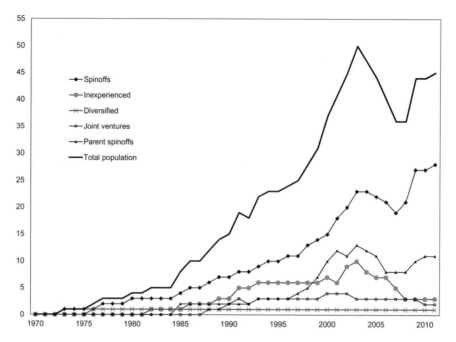

Fig. 4. Firm population by entry type

industry was in crisis, many of the foreign MNCs relocated their development activities to bigger R&D centres. These negative effects of MNCs in clusters is in line with findings in the literature (BIRKINSHAW and HOOD, 2000; GÖRG and STROBL, 2003; CANTWELL and MUDAMBI, 2011).

CONCLUSIONS AND DISCUSSION

Regional clusters are constantly exposed to external disruptions from changes in the industry and the market. A cluster's ability to adapt to these changes determines the evolution of the cluster after such disruptions. This paper analyses the process of cluster decline, which has been a rather neglected subject in cluster research. An in-depth case study on a wireless communication cluster shows that changes in the cluster's adaptive capabilities are important in understanding how and why a well-functioning cluster turns into a declining cluster following several periods of disruption. What is interesting in the NorCOM story is that these adaptive capabilities can change over time, and that a once highly adaptive cluster can decline if some factors diminish its ability to renew itself.

The quantitative data point toward the signs of decline following the second period of disruption, while the qualitative signs of decline becomes evident in the third period of disruption, where large MNCs leave the cluster, the heterogeneity and diversity shrinks and highly skilled employees leaves the cluster. Furthermore, the strong identity as a wireless communications cluster becomes challenged as the dominant firms close down and in particular with the closing of the cluster association

when it merged into a broader association for the regional ICT sector. The longitudinal study on the cluster examined here enhances the understanding of the factors that influence its development over time.

The major force that affected NorCOM's adaptive capabilities was lock-in. The fact that the firms were not able to develop the newly dominant technologies in the industry implies that there was a technological lock-in. Cognitive lock-in among cluster firms have brought about the technological lock-in, as they focused on further development of the already-existing technological competencies in 2G instead of being active in developing new technologies. Organizational lock-in could be found in the operations of subsidiaries of the MNCs, where the R&D divisions in different locations had to compete against each other for headquarters' choice of new products. Sometimes, the new initiatives of local employees were turned down because they did not fit with the headquarters' overall strategy (REINAU, 2011). What happened in the cluster is also in line with the argument by MARTIN and SUNLEY (2006) that processes and configurations built up in the phase of 'positive' lock-in – in this case, the phase when GSM technologies flourished and created positive externalities – become a source of increasing inflexibility and rigidity.

However, it seems that lock-in is only part of the explanation for the cluster's limited adaptive capabilities. While MARTIN and SUNLEY (2011) almost solely focus on the reorientation of existing companies (intra-preneurship) as a source of adaptive change, new-firm creation is also critical to adaptability. One way for a cluster to reorganize itself and recover is entrepreneurship (MENZEL and FORNAHL, 2010). This is proven in the case when the cluster experienced the first crisis in the late 1980s. During this crisis, when firms started to exit, new organizations entered the cluster by either acquiring troubled firms or establishing new entities engaging laid-off employees. Silicon Valley, the Cambridge high-tech cluster, and the Ruhr area all demonstrate the importance of new firms to a cluster's ability to reorganize when facing disruptions.

In addition, the strong presence of foreign MNCs in the cluster also influenced the evolution, yet with some contradictory effects in different time periods. When the cluster was in a growing phase, many foreign firms entered the cluster to get access to its highly skilled labour. After the first disruption, MNCs did in fact save the leading cluster firms that had severe financial troubles by acquiring them. In this way, the technological competencies that otherwise were in danger of being dissolved remained within the cluster. The foreign MNCs also provided access to new markets, financial resources and knowledge (BATHELT *et al.*, 2004; CANTWELL and MUDAMBI, 2005). Entry of MNCs therefore had a positive effect on the cluster's adaptive capabilities in this period. However, during the next disruptions, foreign firm's presence proved vulnerability. They were largely reactive to changes in the industry, as they readily downsized or simply exited the cluster during the crises, proving that they are much more 'footloose' than local firms (GÖRG and STROBL, 2003). The MNCs' decision to withdraw from a location also depended on the overall performance of the company and was also affected by the severity of the third period disruptions that resembles a JOVANOVIC and MACDONALD (1994) industry shakeout. For example, Motorola suffered from a sharp decrease in its market share in the mobile phone market, which directly influenced the company's decision to exit the cluster. Some policy implications can be inferred from the above findings. In terms of creating diversity in the cluster and developing pipelines to other external actors, the attracting MNCs can strengthen the cluster's adaptive capabilities (see also MENZEL and FORNAHL, 2010; MARTIN and SUNLEY, 2011). MNCs can also takeover failing firms and preserve the activities in the cluster in the time of disruption. However, policies towards foreign MNCs should ensure that these firms are embedded in the cluster environment and maintain their commitment to the cluster over time. The existence of foreign firms clearly brings both positive and negative effects to the clusters. The footloose nature might be a challenge when adapting to a major disruption. In order to deal with these issues, policies should also direct attention to supporting the local actors in retaining the technology leadership within the cluster. For a declining cluster, policies could also be directed towards helping the laid off employees entering related industries and avoiding a chaotic decline.

The findings in this paper point to some relevant future research areas. Firstly, studies on evolution of other wireless communication clusters within the same period of time will reveal more location-specific factors that may affect the decline of clusters. Secondly, how the adaptability of a regional economy is related to that of a cluster is an area of study that needs more attention, as this has policy implications for both regional economies and clusters.

Acknowledgements – The authors thank the discussants at: the Danish Research Unit for Industrial Dynamics (DRUID) Society conference 2012; the Regional Innovation Policy conference 2012; and the Association of American Geographers (AAG) Annual meeting 2012; as well as the two anonymous reviewers for their useful comments.

Disclosure statement – No potential conflict of interest was reported by the authors.

Funding – This project was funded by two projects: GONE, sponsored by the Danish Council for Strategic Research; and AEGIS, sponsored by European Union 7th Framework Programme [grant agreement number 225134].

NOTES

1. The average age of the cluster firms is about 11.5 years; the average size in terms of employees is 51; while the average size in terms of gross profit is about €3 million (this figure is only available for 38 firms). Fourteen companies (about 30% of the cluster firms) are foreign owned and their employees account for about 66% of the total employee population in the cluster.
2. The evolution of mobile communication technologies can be explained well by technological life cycles (DALUM *et al.*, 2005). Different generations of mobile communication technology (1G–4G) have life cycles of their own. Within each generation, different systems were developed in different parts of the world (e.g. Nordic countries, Central Europe, the United States and Asia), and competed with each other. The first-generation technology system (1G) was represented by analogue mobile systems. In 1981, the Nordic mobile telephony operators launched the first cross-national public mobile telephony system, called NMT.

ORCID

Christian Richter Østergaard ⓘ http://orcid.org/0000-0003-1782-202X

REFERENCES

BATHELT H., MALMBERG A. and MASKELL P. (2004) Clusters and knowledge: local buzz, global pipelines and the process of knowledge creation, *Progress in Human Geography* **28**, 31–56. doi:10.1191/0309132504ph469oa

BEST M. H. (2001) *The New Competitive Advantage: The Renewal of American Industry.* Oxford University Press, Oxford.

BIRKINSHAW J. and HOOD N. (2000) Characteristics of foreign subsidiaries in industry clusters, *Journal of International Business Studies* **31**, 141–154. doi:10.1057/palgrave.jibs.8490893

BOSCHMA R. and FRENKEN K. (2006) Why is economic geography not an evolutionary science? Towards an evolutionary economic geography, *Journal of Economic Geography* **6**, 273–302.

BOSCHMA R. and MARTIN R. (2007) Editorial: Constructing an evolutionary economic geography, *Journal of Economic Geography* **7**, 537–548. doi:10.1093/jeg/lbm021

BUENSTORF G. and KLEPPER S. (2009) Heritage and agglomeration: the Akron tyre cluster revisited, *Economic Journal* **119**, 705–733. doi:10.1111/j.1468-0297.2009.02216.x

CANTWELL J. and MUDAMBI R. (2005) MNE competence-creating subsidiary mandates, *Strategic Management Journal* **26**, 1109–1128. doi:10.1002/smj.497

CANTWELL J. and MUDAMBI R. (2011) Physical attraction and the geography of knowledge sourcing in multinational enterprises, *Global Strategy Journal* **1**, 206–232. doi:10.1002/gsj.24

CHRISTENSEN C. (1997) *The Innovator's Dilemma.* Harvard Business School Press, Boston, MA.

DAHL M. S. and PEDERSEN C. Ø. R. (2004) Knowledge flows through informal contacts in industrial clusters: myth or reality? *Research Policy* **33**, 1673–1686. doi:10.1016/j.respol.2004.10.004

DAHL M. S., PEDERSEN C. Ø. R. and DALUM B. (2003) *Entry by Spinoff in a High-Tech Cluster.* DRUID Working Paper Series. Danish Research Unit for Industrial Dynamics (DRUID), Copenhagen.

DAHL M. S. and SORENSON O. (2009) The embedded entrepreneur, *European Management Review* **6**, 172–181. doi:10.1057/emr.2009.14

DALUM B. (1993) North Jutland: a 'technology district' in radiocommunication technology, FAST dossier: continental Europe, *Science, Technology and Community* **26**, 1–49.

DALUM B. (1995) Local and global linkages the radiocommunications cluster in Northern Denmark, *Journal of Industry Studies* **2**, 89–109. doi:10.1080/13662719508538557

DALUM B. (1998) Localised learning: university–industry links in the case of the radiocommunications cluster in North Jutland, Denmark. Paper presented at the Association of American Geographers (AAG) 1998 Annual Meeting, Boston, MA, USA, 1998.

DALUM B., HOLMÉN M., JACOBSSON S., PRAEST M., RICKNE A. and VILLUMSEN G. (1999) The formation of knowledge based clusters in North Jutland and Western Sweden. Paper presented at the Danish Research Unit for Industrial Dynamics (DRUID) Conference, Rebild, 9–12 June 1999.

DALUM B. and PEDERSEN C. Ø. R. (2002) *Vision Nordstjernen.* NOVI, Aalborg.

DALUM B., PEDERSEN C. Ø. R. and VILLUMSEN G. (2002) *Technological Life Cycles: Regional Clusters Facing Disruption.* DRUID Working Paper. Danish Research Unit for Industrial Dynamics (DRUID), Copenhagen.

DALUM B., PEDERSEN C. Ø. R. and VILLUMSEN G. (2005) Technological life-cycles: lessons from a cluster facing disruption, *European Urban and Regional Studies* **12**, 229–246. doi:10.1177/0969776405056594

DE PROPRIS L. and DRIFFIELD N. (2006) The importance of clusters for spillovers from foreign direct investment and technology sourcing, *Cambridge Journal of Economics* **30**, 277–291. doi:10.1093/cje/bei059

FALCK O., GUENTHER C., HEBLICH S. and KERR W. R. (2013) From Russia with love: the impact of relocated firms on incumbent survival, *Journal of Economic Geography* **13**, 419–449. doi:10.1093/jeg/lbs035

FLYVBJERG B. (2006) Five misunderstandings about case-study research, *Qualitative Inquiry* **12**, 219–245. doi:10.1177/1077800405284363

GÖRG H. and STROBL E. (2003) 'Footloose' multinationals?, *Manchester School* **71**, 1–19. doi:10.1111/1467-9957.00331

GRABHER G. (1993) The weakness of strong ties: the lock-in of regional development in the Ruhr area, in GRABHER G (Ed.) *The Embedded Firm: On the Socioeconomics of Industrial Networks*, pp. 93–104. Routledge, London.

HERVÁS-OLIVER J. L. and ALBORS-GARRIGÓS J. (2007) Do clusters capabilities matter? An empirical application of the resource-based view in clusters, *Entrepreneurship and Regional Development* **19**, 113–136. doi:10.1080/08985620601137554

HOLM J. R. and ØSTERGAARD C. R. (2015) Regional employment growth, shocks and regional industrial resilience: a quantitative analysis of the Danish ICT sector, *Regional Studies* **49**, 95–112.

JOVANOVIC B. and MACDONALD G. M. (1994) The life cycle of a competitive industry, *Journal of Political Economy* **102**, 322–347. doi:10.1086/261934

KLEPPER S. (2010) The origin and growth of industry clusters: the making of Silicon Valley and Detroit, *Journal of Urban Economics* **67**, 15–32. doi:10.1016/j.jue.2009.09.004

KLEPPER S. and SIMONS K. L. (2005) Industry shakeouts and technological change, *International Journal of Industrial Organization* **23**, 23–43. doi:10.1016/j.ijindorg.2004.11.003

LANGLOIS R. N. and STEINMUELLER W. E. (1999) The evolution of competitive advantage in the worldwide semiconductor industry 1947–1996, 19–78, in MOWERY D. C. and NELSON R. R. (Eds) *Sources of Industrial Leadership*, pp. 19–78. Cambridge University Press, Cambridge.

LORENZEN M. and MAHNKE V. (2002) *Global Strategy and the Acquisition of Local Knowledge: How MNCs Enter Regional Knowledge Clusters.* DRUID Working Paper. Danish Research Unit for Industrial Dynamics (DRUID), Copenhagen.

MARTIN R. and SUNLEY P. (2006) Path dependence and regional economic evolution, *Journal of Economic Geography* **6**, 395–437. doi:10.1093/jeg/lbl012

MARTIN R. and SUNLEY P. (2011) Conceptualizing cluster evolution: beyond the life cycle model?, *Regional Studies* **45**, 1299–1318. doi:10.1080/00343404.2011.622263

Menzel M.-P. and Fornahl D. (2010) Cluster life cycles – dimensions and rationales of cluster evolution, *Industrial and Corporate Change* **19**, 205–238.

Mudambi R. and Swift T. (2012) Multinational enterprises and the geographical clustering of innovation, *Industry and Innovation* **19**, 1–21. doi:10.1080/13662716.2012.649058

Østergaard C. R. (2009) Knowledge flows through social networks in a cluster: comparing university and industry links, *Structural Change and Economic Dynamics* **20**, 196–210. doi:10.1016/j.strueco.2008.10.003

Pedersen C. Ø. R. (2001) *Clusteranalyse af IKT sektoren i Nordjylland*. Aalborg University, Aalborg.

Pedersen C. Ø. R. (2005) *The Development Perspectives for the ICT Sector in North Jutland*. Aalborg University, Aalborg.

Porter M. E. (1998) *On Competition*. Harvard Business School Press, Boston, MA.

Pouder R. and St. John C. H. (1996) Hot spots and blind spots: geographical clusters of firms and innovation, *Academy of Management Review* **21**, 1192–1225.

Reinau K. H. (2011) *Local Clusters in a Globalized World*. Aalborg University, Aalborg.

Romanelli E. and Khessina O. M. (2005) Regional industrial identity: cluster configurations and economic development, *Organization Science* **16**, 344–358. doi:10.1287/orsc.1050.0131

Saxenian A. (1990) Regional networks and the resurgence of Silicon Valley, *California Management Review* **33**, 89–112.

Schmitz H. (1995) Collective efficiency: growth path for small-scale industry, *Journal of Development Studies* **31**, 529–566. doi:10.1080/00220389508422377

Simmie J. and Martin R. (2010) The economic resilience of regions: towards an evolutionary approach, *Cambridge Journal of Regions, Economy and Society* **3**, 27–43. doi:10.1093/cjres/rsp029

Sorenson O. and Audia P. G. (2000) The social structure of entrepreneurial activity: geographic concentration of footwear production in the United States, 1940–1989, *American Journal of Sociology* **106**, 424–62. doi:10.1086/316962

Staber U. and Sautter B. (2011) Who are we, and do we need to change? Cluster identity and life cycle, *Regional Studies* **45**, 1349–1361.

Stam E. and Garnsey E. (2009) Decline and renewal of high-tech clusters: the Cambridge Case. Paper presented at the Danish Research Unit for Industrial Dynamics (DRUID) Conference, Copenhagen, Denmark, 17–9 June 2009.

Storper M. and Walker R. (1989) *The Capitalist Imperative: Territory, Technology, and Industrial Growth*. Basil Blackwell, Oxford.

Ter Wal A. L. J. and Boschma R. (2011) Co-evolution of firms, industries and networks in space, *Regional Studies* **45**, 919–933.

Path Renewal in Old Industrial Regions: Possibilities and Limitations for Regional Innovation Policy

LARS COENEN, JERKER MOODYSSON and HANNA MARTIN
Centre for Innovation and Research in the Learning Economy (CIRCLE), Lund University, Lund, Sweden.
Nordic Institute for Studies in Innovation (NIFU), Research and Education, Majorstuen, Oslo, Norway

COENEN L., MOODYSSON J. and MARTIN H. Path renewal in old industrial regions: possibilities and limitations for regional innovation policy, *Regional Studies*. This paper analyses the potential, barriers and limitations for regional innovation policy to facilitate industrial renewal in old industrial regions. It draws on a case analysis of the policy programme 'Biorefinery of the Future' geared to promote renewal of the forest industry in Northern Sweden. It is shown that infusion of radical emergent technology is necessary for new regional path development, but not sufficient. To avoid a singular focus on technology-push, policy should pay more attention to complementary experimentation processes in relation to demand-side characteristics, firm strategies and business models as well as regulatory aspects. Moreover, coordination between regional innovation policy and adjacent domains and levels of policy-making is needed as some of the most pressing obstacles for renewal are not specific to the region but instead to the industry at large.

COENEN L., MOODYSSON J. and MARTIN H. 旧工业区的路径革新：区域创新政策的可能性与限制, *区域研究*。本文分析区域创新政策促进旧工业区域的产业革新的潜力、障碍与限制。本文将分析一个促进瑞典北部林业革新、名为"未来的生物提炼"的政策计画。本文显示，新的区域路径发展，需要激进的新兴科技，但该科技本身却并不足够。为了避免单一聚焦于科技推力，政策必须更为关注与需求面特徵、企业策略、商业模式及规范面向有关的补充性实验过程。此外，区域创新政策与政策制定的邻近范畴及层级之间，必须进行协调，因为追求革新的最为迫切的障碍之中，部分并不只专属于该区域，而是对整体产业皆然。

COENEN L., MOODYSSON J. et MARTIN H. La voie du renouveau dans les anciennes régions industrielles: les possibilités et les limites en matière de politique en faveur de l'innovation régionale, *Regional Studies*. Cet article analyse le potentiel, les obstacles et les limites quant à la politique en faveur de l'innovation régionale visant le renouveau industriel dans les anciennes régions industrielles. On puise dans une étude de cas, à savoir le programme politique appelé 'La bioraffinerie de l'avenir' qui est axé sur la promotion du renouveau de l'industrie forestière dans le nord de la Suède. On montre que l'apport de la nouvelle technologie radicale est une condition nécessaire mais pas suffisante pour le développement de nouvelles voies régionales. Pour éviter de donner la priorité à une poussée technologique, la politique devrait prêter plus d'attention aux processus d'expérimentation complémentaires par rapport aux caractéristiques de la demande, aux strategies d'entreprises et aux modèles d'affaires ainsi qu'aux aspects réglementaires. Qui plus est, il faut la coordination entre la politique en faveur de l'innovation régionale et les domaines connexes et les niveaux de la mise au point de la politique parce que quelques-uns des principaux obstacles au renouveau ne sont pas spécifiques à la région mais plûtot à l'industrie en général.

COENEN L., MOODYSSON J. und MARTIN H. Pfaderneuerung in alten Industrieregionen: Möglichkeiten und Grenzen der regionalen Innovationspolitik, *Regional Studies*. In diesem Beitrag werden das Potenzial, die Hindernisse und die Grenzen der regionalen Innovationspolitik für eine Industriesanierung in alten Industrieregionen untersucht. Ausgangspunkt ist die Fallanalyse des Politikprogramms 'Bioraffinerie der Zukunft' zur Förderung einer Erneuerung der Waldindustrie in Nordschweden. Wie sich zeigt, ist eine Infusion mit radikalen neuen Technologien zur Entwicklung eines neuen regionalen Pfades zwar erforderlich, aber nicht ausreichend. Um eine ausschließliche Betonung der Einführung von Technologie zu vermeiden, sollte die Politik stärker auf ergänzende experimentelle Prozesse im Zusammenhang mit den Merkmalen auf der Nachfrageseite, den Firmenstrategien und den Geschäftsmodellen sowie auf gesetzliche Aspekte achten. Darüber hinaus ist eine Koordination zwischen der regionalen Innovationspolitik und den angrenzenden politischen Bereichen und Stufen erforderlich, da einige der dringlichsten Hindernisse für eine Erneuerung nicht regionsspezifisch sind, sondern für die Branche als Ganzes gelten.

COENEN L., MOODYSSON J. y MARTIN H. Renovación de las rutas en antiguas regiones industriales: posibilidades y limitaciones de la política de innovación regional, *Regional Studies*. En este artículo analizamos el potencial, las barreras y las limitaciones de la política de innovación regional para facilitar la renovación industrial en antiguas regiones industriales. Nos basamos en un análisis de casos del programa político para la 'Biorrefinería del Futuro' cuyo objetivo es fomentar la renovación de la industria forestal del norte de Suecia. Mostramos que, aunque es necesaria una inyección de tecnología emergente radical para el desarrollo de nuevas rutas regionales, no es suficiente. Para evitar un enfoque único en la introducción de tecnología, las políticas deberían prestar más atención a los procesos de experimentación complementarios con relación a las características de la demanda, las estrategias de las empresas y los modelos comerciales así como los aspectos legislativos. Además, es necesaria una coordinación entre la política de innovación regional y los dominios y niveles adyacentes en la elaboración de políticas dado que algunos de los obstáculos más apremiantes para la renovación no son específicos de la región sino de la industria en general.

INTRODUCTION

Since the early 1990s there has been an ongoing engagement in the field of regional studies with the particular problems, challenges and strategies for renewal of old industrial regions (BOSCHMA and LAMBOOY, 1999; COOKE, 1995; HASSINK, 1993; HASSINK and SHIN, 2005; HUDSON, 1989, 2005; KAUFMANN and TÖDTLING, 2000; MORGAN, 1997; TRIPPL and OTTO, 2009). This literature is primarily geared to identify and analyse the typical problems found in the innovation system of such regions focusing on issues related to path dependence and lock-in. Old industrial regions are typically considered to be those overspecialized in mature industries experiencing decline. A key challenge for regional development strategies concerns the question how such industries and regions may, or may not, be able to break out of locked-in paths of development by pursuing innovation, new technological pathways and industrial renewal.

More recently this debate has gained further momentum through the evolutionary turn in economic geography (BOSCHMA and FRENKEN, 2006; BOSCHMA and MARTIN, 2010; ESSLETZBICHLER and RIGBY, 2007; MARTIN and SUNLEY, 2007). At the core of the agenda in evolutionary economic geography two interrelated issues have been emphasized that are of interest and relevance for discussions on old industrial regions (COE, 2011). Firstly, a shift in the role of agglomeration economies has moved attention away from a predominant focus on specialization within regional clusters towards diversification of regional industrial structures through the notion of related variety (FRENKEN et al., 2007). In particular processes of regional branching seem highly relevant to our understanding of how regions are able to diversify into new areas of industrial

development. Following the argument of regional branching, new industry formation draws on the recombination of different but related knowledge, skills and competences found in existing industries in the region (ASHEIM et al., 2011). Secondly, evolutionary economic geography highlights the path-dependent nature of regional development. The distinguishing feature of path dependence is its emphasis on self-reinforcing mechanisms when explaining the dynamics of narrowing down the scope of alternative actions in and among organizations (SCHREYÖGG and SYDOW, 2011). Translated to regional development, this means that 'the combination of historical contingency and the emergence of self-reinforcing effects steer a regional economy along one "path" rather than another' (MARTIN, 2010, p. 3).

At the same time, various scholars have articulated a critique on evolutionary economic geography for an overriding focus on micro-level firm routines in its analyses of regional development at the expense of other actors and institutions (such as the state) (MACKINNON et al., 2009; MORGAN, 2012). Especially, the role of policy has so far been relatively neglected in the literature (ASHEIM et al., 2013; HASSINK and KLAERDING, 2011; RODRÍGUEZ-POSÉ, 2013). This omission is, to our mind, particularly problematic in the context of old industrial regions. As will be explained below, institutions and the role of the state in particular have been integral to much of the previous research. However, the existing knowledge base tends to be predominantly geared to identifying and explaining the specific problems that these kinds of regions face. While this has led to a solid understanding of the troublesome conditions for innovation in old industrial regions and, consequently, its challenges for renewal and revitalization, actual analyses of policy initiatives that seek to facilitate such renewal are much less developed. Undoubtedly, this is a daunting task as 'the capacity of a region to transform the whole regional innovation system turns out to be the decisive factor for renewal processes' (TRIPPL and OTTO, 2009, p. 1231).

Taking stock with this gap, this paper conducts a case study of an existing regional support programme in an old industrial region in Sweden where mature industries dominate. This policy programme explicitly aims to develop a strong research and innovation environment around emergent biorefining technology in order to promote regional growth in the Örnsköldsvik-Umeå area in the north of Sweden. The objective of the analysis is to further insights on the potentials, barriers and limitations for regional innovation policy to facilitate industrial renewal in locked-in regions.

More specifically, the paper provides a case study of an old industrial region where mature industries dominate and takes a closer look at the VINNVÄXT programme 'Biorefinery of the Future' (BioF). This initiative targets the forest industry that has been a traditionally important and large industry in this region in terms of employment opportunities. However, due to shrinking global demand for paper products and tightening global competition, scarcity and increased prices of forest raw materials, and increased requirements on more sustainable production methods, the local industry is facing challenges to remain competitive. Being strongly dependent on this mature industry, the future development of this region is heavily tied to its fate (as well as many other peripheral regions in Sweden). In recent years the industry is increasingly seeking new, alternative ways to extract and appropriate greater value from biomass, while at the same time improving its energy-efficiency, carbon-emission impact and overall environmental performance. A biorefinery can be seen as a platform technology that integrates biomass conversion processes and equipment to produce a portfolio of environmentally friendly fuels, power, heat and value-added chemicals from biomass (NATIONAL RENEWABLE ENERGY LABORATORY (NREL), 2014). Instead of using the forest biomass exclusively for the production of paper and pulp, biorefinery technologies allow its conversion into additional or substitute products such as low-carbon fuels (e.g. second generation bioethanol, dimethyl ether and biodiesel), green chemicals, substances used in the construction industry, viscose for clothing, or ingredients for the food and pharmaceutical industry, while making more efficient use of the heat in the production process. The notion of a biorefinery is comparable with that of an oil refinery, yet replacing fossil oil by renewable, low-carbon resources (i.e. biomass). As such, a biorefinery offers a possibility for forest industries to increase their efficiency and diversify into different markets. However, this requires cooperation with and establishing linkages to other industries. In doing so, biorefineries are considered to have the potential to contribute to renewing forest

industries (KARLTORP and SANDÉN, 2012; OTTOSSON and MAGNUSSON, 2013). At the same time, previous studies have shown that there has been a fair deal of resistance in the forest industry against what is considered to be a radical and disruptive technological pathway (LAESTADIUS, 2000; OTTOSSON, 2011). The research question guiding this analysis is as follows:

> *How can a regional innovation support programme, and its efforts to foster the adoption of science-based knowledge creation and exploitation, contribute to the renewal of mature industries? How is such a transition constrained and/or enabled by the regional context?*

The remainder of this paper is organized as follows. The next section presents the theoretical framework of the study, drawing on literature on regional innovation policy, old industrial regions and transitions. The third section provides a short outline of the research design and methods applied in the study. This is followed in the fourth section by a presentation of the regional and industrial context of the policy initiative. The fifth section offers the empirical analysis of the regional innovation initiative. Drawing on the empirical analysis, the sixth section discusses the theoretical implications for regional innovation policy targeting old industrial regions, while the seventh section concludes by providing an outlook on how future research may address the challenges of old industrial regions by drawing on a wider framework based on the socio-technical transition literature.

THEORETICAL FRAMEWORK: REGIONAL INNOVATION POLICY, OLD INDUSTRIAL REGIONS AND TRANSITIONS

As this paper deals with renewal of mature industries in a regional context, the theoretical framework departs from the literature on old industrial regions. This literature is primarily geared to identify typical problems found in the innovation system of such regions focusing on issues related to path dependence and lock-in. While this literature provides a useful framework for identifying barriers to renewal in regional economies and how regions can strive to break out of lock-in (TRIPPL and OTTO, 2009), it is somewhat less developed with regard to explaining extra-regional influences to such regional lock-in and, as a consequence, what are the possibilities and limitations of regional innovation policy to address those barriers. To address this gap, a complementary evolutionary-institutional approach to understanding transformative change is suggested as well the role that regional policy plays in facilitating this.

Systemic innovation policy

In the bourgeoning innovation systems literature, which emerged at the start of the 1990s, the regional innovation systems (RIS) approach has been most explicitly concerned with spatial dimensions of innovation and place-based innovation policies (ASHEIM and GERTLER, 2005; ASHEIM and ISAKSEN, 2002; BRACZYK et al., 1998; COOKE et al., 2004). An RIS encompasses the private and public organizations in the region involved in innovation processes, their relationships and networks as well as the institutions guiding their behaviour (COOKE, 1998). In addition to localized networks and relationships, the RIS framework also takes into account relevant non-local linkages and institutions at higher scales. The approach holds the potential for improved 'on-the-ground' policy knowhow about the specific place-based conditions for innovation (NAUWELAERS and WINTJES, 2002).

The approach has been widely used as a framework for the design, implementation and evaluation of regional innovation policy in a variety of countries and regions. Well-known examples are the European RIS/RITTS initiatives[1] as well as current programmes and strategies developed under the banner of smart specialization (LANDABASO et al., 2001; BOSCHMA, 2014; CAMAGNI and CAPELLO, 2013). In terms of the theoretical rationale for the design of policy and choice of instruments, RIS draws on the more general innovation system perspective (LARANJA et al., 2008; BORRAS and EDQUIST, 2013). This implies that public intervention is legitimate and needed if the complex interactions that take place among the different organizations in the RIS do not function effectively. On a general innovation system level, this has been conceptualized through the notion of system failures (SMITH, 2000; KLEIN WOOLTHUIS et al., 2005; BERGEK et al., 2008; WEBER and ROHRACHER, 2012). Examples of such system failures are the lack of appropriate competencies and resources for innovation at the firm level (capabilities failure), weakly developed institutions, both hard and soft, that insufficiently incentivize actors to engage with innovation processes (institutional failures), too closely tied networks leading to myopia (strong network failure), and/or too limited interaction and knowledge exchange between actors (weak network failure).

The general innovation system failure framework informing policy design has been resourcefully translated to the regional level through the seminal work of TÖDTLING and TRIPPL (2005) by looking carefully at specific regional endowments and its relationship to innovation barriers of weak or vulnerable regions (see also TRIPPL and OTTO, 2009; ASHEIM et al., 2011; COENEN, 2007; ISAKSEN, 2001). To avoid a one-size-fits-all, best-practice models to regional innovation policy, they have introduced three main systems failures: organizational thinness, fragmentation and lock-in. Organizational thinness refers to lack of relevant local actors for innovation, fragmentation to lack of regional cooperation and mutual trust, while lock-in refers to regional industry being specialized in outdated technologies (ISAKSEN, 2001). In reality, regions often face a mix of these deficiencies. However, TÖDTLING and TRIPPL (2005) argue that some innovation problems dominate in certain types of regions and, thus, require more attention than others.

Old industrial regions are typically considered as regions overspecialized in mature technologies and industries experiencing decline, thus facing lock-in. Innovation activities in these regions often follow mature technological trajectories mainly of an incremental character. Efforts to introduce radically new products into the market tend to be limited compared with process optimization and other efficiency-oriented activities. Even though, as TÖDTLING and TRIPPL (2005) observe, the region may have a highly developed and specialized knowledge-generation and diffusion system, this is usually oriented towards traditional industries and technology fields. Moreover, small firm innovation and entrepreneurial activity tends to be low given the dominance of larger firms, incumbent to the established and mature industrial and technological specialization (STEINER, 1985). Examples of old industrial regions are frequently found in regions specialized in heavy industries such as the Ruhr area in Germany (GRABHER, 1993), the North East of England (HUDSON, 1994; COENEN, 2007) or Wales (MORGAN, 2012). These regions are also well known for being sites with severe difficulties dealing with environmental waste and pollution (such as, for example, carbon emissions) (GONZÁLEZ-EGUINO et al., 2012).

As TÖDTLING and TRIPPL (2005) acknowledge, regions may face a mix of RIS deficiencies (failures) as suggested in their typology. The present paper therefore also draws partly on a second type of 'problem description' related to RIS, namely that of peripheral regions and its dominant problem of organizational thinness. Similar to the old industrial region typology, the emphasis is on incremental innovation and on process innovations. But now, the main explanation for a lower level of innovation activity is tied to low density as well as a 'thin' and less specialized structure of knowledge suppliers, technology transfer organizations and educational organizations.

In sum, the key problem of old industrial regions can nonetheless be characterized as primarily one of negative lock-in (HASSINK, 2010). Lock-in is closely connected to path dependence, a concept originating from the literature on evolutionary economics and technological change (DAVID, 1985). It is important to note that lock-in per se does not need to have a negative impact on a regional economy (HASSINK, 1997; ESSLETZBICHLER and WINTHER, 1999). Strong specialization in specific industries is a classic feature of clusters and regional competitive advantage (PORTER, 2000). Lock-in becomes however problematic when its path direction steers to (over)specialization in long-established technologies and industries with little scope for further economic exploitation of knowledge while, often simultaneously, curtailing efforts by novel industries or technologies to emerge and develop. A closer look at lock-in is therefore required.

GRABHER (1993) highlights the multidimensionality of regional lock-in by distinguishing between three types of interrelated lock-in: functional, cognitive and political, and states that regional lock-in results from the interplay between these three types of lock-in. Functional lock-in refers to how overly strong and often hierarchical inter-firm networks in declining industries tend to block the development of alternative linkages and reorientations in the value chain. Cognitive lock-in refers to how a common world view or mindset among actors reinforces 'group-think' and precludes creativity and imagination needed for the development of new ideas. Political lock-in is related to the existence of dense relationships between public and private sectors that aim at preserving traditional industrial structures that hamper alternative directions for industrial development (GRABHER, 1993; UNDERTHUN et al., 2014).

Adding analytical precision to address the question why it is that some regional economies become locked into development paths that lose dynamism, HASSINK (2010, p. 455) suggests a set of economic–structural and political–institutional impact factors. Economic–structural impact factors primarily leading to functional lock-in includes the following:

- A marked industrial mono-structure: the leading industry having an employment share of at least 30% of the total manufacturing employment in the region as a rough indicator for a mono-structure.
- A specific leading industry: capital-intensive, high entry and exit barriers, above-average company size, oligopolistic market structure and influential trade unions.

Political–institutional impact factors primarily related to cognitive and political lock-in include the following:

- An institutional constellation at the regional level, consisting of local, regional policymakers, captains of industry, regional trade unionists, representatives of industry associations, that is strongly focused on the leading industry and hence weakly on external relations.
- A national political system that enables regional actors to influence political questions concerning industrial policy.
- Supra-national institutions that strongly affect the conditions of industrial policy relevant to the leading industry.

In engaging with discussions on lock-in, recent studies from evolutionary economic geography have figured prominently, particularly with regard to strategies concerning how to unlock or rejuvenate old industrial regions. MARTIN and SUNLEY (2006) suggest a number of 'sources' for new path development

that regions may draw upon to escape lock-in. Given that our case, related to the adoption of biorefinery technology by an incumbent forest industry in the region, mainly draws on path renewal of already existing industry, as opposed to attraction or development of new industry, two strategies seem to be most pertinent. These escape sources are 'diversification into technologically related industries', which refers to the 'transition where an existing industry goes into decline but its core technologies are redeployed and extended to provide the basis of related new industries in the region' (MARTIN and SUNLEY, 2006, p. 420). Another relevant option is the 'upgrading of existing industries' referring to 'the revitalization and enhancement of a region's industrial base through the infusion of new technologies or introduction of new products and services' (p. 420). While examples of regions are provided for both escape routes, the authors also acknowledge that often they are not mutually exclusive but rather that different mechanisms may be at work simultaneously and in mutually reinforcing ways. Whether these escape routes may also counteract on each other is, however, left open for debate.

These mechanisms relate to a well-known advancement made in evolutionary economic geography around the importance of relatedness in knowledge and competences for innovation and renewal, often referred to as related variety (FRENKEN et al., 2007). Especially in light of transformative change, combinatorial rather than cumulative knowledge dynamics are emphasized to foster radical, path-breaking innovations (STRAMBACH and KLEMENT, 2013). However, such combinatorial knowledge dynamics are characterized by high uncertainties in the pay-off and the time horizon of their outcome, and require high investment to ensure mutual understandings between the actors. Similarly, SIMMIE (2012) highlights the disruptive nature of regional new path development and stresses a process of 'mindful deviation' by innovators when introducing new and replacing old technologies (see also GARUD and KARNØE, 2001). While drawing our attention to the need for disruptive path-breaking innovation and technological change to transition old industrial regions into new pathways, it should also be stressed that this is a particularly cumbersome and challenging process precisely because of the path-dependent nature of technological change.

The path-dependent nature of technological change has been fruitfully explained and theorized in the literature on socio-technical transitions, with the help of the concept of 'socio-technical regimes' (GEELS, 2002; SIMMIE, 2012; TRUFFER and COENEN, 2012). Essentially, this concept extends the previous notion of technological regimes (DOSI and NELSON, 1994; BRESCHI et al., 2000) to include 'the coherent complex of scientific knowledge, engineering practices, production process technologies, product characteristics, skills and procedures, established user needs, regulatory requirements, institutions and infrastructures' (RIP and KEMP, 1998, p. 338). The 'structuration' of this complex is high, providing stable rules and coordinating effects on actors. Reflecting the 'established way of doing things', it primarily enables incremental, cumulative, path-following innovation yet constrains radical path-breaking innovation and helps to explain why combinatorial knowledge dynamics and mindful deviation are indeed difficult to achieve. The concept of socio-technical regimes has been particularly forceful to explain why current energy and transport systems remain locked-in to fossil fuel-based technologies (SMITH et al., 2010; UNRUH, 2000)

The contrasting notion of 'niches' is used to conceptualize the genesis and development of path-breaking and deviant technologies (KEMP et al., 1998; RAVEN, 2005). These niches are 'incubation spaces' for novel, yet immature, emergent technologies that challenge the established regime and, if successful in its maturation process, can replace the incumbent, old technologies. A niche is defined as an application context in which novel technology is temporarily shielded from the structuration forces found in a regime and acts as an important selection environment in which the process of new path creation may be started. As GEELS (2004, p. 912) puts it, '[t]hey provide locations for learning processes, e.g. about technological applications, user preferences, public policies, symbolic meanings. Niches are locations where it is possible to deviate from the rules of the existing regime'. At the same time, it should be stressed that the extent of structuration between the technology, knowledge, skills, user needs, regulatory requirements and institutions in such niches is very loose, at least compared with the structuration effects found in a regime context. In other words, it reflects the uncertainty and heterogeneity found in a situation of combinatorial knowledge dynamics.

Taken together, the literatures on old industrial regions and socio-technical transitions provide an evolutionary perspective, not only on the particular place-specific challenges related to lock-in of mature regional industries but also on the transition pathways to unlock these regions and industries through technological renewal. Here, the transition perspective adds a careful understanding of the room to manoeuvre for policy-making in relation to the introduction of new path-breaking technologies.

The above discussion concerning the challenges for old industrial regions to break-out of lock-in and transition into (re)new(ed) path development is used to frame and identify the challenges that the BioF initiative in Sweden is facing. However, the literature is less developed with regard to questions about whether and how regional innovation policy can in fact contribute to the unlocking and path renewal mechanisms that are needed in light of such a transition, in particular with regard to dealing with the complex interplay between regional and extra-regional impact factors. The analysis of this initiative will therefore contribute

to our understanding about the potentials, barriers and limitations for policy to facilitate industrial renewal in locked-in regions. After the empirical analysis, the paper will revisit the literature concerning old industrial regions and technological path dependence to discuss the role of regional innovation policy as niche experimentation for path renewal.

RESEARCH DESIGN AND METHODS

The analysis is based on a combination of qualitative research methods; document studies and personal in-depth interviews with key stakeholders being the two dominant data sources. Previous research on these and similar industries are used as reference cases, while primary data collection has been focused on publicly available documents such as websites, annual reports, strategy documents and publicly commissioned evaluations. A total number of 20 semi-structured interviews with representatives of the initiative and its target industries were conducted. The group of respondents includes representatives from the public sector (policymakers) as well as universities and industry. Eight interviews were conducted in October 2008 when the initiative in its current form was recently launched. Six more interviews were conducted in January 2012. While the first interviews primarily aimed at collecting information on the industries, the initiative and the various challenges that served as a main rationale for the initiative, the second round of interviews focused more explicitly on activities, outcomes and remaining problems/deficiencies. In addition to those interviews, which explicitly dealt with the initiative and its target industries, another six interviews were made with actors doing research on or representing the industries, but with no specific stake in the initiative as such. These interviews, carried out in the period March–July 2009, are used primarily for reference and cross-check purposes. The interviews were conducted in Swedish, recorded and transcribed. Important quotes were translated into English by the authors.

REGIONAL AND INDUSTRIAL CONTEXT

Region

The area of Örnsköldsvik-Umeå is located on the Swedish east coast, more than 500 km north of the capital, Stockholm. In terms of administrative regions it covers the Swedish counties of Västerbotten and Västernorrland (NUTS-3). These are thinly populated regions with a population density of 4.7 and 11.0 inhabitants/km^2 respectively (2011).

The region suffers from typical problems of peripheral and old industrial regions with serious challenges to cope with renewal and economic growth. Since the mid-1990s the region has been lagging behind the national

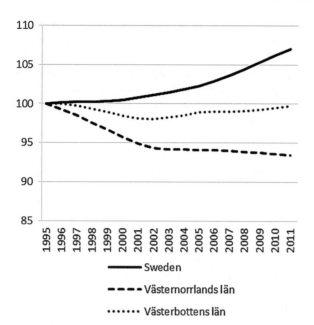

Fig. 1. *Change in average yearly population*
Source: Statistics Sweden

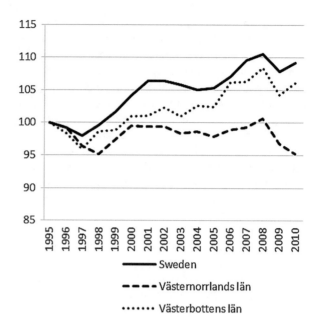

Fig. 3. *Change in employment*
Source: Statistics Sweden

average on most indicators reflecting economic development. While the Swedish population as a whole is constantly growing, as most European countries, the regional population in Västerbotten and Västernorrland is decreasing. A particular strong decrease is identified in Västernorrland, which displays the strongest depopulation trend of all Swedish regions (Fig. 1). Also regional employment is lagging behind the national average in both counties. This indicates not only gradual depopulation in the periphery but also increased challenges of maintaining regionally based economic growth (Fig. 2). Depopulation and decrease in regional employment is

also reflected in the relative change in regional gross value added, where the region is lagging behind the national average, however not as dramatically as could have been expected (Fig. 3). With regard to private research and development (R&D) expenditures particularly, Västernorrland displays negative development compared with the national average, while Västerbotten has managed relatively well despite a severe downturn in connection with the financial crisis in the early 2000s (Fig. 4).

A large part of the problem with regard to regional economic development can be found in the region's

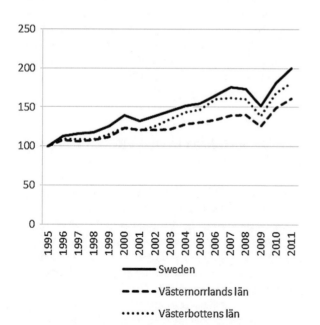

Fig. 2. *Change in gross value added*
Source: Statistics Sweden

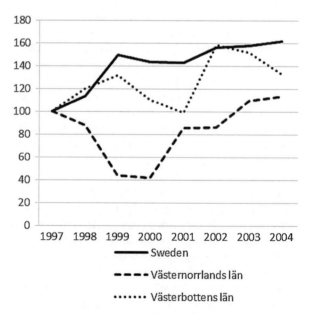

Fig. 4. *Change in private sector research and development*
(R&D) expenditures
Source: Statistics Sweden

relative overspecialization in the declining forest industry. The forest industry represents 30% of the regional economy in Västernorrland and 20% in Västerbotten. This should be compared with the national average of 11%. Almost 30% of the working population is directly employed in the forest industry, which still generates almost 50% of the total regional production value (SKOGSINDUSTRIERNA, 2013). This strong dependence on one industry obviously makes the regional economy vulnerable, particularly when the industry in question is in decline. The total employment in the Swedish forest industry has been reduced by 50% since the 1990s (SKOGSINDUSTRIERNA, 2013).

Industry

As touched upon above, the forest industry has been very important for the northern part of Sweden, and the Örnsköldsvik-Umeå area in particular, since the late 19th century. Prior to the period covered in the descriptive statistics above, important transformation forces were set in motion. Between 1960 and 1990 the industry witnessed a period of structural change. In the 1960s a process of structural rationalization was initiated driven by the need to decrease costs and increase productivity as a result of increased international competition. As a result, production shifted increasingly away from small mills towards large-scale facilities, primarily located along the east coast. This rationalization was paralleled by an increased awareness of the polluting and energy-intensive character of paper and pulp production which, in turn, led to tougher environmental regulation for the industry. As a response to both challenges, the forest industry invested heavily in technology-driven process innovations which resulted in substantial improvements in environmental performance as well as productivity (BERGQUIST and SÖDERHOLM, 2011). During this process of structural change, the Swedish forest industry quickly caught up with North American forest industry and established itself as a dominant global player, capturing increasing shares of the global market (OJALA et al., 2006). As a result of this rationalization process, the regional forest industry became dominated by a few large companies (MELANDER, 1997).

Since the late 1980s a new wave of structural change has started to influence the industry. Similar to the earlier period, environmental and energy concern feature prominently along the factors driving these developments (KARLTORP and SANDÉN, 2012). Concern for climate change and energy security has led to a number of policy measures that have substantially affected energy and feedstock prices for the industry. Exactly how this is going to impact the industry is still an open question. On the one hand, increased demand for bioenergy and biofuels to meet renewable energy objectives has resulted in higher prices for biomass feedstock. On the other hand, the introduction

of green electricity certificates in 2002 has created economic incentives for paper and pulp companies to produce and sell green electricity in their plants (ERICSSON et al., 2014). An additional environment-related factor concerns the introduction of more stringent environmental regulation in the field of waste in Sweden. Increased taxation has created incentives to avoid waste production and, instead, created incentives to refine waste products into tradable products or intermediaries. Increased attention to energy and environmental issues is, however, not the sole source of pressure for change. Substitution of paper-based media by electronic media has led to an absolute decrease in demand for printing paper, traditionally one of the core products of the forest industry. Finally, increased production capacity in South America and Asia and deepening global trade liberalization has led to increased competition from firms with significantly lower production and feedstock costs.[2]

Increasingly, firms realize that they have to diversify their product portfolios to achieve higher value out of their feedstock. In doing so, the biorefinery concept offers new business opportunities but also represents a major challenge as it entails large investments in new process technology, knowledge and networks required to enter or establish new value chains (KARLTORP and SANDÉN, 2012). In this context, firms in the Örnsköldsvik-Umeå area have the advantage that they draw on a historical legacy. As a response to trade blockades during the Second World War and the resulting shortage of chemicals in Sweden, the paper and pulp industry in Örnsköldsvik-Umeå has made early attempts to broaden the range of products produced from forest raw materials. During these years, the production of bio-based chemicals and ethanol entered the scene and led to unique experiences for the industry with regard to product diversification based on forest feedstock. In the post-war years, however, chemicals production relocated back to the west coast of Sweden due to its closer connection to major international ports, which was of strategic importance for the petrochemical industry. The forest industry in Örnsköldsvik-Umeå returned to its traditional business in pulp and paper production. In the mid-1990s, scientific breakthroughs in life science made it possible to start research with dissolving cellulose by applying alternative technology (i.e. enzyme-based biotechnology processes). One of the paper mills in Örnsköldsvik was among the few pioneers worldwide entering into this field.

ANALYSIS

The BioF initiative

The successful application of the BioF initiative to secure support and funding through the VINNVÄXT programme[3] built on existing activities and networks in the region based on a common biorefinery platform.

Following initial research and experiments during the mid-1990s, a technology park located on the site of the pulp and paper industry in Örnsköldsvik was established in 2003. Here, 12 small and medium-sized enterprises related to R&D in pulp and paper technologies, chemicals and energy production started collaborating with two large companies specialized in various applications of forest and chemistry-related production (Domsjö Fabriker AB and AkzoNobel). The primary focus was on energy efficiency, much in line with general trends in industry at this time (see above). The municipality, the county administration, a regional technology transfer agency (Innovationsbron) and a privately owned funding foundation (Kempestiftelsen) with its roots in the region's forest-based industry provided financial support. Over time, linkages to the nearby universities in Luleå and Umeå were established and increasingly formalized. This technology park evolved into a network of related firms and organizations distributed over a territory much wider than its initial core in Örnsköldsvik, encompassing the counties of Västerbotten and Västernorrland. A large grant from the Swedish Energy Agency was used to set up a pilot plant for cellulose-based ethanol production, which gradually developed into a platform for several products, primarily drawing on forest-based feedstock. A central firm in this pilot plant is a producer and developer of ethanol, SEKAB, today considered to be a world leading actor in the field of bioethanol. The pilot plant, the ethanol firm, a small firm specialized in pulp and paper-related R&D (MoRe Research), a large forestry company (Holmen), a sector-specific industry support initiative, and the regional universities can be seen as the nexus for the biorefinery initiative responsible for developing the VINNVÄXT proposal.

In 2008, the consortium with representatives from industry, academia and the regional public sector in Örnsköldsvik made a successful application for VINN-VÄXT and received a ten-year grant for their initiative 'Biorefinery of the Future' (BioF). The aim of this initiative was to become a world-leading research and innovation environment for developing biorefineries based on forest raw material and energy crops by combining historical and current strengths in traditional forestry with new cutting-edge knowledge in science-based technologies. BioF aims to materialize industrial renewal of the local pulp and paper industry towards higher value-added activities as a collective regional strategic response to the aforementioned competitive and climate-related challenges. In this context, the BioF initiative acts as an operational incubation and experimentation space for technological learning processes targeting biorefinery technologies.

Taking a closer look at the supportive activities carried out within BioF reveals that an R&D council plays a central coordinating role. The R&D council is where most project ideas are evaluated to assess whether they can be financed through BioF. The

council consists of two representatives from member companies, two from Umeå University and two from Processum, the holding company for the biorefinery initiative.[4] Its mission is to promote new products and process ideas in the biorefinery area. In funding decisions, the utility for the participating companies is a very important criterion as well as collaboration between industry, academic and public sector stakeholders. In 2012, approximately 100 projects were funded which resulted in ten new processes, 30 new products and prototypes, and just over 30 patent applications. Even though there is a focus on new product and process development, the lion's share of projects can be considered to be applied research with potential for member companies in areas such as green chemicals, products from residual streams, industrial biotechnology, smart processes/process efficiency and energy. More downstream innovation activities are coordinated under the header of 'pilot equipment' to scale up the most promising research, with a view to achieving a commercial scale in the near future. Of these, 11 pilot projects have been carried out in the initiative.

Even though these 'formal' support activities suggest that innovation support is primarily of a technological nature, which can be regarded as rather narrowly defined innovation activities, the interviews revealed that social learning processes have occurred in what could be seen as an indirect effect of the R&D activities and collaborations. The expectations and interests among different actors with regard to the products and processes developed in a biorefinery diverged considerably at the start of the initiative. This had partly to do with the heterogeneity among the firms involved, including paper and pulp companies, ethanol producers, chemical companies and energy utilities. Given their different industrial backgrounds, these firms operate in different markets and draw upon different competences and technologies. Through the BioF initiative, the firms are exploring and assessing the scope for collaborations across industries, which contributes to mutual learning and alignment of expectations within the initiative. For example, in the area of green chemicals, the forest industry is seeking out new applications and wants to learn more about the chemicals market, while the chemical industry is looking for ways how to replace today's fossil-based basic chemicals with a green supply. Another well-known example is the production of bioethanol based on forest material. In this context, the collaborations in the BioF initiative give rise to exploring the possibilities and difficulties in creating new value chains that cut across traditional industry boundaries.

In particular, the BioF initiative has contributed to a better joint understanding or common framing of some of the key challenges which actors in the BioF initiative are facing in their efforts to make products and processes related to biorefineries commercially feasible. As a result of the R&D activities carried out in BioF, a number of technologies have become (technically) sufficiently mature for scaling up to full-scale application. However, this process has proven more difficult than initially expected across the industry, mainly due to non-technical institutional aspects. Challenges particularly concern the large-scale production of ethanol from forest biomass residuals (i.e. second-generation bioethanol) even though they, to a large extent, also apply for other biorefinery products.

One of the main challenges, related to lock-in, has to do with sunk investments in conventional technology and production facilities. Forest industries are very capital intensive, and massive resources have already been invested in facilities drawing on the existing technological paradigm geared to the production of pulp and paper. As stated by one of the interviewees: 'One has invested into a particular production and it is not easy to just change it over one night. The fact that the investments are so huge leads automatically to inertia in the system' (chief executive officer (CEO) of a local R&D company). These investments traditionally targeted the production of bulk products. This constitutes a challenge to the industry in terms of diversifying its outcomes and, by implication, adapting to (and entering) diversified, small-scale markets. To achieve profitability, a commercial, full-scale biorefinery is expected to require new investments of approximately SEK3 billion. Combined with the current lack of possibilities to employ premium pricing strategies for green chemicals and energy (i.e. an insufficiently developed market), this raises an urgent need for subsidies from the public sector.

> An issue that is challenging is up-scaling, to go into full industrial scale, this we have realized over the last 2–3 years. There is very interesting research, but how the rules stand today, it is very difficult to get a commercial viability. [...] The State and the EU should take a more active role. It has become clear to me that it is a political issue.
>
> (CEO, BioF)

This is, however, not exclusively a national, but rather a supranational issue related to a lack of attention on the largely peripherally located forest-related industries within the European Union (EU) policy agenda:

> If you read the EU directive, it is not considered sustainable to cut down forest. There is so much to be done on the information side so that [politicians in Brussels] start to realize. [...] In the EU, it is agriculture that is important. Forest is only seen as spare time activity.
>
> (Professor of Chemistry, Umeå University)

While subsidies exist in Sweden today, they lack a long-term horizon, which makes them uncertain and create critical financial liabilities for investors.

> The problem with these systems and regulatory frameworks is that they are almost on one-year basis, and this is what limits us. [...] First they subsidize and then they

take it away. Ethanol was in for a while, then it was biogas and now it is electric cars. It is impossible to see what is coming as consumer or producer.

> (CEO, ethanol producer)

Government policies are providing unclear and contradictory signals concerning the needs for carbon reductions and a shift to renewable energy and at what costs such needs should be supported. In addition to the direct effect in terms of economic realities for potential investors, these shifting policies also contribute to influencing consumer preferences and societal legitimacy of alternative technologies. It reveals the dependence of the regional actors on a national political system, particularly with regard to learning about demand-side aspects of new technologies. As a result of this lack of a clear future vision, investors hesitate, entrepreneurs are reluctant to take the necessary risks and consumers are ambivalent.

Another barrier to the fulfilment of the aims of BioF has thus to do with the public perception of a new technology. In the public opinion, forest-based biofuels (second generation) are often conflated with agro-based biofuels (first generation), which causes resistance with reference to the crops-for-food-or-fuel debate. In the current public debate, the producers of forest-based biofuels have severe problems explaining the differences in a way that is easy for consumers and investors to understand fully, which again points at the limitations of the regional actors with regard to influencing demand-side-related conditions. As stated by one of the interviewees:

> There is good ethanol and there is bad ethanol. There exists a risk of competition with the food production in the world, and you should not make ethanol from that. [...] These facts are communicated and presented, but it does not have any impact in the press.
>
> (CEO, ethanol producer)

On a more general level, being located in a peripheral part of Sweden seems to play an ambiguous role for the actors in the initiative. On the one hand, the location is seen as an important (positive) factor behind the creation and maintenance of social networks of firms and individuals involved in the initiative. The regional identity is considered to be strong. This means that knowledge exchange both within and across industry boundaries in the region is facilitated by a high degree of interpersonal trust. On the other hand, this also leads to less integration in national and international networks since the regional actors are strongly focused on intra-regional networking and consider themselves to be less connected to the outer world.

> I feel that we have a pretty good situation network-wise and in terms of contacts. [...] The disadvantage of a small town is that it is some distance away, the advantage of a small town is that, with the right atmosphere, a lot

of people help each other. […] But it is a disadvantage that we always have to travel.

(CEO, BioF)

This problem, however, seems to be diminishing, partly as a result of the BioF initiative. Recently, one of the dominant forestry companies, Domsjö Fabriker AB (part of the Holmen Group), has been acquired by an Indian multinational firm (Aditya Birla Group), which has led to an increasing focus on high-value-added products and materials (e.g. textiles) in the initiative. Likewise, the establishment of R&D collaborations between regional actors and universities in other parts of Sweden has increased through the BioF initiative, as well as an intensified collaboration with the petrochemical industry at the Swedish east coast.

DISCUSSION

The case presented in this paper demonstrates that regional innovation policy indeed contributes to 'on-the-ground' policy that addresses the specific challenges for innovation in the region. BioF explicitly seeks to transition existing but declining regional industry into new path development through a process of diversification that is fuelled by infusion with radical new technology (MARTIN and SUNLEY, 2006). The region clearly displays symptoms of functional lock-in (HASSINK, 2010) having a marked industrial mono-structure based on the paper and pulp industry that is characterized by industrial concentration in a number of established firms, high levels of capital intensity and high entry barriers. The initiative seeks to break this lock-in through systematic and concentrated R&D and innovation investments in a biorefinery platform. Through this focus on biorefining technologies, it has established new, but also built further on existing, relationships across related industries (and non-firm actors) in the region in a process of combinatorial innovation. To what extent these efforts will eventually result into processes of regional branching remains, however, to be seen. On the one hand, there is indeed evidence of diversification of incumbent firms into new markets as paper and pulp companies are becoming increasingly interested and active in producing biofuels and, albeit to a lesser extent, green chemicals and biotextiles. On the other hand, the involved firms also encounter severe obstacles to make a fully fledged entry into these markets. Here, the findings confirm the arguments raised by STRAMBACH and KLEMENT (2013) that combinatorial knowledge dynamics are conducive to path-breaking innovation but at the same time fraught with difficulties in light of the high uncertainties and time horizons concerning return on investment. Related to this, the case also points to rather modest levels of activity by new firm start-ups and entrepreneurs. If any entrepreneurial activity is to be observed, this

seems to come primarily from existing firms in the region rather than through new firm formation.

In sum, it can be argued that the initiative has been successful in planting and growing seeds for path renewal. At the same time, the regional actors are facing difficulties to develop and implement a large-scale biorefinery facility, which could be seen as an indicator of a more complete transition process. To understand this relative success as well as its limitations, it is important to acknowledge the regional context in which the initiative is placed. The place-bound historical legacy of the current industrial structure is one important factor. Even if the initiative is composed by a fairly large number of independent and relatively young knowledge-intensive small and medium-sized firms, most of which have their roots in the dominant forest industry in the region, providing a basis for technological relatedness. The same is true for a large share of the capital channelled through the private foundation. Between the late 19th century and the 1970s they were all part of the same organization, MoDo (today renamed as Holmen). This common history has been conducive to forging mutual understandings and expectations among the actors even though they over time have diverged into different fields of specialization (such as energy, chemicals, paper and pulp). Secondly, localized social networks built up over time (prior to and during the BioF initiative) provide important conditions enabling knowledge exchange and interactive learning (within and across industry boundaries), and have contributed to giving the actors a collective voice articulating key challenges with regard to biorefineries.

While there is a common and shared understanding among the regional actors in the initiative about critical challenges, it is doubtful that the actors themselves also will be able to address them effectively. The first challenge refers to mobilizing recourses for full-scale operations that require large amounts of capital investments.[5] This is not untypical for the forest industry. Here, actors obviously need to search for investment possibilities from outside the region. Attracting these kinds of investments remains still very problematic and would require a broader interest and legitimacy for biorefinery technologies within forest and related industries at a national and even international level. The actors seem to be very well-aware of this and are increasingly establishing connections beyond the region. However, its location in a peripheral part of Sweden entails structural disadvantages that a more centrally located region would probably not encounter to a similar degree. Also with regard to the second challenge, the initiative's location in a peripheral region is problematic. This refers to the importance of regulatory frameworks in market creation for typically 'green' products such as biofuels and bioplastics (see also DEWALD and TRUFFER, 2012). Most of the markets targeted by the actors in the BioF initiative are strongly affected by energy and environmental regulations through subsidies and taxations. These regulations are mostly designed and implemented at, again, a national and/or international level. This means that many of the conditions determining the adoption of the new products developed within the initiative are well beyond the reach of influence to regional actors. While the actors collectively argue that compulsory quotas for biofuel or some form of long-term tax relief on green solutions are needed to facilitate the up-scaling of their facility, they lack the means to influence the decision-making process for such regulation. This is part of a political process that is embedded in wider debates and interests in terms of industrial, energy and climate policy. As such, it refers to a lack of coordination and/or integration across policy domains, which has a direct effect on the 'success' of this regional innovation initiative.

It can actually be argued that both these challenges, and the constraints of regional actors to address them effectively, are endemic to the fact that a regional transition from a locked-in mature industry towards related new industries (MARTIN and SUNLEY, 2006) is part and parcel of a wider industrial transition that transcends the regional level. The potential, barriers and limitations for a regional innovation initiative to address lock-in and facilitate industrial renewal should thus be seen in this light. This implies that the difficulties that the regional actors are experiencing to upscale biorefining technologies are not specific to the region, but rather specific to the industry. So far, the regional initiative has indeed been instrumental to technological learning, but ultimately the wider adoption of the technology, its products and processes is contingent on the extent to which the forest industry, and related industries, can deviate from their 'established ways of doing things'. That is, adopting biorefinery technology is not so much a process of technology adoption but would rather require in parallel a change in business models and institutional frameworks.

As such this points to two important limitations to regional innovation policy for industrial renewal, at least the way it is designed and implemented within the BioF initiative. First of all, innovation is still too narrowly defined as primarily relating to technological innovation. The challenge to upscale biorefineries can partly be explained by its tension with the prevalent business models of the paper and pulp industry. In its current form, companies primarily draw on economies of scale, bulk production of commodities and price-based competition. Producing a portfolio of bio-based products, including high-value-added products, as implied by a biorefinery would require economies of scope, a competitive strategy based on product differentiation and quality and ultimately production of niche products. These issues remain, however, beyond the scope of the regional innovation policy initiative alone. Secondly, industrial renewal is strongly contingent on institutional change, specifically in relation to the way markets for green products are to be regulated as well as more normative institutions concerning demand for green products. Currently, the products and processes developed in a biorefinery can hardly compete with fossil alternatives and require support, either through 'greener' regulatory frameworks or because consumers are willing to pay a premium for the environmental externalities offered by these bioproducts. Again, the critical bottlenecks remain beyond the reach of regional innovation policy. Both limitations refer to wider 'regime' based barriers (GEELS, 2002; RIP and KEMP, 1998) that inhibit, or at least counteract, transformative and path-breaking change. How this now feeds into the theoretical development on lock-in old industrial regions will be discussed in the concluding section.

CONCLUSIONS

This study has shown that regional innovation policy has been important in facilitating the development of new biorefinery technology in the region and, thus, offers a diversification path for the forestry industry in the region. At the same time, supra-regional bottlenecks are constraining further advancement towards a more comprehensive industrial and regional transformation in the direction of a bio-based economy. Market-related regulatory barriers as well as industry-specific norms and established ways of doing things limit the development and adoption of radical, path-breaking innovation, thus hampering the ability of the regional economy to break out of its lock-in. It is argued that this is largely a result of inherent limitations of regional innovation policy in a context of locked-in old industrial regions.

It has been shown that infusion of new technology is indeed necessary for new path creation of old industrial regions, but hardly sufficient. The case of BioF illustrates that innovation support typically has focused most attention and resources on technology-related innovation while changing firm routines and institutional adaptation have been overlooked, or at least underemphasized. As an *indirect* result of collaborative innovation activities, however, these dimensions have become more explicitly framed as key challenges among the heterogeneous set of stakeholders in the initiative. This points to the importance of non-technical, social learning processes related to novel, emergent technologies as highlighted in the literature on socio-technical transitions (RAVEN, 2005). Drawing on this literature, and in particular its insights regarding niche dynamics in deviant, immature technological fields (such as biorefineries), this paper argues for a stronger acknowledgement of the *experimental* features of new technology-based path creation in policy-making. In doing so, inherent, fundamental uncertainties involved in path shaping are stressed not just in technological terms but, more importantly, in institutional terms.

Constructing new regional development pathways through regional innovation policy involves a co-evolutionary process of technological, industrial and institutional change. Instead of primarily promoting innovation framed as technological change, as often seems the case especially when such technologies are still in an early stage of development and adoption, policy should focus more explicitly on other learning processes: learning about user characteristics and demand, regulatory aspects, mindsets related to firm strategy. Given the immature state of emergent new technology, this often takes shape through expectations that different stakeholders have about a technology and the new or improved products, processes and services it may give rise to. In such an emergent stage of path development, these expectations are often still rather diffuse and there may be considerable variation among the stakeholders, especially when the technological field cuts across different industries. Through iterative processes of learning-by-using and learning-by-interacting among actors, such expectations are articulated, tested, refuted and modified. On a collective level, this leads over time to alignment of expectations and, consequently, may increase knowledge about and legitimacy for the technology, its application context and institutional embedding.[6] Building such legitimacy is crucial as a selection mechanism to maintain support and mobilize resources for innovation, especially in pre-market stages of development. Regions are seen as key sites to carry out such experimentation due to various proximity effects that compensate for the inherent uncertainties connected to new path creation (COENEN et al. 2010; HEALY and MORGAN, 2012). The case of BioF has shown that such experimentation processes have played an important role as an indirect outcome of more technology focused innovation interactions.

While being conducive to broad experimentation in new path creation, we argue that regional innovation policy should also be mindful of some of its inherent limitations related to the scale and reach of its activities. Our study shows that important bottlenecks to unlock an old industrial region prevailed beyond the local level and outside the direct sphere of innovation policy. Some of the greatest obstacles for renewal are not specific to the region but specific to the industry, which makes them largely out of reach for regional policy measures alone. The region, and its industries, is nested in a wider process of industrial transformation and institutional adaptation. Unless being integrated with measures to influence such industry specific institutions at a global (i.e. regime) level, such regional efforts will have a limited effect on path renewal, not only when seen in a global perspective, but also in the region.

In this context, it is argued that a promising topic for future research is to pay greater attention to the role of policy coordination between regional innovation policy and adjacent domains and levels of policy-making (NILSSON and MOODYSSON, 2014). Even though the region may act as a fruitful space for experimentation, there is a risk that regional innovation policy will only deliver 'small victories' and remain peripheral unless policy coordination and learning beyond the level of regional innovation policy takes place. This study has shown that regional actors (including policy-makers) often are aware of the challenges to break out of the old industrial region 'mould' but are struggling to find ways and practices to effectively do so. This is obviously a long-term endeavour. The evolutionary turn in economic geography has at least opened up for greater attention for the path-dependent nature of regional development and helps avoiding the pitfalls of a quick policy fix in dealing with the problems of old industrial regions. The literature on socio-technical transitions allows for a compatible evolutionary framework to understand the wider context in which such processes of transformative change play out (TRUFFER and COENEN, 2012). More conceptual and empirical studies are, however, needed to arrive at a better integrated framework.

Acknowledgements – The authors would like to thank Michaela Trippl, Markus Grillitsch, Bjørn Asheim, two anonymous referees as well as the editors and guest editors of *Regional Studies* for their comments that helped in improving the paper. Previous versions of this paper were presented at the 3rd Global Conference on Economic Geography 2011 in Seoul, Korea; at the Association of American Geographers Annual Meeting 2012 in New York; and the 3rd International Conference on Path Dependence 2014 in Berlin, Germany: the authors are grateful for all comments received. Finally, the authors extend their gratitude to all the interviewees who facilitated this research.

Funding – Financial support, for which the authors are grateful, was provided by Nordic Energy Research (TOP-NEST project), the Swedish Energy Agency (KIBIOS project) and the Swedish Governmental Agency for Innovation Systems, VINNOVA.

NOTES

1. RITTS = Regional Innovation and Technology Transfer Strategies and Infrastructures.
2. For example, in 2009 softwood prices in Scandinavia were approximately US$350/tonne compared with US$90/tonne in South America (FORNELL, 2010).
3. The VINNVÄXT programme is organized as a competition for regions where winning regions receive funding up to SEK10 million per year for a period of ten years. A prerequisite for the programme is the active participation of actors from private, public and research sectors and from the political sphere. Currently, 12 regional initiatives receive funding.
4. Processum AB is 60% owned by the SP Technical Research Institute of Sweden and 40% owned by 21 member companies.
5. To illustrate, Processum (the holding company for the biorefinery plant) has secured €55 million for an

industrial-scale 200 MWth biofuel facility. However, it nonetheless cancelled the investment plans as an additional investment need for €275 million was considered too risky.

6. For a discussion about this process in connection with institutional entrepreneurship and commercialization of clean technology, see also AVDEITCHIKOVA and COENEN (2015).

REFERENCES

ASHEIM B., BOSCHMA R. and COOKE P. (2011) Constructing regional advantage: platform policies based on related variety and differentiated knowledge bases, *Regional Studies* 45, 893–904. doi:10.1080/00343404.2010.543126

ASHEIM B., BUGGE M., COENEN L. and HERSTAD S. (2013) *What Does Evolutionary Economic Geography Bring to the Policy Table? Reconceptualising regional innovation systems.* CIRCLE Electronic Working Paper No. 2013/5. Centre for Innovation, Research and Competence in the Learning Economy (CIRCLE), Lund University, Lund (available at: http://www.circle.lu.se).

ASHEIM B. and GERTLER M. (2005) The geography of innovation: regional innovation systems, in FAGERBERG J., MOWERY D. and NELSON R. (Eds) *The Oxford Handbook of Innovation*, pp. 291–317. Oxford University Press, Oxford.

ASHEIM B. and ISAKSEN A. (2002) Regional innovation systems: the integration of local 'sticky' and global 'ubiquitous' knowledge, *Journal of Technology Transfer* 27, 77–86. doi:10.1023/A:1013100704794

AVDEITCHIKOVA S. and COENEN L. (Forthcoming 2015) Commercializing clean technology innovations – the emergence of new business in an agency-structure perspective, in KYRÖ P. *et al.* (Eds) *Handbook of Entrepreneurship and Sustainable Development.* Edward Elgar, Cheltenham.

BERGEK A., JACOBSSON S., CARLSSON B., LINDMARK S. and RICKNE A. (2008) Analyzing the functional dynamics of technological innovation systems: a scheme of analysis, *Research Policy* 37, 407–429. doi:10.1016/j.respol.2007.12.003

BERGQUIST A.-K. and SÖDERHOLM K. (2011) Green innovation systems in Swedish industry, 1960–1989, *Business History Review* 85, 677–698. doi:10.1017/S0007680511001152

BORRAS S. and EDQUIST C. (2013) The choice of innovation policy instruments, *Technological Forecasting and Social Change* 80, 1513–1522. doi:10.1016/j.techfore.2013.03.002

BOSCHMA R. (2014) Towards an evolutionary perspective on regional resilience, *Regional Studies* doi:10.1080/00343404.2014.959481.

BOSCHMA R. A. and FRENKEN K. (2006) Why is economic geography not an evolutionary science? Towards an evolutionary economic geography, *Journal of Economic Geography* 6, 273–302. doi:10.1093/jeg/lbi022

BOSCHMA R. and LAMBOOY J. (1999) The prospects of an adjustment policy based on collective learning in old industrial regions, *GeoJournal* 49, 391–399. doi:10.1023/A:1007144414006

BOSCHMA R. and MARTIN R. (2010) *Handbook of Evolutionary Economic Geography.* Edward Elgar, Cheltenham.

BRACZYK H.-J., COOKE P. and HEIDENREICH M. (1998) *Regional Innovation Systems: The Role of Governances in a Globalized World.* UCL Press, London.

BRESCHI S., MALERBA F. and ORSENIGO L. (2000) Technological regimes and Schumpeterian patterns of innovation, *Economic Journal* 110, 388–410. doi:10.1111/1468-0297.00530

CAMAGNI R. and CAPELLO R. (2013) Regional innovation patterns and the EU regional policy reform: toward smart innovation policies, *Growth and Change* 44, 355–389. doi:10.1111/grow.12012

COE N. (2011) Geographies of production I: an evolutionary revolution?, *Progress in Human Geography* 35, 81–91. doi:10.1177/0309132510364281

COENEN L. (2007) The role of universities in the regional innovation systems of the north east of England and Scania, Sweden: providing missing links?, *Environment and Planning C: Government and Policy* 25, 803–821. doi:10.1068/c0579

COENEN L., RAVEN R. and VERBONG G. (2010) Local niche experimentation in energy transitions: a theoretical and empirical exploration of proximity advantages and disadvantages, *Technology in Society* 32, 295–302. doi:10.1016/j.techsoc.2010.10.006

COOKE P. (Ed.) (1995) *The Rise of the Rustbelt.* UCL Press, London.

COOKE P. (1998) Introduction: origins of the concept, in BRACZYK H. J., COOKE P. and HEIDENREICH M. (Eds) *Regional Innovation Systems: The Role of Governance in a Globalized World*, pp. 2–25. UCL Press, London.

COOKE P., HEIDENREICH M. and BRACZYK H.-J. (2004) *Regional Innovation Systems: The Role of Governance in a Globalized World.* UCL Press, London.

DAVID P. (1985) Clio and the economics of QWERTY, *American Economic Review* 75, 332–337.

DEWALD U. and TRUFFER B. (2012) The local sources of market formation: explaining regional growth differentials in German photovoltaic markets, *European Planning Studies* 20, 397–420. doi:10.1080/09654313.2012.651803

DOSI G. and NELSON R. (1994) An introduction to evolutionary theories in economics, *Journal of Evolutionary Economics* 4, 153–172. doi:10.1007/BF01236366

ERICSSON K., HUTTUNEN S., NILSSON L. J. and SVENNINGSSON P. (2004) Bioenergy policy and market development in Finland and Sweden, *Energy Policy* 32, 1707–1721. doi:10.1016/S0301-4215(03)00161-7

ESSLETZBICHLER J. and RIGBY D. (2007) Exploring evolutionary economic geographies, *Journal of Economic Geography* 7, 549–571. doi:10.1093/jeg/lbm022

ESSLETZBICHLER J. and WINTHER L. (1999) Regional technological change and path dependency in the Danish food processing industry, *Geografiska Annaler, Series B: Human Geography* 81, 179–196. doi:10.1111/j.0435-3684.1999.00903.x

FORNELL R. (2010) *Energy Efficiency Measures in a Kraft Pulp Mill Converted to a Biorefinery Producing Ethanol.* Licentiate thesis, Chalmers University of Technology, Gothenburg.

FRENKEN K., VAN OORT F. and VERBURG T. (2007) Related variety, unrelated variety and regional economic growth, *Regional Studies* 41, 685–697. doi:10.1080/00343400601120296

GARUD R. AND KARNØE P. (2001) *Path Dependence and Creation*. Lawrence Erlbaum Associates, Mahwah, NJ.

GEELS F. W. (2002) Technological transitions as evolutionary reconfiguration processes: a multi-level perspective and a case-study, *Research Policy* 31, 1257–1274. doi:10.1016/S0048-7333(02)00062-8

GEELS F. W. (2004) From sectoral systems of innovation to socio-technical systems, *Research Policy* 33, 897–920. doi:10.1016/j.respol.2004.01.015

GONZÁLEZ-EGUINO M., GALARRAGA I. and ANSUATEGI A. (2012) The future of old industrial regions in a carbon-constrained world, *Climate Policy* 12, 164–186. doi:10.1080/14693062.2011.605707

GRABHER G. (1993) The weakness of strong ties: the lock-in of regional development in the Ruhr area, in GRABHER G. (Ed.) *The Embedded Firm*, pp. 255–277. Routledge, London.

HASSINK R. (1993) Regional innovation policies compared, *Urban Studies* 30, 1009–1024. doi:10.1080/00420989320080921

HASSINK R. (1997) What distinguishes 'good' from 'bad' industrial agglomerations?, *Erdkunde* 51, 2–11. doi:10.3112/erdkunde.1997.01.01

HASSINK R. (2010) Locked in decline? On the role of regional lock-ins in old industrial areas, in BOSCHMA R. and MARTIN R. (Eds) *Handbook of Evolutionary Economic Geography*, pp. 450–469. Edward Elgar, Cheltenham.

HASSINK R. and KLAERDING C. (2011) Evolutionary approaches to local and regional development policy, in PIKE A., RODRÍGUEZ-POSÉ A. and TOMANEY J. (Eds) *Handbook of Local and Regional Development*, pp. 139–148. Routledge, London.

HASSINK R. and SHIN D.-H. (2005) The restructuring of old industrial areas in Europe and Asia, *Environment and Planning A* 37, 571–580. doi:10.1068/a36273

HEALY A. and MORGAN K. (2012) Spaces of innovation: learning, proximity and the ecological turn, *Regional Studies* 46, 1041–1053. doi:10.1080/00343404.2012.672725

HUDSON R. (1989) Labour-market changes and new forms of work in old industrial regions: maybe flexibility for some but not flexible accumulation, *Environment and Planning D: Society and Space* 7, 5–30. doi:10.1068/d070005

HUDSON R. (1994) New production geographies? Reflections on changes in the automobile industry, *Transactions of the Institute of British Geographers* 19, 331–345. doi:10.2307/622326

HUDSON R. (2005) Rethinking change in old industrial regions: reflecting on the experiences of North East England, *Environment and Planning A* 37, 581–596. doi:10.1068/a36274

ISAKSEN A. (2001) Building regional innovation systems: is endogenous industrial development possible in the global economy?, *Canadian Journal of Regional Science* 24, 101–120.

KARLTORP K. and SANDÉN B. A. (2012) Explaining regime destabilisation in the pulp and paper industry, *Environmental Innovation and Societal Transitions* 2, 66–81. doi:10.1016/j.eist.2011.12.001

KAUFMANN A. and TÖDTLING F. (2000) Systems of innovation in traditional industrial regions: the case of Styria in a comparative perspective, *Regional Studies* 34, 29–40. doi:10.1080/00343400050005862

KEMP R. SCHOT J. W. and HOOGMA R. (1998) Regime shifts to sustainability through processes of niche formation: the approach of strategic niche management, *Technology Analysis and Strategic Management* 10, 175–198. doi:10.1080/09537329808524310

KLEIN WOOLTHUIS R., LANKHUIZEN M. and GILSING V. A. (2005) A system failure framework for innovation policy design, *Technovation* 25, 609–619. doi:10.1016/j.technovation.2003.11.002

LAESTADIUS S. (2000) Biotechnology and the potential for a radical shift of technology in forest industry, *Technology Analysis and Strategic Management* 12, 193–212. doi:10.1080/713698464

LANDABASO M., OUGHTON C. and MORGAN K. (2001) Innovation networks and regional policy in Europe, in KOSCHATZKY K., KULICKE M. and ZENKER A. (Eds) *Innovation Networks: Concepts and Challenges in the European Perspective*, pp. 243–273. Physica, Heidelberg.

LARANJA M., UYARRA E. and FLANAGAN K. (2008) Policies for science, technology and innovation: translating rationales into regional policies in a multi-level setting, *Research Policy* 37, 823–835. doi:10.1016/j.respol.2008.03.006

MACKINNON D., CUMBERS A., PIKE A., BIRCH K. and MCMASTER R. (2009) Evolution in economic geography: institutions, political economy, and adaptation, *Economic Geography* 85, 129–150. doi:10.1111/j.1944-8287.2009.01017.x

MARTIN R. (2010) Roepke Lecture in Economic Geography: Rethinking regional path dependence: beyond lock-in to evolution, *Economic Geography* 86, 1–27. doi:10.1111/j.1944-8287.2009.01056.x

MARTIN R. and SUNLEY P. (2006) Path dependence and regional economic evolution, *Journal of Economic Geography* 6, 395–437. doi:10.1093/jeg/lbl012

MARTIN R. and SUNLEY P. (2007) Complexity thinking and evolutionary economic geography, *Journal of Economic Geography* 7, 573–601. doi:10.1093/jeg/lbm019

MELANDER A. (1997) *Industrial Wisdom and Strategic Change: The Swedish Pulp and Paper Industry 1945–1990*. JIBS Dissertation Series. Internationella handelshögskolan, Jönköping.

MORGAN K. (1997) The learning region: institutions, innovation and regional renewal, *Regional Studies* 31, 491–503. doi:10.1080/00343409750132289

MORGAN K. (2012) Path dependence and the state: the politics of novelty in old industrial regions, in COOKE P. (Ed.) *Re-framing Regional Development: Evolution, Innovation, Transition*, pp. 318–340. Routledge, Abingdon.

NATIONAL RENEWABLE ENERGY LABORATORY (NREL) (2014) *What is a Biorefinery?* (available at: http://www.nrel.gov/biomass/biorefinery.html) (accessed on 18 September 2014).

NAUWELAERS C. and WINTJES R. (2002) Innovating SMEs and regions: the need for policy intelligence and interactive policies, *Technology Analysis and Strategic Management* 14, 201–215. doi:10.1080/09537320220133866

NILSSON M. and MOODYSSON J. (Forthcoming 2014) Regional innovation policy and coordination: illustrations from Southern Sweden, *Science and Public Policy*.

OJALA J., LAMBERG J. A., AHOLA A. and MELANDER A. (2006) The ephemera of success: strategy, structure and performance in the forestry industries, in LAMBERG J. A. and OJALA J. (Eds) *The Evolution of Competitive Strategies in Global Forestry Industries*, pp. 257–286. Springer, Amsterdam.

OTTOSSON M. (2011) *Opposition and Adjustment to Industrial 'Greening': The Swedish Forest Industry's (Re)actions Regarding Energy Transition, 1989–2009*. Linköping University, Linköping.

OTTOSSON M. and MAGNUSSON T. (2013) Socio-technical regimes and heterogeneous capabilities: the Swedish pulp and paper industry's response to energy policies, *Technology Analysis and Strategic Management* **25**, 355–368. doi:10.1080/09537325.2013.774349

PORTER M. (2000) Location, clusters and company strategy, in CLARK G., FELDMAN M. and GERTLER M. (Eds) *The Oxford Handbook of Economic Geography*, pp. 253–274. Oxford University Press, Oxford.

RAVEN R. (2005) Strategic niche management for biomass. PhD thesis, Technical University Eindhoven, Eindhoven.

RIP A. and KEMP R. (1998) Technological change, in RAYNER S. and MALONE E. L. (Eds) *Human Choice and Climate Change*, vol. 1, pp. 327–399. Batelle, Columbus, OH.

RODRÍGUEZ-POSÉ A. (2013) Do institutions matter for regional development?, *Regional Studies* **47**, 1034–1047. doi:10.1080/00343404.2012.748978

SCHREYÖGG G. and SYDOW J. (2011) Organizational path dependence: a process view, *Organization Studies* **32**, 321–335. doi:10.1177/0170840610397481

SIMMIE J. (2012) Path dependence and new technological path creation in the Danish wind power industry, *European Planning Studies* **20**, 753–772. doi:10.1080/09654313.2012.667924

SKOGSINDUSTRIERNA (2013) *Skogsindustrin – En faktasamling. 2012 års branschstatistik* [The Forest Industry – Facts Collection]. Skogsindustrierna, Stockholm.

SMITH A., VOß J.-P. and GRIN J. (2010) Innovation studies and sustainability transitions: Tthe allure of the multi-level perspective and its challenges, *Research policy Policy* **39(4)**, 435–448. doi:10.1016/j.respol.2010.01.023

SMITH K. (2000) Innovation as a systemic phenomenon: rethinking the role of policy, *Enterprise and Innovation Management Studies* **1(1)**, 73–102. doi:10.1080/146324400363536

STEINER M. (1985) Old industrial areas: a theoretical approach, *Urban Studies* **22**, 387–398. doi:10.1080/00420988520080701

STRAMBACH S. and KLEMENT B. (2013) Exploring plasticity in the development path of the automotive industry in Baden-Württemberg: the role of combinatorial knowledge dynamics, *Zeitschrift für Wirtschaftsgeographie* **57**, 67–82.

TÖDTLING F. and TRIPPL M. (2005) One size fits all? Towards a differentiated regional innovation policy approach, *Research Policy* **34**, 1203–1219. doi:10.1016/j.respol.2005.01.018

TRIPPL M. and OTTO A. (2009) How to turn the fate of old industrial areas: a comparison of cluster-based renewal processes in Styria and the Saarland, *Environment and Planning A* **41**, 1217–1233. doi:10.1068/a4129

TRUFFER B. and COENEN L. (2012) Environmental innovation and sustainability transitions in regional studies, *Regional Studies* **46**, 1–21. doi:10.1080/00343404.2012.646164

UNDERTHUN A., HILDRUM J., SVARE H., FINSRUD H. and VAREIDE K. (2014) The restructuring of the old industrial region of Grenland in Norway: between lock-in, adjustment, and renewal, *Norsk Geografisk Tidskrift – Norwegian Journal of Geography* **68**, 121–132. doi:10.1080/00291951.2014.894566

UNRUH G. C. (2000) Understanding carbon lock-in, *Energy Policy* **28**, 817–830. doi:10.1016/S0301-4215(00)00070-7

WEBER M. and ROHRACHER H. (2012) A systems approach to transition dynamics: providing a foundation for legitimizing goal-oriented policy strategies, *Research Policy* **41**, 1037–1047. doi:10.1016/j.respol.2011.10.015

Education–Job (Mis)Match and Interregional Migration: Italian University Graduates' Transition to Work

SIMONA IAMMARINO and ELISABETTA MARINELLI

Department of Geography and the Environment, London School of Economics and Political Science, Houghton Street, London, UK.

European Commission JRC-IPTS, C/ Inca Garcilaso 3, Spain.

IAMMARINO S. and MARINELLI E. Education–job (mis)match and interregional migration: Italian university graduates' transition to work, *Regional Studies*. This paper analyses the micro-level determinants of the education–job (mis)matches of recent university graduates in Italy. As the Italian graduate population has experienced increasing internal migration, this paper focuses in particular on the role of interregional migration in driving education–job match. The methodology takes into account both the endogenous relationship between migration and employment, and the self-selection bias between employment and education–job (mis)match. Using a survey on Italian graduates' entry into the labour market, it is found that whilst migration at the national level is confirmed to have a positive role in both finding a job and decreasing the probability of over-education, robust differences emerge when looking at the sub-national dimension. Indeed, the Northern regions by receiving inflows of Southern graduates who manage to attain a good education–job match in the recipient labour markets are apparently reaping part of the return to the investment in university education borne in the South.

IAMMARINO S. and MARINELLI E. 教育—职业（不）对称与跨区域迁徙：意大利大学毕业生过渡至就业，*区域研究*。本文分析意大利晚近的大学毕业生教育—职业（不）对称的微观层级决定因素。意大利的大学毕业生人口，经历了逐渐成长中的内部移民，本文于是特别聚焦跨区域迁徙之于驱动教育—工作匹配的角色。本研究方法，将迁徙与就业之间的内生关系，以及就业和教育—职业（不）对称之间的自我选择偏误同时纳入考量。本研究运用意大利大学毕业生进入劳动市场的调查，发现当全国层级的迁徙确定同时对找工作与减少过度教育的可能性具有正面的作用时，坚实的差异却在次国家层级方面浮现。北方区域，透过接受在接收性的劳动市场中获得良好教育—就业配对的南方大学毕业生的涌入，显然收割了南方大学教育所承担的投资之部分回收。

IAMMARINO S. et MARINELLI E. L'(in)adéquation entre l'éducation et l'emploi et la migration interrégionale: l'entrée sur le marché du travail des diplômés universitaires italiens, *Regional Studies*. Cet article analyse les déterminants microéconomiques de l'(in)adéquation entre l'éducation et l'emploi des diplômés universitaires italiens au cours des années récentes. Étant donné que la population diplômée italienne a fait preuve d'une hausse de la migration interne, cet article porte notamment sur le rôle de la migration interrégionale comme force motrice de l'adéquation entre l'éducation et l'emploi. La méthodologie tient compte à la fois du rapport endogène entre la migration et l'emploi, et du biais d'auto-sélection entre l'emploi et l'(in)adéquation entre l'éducation et l'emploi. À partir d'une enquête sur l'entrée des diplômés italiens sur le marché du travail, il s'avère que d'importantes différences voient le jour au moment où on considère le point de vue infranational, alors qu'il est confirmé que la migration à l'échelle nationale joue un rôle positif à la fois pour rechercher un emploi et réduire la probabilité d'être surqualifié. En effet, il semble que les régions septentrionales qui reçoivent des flux de diplômés en provenance des régions méridionales, forts d'une bonne adéquation entre l'éducation et l'emploi sur le marché du travail des régions d'accueil, obtiennent en partie un retour à l'investissment dans l'éducation universitaire supporté par les régions méridionales.

IAMMARINO S. und MARINELLI E. (Fehlende) Übereinstimmung zwischen Ausbildung und Arbeitsstellen und interregionale Migration: der Übergang von italienischen Hochschulabsolventen in den Arbeitsmarkt, *Regional Studies*. In diesem Beitrag analysieren wir auf Mikroebene die Determinanten für eine (fehlende) Übereinstimmung zwischen der Ausbildung und den Arbeitsstellen von neuen Hochschulabsolventen in Italien. Aufgrund der gestiegenen internen Migration unter italienischen Hochschulabsolventen konzentrieren wir uns insbesondere auf die Rolle der interregionalen Migration für die Übereinstimmung zwischen Ausbildung und Arbeitsstelle. Bei der Methodologie werden sowohl die endogene Beziehung zwischen Migration und Beschäftigung als auch die durch Selbstauswahl verursachte Verzerrung hinsichtlich der Beschäftigung und der (fehlenden) Übereinstimmung zwischen Ausbildung und Arbeitsstelle berücksichtigt. Anhand einer Umfrage über den Zugang von italienischen Hochschulabsolventen zum Arbeitsmarkt stellen wir fest, dass sich die Migration auf nationaler Ebene zwar tatsächlich positiv auf den Erfolg bei der Arbeitssuche auswirkt und die Wahrscheinlichkeit einer Überqualifikation senkt, doch dass auf subnationaler Ebene robuste Unterschiede deutlich werden. Die Regionen des Nordens scheinen in der Tat einen Teil des Ertrags der im Süden getätigten Investitionen in die Hochschulbildung zu ernten, da sie Ströme von Hochschulabsolventen aus dem Süden aufnehmen, die in den Arbeitsmärkten der Empfangsregionen eine gute Übereinstimmung zwischen Ausbildung und Arbeitsstelle erzielen können.

IAMMARINO S. y MARINELLI E. (Des)ajuste entre educación y empleo y la migración interregional: la transición al trabajo de los licenciados universitarios italiano, *Regional Studies*. En este artículo analizamos los determinantes a nivel micro de los (des)ajustes entre la educación y el empleo de los recientes licenciados en Italia. Considerando el aumento de la migración interna entre los licenciados italianos, destacamos especialmente el papel de la migración interregional al buscar una concordancia entre la formación y los puestos de trabajo. En esta metodología se tiene en cuenta la relación endógena entre la migración y el empleo, y el sesgo autoselectivo que afecta al empleo y al (des)ajuste entre la formación y los puestos de trabajo. A partir de una encuesta sobre el acceso al mercado laboral de licenciados italianos, observamos que si bien se confirma que la migración de ámbito nacional tiene un papel positivo a la hora de encontrar trabajo y disminuir la probabilidad de caer en la sobre cualificación, surgen grandes diferencias cuando se analiza a nivel subnacional. De hecho, parece que las regiones del norte aprovechan parte del lucro obtenido a través de la inversión en educación universitaria por parte del sur porque reciben influjos de licenciados del sur que consiguen un buen ajuste entre educación y trabajo en los mercados laborales de destino.

INTRODUCTION

It is largely acknowledged that graduates' entry into the labour market is a critical mechanism through which public investment in higher education generates its returns (e.g. PAVITT, 1991; SALTER and MARTIN, 2001). As well as carrying up-to-date knowledge, graduates possess competencies and capabilities to combine and use knowledge in new productive ways (e.g. WALTERS, 2004; VON TUNZELMANN and WANG, 2007). It follows that the returns to public, as well as private, investment in human capital crucially depend on the use that graduates can make of their education in the labour market, that is, on the degree of their education–job match.

From a regional perspective, a crucial question becomes whether university graduates' education–job match or mismatch – the latter commonly indicated as over-education – vary across regions within countries, leading to different returns to investments in higher education across space. Following the seminal work of BÜCHEL and VAN HAM (2003), recent contributions have shown that geographical characteristics are likely to affect labour market outcomes such as match or over-education. At the same time, the literature on technological change has long posited that an alignment between the local stage of socio-economic development

and the quality of local human capital is a necessary condition for the latter to generate regional economic growth (e.g. NELSON and PHELPS, 1966; VON TUNZELMANN, 2009). The rationale behind this view crucially depends on the assumption that graduates remain within the region where the investment in learning and education was carried out, or that gaps between the local demand and supply of human capital are met by adequate migration flows. Indeed, one of the explanations for the existence of education–job mismatch indicated by the literature is the limitation in the geographical scope of the graduates' job search.

Despite the links between the literature on skills/education and regional/spatial perspectives, the geographical dimension of graduates' skill use and their sub-national mobility are still underexplored. This paper addresses this gap focusing on the case of Italy, testing whether spatial mobility has an impact on education–job matching in the early stage of the graduate's professional career. Indeed, one of the tasks of evolutionary economic geography is to understand how a territorial perspective can shed light on the learning processes underpinning economic evolution. By showing that geography shapes the relationship between migration and education–job match, this paper provides critical insights to the field, further supporting the need to look at migration not simply as a mechanism for labour reallocation but also in terms of the knowledge flows it generates.

Italy, with its marked sub-national disparities and increasing internal graduate migration, allows important insights to emerge by framing the phenomenon under scrutiny against the geographical context that produces and employs graduate skills. The exercise adds novel empirical evidence to a crucial area of research and policy interest, so far largely investigated with reference to Anglo-Saxon or Northern European countries (CONSOLI et al., 2013).

The data used in this paper come from the survey on graduates' entry into the labour market carried out by the Italian National Statistical Institute (ISTAT, 2010). Originally developed indicators of education–job (mis) match are used, and ordered logit models are applied. In so doing one takes into account both the endogeneity between migration and labour market outcomes, and the graduates' self-selection into employment, issues normally not tackled simultaneously in the current literature.

The paper is organized as follows. The second section reviews the relevant strands of literature that provide the background of the study, and identifies the contribution of the paper; at the same time, it briefly sketches the Italian context and its territorial dualism. The third section introduces the data, defines the indicators of education–job match and over-education, and provides some descriptive statistics. The fourth section describes the econometric strategy and specification; whilst the fifth section discusses the empirical findings. The sixth section concludes with a summary of the main results and their possible implications, and some future research directions.

BACKGROUND LITERATURE AND CONTEXT OF THE STUDY

Graduate education–job match, over-education and spatial mobility

The vast literature on education–job (mis)match, and in particular on over-education, has been stimulated by the observation that generalized increases in education levels have not been always mirrored by rises in skills' use and remuneration (SLOANE, 2003; and McGUINNESS, 2006, have excellent reviews). Although in the seminal work of ROSEN (1972) over-education emerges as a rather transitory phenomenon – as workers accept jobs requiring less education than that they actually possess in order to gain experience and improve their chances of a more suitable occupation in the future – the debate on the nature and persistence of education–job mismatch is still far from being conclusive, with disconcerting evidence particularly with respect to university graduates (e.g. DOLTON and VIGNOLES, 2000; McGUINNESS, 2006; McGUINNESS and WOODEN, 2009).

There are several reasons why understanding education–job (mis)match in relation to university graduates is important (BOUDARBAT and CHERNOFF, 2010). At the micro-level, it is well established that an inadequate alignment between acquired and required competences is associated to worse employment conditions (SICHERMAN, 1991), such as, for instance, lower salary (e.g. BATTU et al., 2000; HEIJKE et al., 2003; DI PIETRO and URWIN, 2006; ROBST, 2007; DOLTON and SILLES, 2008) and employee dissatisfaction (e.g. GARCIA-ESPEJO and IBANEZ, 2006; IAMMARINO and MARINELLI, 2011; GREEN and ZHU, 2010). At the organization or firm level, on the other hand, over-education is reflected in lower productivity and higher labour turnover (e.g. WOLBERS, 2003).

The literature that has tried to disentangle the determinants of graduate over-education at the micro-level has found that this condition is more common in part-time or temporary jobs, in which graduates may often find themselves at the beginning of their career – the so-called *waiting room effect* (DEKKER et al., 2002). In the same line, other empirical contributions indicate that over-education decreases with tenure within a job (GROOT and MAASSEN VAN DER BRINK, 2000). Scholars have also shown that graduates' education–job match depends on the field of study (BOUDARBAT and CHERNOFF, 2010; VENHORST and CÖRVERS, 2011) and, although the results are more mixed, on study performance measured by final grades (BATTU et al., 1999; BIGGERI et al., 2001; VAN DER KLAAUW and VAN VUREN, 2010).

Notably, on the basis of the high heterogeneity of graduates' conditions, some recent studies have pointed to the distinction between two different components of over-education: the first can be related to the mismatch of the formal qualification, while the second refers to the underutilization of skills and competencies acquired through the university study. These two components are conceptually and empirically different (for various interpretations, see ALLEN and VAN DER VELDEN, 2001; CHEVALIER, 2003; GREEN and McINTOSH, 2007; and GREEN and ZHU, 2010) and have been used in the attempt to disentangle between different degrees of mismatching, some deemed more serious than others.

Along with the interest for the micro-level drivers and implications of education–job match, in the last decades emphasis has been put on the alignment, at the macro- or meso-level of the country or the region, between the skills demanded and the skills produced in a territory. Such debate has been framed within the discussion on the developmental role of universities and their explicit mission towards the generation and dissemination of knowledge and innovation (e.g. ROSENBERG and NELSON, 1994; ETZKOWITZ and LEYDESDORFF, 1997; MORGAN, 1997; SALTER and MARTIN, 2001; MOWERY and SAMPAT, 2005; GULBRANDSEN et al., 2011). Scholars have emphasized that the impact of graduates on economic performance and knowledge creation depends on the overall level of social, technological and economic development of the regional system where they are employed (e.g. NELSON and PHELPS, 1966; VANDEBUSSCHE *et al.*, 2006; VON TUNZELMANN, 2009; CRESCENZI *et al.*, 2013). A regional system with a strong knowledge base will thus benefit more from a highly skilled labour force than a backward one, as for higher education investment to translate into local socio-economic benefits, the knowledge embodied in graduates needs to match or complement that embedded in the region (e.g. FRENKEN *et al.*, 2007; FAGGIAN and McCANN, 2009; RODRÍGUEZ-POSE and TSELIOS, 2010; KRABEL and FLÖTHER, 2014; CONSOLI *et al.*, 2013).

Whilst the importance of education–job match at the individual and systemic levels have been recognized as critical to understand the evolutionary mechanisms of learning and knowledge creation processes (HEALY and MORGAN, 2009; RODRÍGUEZ-POSE and TSELIOS 2010, 2012; CONSOLI *et al.*, 2013), more needs to be done to appreciate fully how geography shapes these phenomena.

In this respect, the study of the link between interregional migration and education–job match can shed light on how spatial conditions, by affecting the opportunity to apply, or not, skills, generate – or fail to do so – virtuous cycles of accumulation, creation and diffusion of knowledge.[1] Whilst the literature covering the links between migration and education–job match has not specifically taken this perspective, the current wealth of results indirectly encourage this line of analysis. For instance, one of the explanations for over-education has been identified in the limited spatial scope of the job search (SLOANE, 2003). BÜCHEL and VAN HAM (2003) and RAMOS and SANROMÀ (2011) show how spatial constraints are very likely to affect labour market outcomes. The former, focusing on the effect of regional characteristics and spatial mobility across labour markets in West Germany, point to a negative relationship between mobility (i.e. in terms of possibility of commuting by car) and over-education. The latter show that young graduates may be forced into over-education conditions by the peripherality and lack of effective connections of their location, highlighting the importance of geographical characteristics such as city size and access to larger labour markets. Similar results are found by CROCE and GHIGNONI (2011) in Italy, and by HENSEN *et al.* (2009) and VENHORST and CÖRVERS (2011) in the Netherlands.

The above empirical studies, while mostly confirming that spatial mobility/migration can be a means of reducing over-education, invariably demand to look more in depth into geographic-specific explanations for over-education. As the full use of competencies and skills is a crucial input to both regional innovative activity and economic growth, graduates' spatial movements can potentially affect the long-term dynamics of regional development (see also FAGGIAN and McCANN, 2006; MARINELLI, 2011, 2013).

The Italian case

This paper aims to shed light on the links between education–job match and interregional migration by focusing on the case of Italy. The country is an interesting example for this purpose, as its dualistic socio-economic structure, with the South lagging historically behind the rest of the country (among a vast literature, see VACCARO, 1995; VIESTI, 2003; IAMMARINO, 2005; BARCA, 2006; and ASSOCIAZIONE PER LO SVILUPPO DELL'INDUSTRIA NEL MEZZOGIORNO (SVIMEZ), 2009), results in strongly geographically differentiated skill markets. Broadly speaking, the North comprises, on the one hand, some highly innovative regions, with strong interactions among local economic actors and institutions, good scientific and technological infrastructure, and effective policies; on the other hand, a group of *learning regions* (particularly in the North East) with strong endogenous competences, despite the relatively low formal research and development (R&D). The Centre is dominated by Lazio, the capital-region, which although it captures a large proportion of the national public R&D, it does not show the same dynamic industrial structure and specialization of the North. The regions of the South (or Mezzogiorno) are largely lagging behind, with scattered specialization mostly in traditional and low-technology industries, and weak innovation and systemic linkages. Furthermore, in recent years these geographical disparities have been accompanied by an increasing internal brain-drain. Since the mid-1990s, the Mezzogiorno regions have experienced substantial outflow of graduates (e.g. PIRAS, 2005, 2006; D'ANTONIO and SCARLATO, 2007), particularly towards more innovative and dynamic regions that offer wider and better opportunities to apply competences and skills (SVIMEZ, 2009; MARINELLI, 2011; DOTTI *et al.*, 2012; MELICIANI and RADICCHIA, 2014).

A further reason that makes Italy an interesting case study is that whilst the typical Italian dualism is not reflected in university educational attainment, with the Centre and the North showing levels of higher education similar to those of the Mezzogiorno (e.g. PIRAS, 2005, 2006; DI LIBERTO, 2007), there are large differences in the employment opportunities open to graduates from different parts of the country (CONIGLIO and PERAGINE, 2007). Three years after graduation the proportion of employed graduates is 74% in the country as a whole, while in the South it drops to 59.2% (ISTAT, 2005; 2006). Moreover, jobs are often not accessible by merit alone, as the area is characterized by very low social mobility (CHECCHI and DARDANONI, 2002) with the family upbringing influencing the access to the labour market (CHECCHI and PERAGINE, 2005).

Against this background, the present paper aims to contribute to the still overlooked spatial dimension of over-education by focusing on the empirical investigation of two research questions:

- Does interregional migration impact on education–job match and over-education in the early stages of graduates' integration in the labour market?
- Does such a link differ according to the geographical area the graduates are moving from and towards?

DATA AND INDICATORS

Data set

The paper uses the *Indagine sull'Inserimento Professionale dei Laureati* (ISTAT, 2010) carried out periodically by ISTAT, the Italian National Statistical Institute. The survey investigates the entrance of graduates into the labour market three years after they completed their studies. What follows uses the seventh edition of the survey, carried out in 2007 and covering 2004 graduates. At the time, the Italian system was in transition from the old *Laurea degree* (a longer degree comprising bachelor's and master's) to the new system aligned to the Bologna process, based on bachelor's and master's at two different stages. Here the focus will be exclusively on graduates from the old system: they account for 167 886 of the total universe of 260 070 Italian graduates in 2004, and for 26 570 of the *Indagine*'s sample of 47 300.

The *Indagine* is characterized by one-stage stratification by gender, university and type of degree. Each of the surveyed individuals is attributed a sampling weight, which allows one to build indicators representative at the level of nation, field of study and, most importantly for the objective of the present work, region of study and current region of residence and employment.

Education–job (mis)match: indicators

Different indicators and methods of measuring education–job match have been applied in the literature. According to VERHAEST and OMEY (2006), three categories of indicators can be identified:

- Those based on a professional job analyst's definition of the skills or educational requirements for each occupation, labelled as 'objective' measures.
- Those based on the 'subjective' assessment of the educational requirements (i.e. the graduate's or the employer's) of the job.
- Those based on the distance between the worker's education and the mean or modal education level of her/his occupational group, labelled as 'empirical method'.[2]

The indicators used here fall in the second category of subjective or self-reported measures. In particular this paper uses, both separately and in conjunction, information on (1) the formal educational requirements of the employer (referred in the literature as indirect self-assessment); and (2) the graduates' self-assessment with respect to the competences and skills required to perform their job (direct self-assessment). According to WALD and FANG (2008), this type of measure has the advantage of being job specific. However, being subjective, it may be biased by the individual's attitudes, for instance when the graduate wishes to increase the standing of the job (HARTOG, 2000; SGOBBI and SULEMAN, 2013).

The *Indagine* asks graduates the following question related to the employers' educational requirement (indirect self-assessment):

1a. Was the Laurea degree formally required by the employer to apply for the job?

As for the direct self-assessment, the question from the survey is:

1b. Is the Laurea degree effectively necessary to carry out the job?

Both questions generate a yes/no dichotomous variable. However, whilst question 1a gives insights on the qualification required, question 1b provides information on the graduate's perception of the use of her/his competences and skills acquired through university education. A combined indicator is employed – building on ALLEN and VAN DER VELDEN (2001), CHEVALIER (2003), UNGARO and VERZICCO (2005), and IAMMARINO and MARINELLI (2011) – incorporating the crucial distinction between qualification and competencies/skills utilization discussed in the second section above.[3]

A matrix of four possible education–job (mis)matches is obtained, as described in Fig. 1. Following the literature, a match or mismatch (over-education) are defined as *real* when the opinion of the graduate on the effective need of her/his qualifications is coherent with the perception of the formal requirement of the job. A *real match* (*real over-education*) therefore arises when the graduate believes (does not believe) that her/his education level is effectively needed in the job, and when the degree was also (was not) a formal requirement of the employer. Whenever the opinion of the graduate and the employer's condition differ, on the other hand, *apparent match* (*apparent over-education*) arises. Specifically, when a graduate feels that the degree is needed in her/his work, though the employer did not formally require it, the graduate is experiencing *apparent education–job match*. Conversely, when the graduate is in a job for which the degree was formally required but is perceived unnecessary she/he is experiencing *apparent over-education*.

In other words, of the two typologies of the matrix above that correspond to overqualification (i.e. those for which, according to the indirect self-assessment, the degree was *not* formally required by the employer), only the situation in which the graduate is both

		Was the degree effectively necessary to carry out the job?	
		YES	NO
Was the degree formally required?	YES	REAL MATCH: matched qualification, full skill utilization	APPARENT OVER-EDUCATION: matched qualification, skill under-utilization
	NO	APPARENT MATCH: overqualification, full skill utilization	REAL OVER-EDUCATION: overqualification, skill under-utilization

Fig. 1. Matrix of education–job (mis)match

overqualified and over-skilled represents what the literature has indicated as *real over-education*; the other category is instead indicated as *apparent match*, as it implies a full skills' utilization. Conversely, *apparent over-education* is the category where graduates have a matched qualification but their competences and skills are perceived as underutilised: these graduates may be hired by employers who want to benefit from highly qualified labour force even in low-skilled and low-salary jobs (a phenomenon already discussed for Italy by DI PIETRO and URWIN, 2006). On the other hand, *apparently matched* graduates may be frustrated with their economic treatment, because employers are labelling the occupation as 'non-graduate' in order to pay lower wages, but employees perceive their skills as necessary to perform the job.

The above four typologies can be ordered in the following way: *real over-education* indicates the lowest (or worst) degree of education–job match, followed by *apparent over-education*, *apparent match* and a *real match*.[4] An ordinal variable of education–job (mis)match is thus created, comprising the following levels:

1. Real over-education.
2. Apparent over-education.
3. Apparent match.
4. Real match.

Descriptive statistics

Interregional migrants are here defined as graduates whom, three years after graduation, are residing in a region different than the one in which they studied, and represent about a quarter of Italian graduates: such proportion is similar across the three Italian macro-regions (see Fig. 2 for the geographical definition).[5]

As Table 1 shows, whilst nearly 25% of total migrants move from the South to the Centre or North of the country (9.6% and 14.9% respectively), the proportion of those who leave the North for the Centre or the South is less than 15% in total: to be noted that nearly 27% of total migrants are intra-North. The proportion of total migrants that leave the Centre for another macro-region is slightly above 19% (8.9% for North and 10.2% for the South).

Table 2 firstly highlights the remarkable differences among the three macro-regions in terms of employment

rate. In the South only 59.8% of graduates are employed, as compared with 83.4% in the North and 72% in the Centre. Although employment opportunities are significantly lower in the Mezzogiorno, the proportion of graduates with favourable education–job match is slightly higher in the South than in the other parts of Italy, whilst the shares are lower for over-education (both real and apparent). Overall, those who qualify for having achieved real over-education (real match) according to the composite indicator based on the matrix reported in Fig. 1 are 18.3% (61%) in the South, versus 21.7% (55.3%) in the Centre and 20.2% (58.3%) in the North.

Finally, Table 3 compares stayers, migrants and South-to-Centre/North migrants across the main indicators of education–job (mis)match. Remarkably, the values for graduates migrating after university from the South to work in other regions are higher across all indicators but for over-education (both real and apparent), indicating an overall better education–job matching for these southern migrants as compared with other migrants and stayers.

ECONOMETRIC STRATEGY AND SPECIFICATION

Endogeneity and sample selection

In exploring the research questions, one needs to take into account two possible biases:

- The endogenous relationship between mobility behaviour and employment.
- The issue of self-selection into employment.

As a long scholarly debate has explored whether migration is the cause or the consequence of employment and other labour market outcomes (see HOOGSTRA *et al.*, 2011, for a meta-review), such an issue is taken into account in the methodology. As for self-selection, the degree of education–job (mis)match is observable only for those graduates who are actually employed (e.g. BUCHEL and VAN HAM, 2003; JAUHIAINEN, 2011; DEVILLANOVA, 2013). Thus, if unobserved factors affecting the outcome (in the case here, the education–job (mis) match) are correlated with unobserved factors affecting

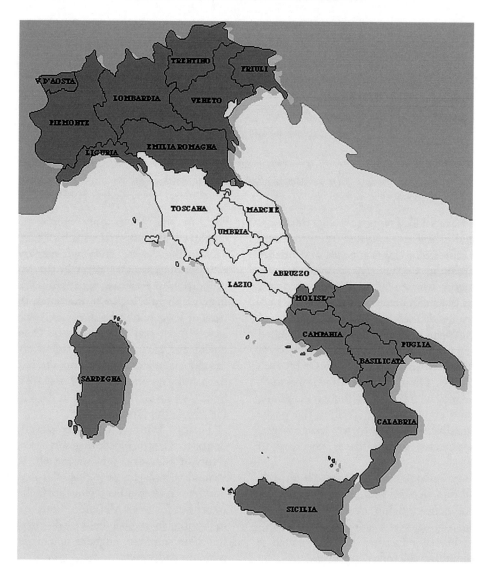

Fig. 2. Italian macro-regions

Table 1. *Graduate migration flows by macro-area*

	Destination		
Origin	North	Centre	South
North	26.9%	7.4%	7.2%
Centre	8.9%	5.8%	10.2%
South	14.9%	9.6%	9.1%

the selection process (i.e. whether graduates are employed or not) standard regression techniques deliver inconsistent estimators (HECKMAN, 1979).

To tackle both issues, the methodology devised by ARENDT and HOLM (2006), which is an extension of the Heckman correction (HECKMAN, 1979), is applied.[6] Specifically, these three logical steps are followed: first, an equation explaining the migration decision is estimated; based on this, the inverse Mills ratio (IMR) is calculated,[7] which becomes an explanatory variable for the employment equation, accounting

for the endogeneity between the latter and migration. Secondly, the employment equation is estimated, and its own IMR is calculated, which then becomes one explanatory variable of the third step, to account for self-selection between employment and education–job match. Finally, the education–job match equation is estimated.

As the software STATA allows probit and ordered probit with sample selection to be estimated, empirically the three steps are collapsed into two stages as follows:

- Stage 1: The migration equation is estimated and IMR is calculated.
- Stage 2: Both ordered (MIRANDA and RABE-HESKETH, 2006) and binary probit are run with sample selection. These models estimate two equations simultaneously: one selection equation, which accounts for the probability of the graduate being employed; and one outcome equation, where the level of education–job match is estimated.

Table 2. Employment rate and indicators of education–job (mis)match by macro-area

	% Employment rate	% Degree necessary for job (question 1b)	% Degree formally required (question 1a)	% Real over-education	% Apparent over-education	% Apparent match	% Real match
North	83.4%	68.5%	69.5%	20.2%	11.3%	10.3%	58.3%
Centre	72.0%	67.4%	66.2%	21.7%	10.9%	12.1%	55.3%
South	59.8%	72.6%	70.0%	18.3%	9.1%	11.7%	60.9%

Table 3. Education–job (mis)match indicators by mobility category

	% Degree necessary for job (question 1b)	% Degree formally required (question 1a)	% Real over-education	% Apparent over-education	% Apparent match	% Real match
Stayers	68.5%	68.1%	20.7%	10.2%	12.2%	56.9%
All other migrants	70.4%	70.7%	19.1%	9.6%	12.9%	57.4%
South to Centre/ North migrants	75.4%	72.3%	15.9%	8.7%	11.8%	63.6%

To assess whether there is effectively a selection bias, parameter ρ is looked at, which measures the correlation between the error terms of the two equations: when ρ is significantly different from zero, then the Heckman selection model is appropriate. When ρ is not significantly different from zero, only the outcome equation, including the IMR from the migration equation among the independent variables, is estimated.

Econometric specification

As mentioned above, three equations need to be specified, explaining migration, employment status and education job match respectively. The complete list of variables and their explanation for all three equations is reported in Table 4.

Step 1: Migration equation. The probability of being a migrant versus being a stayer (Migr) is estimated, where migrant is defined as a graduate whom, three years after graduation, is residing in a region different than the one in which she/he studied (conversely a graduate who remained in the same region of study is classified as a stayer).[8] The migration equation is specified as follows:

$$\text{Migr} = f(\text{Field1, Mark, High\_school\_mark,}$$
$$\text{Prev\_degree, Study\_migr, Erasmus, Work,}$$
$$\text{Study\_father, Uni\_city, Uni\_regio})$$

Following the literature discussed in the second section, among the explanatory variables for the migration equation are included covariates accounting for the geographical origin (i.e. of study, Uni_city, Uni_regio) and academic (Field1, Mark, High_school_mark, Prev_degree) and social background (Study_father) of the graduate. Furthermore, included are experience of previous migration, of study abroad and work (Study_migr, Erasmus, Work), as these factors have been

shown to affect the likelihood of future moves (e.g. DE GRIP *et al.*, 2010).[9]

Stage 2: Selection and outcome equations. The selection equation, which explains graduates' employment status (a binary variable, expressing whether the graduate is employed or not), is specified as follows (for the detailed list of variables, see Table 4):

$$\text{Employment} = f(\text{Migr, Field2, PERSONAL,}$$
$$\text{CURR\_EDU, Macro\_Region,}$$
$$\text{Uni\_city, IMR})$$

where Migr is a binary variable defined as in the migration equation; Field2 captures the broad field of university study (including five disciplinary groups);[10] PERSONAL is a vector of variables on personal characteristics of graduates; and CURR_EDU is a vector on engagement in further education. Two other controls take into account the location of study of the graduate (Macro_Region and Uni_city); IMR is the inverse Mills ratio, derived from the migration equation.

Finally, the outcome equation, explaining the education–job (mis)match – expressed as an ordinal variable with four levels as described in the third section above – is specified as follows:[11]

$$\text{Edu-job match} = f(\text{Mobility, Field2, Mark,}$$
$$\text{ATTITUDE, JOB, Female, IMR})$$

where Mobility, the regressor of interest, is a categorical variable that distinguishes between migrants from the South to the Centre and North of Italy (StoCN), and the rest of interregional migrants (i.e. either within each macro-region or between the Centre and the North in either direction, or from them to the South). Other independent variables are: Field2, defined as in

Table 4. Variables included in the migration equation, selection and outcome equations (in alphabetical order)

ATTITUDE	Vector of variables that capture the graduates' attitude towards their field of studies. It includes: • Interest: dummy variable that identifies those graduates who chose their degree because they were interested in the topic • Job prospects: dummy variable that identifies those graduates who chose their degree because of the job prospects it offered
CURREDU	Vector of variables capturing those graduates currently engaged in further education, and includes: • PhD: the graduate is currently enrolled in a doctoral programme • Training: the graduate is currently enrolled in training/an internship • Otheredu: the graduate is currently enrolled in other qualifications/courses
Edu–job match	Ordered indicator of education–job (mis)match based on Fig. 1. It is the dependent variable of the outcome equation
Employment	Binary variable identifying graduates who are employed versus those unemployed. It is the dependent variable of the selection equation
Erasmus	Binary variable capturing whether the graduate participated in international mobility programmes, such as Erasmus, during the degree
Female	Dummy variable identifying the gender of the graduate (also in PERSONAL in the selection equation)
Field1	Captures the fields of study of the graduate and it is a covariate in the migration equation: • Humanities (base category) • Economics and statistics • Social and political sciences • Law • Sciences • Engineering • Architecture • Medicine • Sports
Field2	Captures the broad field of study and includes five groups, which collapse the nine fields of Field1 (in parenthesis): • Sports (base category) • Humanities • Social sciences (Economics and statistics, Social and political sciences and Law) • Hard and technical sciences (Sciences, Engineering and Architecture) • Medicine
High_school_M	Captures the high-school graduation mark and is expressed on a scale from 36 to 60
IMR	Inverse Mills ratio derived from the migration equation
JOB	Vector of job-specific characteristics and includes: • Previous_job: dummy variable that identifies graduates who had job experience before the current employment • Self_emp: dummy variable that identifies graduates who are self-employed • Seniority: number of years the graduate has been in the job (from zero to three, as this question is asked exclusively to graduates who started their job after graduating and the *Indagine* targets graduates after the end of their studies) • Salary: monthly salary (€) of graduates
Macro_Region	Categorical variable identifying whether the graduate obtained the university degree in the North (the base category), Centre or South
Mark	Continuous variable that expresses the graduation mark of the graduate (in the Italian system from 70 to 110 *cum laudem*, the latter coded 111)
Migr	Binary variable that distinguishes migrants (those who live in a region different than the one in which they graduated) from stayers (those who live in the same region of graduation). It is the dependent variable of the migration equation and one of the covariates in the selection equation. For the education–job match equation, a more complex indicator (mobility) accounting for the direction of migration is adopted

Mobility	Categorical variable that distinguishes between migrants from the South to the Centre and North of Italy, and the rest of interregional migrants (i.e. either within each macro-region or between the Centre and the North, or from there to the South). Specifically it distinguishes between:
	• Stayers (base category; those who remain in the same region in which they studied)
	• Migr_Italy: those who live in a different region than that of graduation, excluding South-to-Centre/North migrants (Migr_StoCN)
	• Migr_StoCN: those who left a region of the South to move to a region in the Centre–North
	As separate models are run for Italy and its three macro-areas, this latter variable is then split into the following:
	• Migr_StoN: those who left a region of the South to move to a region in the North
	• Migr_StoC: those who left a region of the South to move to a region in the Centre
PERSONAL	Vector of variables capturing personal characteristics of graduates, including:
	• Age: age of the graduate (years)
	• Female: dummy variable that identifies female graduates
	• Par_uni: dummy variable that captures the social background of the graduate by identifying whether she/he has at least one parent with a university education
Prev_degree	Categorical variable that captures whether the graduate had other university titles before her/his graduation in 2004
Study_migr	Dummy variable that identifies whether the graduate attended university in the same region where she/he was residing before starting university
Study_father	Ordered variable, inserted into the regression as a continuous one, capturing the level of education of the father, with the following values: no title, elementary school, middle or vocational school, high school or high vocational school; university degree or doctorate
Uni_city	Binary variable that identifies graduates from the largest nine cities in Italy: Torino, Genova, Milano, Bologna, Firenze, Roma, Napoli, Bari and Palermo
Work	Categorical variable that identifies whether the graduate worked during her/his studies. It can take three values:
	• Occasional work (base category)
	• Continuous work
	• Never worked

the selection equation; Mark; ATTITUDE, which is a vector of variables that capture the graduates' attitude towards their field of study; JOB, a vector of job-specific characteristics;[12] Female and IMR, both as in the employment equation.

The regressions for the ordinal indicator of education–job (mis)match identified in the third section were run for Italy as whole, and then separately for the North, Centre and South to evaluate whether differences emerge with respect to the integration of migrant graduates in the recipient labour markets.

RESULTS

The results of the migration equation are reported in Table A1 in Appendix A in the Supplemental data online. As this stage is only instrumental to the main selection and outcome regressions, commenting in detail the results is not deemed necessary. However, it is interesting to note that previous geographical mobility impacts on the chances of future relocation, with those who changed region to attend university (Study_migr) and those who took part in programmes of student mobility abroad (Erasmus) being more likely to move subsequently. In addition, and in line with expectations, graduates who studied in large cities (Uni_city) are less likely to move, as they are more easily absorbed by the local labour market. The regional dummies highlight that Southern regions are invariably losing graduates to other Italian regions (with the only exception of Sardinia), while the results are far more mixed (and largely non-significant) for the North and Centre of the country.

Turning to the core research issue – the impact of interregional migration on education–job match – Table 5 shows the results of the ordered logit regressions for the four models: Italy as a whole, North, Centre and South. In the latter case, however, ρ was not significant, thus only the outcome equation, which includes the IMR from the migration equation among the explanatory variables, is reported.

First of all, in line with the empirical evidence reported in the second section on the overall positive effects of spatial mobility, the results indicate that for the country as a whole interregional migration increases both the probability of being employed and the probability of a better education–job match. Interestingly, migrating from the Mezzogiorno's regions towards the Centre–North of the country (Migr_StoCN) raises the likelihood to achieve a good education–job match relative to stayers and other migrants. It has to be noted that in the sets of regressions the cut-offs across the four categories of the education–job matrix represented in Fig. 1 are all highly statistically significant and with coefficients of remarkable magnitude (bottom of Table 5), supporting the choice to rank the matching

Table 5. Regression results: order logit equations with an ordered dependent variable in the outcome equations (education–job (mis)match, four levels)

	Italy	North	Centre	South[a]
Outcome equations				
Migr_Italy	0.117***	0.167***	0.146	0.371*
	(3.11)	(3.07)	(1.64)	(1.76)
Migr_StoCN	0.195***			
	(3.16)			
Migr_StoN		0.364***		
		(4.77)		
Migr_StoC			0.0858	
			(0.81)	
Migr_StoS				0.0227
				(0.10)
Humanities	−0.261***	−0.264***	−0.285	−0.0270
	(−3.43)	(−2.74)	(−1.26)	(−0.10)
Soc Sciences	−0.337***	−0.328***	−0.144	−0.588**
	(−4.86)	(−3.88)	(−0.66)	(−2.34)
Hard Sciences	0.261***	0.235***	0.415*	0.556**
	(3.81)	(2.79)	(1.87)	(2.18)
Medicine	1.451***	1.531***	1.356***	2.487***
	(12.60)	(8.45)	(4.46)	(6.30)
Mark	0.0171***	0.0150***	0.0205***	0.0289***
	(7.93)	(5.34)	(4.28)	(3.59)
Interest	0.165***	0.158***	0.252**	0.216
	(3.68)	(2.63)	(2.57)	(1.39)
Job_prospects	0.176***	0.208***	0.306***	−0.0723
	(4.37)	(3.78)	(3.52)	(−0.52)
Previous_job	−0.132***	−0.112**	−0.134*	−0.321***
	(−3.97)	(−2.45)	(−1.82)	(−2.88)
Self_emp	0.417***	0.428***	0.376***	0.817***
	(9.83)	(7.10)	(4.62)	(5.32)
Seniority	−0.0103	−0.0496**	0.0476	0.0192
	(−0.64)	(−2.23)	(1.46)	(0.37)
Salary	0.000136***	0.000136***	0.0000763	0.000148
	(4.27)	(2.82)	(1.20)	(1.36)
Female	0.000675	0.0194	−0.0586	−0.0310
	(0.02)	(0.44)	(−0.89)	(−0.29)
IMR				0.366**
				(2.01)
Selection equations (employment)				
Migr	0.195***	0.0364	−0.0487	
	(4.38)	(0.39)	(−0.28)	
Humanities	0.227***	0.437***	0.336	
	(2.61)	(3.63)	(1.45)	
Soc Sciences	−0.121	−0.0872	0.211	
	(−1.63)	(−0.84)	(0.99)	
Hard Sciences	0.405***	0.282***	0.668***	
	(5.23)	(2.65)	(2.98)	
Medicine	−0.938***	−1.089***	−0.615***	
	(−11.21)	(−8.93)	(−2.79)	
Par_uni	−0.0492	−0.152**	−0.0561	
	(−1.07)	(−2.31)	(−0.52)	
Age	0.00317	−0.00515	0.00795	
	(0.39)	(−0.50)	(0.37)	
Female	−0.260***	−0.276***	−0.238***	
	(−7.69)	(−5.14)	(−3.23)	
PhD	−1.556***	−1.703***	−1.435***	
	(−21.88)	(−16.79)	(−10.23)	
Training	−0.831***	−0.931***	−1.002***	
	(−14.17)	(−9.80)	(−7.87)	
Other_Edu	−0.398***	−0.391***	−0.435***	
	(−6.62)	(−4.50)	(−3.18)	
Centre	−0.413***	−0.0169	−0.0163	
	(−7.60)	(−0.13)	(−0.08)	

(Continued)

Table 5. Continued

	Italy	North	Centre	South[a]
Selection equations (employment) *continued*				
South	−0.605***	−0.0301	0.267	
	(−16.35)	(−0.24)	(1.59)	
Uni_city	0.00955	0.132**	−0.0446	
	(0.27)	(2.52)	(−0.59)	
IMR	0.149***	0.0703	−0.109	
	(3.82)	(1.30)	(−1.34)	
_cons	0.914***	1.285***	0.628	
	(4.11)	(4.43)	(1.05)	
Auxiliary parameters				
cut1	1.217***	0.970***	1.997***	2.208**
	(5.30)	(3.29)	(3.73)	(2.39)
cut2	1.575***	1.339***	2.337***	2.803***
	(6.86)	(4.53)	(4.37)	(3.03)
cut3	1.891***	1.631***	2.663***	3.400***
	(8.23)	(5.51)	(4.98)	(3.68)
load	0.391***	0.655**	1.781***	
	(3.14)	(2.21)	(3.75)	
Rho	0.257 ***	0.387***	0.617***	0.127
	(0.071)	(0.122)	(0.039)	(0.114)
N	26 570	12 093	5929	3005

Notes: t-statistics are given in parentheses: *$p < 0.10$, **$p < 0.05$, ***$p < 0.01$.

[a]In the South model, ρ was not significant and thus the results of a simple ordered logit are reported.

according to ordinal degrees of importance, from real over-education to real match.

This main result at the national level, though, tends to average down different geographical peculiarities. In the regression for the North, whilst migrants and stayers have, other things being equal, the same chance of being employed (i.e. Migr is not significant in the selection equation), migrants are overall more likely to improve their education job match. Furthermore, as in the case of Italy as a whole, migrants from the South (Migr_StoN) are more likely than all the other graduates (both stayers and other migrants) to achieve a good match (the coefficient is highly significant and of notable magnitude). Conversely, in the regression for the Central regions the results at the national level are neither confirmed in the employment equation nor in the outcome equation: interregional mobility of graduates seems to have no impact on employability, or on the education–job match. Although the results for the South (outcome equation only) have to be interpreted with caution, some positive effect of overall inflows of migrants from the rest of Italy in the Mezzogiorno is exerted on the probability of a better match. A tentative explanation may be that migration from the Centre–North to the South occurs under specific circumstances in which a good education–job match is likely for graduate profiles that are lacking in the local market.

Looking at the other explanatory variables, note that in the outcome equation graduates in Medicine and Science are more likely to experience a good education–job match, independently on geography. On the contrary, graduates in Humanities and Social sciences have always negative coefficients, which turn out to be highly significant in the regressions for Italy and the North, indicating that graduates in such fields are less likely to achieve a good education–job match (graduates in sport constitute the base category). As for the selection/employment equation, graduates in Medicine are the least likely to work within three years after graduation, reflecting the fact that the most common path for them is to enter further medical training, whereas those who studied Science are, consistently, the most likely to be employed; graduates with a degree in Humanities find more easily employment in the models for Italy and the North, both not in the Centre, whilst Social sciences seems to have no impact at all on employability. Overall, these findings confirm the widespread perception that while hard and technical science graduates incontrovertibly tend to have significantly better education–job matches, showing a shortage of such specializations, social scientists tend to experience a much worst underutilization of their competencies, but in the case of the Centre (where the variable is never significant), possibly due to the wide use of these backgrounds in the public sector.

As expected, graduates who chose their degree out of interest and because of the job prospects it provides are more likely to have a better match (coefficients of Interest and Job_prospects positive and significant in all equations but that for the South). In line with some previous findings, graduates with a higher grade are found to be more likely to be matched in all four models.

Job-specific characteristics seem to matter considerably in influencing over-education. Not surprisingly, those who are self-employed are always far better matched than the other graduates in all regions of employment, conceivably demonstrating the rewarding role of entrepreneurship in terms of skill application across geographical areas (the magnitude of the coefficients of the variable Self_emp is impressive in all cases, and particularly in the equation for the South). The opposite is true for graduates who had previous job experience, who seem invariably less likely to achieve a good education–job match independently on geography: this might hint to a worse capacity of integrating in the labour markets of those who had to work before and/or during their university studies, presumably because of personal financial constraints. Whilst the coefficient for salary is, as expected, generally positive, it is significant only for the models for Italy and the North; seniority does not seem to impact on education job match, and actually it even shows a negative and significant role in the North regression.

Turning to personal characteristics, whereas gender has no effect on education–job match in any of the four models, in line with previous results being a female graduate definitely decreases the probability of finding a job across geographical boundaries. Among the explanatory variables inserted only in the selection equations – insofar as, following the literature, they are likely to bear an impact on employability, more than determining over-education versus a more favourable match – age does not show any impact on the probability of being employed, as well as the social background of the graduate (in terms of having at least one parent with university degree, i.e. Par_uni), which even turns out to exert a negative and significant effect on in the regression for the North. The variables PhD, Training and Otheredu, are – as expected – negative and significant across the models. Finally, geographical differences are reflected in the remarkably lower probability of graduates from the Centre and the South (as regions of university study) to be employed than those from the North, whereas having studied in a large city (Uni_city) seems to exert a positive and significant effect on employability in the regression for the North.[13]

DISCUSSION AND CONCLUSIONS

The aim of this paper was to test empirically whether and where interregional migration has an impact on the education job matches at the early stage of graduates' professional career. In so doing, particular attention was paid to graduates leaving the Southern regions of Italy, adding a more geographic-specific perspective on the determinants of over-education. Such a perspective has indeed proved to be critical in understanding the learning processes and outcomes associated with

graduate migration, and ultimately underpinning regional economic evolution.

The findings confirm, for the national model, previous empirical literature on the positive role that interregional migration exerts both on decreasing the probability of real over-education – i.e. the combination of both overqualification and underutilization of the graduate's skills and capabilities – and on increasing the likelihood of finding a job. However, remarkable differences emerge when looking at the sub-national dimension: whilst in the North – characterized by the most dynamic regional economic and innovation systems – migration significantly increases the likelihood of achieving a better education–job match, this is not the case for migrants to the Centre, in spite of the weight of the capital region in terms of employment in the public sector, structurally associated with a lower level of over-education (DEVILLANOVA, 2013). Furthermore, whilst the North does not provide more job opportunities to migrants with respect to the local graduates, here the inflows of human capital, and particularly those from the Southern regions, seem to find a better fit between their own competences and the highly diversified economic structure of the area. Hence, the benefits of migration – general, if looking at the national case – seem to be particularly pronounced for those migrants coming to work in the North after graduating in the more peripheral and disadvantaged Mezzogiorno regions.

In the traditional role of 'vector of regional convergence' assigned to labour mobility by classical economics, the North of Italy emerges, once again, as a net winner: not only it gains from public investment in higher education made in other regions of the country, but it is also able to ensure a more productive use of such an investment than other areas. On the other hand, the analysis offers support to the more general story that the Mezzogiorno's enduring productive capacity constraint pushes part of its endogenously created human capital somewhere else in order to be employed (see also CRESCENZI et al., 2014). However, graduates who stayed seem to incur less in over-education, while those who leave finds a more favourable application of their own competences in other parts of the country – indicating an overall strong capacity of getting integrated in the local job markets of destination.

These preliminary results need obviously further validation and extension: yet, they do seem to put in question the common perception of a lower quality of Southern university systems. Graduates from the South of Italy seem relatively better off in terms of education–job match if they do find a job in the same area: often, however, this is not the case, as the very low employment rate shows, consistently with the unemployment rate in the Mezzogiorno compared with the rest of the country: in the year of the survey, 2007, whilst the national average was 6.1%, the North displayed an unemployment rate of 3.5%, against the

11% in the South (ISTAT, 2014).[14] Those graduates that then decide to move to other parts of the country, and especially to the Northern regions, are benefitting from such an interregional mobility far more than the others, either migrants or stayers.

Future research should dig further in the distinction between qualification and skill utilization, and in the four categories of real and apparent over-education and match. Following DEVILLANOVA (2013), it is concluded that the positive effect of spatial mobility on education–job match needs additional investigation, particularly by assuming geographically specific research perspectives. A better understanding of the profiles needed at the territorial level should have critical implications for public policies targeting the gap between the demand and the supply of competences and skills. At the same time, more effective regionally designed interventions for the expansion and diversification of the Southern economic and innovation systems are extremely urgent, especially in light of the rising competition from global markets, which has made even more apparent the vulnerability of the Mezzogiorno's productive system as a whole. Education–job match is likely to be achieved only by enabling complementary and coordinated efforts on both demand and supply of skills and upgrading and diversification of local economic structures.

Acknowledgements – The authors thank the participants at: the European Seminar EuroLIO Geography of Innovation, St Etienne, France, January 2012; the AAG 2012 Annual Meeting, New York, United States, February 2012; and the Regional Studies Association European Conference, Delft, Netherlands, May 2012. All errors and omissions remain the own.

Funding – The authors gratefully acknowledge funding from the European Community's Seventh Framework Programme (FP7/2007-2013) [grant agreement number 266959].

SUPPLEMENTARY DATA

Supplemental data for this article can be accessed at http://dx.doi.org.10.1080/00343404.2014.965135

NOTES

1. A rather abundant stream of literature refers to international migration and general over-education (i.e. not specifically at the university level) (e.g. QUINN and RUBB, 2005; CHISWICK and MILLER, 2009).
2. On the limitations of all three measures of education–job match, see SLOANE (2003) and SGOBBI and SULEMAN (2013).

3. For alternative indicators based on the *Indagine*, see also DI PIETRO and URWIN (2006) and QUINTANO *et al.* (2008).
4. In placing *apparent over-education* below *apparent match* in the ordered scale, it was assumed that the a graduate's judgement on skills use is more relevant than the employer's assessment. This choice is supported in the results by strongly significant coefficients for the cut-off points. Nevertheless, the robustness tests collapsed the two categories and the key results of the analysis remain stable (see note 13).
5. For the definition of the mobility categories, see the variable list in Table 4.
6. Current routines available in STATA do not allow accounting, at the same time, for self-selection and endogeneity in ordered models. It is thus necessary to use an approximation and, to do so, the approach of ARENDT and HOLMES (2006) – who focus on a binary dependent – was extended into the ordered dependent variable.
7. IMR is the ratio of the probability density function to the cumulative distribution function of a distribution.
8. This definition of interregional mobility (as well as that more articulated used in the outcome equation) is clearly limited, as it does not distinguish between those who moved to return to their home region – having studied somewhere else – from the rest. Unfortunately, the *Indagine* does not allow such a distinction to be performed; however, one robustness check takes this aspect into account, following the methodology devised by MARINELLI (2013).
9. Different specifications were explored: the final choice was based on indicators of goodness of fit, such as pseudo-R^2 (0.3007) and the percentage of correctly predicted cases (83.7%).
10. The migration regression uses the expanded version for this variable (nine fields). The reason is that whilst in the migration equation the main concern was the predictive power of the model, in the employment and education–job match models the option was for a more parsimonious specification.
11. As a robustness check, regressions were also run on the binary indicators based on the questions of the survey (see the third section). The results are available from the authors on request.
12. In the analysis, graduates who are in seasonal employment are excluded as well as graduates who started their current job before the end of their degree (about 9% of the total sample), as the *Indagine* does not provide information on their education–job match.
13. To check further the robustness of the findings and the indicators, the ordered models were also estimated with an alternative variable, collapsing the categories of Apparent over-education and Apparent match. Furthermore, given the aforementioned limitations of the used definition of migration, a method was applied to distinguish (and exclude) tentatively returners from migrants in the *Indagine*, as defined by MARINELLI (2013). The results across the different specifications confirm the main results on interregional migration as a means to reduce over-education, particularly when migrating from the South.

14. Unemployment has not improved after the recent crisis, and for 2013, while Italy as a whole reported a rate of 12.2%, the Southern regions had a share around 20%, double and more than double than those for the Centre (10.9%) and for the North (8.4%) respectively.

REFERENCES

ALLEN J. and VAN DER VELDEN R. (2001) Educational mismatches versus skill mismatches: effects on wages, job satisfaction and on-the-job search, *Oxford Economic Papers* **53**, 434–452. doi:10.1093/oep/53.3.434

ARENDT J. N. and HOLM A. (2006) *Probit Models with Binary Endogenous Regressors.* CAM Working Paper No. 2006–06.

ASSOCIAZIONE PER LO SVILUPPO DELL'INDUSTRIA NEL MEZZOGIORNO (SVIMEZ) (2009) *Rapporto sull'economia del Mezzogiorno 2008.* Il Mulino, Bologna.

BARCA F. (2006) *Italia Frenata, Paradossi e Lezioni della Politica per lo Sviluppo.* Donzelli, Rome.

BATTU H., BELFIELD C. R. and SLOANE P. (1999) Overeducation among graduates: a cohort view, *Education Economics* **7**, 21–38. doi:10.1080/09645299900000002

BATTU H., BELFIELD C. R. and SLOANE P. J. (2000) How well can we measure graduate over-education and its effects?, *National Institute Economic Review* **171**, 82–93. doi:10.1177/002795010017100107

BIGGERI L., BINI M. and GRILLI L. (2001) The transition from university to work: a multilevel approach to the analysis of the time to obtain the first job, *Journal of the Royal Statistical Society: Series A (Statistics in Society)* **164**, 293–305. doi:10.1111/1467-985X.00203

BOUDARBAT B. and CHERNOFF V. (2010) *The Determinants of Education–Job Match among Canadian University Graduates.* Scientific Series, Ciranos Working Paper No. 14–2010.

BÜCHEL F. and VAN HAM M. (2003) Overeducation, regional labor markets and spatial flexibility, *Journal of Urban Economics* **53**, 482–493.

CHECCHI D. and DARDANONI V. (2002) Mobility comparisons: does using different measures matter?, *Research on Economic Inequality* **9**, 113–145. doi:10.1016/S1049-2585(03)09008-2

CHECCHI D. and PERAGINE V. (2005) *Regional Disparities and Inequality of Opportunity: The Case of Italy.* IZA Discussion Papers No. 1874. Institute for the Study of Labor (IZA), Bonn.

CHEVALIER A. (2003) Measuring over-education, *Economica* **70**, 509–531. doi:10.1111/1468-0335.t01-1-00296

CHISWICK B. R. and MILLER P. W. (2009) The international transferability of immigrants' human capital, *Economics of Education Review* **28**, 162–169. doi:10.1016/j.econedurev.2008.07.002

CONIGLIO N. and PERAGINE V. (2007) Giovani al Sud: tra immobilità sociale e mobilità territoriale, in CONIGLIO N. and FERRI G. (Eds) *Primo Rapporto Banche e Mezzogiorno.* Banca Carime-University of Bari, Bari.

CONSOLI D., VONA F. and SAARIVIRTA T. (2013) Analysis of the graduate labour market in Finland: spatial agglomeration and skill–job match, *Regional Studies* **47**, 1634–1652. doi:10.1080/00343404.2011.603721

CRESCENZI R., GAGLIARDI L. and PERCOCO M. (2013) Social capital and the innovative performance of Italian provinces, *Environment and Planning A* **45**, 908–929. doi:10.1068/a45221

CRESCENZI R., GAGLIARDI L. and ORRU' E. (2014) *Learning Mobility Grants and Skill (Mis)Matching in the Labour Market. The Case of the 'Master and Back' Programme.* Mimeo. London School of Economics and Political Science (LSE), London.

CROCE G. and GHIGNONI E. (2011) *Overeducation and Spatial Flexibility in Italian Local Labour Markets.* MPRA Working Paper No. 29670, October.

D'ANTONIO M. and SCARLATO M. (2007) *I Laureati del Mezzogiorno: Una Risorsa Sottoutilizzata o Dispersa.* Quaderni SVIMEZ. Associazione per lo Sviluppo dell'Industria nel Mezzogiorno (SVIMEZ), Rome.

DE GRIP A., FOUARGE D. and SAUERMANN J. (2010) What affects international migration of European science and engineering graduates?, *Economics of Innovation and New Technology* **19**, 407–421. doi:10.1080/10438590903434828

DEKKER R., DE GRIP A. and HEIJKE H. (2002) The effects of training and overeducation on career mobility in a segmented labour market, *International Journal of Manpower* **23**, 106–125. doi:10.1108/01437720210428379

DEVILLANOVA C. (2013) Over-education and spatial flexibility: new evidence from Italian survey data, *Papers in Regional Science* **92**, 445–464.

DI LIBERTO A. (2007) Education and Italian regional development, *Economics of Education Review* **27**, 94–107. doi:10.1016/j.econedurev.2006.08.004

DI PIETRO G. and URWIN P. (2006) Education and skills mismatch in the Italian graduate labour market, *Applied Economics* **38**, 79–93. doi:10.1080/00036840500215303

DOLTON P. J. and SILLES M. A. (2008) The effects of over-education on earnings in the graduate labour market, *Economics of Education Review* **27**, 125–139. doi:10.1016/j.econedurev.2006.08.008

DOLTON P. J. and VIGNOLES A. (2000) The incidence and effects of overeducation in the U.K. graduate labour market, *Economics of Education Review* **19**, 179–198. doi:10.1016/S0272-7757(97)00036-8

DOTTI N. F., FRATESI U., LENZI C. and PERCOCO M. (2012) *Local Labour Markets and the Interregional Mobility of Italian University Students.* Working Paper BEST. Politecnico di Milano, Milan.

ETZKOWITZ H. and LEYDESDORFF L. (Eds) (1997) *Universities in the Global Economy: A Triple Helix of University–Industry–Government Relations.* Cassell Academic, London.

FAGGIAN A. and MCCANN P. (2006) Human capital flows and regional knowledge assets: a simultaneous equation approach, *Oxford Economic Papers* **58**, 475–500. doi:10.1093/oep/gpl010

FAGGIAN A. and McCANN P. (2009) Human capital, graduate migration and innovation in British regions, *Cambridge Journal of Economics* **33**, 317–333.

FRENKEN K., VAN OORT F. G. and VERBURG T. (2007) Related variety, unrelated variety and regional economic growth, *Regional Studies* **41**, 685–697.

GARCÍA-ESPEJO I. and IBÁÑEZ M. (2006) Educational–skill matches and labour achievements among graduates in Spain, *European Sociological Review* **22**, 141–156. doi:10.1093/esr/jci048

GREEN F. and McINTOSH S. (2007) Is there a genuine under-utilization of skills amongst the over-qualified?, *Applied Economics* **39**, 427–439. doi:10.1080/00036840500427700

GREEN F. and ZHU Y. (2010) Overqualification, job dissatisfaction, and increasing dispersion in the returns to graduate education, *Oxford Economic Papers* **62**, 740–763.

GROOT W. and MAASSEN VAN DEN BRINK H. (2000) Overeducation in the labor market: a meta-analysis, *Economics of Education Review* **19**, 149–158. doi:10.1016/S0272-7757(99)00057-6

GULBRANDSEN M., MOWERY D. and FELDMAN M. (2011) Introduction to the special section: Heterogeneity and university–industry relations, *Research Policy* **40**, 1–5. doi:10.1016/j.respol.2010.09.007

HARTOG J. (2000) Mismatch and earnings: where are we, where should we go?, *Economics of Education Review* **19**, 131–147. doi:10.1016/S0272-7757(99)00050-3

HEALY A. and MORGAN K. (2009) *Spaces of Innovation: Learning, Proximity and the Ecological Turn*. Papers in Evolutionary Economic Geography (PEEG) No. 0918. Utrecht University, Utrecht.

HECKMAN J. J. (1979) Sample selection bias as a specification error, *Econometrica* **47**, 153–161. doi:10.2307/1912352

HEIJKE H., MENG C. and RIS C. (2003) Fitting to the job: the role of generic and vocational competencies in adjustment and performance, *Labour Economics* **10**, 215–229. doi:10.1016/S0927-5371(03)00013-7

HENSEN M. M., DE VRIES M. R. and CÖRVERS F. (2009) The role of geographic mobility in reducing education–job mismatches in the Netherlands, *Papers in Regional Science* **88**, 667–682. doi:10.1111/j.1435-5957.2008.00189.x

HOOGSTRA G. J., VAN DIJK J. and FLORAX R. J. G. M. (2011) Determinants of variation in population–employment interaction findings: a quasi-experimental meta-analysis, *Geographical Analysis* **43**, 4–37. doi:10.1111/j.1538-4632.2010.00806.x

IAMMARINO S. (2005) An evolutionary integrated view of regional systems of innovation. Concepts, measures and historical perspectives, *European Planning Studies* **13**, 495–517.

IAMMARINO S. and MARINELLI E. (2011) Is the grass greener on the other side of the fence? Graduate mobility and job satisfaction in Italy, *Environment and Planning A* **43**, 2761–2777. doi:10.1068/a44126

ISTITUTO NAZIONALE DI STATISTICA (ISTAT) (2005) *L'Istruzione della Popolazione al 2001. Dati Definitivi del Censimento.* ISTAT, Rome.

ISTITUTO NAZIONALE DI STATISTICA (ISTAT) (2006) *I Laureati e il Mercato del Lavoro.* ISTAT, Rome.

ISTITUTO NAZIONALE DI STATISTICA (ISTAT) (2010) *Indagine Campionaria sull'Inserimento Professionale dei Laureati.* ISTAT, Rome.

ISTITUTO NAZIONALE DI STATISTICA (ISTAT) (2014) *Tasso di disoccupazione – livello ripartizionale* (available at: http://dati.istat.it/Index.aspx?DataSetCode=DCCV_TAXDISOCCU).

JAUHIAINEN S. (2011) Overeducation in the Finnish regional labour markets, *Papers in Regional Science* **90**, 573–588. doi:10.1111/j.1435-5957.2010.00334.x

KRABEL S. and FLÖTHER C. (2014) Here today, gone tomorrow? Regional labour mobility of German university graduates, *Regional Studies* **48**, 1609–1627. doi:10.1080/00343404.2012.739282

MARINELLI E. (2011) Graduates on the move: knowledge flows and Italian regional disparities. Migration patterns of 2001 graduates. PhD thesis, London School of Economics and Political Sciences (LSE), London.

MARINELLI E. (2013) Sub-national graduate mobility and knowledge flows: an exploratory analysis of onward- and return-migrants in Italy, *Regional Studies* **47**, 1618–1633. doi:10.1080/00343404.2012.709608

McGUINNESS S. (2006) Overeducation in the labour market, *Journal of Economic Surveys* **20**, 387–418. doi:10.1111/j.0950-0804.2006.00284.x

McGUINNESS S. and WOODEN M. (2009) Overskilling, job insecurity, and career mobility, *Industrial Relations: Journal of Economy and Society* **48**, 265–286. doi:10.1111/j.1468-232X.2009.00557.x

MELICIANI V. and RADICCHIA D. (2014) Informal networks, spatial mobility and overeducation in the Italian labour market. Paper presented at the CIMR Workshop on Scientific Labour Markets and Innovation Systems, CIMR, Birkbeck, University of London, London, UK, 4 July 2014.

MIRANDA A. and RABE-HESKETH S. (2006) Maximum likelihood estimation of endogenous switching and sample selection models for binary, ordinal, and count variables, *Stata Journal* **6**, 208–308.

MORGAN K. (1997) The learning region: institutions, innovation and regional renewal, *Regional Studies* **31**, 491–503.

MOWERY D. C. and SAMPAT B. N. (2005) The Bayh–Dole Act of 1980 and university–industry technology transfer: a model for other OECD governments?, *Journal of Technology Transfer* **30**, 115–127. doi:10.1007/s10961-004-4361-z

NELSON R. R. and PHELPS E. S. (1966) Investments in humans, technology diffusion and economic growth, *American Economic Review* **1/2**, 69–75.

PAVITT K. (1991) What makes basic research economically useful?, *Research Policy* **20**, 109–119. doi:10.1016/0048-7333(91)90074-Z

PIRAS R. (2005) Il contenuto di capitale umano dei flussi migratori interregionali: 1980–2002, *Politica Economica* **21**, 461–491.

PIRAS R. (2006) I movimenti migratori interregional per titolo di studio: una stima dei tassi migratori ed un'analisi dei flussi, *Studi di Emigrazione* **43**, 153–170.

QUINN M. A. and RUBB S. (2005) The importance of education–occupation matching in migration decisions, *Demography* **42**, 153–167. doi:10.1353/dem.2005.0008

QUINTANO C., CASTELLANO R. and D'AGOSTINO A. (2008) Graduates in economics and educational mismatch: the case study of the university of Naples 'Parthenope', *Journal of Education and Work* **21**, 249–271. doi:10.1080/13639080802214118

RAMOS R. and SANROMÀ E. (2011) *Overeducation and Local Labour Markets in Spain*. IZA DP No. 6028, October 2011. Institute for the Study of Labor (IZA), Bonn.

ROBST J. (2007) Education and job match: the relatedness of college major and work, *Economics of Education Review* **26**, 397–407. doi:10.1016/j.econedurev.2006.08.003

RODRÍGUEZ-POSE A. and TSELIOS V. (2010) Returns to migration, education and externalities in the European Union, *Papers in Regional Science* **89**, 411–434. doi:10.1111/j.1435-5957.2010.00297.x

RODRÍGUEZ-POSE A. and TSELIOS V. (2012) Individual earnings and educational externalities in the European Union, *Regional Studies* **46**, 39–57.

ROSEN S. (1972) Learning and experience in the labour market, *Journal of Human Resources* **7**, 326–42. doi:10.2307/145087

ROSENBERG N. and NELSON R. R. (1994) American universities and technical advance in industry, *Research Policy* **23**, 323–348. doi:10.1016/0048-7333(94)90042-6

SALTER A. J. and MARTIN B. R. (2001) The economic benefits of publicly funded basic research: a critical review, *Research Policy* **30**, 509–532. doi:10.1016/S0048-7333(00)00091-3

SGOBBI F. and SULEMAN F. (2013) A methodological contribution to measuring skills (mis)match, *Manchester School* **81**, 420–437. doi:10.1111/j.1467-9957.2012.02294.x

SICHERMAN N. (1991) 'Overeducation' in the labor market, *Journal of Labor Economics* **9**, 101–122. doi:10.1086/298261

SLOANE P. J. (2003) Much ado about nothing? What does the over-education literature really tell us?, in BÜCHEL F., DEGRIP A. and MERTENS A. (Eds) *Overeducation in Europe: Current Issues in Theory and Policy*, pp. 11–48. Edward Elgar, Cheltenham.

UNGARO P. and VERZICCO L. (2005) Misura e analisi del rendimento dei titoli di studio superiori nella fase di primo inserimento nel mondo del lavoro. Paper presented at the XXth Convegno Nazionale di Economia del Lavoro, Rome, Italy, 22–23 September 2005.

VACCARO R. (1995) *Unità Politica e Dualismo Economico in Italia: 1861–1993*. Cedam, Padua.

VAN DER KLAAUW B. and VAN VUUREN A. (2010) Job search and academic achievement, *European Economic Review* **54**, 294–316. doi:10.1016/j.euroecorev.2009.07.001

VANDENBUSSCHE J., AGHION P. and MEGHIR C. (2006) Growth, distance to frontier and composition of human capital, *Journal of Economic Growth* **11**, 97–127.

VENHORST V. A. and CÖRVERS F. (2011) *Entry into Working Life: Spatial Mobility and Job Match Quality of Higher Educated Graduates*. Mimeopn. Faculty of Spatial Science, University of Groningen, Groningen.

VERHAEST D. and OMEY E. (2006) The impact of overeducation and its measurement, *Social Indicators Research* **77**, 419–448. doi:10.1007/s11205-005-4276-6

VIESTI G. (2003) *Abolire il Mezzogiorno*. Laterza, Bari.

VON TUNZELMANN N. (2009) Regional capabilities and industrial regeneration, in FARSHCHI M., JANNE O. and MCCANN P. (Eds) *Technological Change and Mature Industrial Regions: Firms, Knowledge and Policy*, pp. 11–28. Edward Elgar, Cheltenham.

VON TUNZELMANN N. and WANG Q. (2007) Capabilities and production theory, *Structural Change and Economic Dynamics* **18**, 192–211. doi:10.1016/j.strueco.2006.11.002

WALD S. and FANG T. (2008) Overeducated immigrants in the Canadian labour market: evidence from the workplace and employee survey, *Canadian Public Policy* **34**, 457–479. doi:10.3138/cpp.34.4.457

WALTERS D. (2004) The relationship between postsecondary education and skill: comparing credentialism with human capital theory, *Canadian Journal of Higher Education* **34**, 97–124.

WOLBERS M. H. J. (2003) Job mismatches and their labour-market effects among school-leavers in Europe, *European Sociological Review* **19**, 249–266. doi:10.1093/esr/19.3.249

Knowledge Neighbourhoods: Urban Form and Evolutionary Economic Geography

GREGORY M. SPENCER

Munk School of Global Affairs, University of Toronto, 1 Devonshire Place, Toronto.

SPENCER G. M. Knowledge neighbourhoods: urban form and evolutionary economic geography, *Regional Studies*. This paper examines connections between the urban form of neighbourhoods in relation to the evolutionary economic geography of knowledge-intensive industries. The data presented show that firms in 'creative' industries tend to be located in dense, mixed-use neighbourhoods near the city core, while 'science-based' industries tend to be concentrated in low-density, single-use neighbourhoods in the suburbs. It is argued that these spatial patterns are related to the fact that inter-firm networks are more important in the 'creative' industries, while 'science-based' industries rely more heavily on intra-firm interactions and learning.

SPENCER G. M. 知识的邻里：城市形态与演化经济地理学，区域研究。本文检视邻里的城市形态与知识密集产业的演化经济地理之间的连结。本文呈现的数据显示，"创意"产业中的企业，倾向座落于临近市中心的高密度、混合使用的邻里，而"以科技为基础"的产业，则倾向聚集于郊区中低密度、单一使用的邻里。本文主张，这些空间形式，与企业间的网络对"创意"产业更为重要、"以科技为基础"的产业则更大量倚赖企业内部的互动与学习的事实相关。

SPENCER G. M. Les quartiers de la connaissance: la forme urbaine et la géographie économique évolutionniste, *Regional Studies*. Ce présent article cherche à examiner les liens entre la forme urbaine des quartiers par rapport à la géographie économique évolutionniste des industries à haute intensité de connaissance. Les données présentées montrent que les entreprises des industries 'créatives' ont tendance à s'implanter dans les quartiers très peuplés à usages mixtes situés près du noyau urbain, alors que les industries 'à vocation scientifique' tendent à se concentrer dans les quartiers de banlieue à population faible et à usage unique. On affirme que ces configurations spatiales se rapportent au fait que les réseaux interentreprises s'avèrent plus importants dans les industries 'créatives', tandis que les industries 'à vocation scientifique' sont fortement tributaires des interactions intraentreprises et de l'apprentissage.

SPENCER G. M. Nachbarschaften des Wissens: urbane Form und evolutionäre Wirtschaftsgeografie, *Regional Studies*. In diesem Beitrag werden die Verbindungen zwischen der urbanen Form von Nachbarschaften in Beziehung auf die evolutionäre Wirtschaftsgeografie von wissensintensiven Branchen untersucht. Aus den gezeigten Daten geht hervor, dass sich Firmen in 'kreativen' Branchen tendenziell eher in dicht besiedelten Nachbarschaften mit gemischter Nutzung in der Nähe des Stadtkerns ansiedeln, während sich 'wissenschaftsbasierte' Branchen eher in dünn besiedelten Nachbarschaften mit einzelner Nutzung in den Vorstädten konzentrieren. Es wird argumentiert, dass diese räumlichen Muster mit der Tatsache zusammenhängen, dass Netzwerke zwischen Firmen in den 'kreativen' Branchen wichtiger sind, während 'wissenschaftsbasierte' Branchen stärker auf Wechselwirkungen und Lernprozesse innerhalb der Firma angewiesen sind.

SPENCER G. M. Barrios de conocimiento: forma urbana y geografía económica evolutiva, *Regional Studies*. En este artículo se analizan las conexiones entre la forma urbana de los barrios con relación a la geografía económica evolutiva de las industrias de conocimiento intensivo. Los datos presentados indican que las empresas en industrias 'creativas' tienden a ubicase en barrios densamente poblados de uso mixto cerca de centros urbanos, mientras que las industrias 'basadas en la ciencia' suelen estar concentradas en barrios con una baja densidad de población de uso individual en los suburbios. Se argumenta que estos patrones espaciales están relacionados con el hecho de que las redes entre empresas son más importantes en las industrias 'creativas', mientras que las industrias 'basadas en la ciencia' confían más en las interacciones y el aprendizaje dentro de cada empresa.

INTRODUCTION

Diversity is a central principle of evolutionary theory. Specifically, it is a central component of branching and recombination processes that tend to reinforce one another over time. Jane Jacobs (JACOBS, 1961, 1969, 2000) is often credited with making explicit the connections between evolutionary economic processes and local diversity arguing that sustained urban vitality depends on a constant churn of people and ideas. This view is often contrasted with what has become known as the Marshall–Arrow–Romer (MAR) view (MARSHALL, 1890; ARROW, 1962; ROMER, 1986) that local specialization is essential for sustained growth. Research from the emerging field of evolutionary economic geography has directly entered the Jacobs–MAR debate particularly with an effort to find a middle ground with the concept of 'related variety' (FRENKEN et al., 2007). Many studies have attempted to address this debate empirically but without achieving any semblance of consensus (BEAUDRY and SCHIFFAUEROVA, 2009). The majority of such research involves using structural indicators of industrial diversity/specialization at the regional scale in order to find statistical relationships with growth. This type of analysis, however, represents only half of the formulation presented by Jacobs who was at least as, if not more, concerned with how specific urban environments have a direct impact on social interaction and ultimately the production of knowledge. This paper takes a closer look at the evolutionary social processes of knowledge production by taking a closer look at the urban form of the neighbourhoods in which particular knowledge-intensive industries tend to be spatially concentrated.

Specifically, detailed firm-level data are mapped onto three city regions (Montreal, Toronto and Vancouver) in order to demonstrate stark differences in sub-regional spatial patterns of industrial location. The results show that creative firms are heavily concentrated in central areas that are highly congruent with Jacobs's notion of vibrant and diverse urban environments that she contends play a direct and important role in evolutionary socio-economic processes. Conversely, science-based firms tend to locate in more homogeneous suburban neighbourhoods that Jacobs suggests are detrimental to the same knowledge-based processes of social interaction and learning. This provokes some important questions pertaining to the further development of evolutionary economic geography:

- How might urban form impact evolutionary economic and learning processes? Are certain industries influenced by urban form to a greater degree?

- How might one detect the impact of urban form on the evolutionary and learning processes of various industries? Does one need to consider sub-regional scales?
- Can/should planners and designers work with economic development practitioners to create urban environments that facilitate these processes?

These questions are addressed from a theoretical perspective by drawing connections between the evolutionary economic geography literature with emerging work on different knowledge bases as well as sub-regional explorations of knowledge-intensive industries. From an empirical perspective these connections are investigated using address-level firm data in conjunction with detailed contextual data on various aspects of urban form in order to highlight the differences in local environments between 'creative neighbourhoods' and 'science neighbourhoods'. This paper presents each of these in turn before discussing the possible implications to the development of evolutionary economic geography theory and future research.

EVOLUTIONARY PROCESSES AND ECONOMIC GEOGRAPHY

A basic and central question to economic geography is 'why does economic activity occur where it does?'. Putting neo-classical economic theories into spatial context is one of the traditional approaches that is widely practised. Specifically, models of the increasing returns to agglomeration are a major contribution to economic geography. Institutional approaches also have a long history of offering explanations to uneven spatial development particularly in conjunction with the notion that economic activity is embedded with social relations (GRANOVETTER, 1985) and local cultures (GERTLER, 1995). More recently, these dominant paradigms have been increasingly questioned on the basis that they are not able to account fully for the complex path-dependent processes that (re)produce the spatial distribution of economic activities (MARTIN and SUNLEY, 2007). To this point BOSCHMA and FRENKEN (2006) propose that an evolutionary science approach to economic geography is warranted on the basis that it combines formal modelling (neo-classical) with the recognition of heterogeneity (institutional) while directly addressing processes such as search (MASKELL and MALMBERG, 2007), recombination (WEITZMAN, 1998; DESROCHERS, 2001), and branching (FRENKEN and BOSCHMA,

2007) that have the potential to provide detailed explanations of economic activities and their geographies.

In a general sense, the recent attempts to develop a more formal evolutionary economic geography approach needs to be placed in context of the wider movement that explores the role of knowledge and its production in economic growth and regional development. SCHUMPETER (1942) in particular, initiated a great deal of thought and research on technological innovation and its impact on economic growth. One of the key aspects of this work is the recognition that innovation is both path dependent and, at times, disruptive. There are a great deal of similarities between DARWIN'S (1859) evolutionary processes and innovation processes such as recombination and branching. JACOBS (1969) also seized on these ideas in her application of these processes to diversity within urban contexts due to divisions of labour based on increasing specializations. With each of these examples a central notion is that the evolutionary processes are fundamentally concerned with social interaction, and specifically the collision of differentiated knowledge. Such notions have a longstanding tradition in urban sociology, exemplarily represented by Wirth's understanding that the city has

> been the melting-pot of races, people, and cultures, and a most favorable breeding-ground of new biological and cultural hybrids. It has not only tolerated but rewarded individual differences. It has brought together people from the ends of the earth because they are different and thus useful to one another, rather than because they are homogeneous and like-minded.
>
> (WIRTH, 1938, p. 10)

This is also the point at which geography becomes an essential component of the equation in that social interaction is not a-spatial. Despite advances in information and communications technologies, face-to-face contact (STORPER and VENABLES, 2004) and proximity (BOSCHMA, 2005) remain vital to processes of social interaction and learning. In short, the geography of knowledge is both persistent and changing.

BOSCHMA and FRENKEN (2006) propose that this geography is generated across a variety of scales, from the micro/firm level at which routines are constructed, to the meso-level of industrial sectors (related firms) and networks (relationships), to the macro-level geography of the spatial system. This model provides a useful framework to explain where this paper seeks to make a contribution. The contention in this paper is that at the meso-level there are significant differences in the knowledge bases that constitute the different industrial sectors. Furthermore, there are key differences in the social processes (and network structures) that produce each type of knowledge. This in turn suggests that the role of the firm may vary depending on the specific type of knowledge, and that ultimately there are important implications for the overall spatial system.

KNOWLEDGE TYPES AND SOCIAL PROCESSES

There are a number of literatures that explore the differences between types of knowledge. While there is no specific model that can integrate each perspective, they do generally conform to the notion of a spectrum between artistic/cultural knowledge and scientific knowledge. There is also general agreement that the underlying social process vary somewhat across this spectrum. These differences are also reflected semantically as 'creativity' is most often associated with the arts, 'innovation' with technology, and 'discovery' is most often used in conjunction with science. The psychology literature on creativity offers some detailed insights into how the production of artistic-based knowledge may vary from the production of science-based knowledge. STERNBERG and LUBART (1996) make a distinction between 'open' and 'closed' problem solving whereby 'closed' problems have specific answers while 'open' ones do not. AMABILE (1996) makes a similar distinction between heuristic knowledge production and algorithmic knowledge production, whereby the former can only be truly considered 'creativity'. The key difference is that heuristic knowledge production is based on the subjective values of both the creator and the evaluators, while algorithmic knowledge production is observable and repeatable by others who should come to the same conclusions. Little if any knowledge production can be purely subjective or objective, but these two ideal types can prove useful as ends of a conceptual spectrum of knowledge production. For example, FIEST (1999) employs such a framework when examining the differences in the personality traits of highly respected artists and scientists.

The economic geography literature recognizes these distinctions in similar ways. SANTAGATA (2004), for instance, claims that creativity is 'non-utilitarian' as opposed to innovation which is motivated by specific and measurable *improvement*. Furthermore, he suggests that creativity is less path dependent than scientific endeavours. Different types of knowledge have also been directly applied to classifying industries. A leading example of this uses three distinct 'knowledge bases' (symbolic, synthetic and analytic) (ASHEIM and GERTLER, 2005; ASHEIM and HANSEN, 2009) as its organizing framework. Symbolic knowledge is ascribed to cultural and creative industries as it involves a high level of aesthetic value. Analytic knowledge is associated with science-intensive industries in that it requires a firmly rational, deductive approach. As its name suggests, synthetic knowledge is driven by making new combinations of existing knowledge in new and valuable ways and is mainly connected to industries with a technological focus. SPENCER (2011) proposes a similar classification system that emphasizes variations in knowledge production processes. He proposes a spectrum of processes from (artistic) creativity which is based on human experience and one's understanding of it to (scientific) discovery which is based on the material world and one's ability to explain it. Situated between these poles is (technological) innovation which is based on applying scientific knowledge in order to somehow improve human experience. The key message of these literatures is that 'knowledge' needs to be conceived in a pluralistic manner. Furthermore, this has important implications for understanding how knowledge is produced by a variety of processes.

CONVERGENT VERSUS DIVERGENT THINKING, NETWORKS AND FIRMS

While there are a number of ways to segment types of knowledge perhaps the most important to the main argument being made in this paper is the degree to which types of knowledge require divergent thinking versus convergent thinking. Divergent thinking is typically associated with the creative process whereby there is no single answer to a problem and so many possible solutions are sought. With convergent thinking there is a single optimal way to solve a problem and which involves bringing together existing knowledge in a novel way. If one can agree to the stylized fact that creative and cultural industries rely more heavily on divergent thinking and science and technology industries depend more on convergent thinking then this has potential implications for both networks and the role of the firm. From a network perspective this suggests that it may be more of an imperative for people in creative and cultural industries to cast a wider net for knowledge and information. To this end, more weak ties (GRANOVETTER, 1973) and bridging of structural holes in networks (BURT, 1992) would be considered more important. In this case it would be crucial for firms to place themselves in a position to maximize exposure to as wide a range of influences as possible. From a spatial system perspective this would mean being situated in a highly diverse environment. For science and technology firms the key impetus may be to locate in a region where the range of specialized skills. In this case the role of the firm is to access and organize these skills in order to solve specific problems. Indeed, BROWN and DUGUID (2000) suggest that within Silicon Valley, one of the most important roles of the firm is to organize and connect skilled people that would otherwise not likely interact. Diversity at the regional level may be important to both creative and science-based industries, but they may differ significantly in terms of how they access and organize it.

There is a modest amount of evidence that suggests real and significant structural differences between creative industries and science-based industries that map onto the three-scale model of evolutionary processes

proposed by BOSCHMA and FRENKEN (2006). At the network level the 2008 Canadian General Social Survey shows that individuals working in creative and cultural occupations ($N = 277$) have the largest social networks of any occupational group. On average these individuals report maintaining 60 relationships with family, friends, and acquaintances while those working in science and technology occupations ($N = 732$) have on average only 46 connections. Furthermore, the data shows that this disparity is almost entirely accounted for by the number of local (same region) acquaintances that each group maintains relationships with. In network language this can be interpreted as meaning that creative and cultural workers require much larger weak-tie networks than science-based workers. The second key difference detected in the data is that science-based firms are on average 2.5 times larger than firms in creative industries. Data from Dun & Bradstreet indicate that creative[1] firms[2] have on average seven employees while the average for science-based firms is 17 employees. They key implication of these two basic pieces of data is that there are likely significant differences in the scale at which social processes of interaction and learning tend to occur. Creative industries are characterized by larger social networks but smaller firms while science-based industries tend to involve smaller social networks but larger firms. The main point here is that a greater amount of social interaction/learning is more likely to occur between firms in the case of creative industries and conversely social interaction/learning within firms is more prevalent in the case of science-based industries. To the extent that these processes are vital to the knowledge production and vitality of firms in each set of industries there are bound to have significant interrelationships with their respective spatial systems. It is this connection that is investigated in the empirical analysis of this paper.

JACOBS EXTERNALITIES

The role of diversity in urban economic growth and development remains an open question. Often formulated as contrasting the views of Jacobs with the MAR perspective that favours local specialization. They tend wholly to assume interaction between similar/dissimilar agents within local settings. This largely ignores the wider formulation proposed by JACOBS (1961) that the specific characteristic of urban form play a direct and important role in the social interaction and mixing of ideas that generate local dynamism. Arguably, the scale that mattered more to Jacobs was the neighbourhood. In particular, she argued that mixed land uses and a variety of building types within close proximity meant that not only would there be more social interaction but that diverse people would mix as a matter of course. Scott offers a contemporary take on this notion and adds that cities and their environments are not just containers of social interaction but directly reflect cultural norms and values. He relates that

> the creative field of the city can be seen, in short, as a system of cues and resources providing materials for imaginative appropriation by individuals and groups as they pursue the business of work and life in urban space. But it is also a sort of canvas on which creative and innovative acts are variously inscribed. Within this field, individuals are continually if intermittently entangled in transactional exchanges with one another, and in this manner they receive and emit signals that are variously charged with information.
>
> (SCOTT, 2010, p. 121)

A key point made by Scott is that the city does not simply act as a focal point for social interaction and learning but that there is are continual iterative processes between people and the environments which they inhabit. The main implication for the ideas proposed in this paper is that the particularities of urban environments play an active role in the creative process.

While the role of urban environments in knowledge-production processes has been frequently tested at the regional scale, there are also a number of examples of sub-regional research (CURRID and CONNOLLY, 2008). For science-based industries this research has often focused on science parks and includes a significant policy component and associated criticisms (MASSEY, QUINTAS, and WIELD, 1992; SHEARMUR and DOLOREUX, 2000). Furthermore, the effectiveness of science park developments in terms of increased knowledge production and economic competitiveness (WESTHEAD and BATSTONE, 1998). For the creative industries sub-regional geographies are commonly viewed as 'scenes' which take into account surrounding supporting activities and amenities such as cafes, restaurants, bars, and performance venues that blur the lines between production and consumption of cultural products (MOLOTCH, 2002; CURRID and WILLIAMS, 2010; SILVER et al., 2011). The literatures on science parks and creative scenes give mention to urban form, in neither instance is it often considered a central aspect of each place. This seems somewhat at odds with the role that space has in bringing people together (or keeping them apart) and how vital social interaction is to the production of knowledge. The empirical section of this paper examines the spatial arrangements of creative industries and science-based industries in three Canadian city-regions. Specifically, the urban form of 'creative' and 'science-based' neighbourhoods are compared on the basis of how they may affect patterns of social interaction, with a focus on interaction between firms.

AN ASSESSMENT OF URBAN FORM AND KNOWLEDGE TYPOLOGIES

Quantitative research on industrial clusters often utilizes data at the regional scale that enables comparisons to be made *between* places. A problem with this approach can be that nuances and variation *within* regions. This paper addresses this problem by using comprehensive firm-level data provided by Dun & Bradstreet in order to demonstrate stark differences of the spatial arrangements of creative industries and science-based industries within the three largest city-regions in Canada (Toronto, Montreal and Vancouver). Clear and consistent patterns of spatial concentration of these industries are evident in all three regions. Creative industries are found on the edge of the central business districts while the science industries tend to be located in suburban industrial and office parks. By examining the common characteristics of these distinct neighbourhoods one can begin to make inferences about the patterns of social interaction between workers in these firms.

The latest census figures report that the Toronto (5.6 million), Montreal (3.8 million) and Vancouver (2.3 million) regions account roughly one-third of the population of Canada. They are also the most economically diverse (BECKSTEAD and BROWN, 2003) and as they are the main gateways for immigrants to the country they are also home to the most culturally diverse populations. 'Creative' industries and 'science' industries are defined using a similar method to SPENCER (2011) that cross-tabulates the percentage of workers with post-secondary qualifications and the field of study in which their highest qualification was earned for detailed industries (four-digit NAICS; $N = 300$). From this method six creative industries and five science industries are identified (Table 1) as being the most archetypical cases that align with the twin concepts of creative and scientific knowledge production. Over half of all employment in 'creative' industries (57.1%) and 'science' industries (54.7%) in Canada is located in the three largest city-regions. This is a significantly disproportionate share as the location quotients for the two sets of industries across the three cities are 1.65 for the 'creative' industries and 1.58 for the 'science' industries. These results are similar for each group of industries for each individual city-region.

The data provided by Dun & Bradstreet include roughly 1.4 million individual records of establishments for the years 2001, 2006 and 2011 representing an estimated 98% of all establishments across all sectors. All three regions display similar industrial location patterns with the creative industry establishments heavily concentrated on the edge of the central business districts and the science industry establishments predominantly situated in suburban areas (see Appendices A–C in the Supplementary data online). These patterns are characterized by a series of contrasting traits. The creative industry neighbourhoods tend to be centrally located in older and denser areas that are highly accessible by public transportation, while the science industry neighbourhoods tend to be located in newer lower density areas, often in close proximity to the junctions of

Table 1. Overview of 'creative' and 'science' industries

	'Creative' industries			'Science' industries		
NAICS Codes' definitions	5121 Motion picture and video industries			3254 Pharmaceutical and medicine manufacturing		
	5122 Sound recording industries			5112 Software publishers		
	5151 Radio and television broadcasting			5415 Computer systems design and related services		
	5414 Specialized design services			5417 Scientific research and development services		
	7111 Performing arts companies			6215 Medical and diagnostic laboratories		
	7115 Independent artists, writers and performers					
	Employment	LQ	National share (%)	Employment	LQ	National share (%)
Montreal	43 550	1.62	18.4	68 455	1.61	18.4
Toronto	62 855	1.63	26.6	98 505	1.62	26.4
Vancouver	28 385	1.76	12.0	37 075	1.46	9.9
Three-region total	134 790	1.65	57.1	204 035	1.58	54.7

Note: LQ, location quotient.

major highways. There are also localized clusters of science industry firms in the city cores, which are mainly software businesses that have relationships to the finance industry and similar local customers. Average gross rents tend to be higher in creative neighbourhoods than in science neighbourhoods, although many creative firms choose the lower cost areas within the sub-markets of central areas while the opposite is true for science firms seeking higher quality and more expensive space in suburban markets. The urban/suburban patterns of creative/science firms seems to be irrespective of firm size and revenue. This suggests that traditional urban economic cost-based factors are not the main drivers of location decisions. Rather there seems to be a willingness, particularly of creative firms, to pay more in order to be in close physical proximity to similar businesses. The dense sub-regional agglomeration patterns of creative industries appear to be more relational in nature than economic. Both types of neighbourhoods usually have local anchors, but with the creative industries the anchors are just as likely to be institutional (higher education, public galleries and theatres) rather than large firms as is the tendency with the science-based industries.

There are also stark patterns associated with the residential patterns of professionals who work in each type of industry (see Appendix D in the Supplementary data online). Creative and cultural workers live in high numbers in the same neighbourhoods where creative industries are located. There is a high degree of overlap between home location and work location that suggests a high degree of overlap between home life and work life. This is congruent with research on various creative 'scenes' that expand on the notion that the economic and social dimensions of creative work are often inseparable. Perhaps the more surprising finding is that scientists also display residential preferences that appear to be in close proximity to areas with high level science industry employment. The difference, however, is that rather than being a symbiotic overlapping geography, scientists tend to live in

suburban neighbourhoods that are *adjacent to* locations with heavy concentrations of science industries. The lack of any direct overlap is mainly due to the strict separation of land uses in the suburban areas of these city regions. It is unclear as to whether a greater mixing of land uses would engender a similar pattern of overlap as seen with the creative industries. From such general spatial analysis there does not seem to be any compelling evidence of significant integration of work life in the science industry neighbourhoods.

The main implication of these patterns is the degree to which the spatial arrangements of work and residence may affect the probabilities of social interaction and learning beyond the intentional connection made through the course of a traditional workday. The denser, more urban, and overlapping geographies of the 'creative' industry workplaces and the homes of their workers suggests that the likelihood of interaction is greater than it is for the less dense, more suburban, and separated geographies of 'science' industry workplaces and residential neighbourhoods.

A more detailed examination of specific neighbourhoods in each of the regions helps to reveal even greater nuances in the contrasting spatial arrangements of science industries and creative industries. Figs 1–5 highlight pairs of science and creative neighbourhoods for each of the three regions in order to provide additional visual clues as to their specific characteristics. All maps are to the same scale, representing 4 km^2, so that direct comparisons can be made. Specifically, Fig. 1 shows that the densities of firms and employment are much higher in creative neighbourhoods than in science neighbourhoods. In many cases multiple creative business establishments are located in the same buildings and blocks, whereas the science firms are much more spatially diffused. These contrasting proximities suggest a higher probability of direct face-to-face interaction as well as serendipitous encounters in the creative neighbourhoods than in the science neighbourhoods. As was stated above, a great deal of this has to do with the differences in

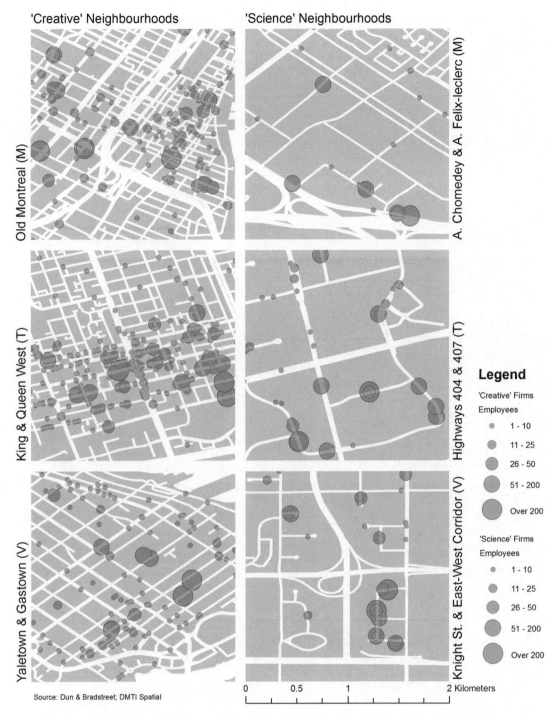

Fig. 1. Firm locations in 'creative' and 'science' neighbourhoods in Montreal, Toronto and Vancouver

land use and zoning between the central areas and suburbs. Fig. 2 shows the land use patterns of the creative and science in neighbourhoods in each of the three regions. In each case the creative neighbourhoods show a distinctly mixed residential, commercial, institutional, and recreational land-use pattern while the science neighbourhoods tend to be exclusively zoned for commercial purposes. Mixed land-use patterns are an indication that people are performing all manners of activities within the neighbourhood. Being directly physically integrated into such a diverse landscape is

bound to have knowledge spillover effects, many of which are unintentional. Land use is not only more mixed in creative neighbourhoods but the neighbourhood structure is also more finely grained which suggests greater variation in the landscape. Fig. 3 displays the block patterns for both types of neighbourhood. The street patterns of the creative neighbourhoods are clearly more finely grained and differentiated while the science neighbourhoods are defined by much larger blocks. These patterns are suggestive of greater walkability in the former which, in

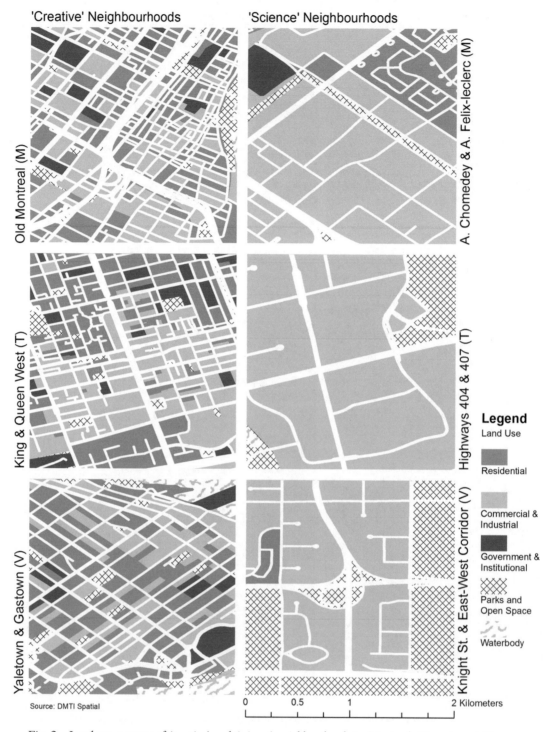

'Creative' Neighbourhoods   'Science' Neighbourhoods

Old Montreal (M)

A. Chomedey & A. Felix-leclerc (M)

King & Queen West (T)

Highways 404 & 407 (T)

Legend
Land Use

Residential

Commercial & Industrial

Government & Institutional

Parks and Open Space

Waterbody

Yaletown & Gastown (V)

Knight St. & East-West Corridor (V)

Source: DMTI Spatial

0   0.5   1   2 Kilometers

Fig. 2. Land-use patterns of 'creative' and 'science' neighbourhoods in Montreal, Toronto and Vancouver

combination with a mixed land use pattern, opens up more possibilities for diverse and serendipitous encounters. Fig. 4 provides further evidence of greater variation in the creative neighbourhoods by comparing the patterns of building footprints. JACOB's (1969) suggestion that new economic uses demand old buildings seems to hold true for the creative industries which tend to reside in buildings adapted from their original purposes, but not for the science industries which are more likely to be in purpose-built office and light

industrial premises. A final note of comparison between these two types of neighbourhoods is the relative opportunities for consumption. Fig. 5 shows the locations of cafes, restaurants, and bars in each neighbourhood. They are differentiated according to whether they are single locations or multiple/chain locations. There are vastly more consumption opportunities in the creative neighbourhoods which reinforces the notion that such places are intense sites of social interaction. Additionally, the cafes, restaurants, and

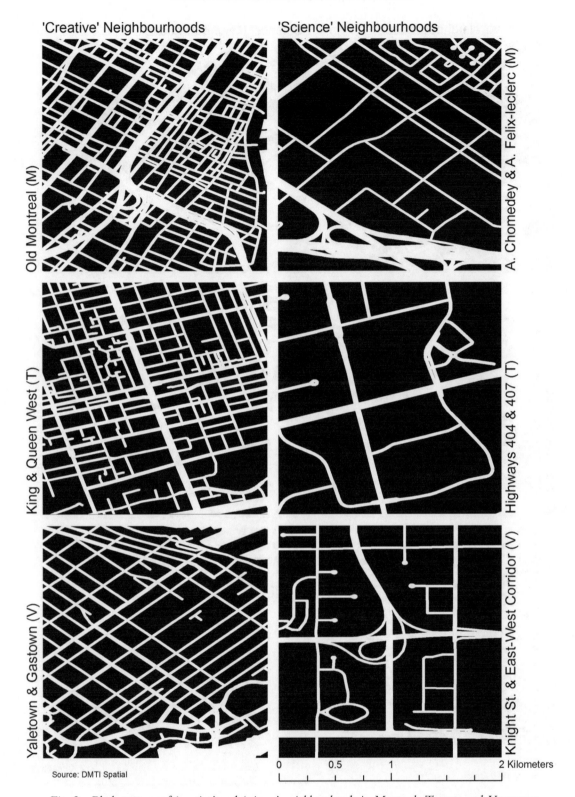

'Creative' Neighbourhoods   'Science' Neighbourhoods

Old Montreal (M)

A. Chomedey & A. Felix-leclerc (M)

King & Queen West (T)

Highways 404 & 407 (T)

Yaletown & Gastown (V)

Knight St. & East-West Corridor (V)

Source: DMTI Spatial

0   0.5   1   2 Kilometers

Fig. 3. Block patterns of 'creative' and 'science' neighbourhoods in Montreal, Toronto and Vancouver

bars are more likely to be single locations. This suggests a greater degree of authenticity in consumption opportunities, meaning that the offerings are more likely to be produced locally and reflective of the local culture in which they are integrated. One further, importance of the presence of cafes, restaurants, and bars is that they attract people from other neighbourhoods and by doing so extend the time period during each day that the neighbourhoods. This adds to the social vibrancy of the creative neighbourhoods and possibilities for social interactions that are less available in the places that science industries tend to inhabit.

'Creative' Neighbourhoods   'Science' Neighbourhoods

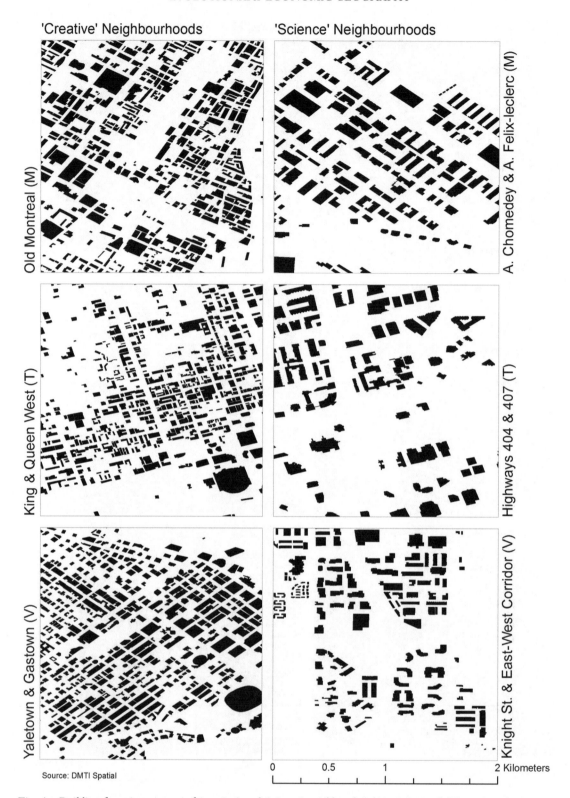

Fig. 4. Building footprint patterns of 'creative' and 'science' neighbourhoods in Montreal, Toronto and Vancouver

Beyond the static picture of the creative and science neighbourhoods in the three regions, growth and change dynamics also lend some insights into the social mechanisms in each type of industry. There is a relatively consistent spatial pattern of change in the number of firms for each set of industries in each region (see Appendix E in the Supplementary data online). Change in the spatial patterns of the science-based industries seems to occur between competing suburban office markets. While the specific reasons cannot be well explained with the data in this paper, possible underlying causes for these shifts include new office

'Creative' Neighbourhoods   'Science' Neighbourhoods

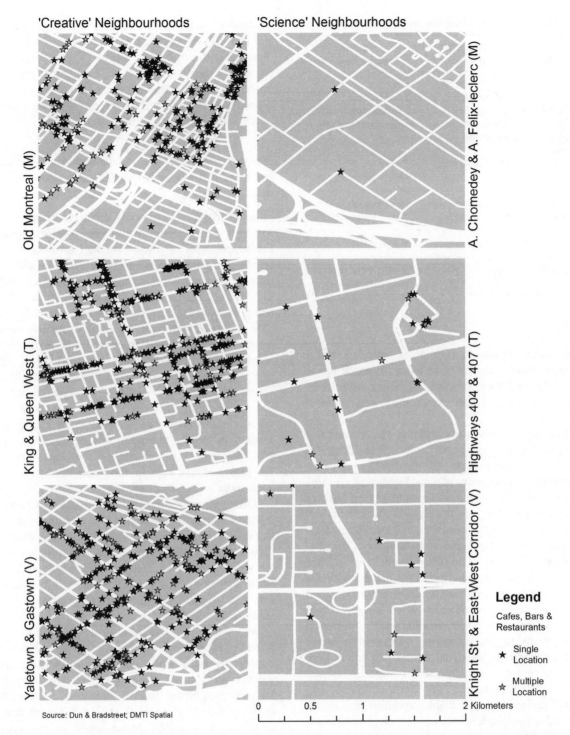

Source: Dun & Bradstreet; DMTI Spatial

Fig. 5. Cafe, restaurant and bar locations in 'creative' and 'science' neighbourhoods in Montreal, Toronto and Vancouver

construction that offers superior facilities as well as price variations. The important point in this respect is that while there are shifts between suburban sub-markets, they do not vary significantly by the characteristics discussed in the previous sections. The pattern of local change for the creative industries in two of the three regions is more specific and clear. In Montreal and Toronto creative industry firms are moving from directly next to the financial district to areas slightly further away. In Montreal the movement is mainly

from Old Montreal to Le Plateau and Mile End, while in Toronto it is from Queen West to Parkdale and the Junction. In Vancouver there some evidence of a move from Yaletown and Gastown to the Broadway Corridor, but this picture is less clear. This push away from the centre is congruent with notions of the creative industries requiring both central and inexpensive locations. This combination of traits however, makes such firm locations highly susceptible to forces of gentrification. This is somewhat detectable in the

Table 2. Summary of neighbourhood characteristics

Characteristics	'Creative' neighbourhoods	'Science' neighbourhoods
Firm location	Edge of core	Suburban
Office rents	Medium–high	Low–medium
Firm structure	Micro-small	Medium–large
Anchors	Venues; institutions	Large firms; institutions
Workforce location	Overlapping	Adjacent
Transportation	Public; walk; bike	Private (cars)
Density	Very high	Low–medium
Land use	Mixed	Mono
Building types	Varied; adapted reuse	New; purpose built
Bars, restaurants, cafes	Dense; authentic	Sparse; inauthentic
Change/ evolution	Gentrification	Sprawl
Social dynamics	Larger social networks; inter-firm (?)	Smaller social networks; intra-firm (?)

data on cafes, restaurants, and bars as there is a similar pattern of more multiple/chain locations entering the areas in the traditional creative neighbourhoods. Subsequently the areas of high growth show a higher level of authenticity.

While none of the many defining characteristics of creative and science neighbourhoods evident from this data on their own provide any direct observations of different types and amounts of social interaction, in combination they offer a strong circumstantial case that there are direct linkages between the physical characteristics of neighbourhoods, social interaction, and knowledge producing activities. Table 2 outlines a summary of the relative traits of creative neighbourhoods and science neighbourhoods. The characteristics associated with the creative neighbourhoods, namely dense, mixed use, and diverse landscapes, are suggestive of environments that provide abundant opportunities for social interaction outside of the regular workplace. Conversely, science neighbourhoods display characteristics that imply very few opportunities for social interaction outside of business premises. While it is clear that both creativity- and science-based industries are highly dependent on knowledge production which in both cases involves social interaction, the differences between the specific contexts that they tend to inhabit suggests that the spatial patterns of these social processes vary significantly.

THREE QUESTIONS CONCERNING EVOLUTIONARY PROCESSES, URBAN FORM AND KNOWLEDGE TYPOLOGIES

The empirical section of this paper demonstrates that there are stark differences in the spatial systems of creative industries and science-based industries. Distinct knowledge production processes appear to have significant

implications to the characteristics of constituent networks and firms. Furthermore, these differences are not easily detected at the traditional regional scale of analysis but require a closer look at sub-regional spatial patterns of economic activities. In order to discuss the possible implications of these findings the paper returns to the questions posed at the beginning of the paper.

How might urban form impact evolutionary economic and learning processes? Are certain industries influenced by urban form to a greater degree?

From a theoretical perspective urban environments play a role in knowledge production processes by influencing the probabilities of interaction and learning between agents. As SCOTT (2010) suggests, cities are also made from human knowledge and thus reflect back cultural information to their inhabitants. Cities are highly complex entities that offer many possibilities for novel ideas to form and grow. Evolutionary processes are fundamentally probabilistic in nature and certain spatial arrangements of workplaces, residences, and 'third spaces' such as streets, parks, restaurants, and cafes, are certain affect the likelihood of interaction and subsequent learning. It is also essential to consider what types of knowledge may be more likely exchanged as a result of largely unintentional encounters in urban settings. Scott seems to suggest that cities are more apt play a direct role in the production of cultural knowledge.

There are indications from the data that particular types of urban environments are an important factor in the location of creative industries within dense and diverse areas of cities that offer maximum opportunities for social interaction between individuals and across firms. The intense spatial clusters in the three cities indicate that specific neighbourhoods provide particular ecosystems which creative scenes require in order to thrive. These are mixed-use neighbourhoods that provide a plethora of opportunities for social interaction outside the walls of the firm. Residential locations of workers are almost totally congruent with workplace locations suggesting that the live–work relationship is deeply intertwined. Overall, there is the sense that the city itself is a much greater input to the creative process and that cultural knowledge can be obtained by simply walking down the street. The large amount and variety of such knowledge can be directly incorporated into the knowledge production process through forging novel combinations of such experiences. These experiences are often not consciously planned but rather owe to the serendipity of highly complex environments from which the unexpected arises. Based on these observations it certainly can be argued that the creative industries involve evolutionary processes in which the city itself plays an important role.

Science-based firms are typically located in much different types of neighbourhoods than creative firms.

Often single use and car centric, they do not present very many opportunities for social interaction outside the walls of the firm. People who work in such neighbourhoods do not likewise live in them suggesting a greater separation between home life and the workplace. As the neighbourhoods have typically been produced in an intentional and highly planned manner they do not provide the same sort of opportunities for serendipitous interaction and mixing. With these factors in mind, it is difficult to observe any sense of how Jacobs-type externalities play a day-to-day functioning of science-based industries. That being said, it would be a mistake to claim that there are not evolutionary processes at work within these industries. Instead, it would be more prudent to suggest that the social dimensions of the evolutionary process in each type of industry vary in their respective natures but also vary according to scale. It seems that social networks play a larger role in the creative industries which involves more inter-firm interaction while science-based firms *contain* more interaction and learning processes. This does not mean that local externalities do not play an important role in the evolution of science based but rather they may be more difficult to detect as they may happen on a less frequent basis. As a result, the specific neighbourhood level characteristics may not matter as much and hence the difference in the sub-regional spatial patterns.

How might one detect the impact of urban form on the evolutionary and learning processes of various industries? Does one need to consider sub-regional scales?

While science-based industries cluster in the same type of regions as creative industries they occupy very different types of neighbourhoods within those regions. While the emerging evolutionary economic geography literature does not place a greater importance on the traditional regional scale, there seems to be a tendency to use this scale empirically. There are certainly a number of pragmatic reasons for this that relate to data availability and how labour market areas are defined. It would be remiss however, to adopt the traditional regional scale as the main unit of analysis as it tends to obfuscate the actual social interactions that fuel the evolutionary processes that are the ultimate aim of such inquiry. There has been a large amount of research undertaken both the firm-level and (regional) spatial systems, it may be that the meso-level of industries and networks (GLÜCKLER, 2007) might provide the greatest future insights.

With this in mind, there is perhaps somewhat of an emerging tendency to focus on science and technology industries while neglect others. These sectors do tend to drive long-run economic growth and have been well discussed in the literature. Technological evolution has arguably a longer and richer history in the literature particularly as it pertains to economic development

(SCHUMPETER, 1942; NELSON and WINTER, 1982; ARTHUR, 1989). The danger in this respect is that cultural evolution will be viewed in a lesser role, one which it may not deserve especially in light of theoretical advances in economic geography since the 'cultural turn'. More to the point, it may be preferable that the co-evolution of technology and culture be studied within economic geography as the two are often difficult to untangle. Specifically, this could involve research that spans multiple types of economic sectors and understanding how evolutionary processes occur across multiple scales.

Can/should planners and designers work with economic development practitioners to create urban environments that facilitate these processes?

There is always a danger with using concepts and rhetoric such as evolution that are derived from the language of the natural sciences as it can lead to a laissez-faire approach to policy making. Any process that can be described in such ways can lead to the opinion that it be best left alone to take its 'natural course'. Evolution can be unforgiving and harsh, especially to the 'weak'. This is not how progressive societies are built. It would also be false to assume that such processes can be fully managed, as complex self-organizing systems tend to defy such attempts over the longer term. Instead, a more suitable approach may be to understand the evolutionary principles that generate knowledge and spur economic growth with the aim of working with these processes in order to achieve optimal outcomes that involve a balance between growth and equality (MACKINNON *et al.*, 2009). A practical example in relation to the findings of this paper is the notion that neighbourhoods can be designed in ways that increase social interaction and learning. This means implementing design guidelines that follow the principles of urbanism promoted by Jacobs and others, specifically creating arranging buildings and the spaces between them in a way that encourages people to come into direct contact with one another. Small walkable blocks, mixed uses, and public spaces are all key ingredients. The practice of urban design at the neighbourhood level is more often concerned with issues of 'liveability' rather than economic vitality. There may indeed be cases where urban design decisions lead to more mixed uses and greater levels of social interaction, but it is not usually motivated from an economic development perspective. In order to accomplish this better, more research is needed on how people and firms relate to one another in urban (versus suburban) environments. One first needs a more nuanced understanding of what physical forms foster more interaction which underpins evolutionary economic activities.

While the evidence in this paper suggests that creative industry firms have more to gain from Jacobs externalities at the neighbourhood scale – this should not be interpreted that other types of economic activity do not benefit at all. There is a growing recognition that even in science-based industries working in close proximity that increases social interaction between firms (and related institutions) can provide advantages. Examples of such thinking include the MaRS Discovery District in Toronto and New York's 'Tech City' on Roosevelt Island that each involves situating science-based start-up businesses in the immediate vicinity of universities (and other related institutions) near the downtown core. It may be too early to deem these attempts successful but it shows instincts towards building environments that may foster the evolution of firms and industries. A possible danger in this respect is that it may not be possible to design and engineer such environments. Most of the creative neighbourhoods highlighted in this paper were not produced intentionally but rather evolved into what they are due to their highly flexible and adaptable characteristics. This in the end may hold the secret to any successful marriage between urban design and economic development.

CONCLUSIONS

While there is general recognition that cities act to magnify social interaction, particularly between heterogeneous agents, and thereby stimulate learning, many of the precise details of how this happens are still relatively unclear. Cities are highly complex entities and it is certainly not possible to map all of the relationships and exchanges that occur within them. Much of one's knowledge and understanding of how urban environments influence human activity (and vice versa) can only be extrapolated from a smaller scale or indirect observation. In relation to evolutionary processes of learning from interaction within and between urban regions there are many questions that one can ask even though one never will be able to answer them fully. For example, who interacts with who? How often do exchanges take place? Where do they take place? What is learned from these interactions? What is the impact of information and communication technologies? Again, on a city-wide systematic level these questions can never be comprehensively addressed empirically, but instead one can build up fuller pictures from smaller studies. The danger in doing so is making generalizations that are not accurate or representative.

Creative industries and science industries tend to be found in high concentrations in the same urban regions. One could suppose then that the underlying dynamics are also similar. This paper examines the sub-regional locations of these industries (and their workforces) and finds quite divergent patterns suggesting that quite different dynamics are at work. While firm location is not 'everything' nor is it

deterministic in terms of outcomes, it can say a great deal about the relational aspirations of economic activity in a more probabilistic fashion. The dense neighbourhood-level clusters of creative industry firms in close proximity to the residences of their workers means that the individuals engaged in these economic activities are in the same spaces with one another for a greater amount of time. This suggests that there is a higher likelihood of more social interaction in such environments. This is accentuated by the observations that there are also more 'third spaces' such as parks, restaurants, cafes, and vibrant streets in creative neighbourhoods that provide specific places for such opportunities. Highly contrasting observations are made of the characteristics of the neighbourhoods where science-based industries locate. These are typically low density suburban locations with little space provided for social interaction to occur outside of the premises of firms. Furthermore, there is no immediate relationship between where science workers live and where they live, thus reducing the space–time overlap and the probability of interaction. These contrasting sub-regional geographies may in part reflect contrasts underlying social dynamics and how they are influenced by particular urban environments. To date much of evolutionary economic geography has explored the evolution of science and technology and it should not be assumed that the dynamics of cultural evolution are similar in character. Furthermore, the relationship of creative industries to the city should not be taken on par with the relationship of science industries to the city.

There is have an improving understanding as to how the specific design of buildings, and in particular the space between buildings, influences how people relate to one another. There is also a decent understanding that evolutionary processes of social interaction and learning as they pertain to creativity and innovation in the economy. However, the link between these two areas of research could certainly be made stronger. As noted above, for reasons of complexity, research on the social dynamics of urban economic processes is extremely difficult to do on a systematic multi-sectoral basis. A research instrument that does hold potential for this agenda is the Canadian General Social Survey.[3] In particular, there are special topics on both social engagement (i.e. networks) and time use that provide rich detail on how individuals interact with one another as well as what they do over the course of a typical day. The traditional drawback of such datasets is that the geography variables are extremely limited (i.e. rural/urban; province) and thus cannot lend any further insights into the influences of specific urban settings. That being said the underlying survey instrument asks respondents for their postal codes which means the possibility exists for the generation of variables based on more nuanced geographical data. Examples, of this could be population density, or walkability scores. Such variables when cross-tabulated with social network and time-use variables could go further in addressing question of how urban settings influence social dynamics. When cross-tabulated by the economic activity of the respondent this could then be linked to questions pertaining to particular industries and occupations. Ideally, there would be additional work related questions in the General Social Survey (GSS) such as work postal code and a differentiation between social engagement with colleagues and friends/family. If such variables were included in the future there could be a much richer economic dimension to the survey which could greatly enhance research connecting local environments, networks, and creativity and innovation.

Acknowledgements – The author would like to thank five anonymous reviewers for their insightful comments. He also thanks all members of the local IDEAs team. Additional thanks to Dun & Bradstreet for providing the data. A previous version of this paper was presented at the Association of American Geographers Annual Meeting in New York, NY, USA, February 2012.

Disclosure statement – No potential conflict of interest was reported by the author.

Funding – Funding for this research was generously provided by the Canadian Foundation for Innovation and the Ontario Research Fund.

Supplemental data – Supplemental data for this article can be accessed at http://dx.doi.org/10.1080/00343404.2015.1019846

NOTES

1. Defined in detail in the next section of this paper.
2. Data are at the establishment level.
3. The Canadian General Social Survey differs from the American General Social Survey in a key respect in that special topic questions are asked of all respondents ($N = 25\,000$) rather than a smaller subset ($N = 1000$) allowing for more robust cross-tabulations.

REFERENCES

AMABILE T. (1996) *Creativity in Context.* Westview, Boulder, CO.

ARROW K. J. (1962) The economic implications of learning by doing, *Review of Economic Studies* **29**, 155–173. doi:10.2307/2295952

ARTHUR W. B. (1989) Competing technologies, increasing returns, and lock-in by historical events, *Economic Journal* **99**, 116–131. doi:10.2307/2234208

ASHEIM, B. T. and GERTLER M. S. (2005) The geography of innovation: regional innovation systems, in FAGERBERG J., MOWERY D. C. and NELSON R. (Eds) *The Oxford Handbook of Innovation*, pp. 291–317. Oxford University Press, Oxford.

ASHEIM B. and HANSEN H. K. (2009) Knowledge bases, talents, and contexts: on the usefulness of the creative class approach in Sweden, *Economic Geography* **85**, 425–442. doi:10.1111/j.1944-8287.2009.01051.x

BEAUDRY C. and SCHIFFAUEROVA A. (2009) Who's right, Marshall or Jacobs? The localization versus urbanization debate, *Research Policy* **38**, 318–337. doi:10.1016/j.respol.2008.11.010

BECKSTEAD D. and BROWN M. (2003) *From Labrador City to Toronto: The Industrial Diversity of Canadian Cities 1992–2002.* Statistics Canada, Ottawa, ON.

BOSCHMA R. (2005) Proximity and innovation: a critical assessment, *Regional Studies* **39**, 61–74. doi:10.1080/0034340052000320887

BOSCHMA R. A. and FRENKEN K. (2006) Why is economic geography not an evolutionary science? Towards an evolutionary economic geography, *Journal of Economic Geography* **6**, 273–302. doi:10.1093/jeg/lbi022

BROWN J. S. and DUGUID P. (2000) Mysteries of the region: knowledge dynamics in Silicon Valley, in MILLER W. F., HANCOCK M. G. and ROWEN H. S. (Eds) *The Silicon Valley Edge: A Habitat for Innovation and Entrepreneurship*, pp. 16–39. Stanford University Press, Stanford, CA.

BURT R. S. (1992) *Structural Holes.* Harvard University Press, Cambridge, MA.

CURRID E. and CONNOLLY J. (2008) Patterns of knowledge: the geography of advanced services and the case of art and culture, *Annals of the Association of American Geographers* **92**, 414–434. doi:10.1080/00045600701879458

CURRID E. and WILLIAMS S. (2010) Two cities, five industries: similarities and differences within and between cultural industries in New York and Los Angeles, *Journal of Planning Education and Research* **29**, 322–335. doi:10.1177/0739456X09358559

DARWIN C. (1859) *On the Origin of Species by Means of Natural Selection, Or the Preservation Of Favoured Races in the Struggle for Life.* London.

DESROCHERS P. (2001) Local diversity, human creativity, and technological innovation, *Growth and Change* **32**, 369–394. doi:10.1111/0017-4815.00164

FIEST G. (1999) The influence of personality on artistic and scientific creativity, in STERNBERG R. (Ed.) *Handbook of Creativity*, pp. 273–296. Cambridge University Press, Cambridge.

FRENKEN K. and BOSCHMA R. (2007) A theoretical framework for evolutionary economic geography: industrial dynamics and urban growth as a branching process, *Journal of Economic Geography* **41**, 635–649. doi:10.1093/jeg/lbm018

FRENKEN K., VAN OORT F. and VERBURG T. (2007) Related variety, unrelated variety and regional economic growth, *Regional Studies* **41**, 685–697. doi:10.1080/00343400601120296

GERTLER M. (1995) 'Being there': proximity, organization, and culture in the development and adoption of advanced manufacturing technologies, *Economic Geography* **75**, 1–26. doi:10.2307/144433

EVOLUTIONARY ECONOMIC GEOGRAPHY

GLÜCKLER J. (2007) Economic geography and the evolution of networks, *Journal of Economic Geography* **7**, 619–634. doi:10.1093/jeg/lbm023

GRANOVETTER M. (1973) The strength of weak ties, *American Journal of Sociology* **78**, 1360–1380. doi:10.1086/225469

GRANOVETTER M. (1985) Economic action and social structure: the problem of embeddedness, *American Journal of Sociology* **91**, 481–510. doi:10.1086/228311

JACOBS J. (1961) *The Death and Life of Great American Cities*. Vintage/Random House, New York, NY.

JACOBS J. (1969) *The Economy of Cities*. Random House, New York, NY.

JACOBS J. (2000) *The Nature of Economies*. Random House, New York, NY.

MACKINNON D., CUMBERS A., PIKE A., BIRCH K. and McMASTER R. (2009) Evolution in economic geography: institutions, political economy, and adaptation, *Economic Geography* **85**, 129–150.

MARSHALL A. (1890) *Principles of Economics*. Macmillan, London.

MARTIN R. and SUNLEY P. (2007) Complexity thinking and evolutionary economic geography, *Journal of Economic Geography* **7**, 573–601. doi:10.1093/jeg/lbm019

MASKELL P. and MALMBERG A. (2007) Myopia, knowledge development and cluster evolution, *Journal of Economic Geography* **7**, 603–618. doi:10.1093/jeg/lbm020

MASSEY D., QUINTAS P. and WIELD D. (1992) *High Tech Fantasies: Science Parks in Society, Science and Space*. Routledge, London.

MOLOTCH H. (2002) Place in product, *International Journal of Urban and Regional Research* **26**, 665–688. doi:10.1111/1468-2427.00410

NELSON R. R. and WINTER S. (1982) *An Evolutionary Theory of Economic Change*. Belknap/Harvard University Press, Cambridge, MA.

ROMER P. M. (1986) Increasing returns and long-run growth, *Journal of Political Economy* **94**, 1002–1037. doi:10.1086/261420

SANTAGATA W. (2004) Creativity, fashion, and market behaviour, in POWER D. and SCOTT A. J. (Eds) *Cultural Industries and the Production of Culture*, pp. 75–90. Routledge, New York, NY.

SCHUMPETER J. A. (1942) *Capitalism, Socialism, and Democracy*. Taylor & Francis, New York, NY.

SCOTT A. J. (2010) Cultural economy and the creative field of the city, *Geografiska Annaler: Series B, Human Geography* **92**, 115–130.

SHEARMUR R. and DOLOREUX D. (2000) Science parks: actors or reactors? Canadian science parks in their urban contexts, *Environment and Planning A* **32**, 1065–1082. doi:10.1068/a32126

SILVER D., NICHOLS CLARK T. and GRAZIUL C. (2011) Scenes, innovation, and urban development, in ANDERSSON D. E., ANDERSSON A. E. and MELLANDER C. (Eds) *Handbook of Creative Cities*, pp. 229–258. Edward Elgar, Cheltenham.

SPENCER G. M. (2011) Local diversity and the spatial concentration of creative economic activity in Canadian city-regions, in BATHELT H., FELDMAN M. and KOGLER D. (Eds) *Dynamic Geographies of Knowledge Creation and Innovation*, pp. 46–63. Taylor & Francis, Abingdon.

STERNBERG R. and LUBART T. (1996) Investing in creativity, *American Psychologist* **51**, 677–688. doi:10.1037/0003-066X.51.7.677

STORPER M. and VENABLES A. J. (2004) Buzz: face-to-face contact and the urban economy, *Journal of Economic Geography* **4**, 351–370. doi:10.1093/jnlecg/lbh027

WEITZMAN M. (1998) Recombinant growth, *Quarterly Journal of Economics* **113**, 331–360. doi:10.1162/003355398555595

WESTHEAD P. and BATSTONE S. (1998) Independent technology-based firms: the perceived benefits of a science park location, *Urban Studies* **35**, 2197–2219. doi:10.1080/0042098983845

WIRTH L. (1938) Urbanism as a way of life, *American Journal of Sociology*, 1–24. doi:10.1086/217913

Index